MW01622162

Matisse/Diebenkorn

Matisse/Diebenkorn

Edited by Janet Bishop and Katherine Rothkopf

The Baltimore Museum of Art and the San Francisco Museum of Modern Art
in association with DelMonico Books • Prestel Munich, London, New York

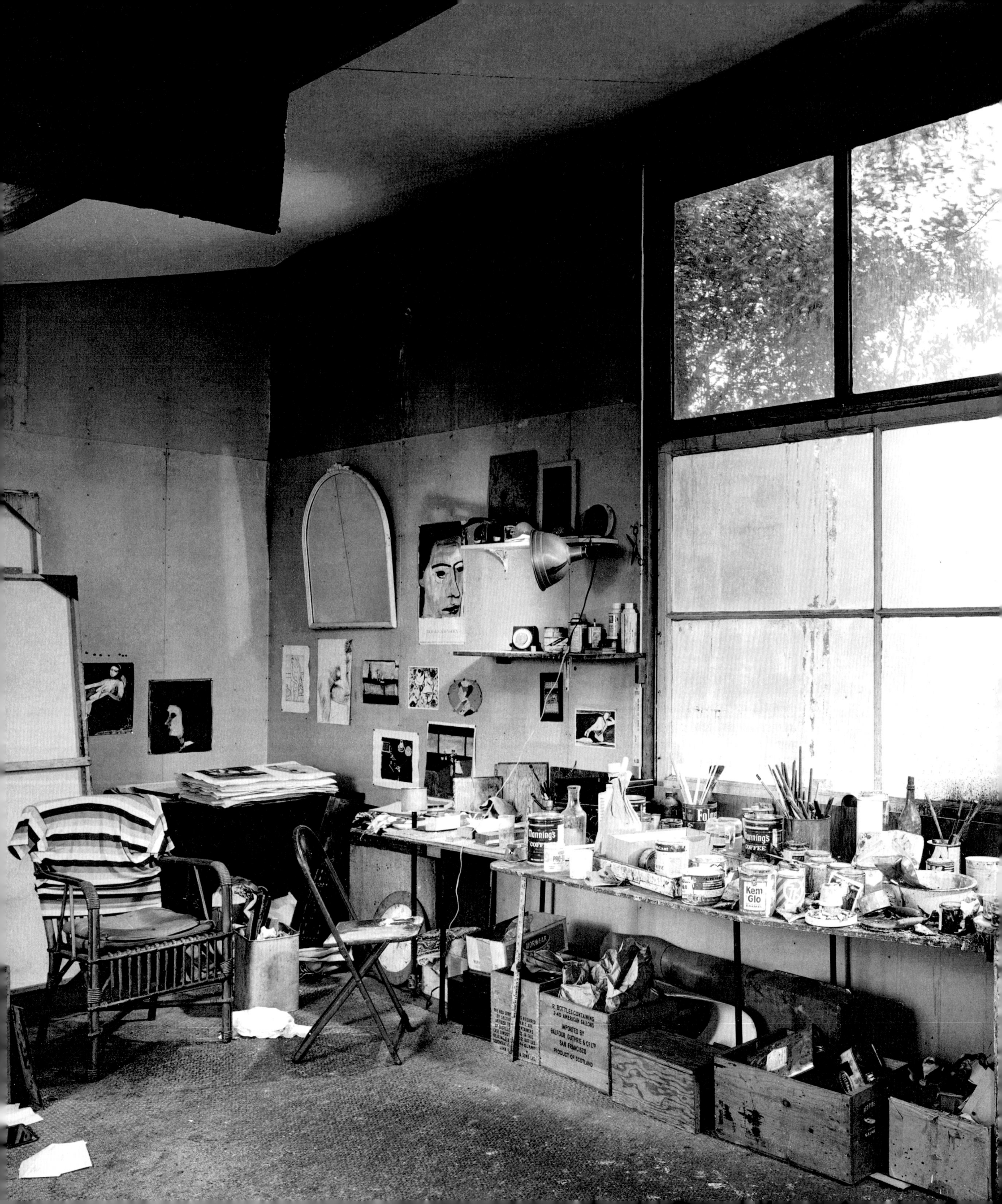
Manning's COFFEE
Manning's COFFEE
Kem Glo
12 BOTTLES CONTAINING
2.40 AMERICAN GALLONS
IMPORTED BY
BALFOUR GUTHRIE & CO LTD
SAN FRANCISCO
PRODUCT OF SCOTLAND

Directors' Foreword

With *Matisse/Diebenkorn*, The Baltimore Museum of Art (BMA) and the San Francisco Museum of Modern Art (SFMOMA) have come together to offer a groundbreaking look at the ways the postwar American painter Richard Diebenkorn (1922–1993) drew inspiration from the French modernist Henri Matisse (1869–1954). Although Matisse's influence has long been recognized in the Diebenkorn literature, *Matisse/Diebenkorn* is the first large-scale exhibition to explore the profound connection between the two artists in depth.

Matisse left an indelible impression on Diebenkorn that is most readily visible in the younger artist's representational works from the 1950s and 1960s but can also be seen in the structure, composition, and light of both his earlier and his later abstractions. The exhibition and catalogue trace these connections by following Diebenkorn's trajectory, charting the impact of important moments when he was able to study Matisse's paintings and drawings closely—when he was a college student and on his trips to East Coast museums as a Marine during World War II; his visits to major Matisse exhibitions in 1952 and 1966; and his travels to significant public collections throughout the United States, Europe, and the former Soviet Union.

That our two museums have partnered on this project could not be more fitting. Both institutions are committed to organizing exhibitions that build upon the strengths of our holdings and extend our histories with core artists. The BMA's impressive collection of works by Matisse is anchored by pieces that sisters Claribel and Etta Cone acquired directly from his studio in the early twentieth century. Since then, the BMA's holdings have grown substantially through many gifts from the Matisse family and others to become the largest public collection of the artist's work in the world. The BMA also has a strong group of Diebenkorn drawings. SFMOMA's Matisse holdings have their roots in the collection built by Sarah and Michael Stein, who were among the artist's most significant early champions as well as great friends of and mentors to the Cones. Many of SFMOMA's finest Matisse works entered the collection through the generosity of Sarah Stein's friend Elise S. Haas, a local art patron. And it was upon a visit to Mrs. Stein's home in Palo Alto in 1943 that Diebenkorn—then a student at nearby Stanford University—first saw Matisse's work in person. Diebenkorn is exceptionally well represented in the SFMOMA collection and much beloved in the Bay Area, where he grew up, spent the first half and latter part of his career, and exhibited throughout his lifetime.

Matisse/Diebenkorn realizes the deep and long-held belief of its curators—the BMA's Katherine Rothkopf, Senior Curator of European Painting and Sculpture, and SFMOMA's Janet Bishop, Thomas Weisel Family Curator of Painting and Sculpture—in the value of exploring the two artists' connection by placing their work in direct dialogue. This collaboration was formalized in 2011 after Katy and Janet discovered that they had independently been conceptualizing such a project. For Katy, who by that time had already spent several years exploring the topic and honing a list of possible works, the idea arose as part of an initiative to increase the focus on Matisse in the BMA's programming and research. The kinship between two drawings from the BMA collection was a particular impetus for this project: Matisse's *Reclining Model with a Flowered Robe* (ca. 1923–24, plate 59) and Diebenkorn's *Untitled (Woman Seated in a Chair)* (1963, plate 60). For Janet, the exhibition offered a chance to look afresh at the two artists, who bracketed the first presentation of SFMOMA's painting and sculpture collection when the museum opened on Third Street in 1995, and to consider the notion of artistic inspiration more broadly. (In San Francisco, *Matisse/Diebenkorn* is accompanied by a single-gallery installation of contemporary works that respond to one or both of the featured artists.) For the exhibition Katy and Janet have carefully sought out Matisse works that Diebenkorn would have known from both direct experience and publications, presenting them for the first time alongside paintings and drawings by the American artist. As a result of these spectacular pairings and groupings, visitors to the exhibition and readers of this publication have an unprecedented opportunity to discover Matisse through Diebenkorn's eyes.

We congratulate Katy and Janet for their exemplary collaboration throughout this project, and we join them in offering profound gratitude to the late Phyllis Diebenkorn, who shared with the curators how enormously pleased her husband would have been with this exhibition and was a great help with key loans, and to Gretchen Diebenkorn Grant, Richard Grant, and the dedicated staff of the Richard Diebenkorn Foundation. Their absolutely unparalleled support throughout the process of realizing this exhibition and producing this publication has been invaluable. Thanks are also due to Barbara Duthuit and the late Claude Duthuit, who expressed special enthusiasm for the exhibition when Katy met with them, and to Georges Matisse for his exceptional partnership on this publication. We also wish to acknowledge the teams at both institutions who are thanked by the curators on pages 9–11; we could not be prouder of their close and thoughtful work together on every aspect of the project, and we applaud their efforts and commitment.

We are profoundly thankful for financial support from many sources, which has enabled us to undertake the scholarship and planning required to bring this ambitious project to fruition. Special acknowledgment is due to the Henry Luce Foundation and the Terra Foundation for American Art. We are also very grateful for an indemnity from the Federal Council on the Arts and the Humanities, and we would like to particularly recognize Patricia Loiko, indemnity administrator at the National Endowment for the Arts. At the BMA generous support has been provided by Ellen W. P. Wasserman, Jeanette C. and Stanley H. Kimmel, the National Endowment for the Arts, corporate sponsor Bank of America, and education partner Transamerica. At SFMOMA the presentation is generously supported by the Evelyn D. Haas Exhibition Fund with additional support from The Bernard and Barbro Osher Exhibition Fund. We also extend sincere thanks to the lenders to this exhibition, listed on page 8. It is their enthusiasm that has enabled us to produce an exhibition and publication that will forever transform the ways we see the art of both Henri Matisse and Richard Diebenkorn.

Christopher Bedford
Dorothy Wagner Wallis Director
The Baltimore Museum of Art

Neal Benezra
Helen and Charles Schwab Director
San Francisco Museum of Modern Art

Lenders to the Exhibition

Albright-Knox Art Gallery, Buffalo
Harry W. and Mary Margaret Anderson
The Art Institute of Chicago
Barbara and Gerson Bakar
The Baltimore Museum of Art
Eve Benesch-Goldschmidt
Gretchen and John Berggruen, San Francisco
U.C. Berkeley Art Museum and Pacific Film Archive
Brooklyn Museum
Iris & B. Gerald Cantor Center for Visual Arts at Stanford University, Stanford, California
Colorado Springs Fine Arts Center
Dallas Museum of Art
Christopher Diebenkorn
Estate of Richard Diebenkorn
Leslie A. Feely, New York
The Doris and Donald Fisher Collection at the San Francisco Museum of Modern Art
Susan and David Gersh, Los Angeles
The Lisa and Douglas E. Goldman family
Grand Rapids Art Museum
The Grant Family Collection
Hirshhorn Museum and Sculpture Garden, Smithsonian Institution, Washington, D.C.
Kalamazoo Institute of Arts, Michigan
Mildred Lane Kemper Art Museum, Washington University in St. Louis
The Metropolitan Museum of Art, New York
Modern Art Museum of Fort Worth
Musée national d'art moderne/Centre de création industrielle, Centre Georges Pompidou, Paris
Museum of Fine Arts, Boston
The Museum of Modern Art, New York
National Gallery of Art, Washington, D.C.
New Orleans Museum of Art
Pennsylvania Academy of the Fine Arts, Philadelphia
Philadelphia Museum of Art
Joann K. Phillips
The Phillips Collection, Washington, D.C.
San Francisco Museum of Modern Art
Santa Cruz Island Foundation
Smithsonian American Art Museum, Washington, D.C.
Statens Museum for Kunst, Copenhagen
Tate, London
University Art Museum, University at Albany, State University of New York
John and Sally Van Doren
Jane Wenner
Private collections

Acknowledgments

An exhibition of this kind would not be possible without the efforts and talents of many individuals from both inside and outside of our institutions. *Matisse/Diebenkorn* had its origins in Baltimore fifteen years ago in conversations with Jay Fisher, Deputy Director for Curatorial Affairs at The Baltimore Museum of Art (BMA), about developing exhibition programming focused on Matisse's influence on subsequent generations of artists. Both Jay and former BMA Director Doreen Bolger supported the exhibition concept from the start, and Jay in particular has been an ongoing champion of the project, which today holds the happy distinction of being the first special exhibition presented during the tenure of Christopher Bedford, the BMA's newly appointed Dorothy Wagner Wallis Director. We thank Jay, Doreen, and Christopher, as well as the San Francisco Museum of Modern Art's (SFMOMA's) Neal Benezra, Helen and Charles Schwab Director; Ruth Berson, Deputy Museum Director for Curatorial Affairs; and Gary Garrels, Elise S. Haas Senior Curator of Painting and Sculpture. Since 2010, when we first discussed the possibility of collaborating on this project, we have benefited tremendously from the enthusiasm and encouragement of the leadership teams at both museums, and we could not be more grateful.

We have also had the good fortune to find many advocates beyond our museums' walls. First and foremost, we offer profound thanks to the Diebenkorn family and the staff of the Richard Diebenkorn Foundation. The late Phyllis Diebenkorn, Gretchen Diebenkorn Grant, Richard Grant, Andrea Liguori, Carl Schmitz, and Daisy Murray Holman have been beyond generous in sharing insights, archival materials, and access to their comprehensive chronology and proprietary database, as well as in offering critical assistance with potential loans. In addition, they provided images of the bulk of the works by Diebenkorn illustrated in this publication and worked closely with the catalogue team to ensure the accuracy of the color reproductions. The project has been further enriched by the participation and perspective of Christopher Diebenkorn. We are also very grateful for the assistance of the Archives Matisse and offer warm thanks to Georges Matisse at Les Héritiers Matisse for his efforts to help us accurately represent the color of the Matisse works in the catalogue.

We are deeply indebted to our colleagues at the many museums and institutions that generously lent works of art to the exhibition: Janne Sirén, Albright-Knox Art Gallery; Stephanie D'Alessandro, Douglas Druick, and James Rondeau, The Art Institute of Chicago; Lucinda Barnes and Lawrence Rinder, U.C. Berkeley Art Museum and Pacific Film Archive; Arnold Lehman and Anne Pasternak, Brooklyn Museum; Alison Gass and Connie Wolf, Iris & B. Gerald Cantor Center for Visual Arts at Stanford University; Blake Milteer, Colorado Springs Fine Arts Center; Maxwell Anderson and Walter Elcock, Dallas Museum of Art; Dana Friis-Hansen, Grand Rapids Art Museum; Melissa Chiu, Hirshhorn Museum and Sculpture Garden, Smithsonian Institution; Belinda Tate, Kalamazoo Institute of Arts; Sabine Eckmann, Mildred Lane Kemper Art Museum, Washington University in St. Louis; Thomas Campbell and Rebecca Rabinow, The Metropolitan Museum of Art; Marla Price, Modern Art Museum of Fort Worth; Bernard Blistène, Jean-Michel Bouhours, Cécile Debray, Brigitte Leal, and Alfred Pacquement, Musée national d'art moderne/Centre de création industrielle, Centre Georges Pompidou; Helen Burnham and Matthew Teitelbaum, Museum of Fine Arts, Boston; Glenn Lowry, Cora Rosevear, Ann Temkin, and Anne Umland, The Museum of Modern Art; Harry Cooper and Earl Powell, National Gallery of Art; Susan Taylor, New Orleans Museum of Art; Robert Cozzolino and Harry Philbrick, Pennsylvania Academy of the Fine Arts; Carlos Basualdo and Timothy Rub, Philadelphia Museum of Art; Sue Frank, Dorothy Kosinski, and Eliza Rathbone, The Phillips Collection; Marla Daily, Santa Cruz Island Foundation; Elizabeth Broun, Smithsonian American Art Museum; Dorthe Aagesen and Mikkel Bogh, Statens Museum for Kunst; Caroline Collier and Nicholas Serota, Tate; and Janet Riker, University Art Museum,

University at Albany, State University of New York. Tremendous thanks are also due to the many collectors, listed on page 8, who have lent deeply treasured paintings and drawings to our exhibition. We are grateful to John Van Doren and Dorsey Waxter of Van Doren Waxter, New York, for assisting us with securing a number of these loans.

Our understanding of Matisse's importance to Diebenkorn has been greatly enhanced by the knowledge and reminiscences of people beyond his immediate family who knew Diebenkorn personally, whether as a friend, teacher, or colleague. We are especially grateful to Robert Bechtle, Adelie Bischoff, John Elderfield, Martin Facey, William Luers, Gerald Nordland, Wayne Thiebaud, Phyllis Tuchman, and Jan Wurm. We are also thankful to our myriad colleagues at museums, galleries, auction houses, and archives who supported this project by sharing research or advice, or assisted in various other ways. We wish to particularly acknowledge Barbara Anne Beaucar, Eliza Bjorkman, and Martha Lucy, Barnes Foundation; Sharon Kim, Laura Nagle, Ellanor Notides, Laura Paulson, Morgan Schoonhoven, and Barrett White, Christie's; Timothy Anglin Burgard, Fine Arts Museums of San Francisco; Laura Satersmoen, Fisher Art Foundation; Michael Hackett and Francis Mill, Hackett | Mill; Scott Canty, Los Angeles Municipal Art Gallery; María Isabel Molestina-Kurla, The Morgan Library & Museum; Sylvie Ramond and Isabelle Monod-Fontaine, Musée des Beaux-Arts de Lyon; Anne Halpern, National Gallery of Art; Kenneth Grossi, Oberlin College Archives, and Lucille Stiger, Allen Memorial Art Museum, Oberlin College; Susan K. Anderson and Joseph Rishel, Philadelphia Museum of Art; Michele De Shazo and Karen Schneider, The Phillips Collection; Jeff Gunderson, San Francisco Art Institute Library; Leslie Cozzi, Hammer Museum, University of California, Los Angeles (UCLA), and Julianna Jenkins, UCLA Library; and Bruce Grenville, Vancouver Art Gallery. Gail Stavitsky of the Montclair Art Museum was particularly generous in sharing research while developing her exhibition *Matisse and American Art*.

Closer to home, we thank our many colleagues at the BMA and SFMOMA who have lent their expertise to all aspects of this endeavor. At the BMA, Christopher Wayner, Director of Program Planning and Administration, skillfully coordinated the project. The complicated logistics of loans and shipping were overseen by Senior Registrar Melanie Harwood. Judy Gibbs, Deputy Director for Development, and Laura Wolf, Grants Writer, led fundraising efforts. Christine Dietze, Deputy Director for Finance and Administration, oversaw the financial coordination. Karen Nielsen, Director of Exhibition Design and Installation, and her team provided an inspired setting in which to display the works of art. Gamynne Guillotte, Director of Interpretation and Public Engagement, and Elizabeth Benskin, Director of School and Teacher Programs, worked with their colleagues to organize engaging programs and interpretive materials. Mary Sebera, The Stockman Family Foundation Senior Conservator, and Emily Rafferty, Head Librarian and Archivist, provided great assistance for the project. Megan McCarthy, Senior Graphic Designer, superbly managed the creative campaign, and Anna Fitzgerald and Zoe Gensheimer, Coordinators for Image Services and Rights, helped source images for the exhibition and catalogue. Public relations, marketing, and social media efforts to promote the exhibition far and wide were handled by Anne Mannix Brown, Senior Director of Communications and Marketing; Suse Cairns, Director of Audience Experience; and their teams. Greg Ferrara, Director of Retail Operations, and Mary Sheehan-Moore, Manager of Retail Operations and Buyer, produced exciting merchandise for the BMA Shop, and Tim Hurlburt, Director of Security, worked closely with his staff to protect the works of art.

At SFMOMA the management of the exhibition was very ably overseen by Jessica Woznak, Co-Director of Exhibitions, with the assistance of Clarissa Morales and Annie Hagar. Other key contributors from SFMOMA's exceptionally talented professional team include Sriba Kwadjovie and Layna White in Collections Information and Access; Paula De Cristofaro and Amanda

Hunter Johnson in Conservation; Chad Coerver, Bridget Carberry, Erin Fleming, Stephanie Pau, and Maggie Wallace in Content Strategy and Digital Engagement; James Provenza and Jennifer Sonderby in the Design Studio; Rehana Abbas, David Blinder, Jess Dang, Beth Harker, Richard Havens, Samantha Leo, Amanda Spector, Caroline Stevens, and Elizabeth Waller in Development; Gina Basso, Megan Brian, Deena Chalabi, Julie Charles, Frank Smigiel, and Dominic Willsdon in Education and Public Practice; Sarah Choi and Kent Roberts in Exhibition Design; Brandon Larson, Rico Solinas, and Greg Wilson in Installations; Dana Goldberg, Clara Hatcher, Jill Lynch, Wynter Martinez, Magnolia Molcan, Jennifer Northrop, and Chris Pacheco in Marketing and Communications; Anne-Marie Conde, Jana Machin, and Tobey Martin in the Museum Store; Jennifer Hing in Registration; and Kelly Bishop and Christopher Lentz in Visitor Experience. Along with SFMOMA's director and deputy director for curatorial affairs, mentioned above, Janet Alberti, Deputy Museum Director for Administration and Finance, and Nan Keeton, Deputy Museum Director for External Relations, have been incredibly supportive of this project.

We also extend special thanks to the dedicated curatorial staff who so ably and enthusiastically worked alongside us in the development of the exhibition. At the BMA we acknowledge Laura Albans, Curatorial Assistant in the Department of European Painting and Sculpture, who has worked tirelessly on this project since its inception. At SFMOMA we are grateful to Jared Ledesma, Curatorial Assistant, who made invaluable contributions to our research efforts; Lily Pearsall, Curatorial Project Manager, and Kate Mendillo, former Assistant Curator and Curatorial Project Manager, for their oversight of loan requests and many other aspects of the exhibition; and Craig Corpora, who provided very capable administrative support. Their collective help was truly indispensable.

This beautiful catalogue was produced by SFMOMA's Publications Department, headed by Kari Dahlgren. Amanda Glesmann, Senior Editor, managed and edited the publication with extraordinary skill and good cheer. Lucy Medrich, Publications Associate, ably assisted with every facet of the project, and both Dianne Woo and Jennifer Knox White contributed valuable editorial insights. We are grateful to Miko McGinty and Claire Bidwell for the book's elegant design and to Mary DelMonico of DelMonico Books • Prestel for her enthusiastic interest in this title and her commitment to shepherding it to a wide audience. On behalf of the catalogue team we thank John Elderfield, whose impact on our thinking on this topic is also noted above, and Jodi Roberts; the wonderful texts they contributed greatly enrich this publication. We have benefited enormously from John's expertise on the work of both artists, and his firsthand knowledge of Diebenkorn's interest in Matisse has been a wonderful asset to our project.

Of course, major financial support is essential to realizing such an ambitious enterprise. We echo our directors' thanks to all the exhibition's funders and express our deep appreciation for their generosity.

Janet Bishop
Thomas Weisel Family Curator of Painting and Sculpture
San Francisco Museum of Modern Art

Katherine Rothkopf
Senior Curator of European Painting and Sculpture
The Baltimore Museum of Art

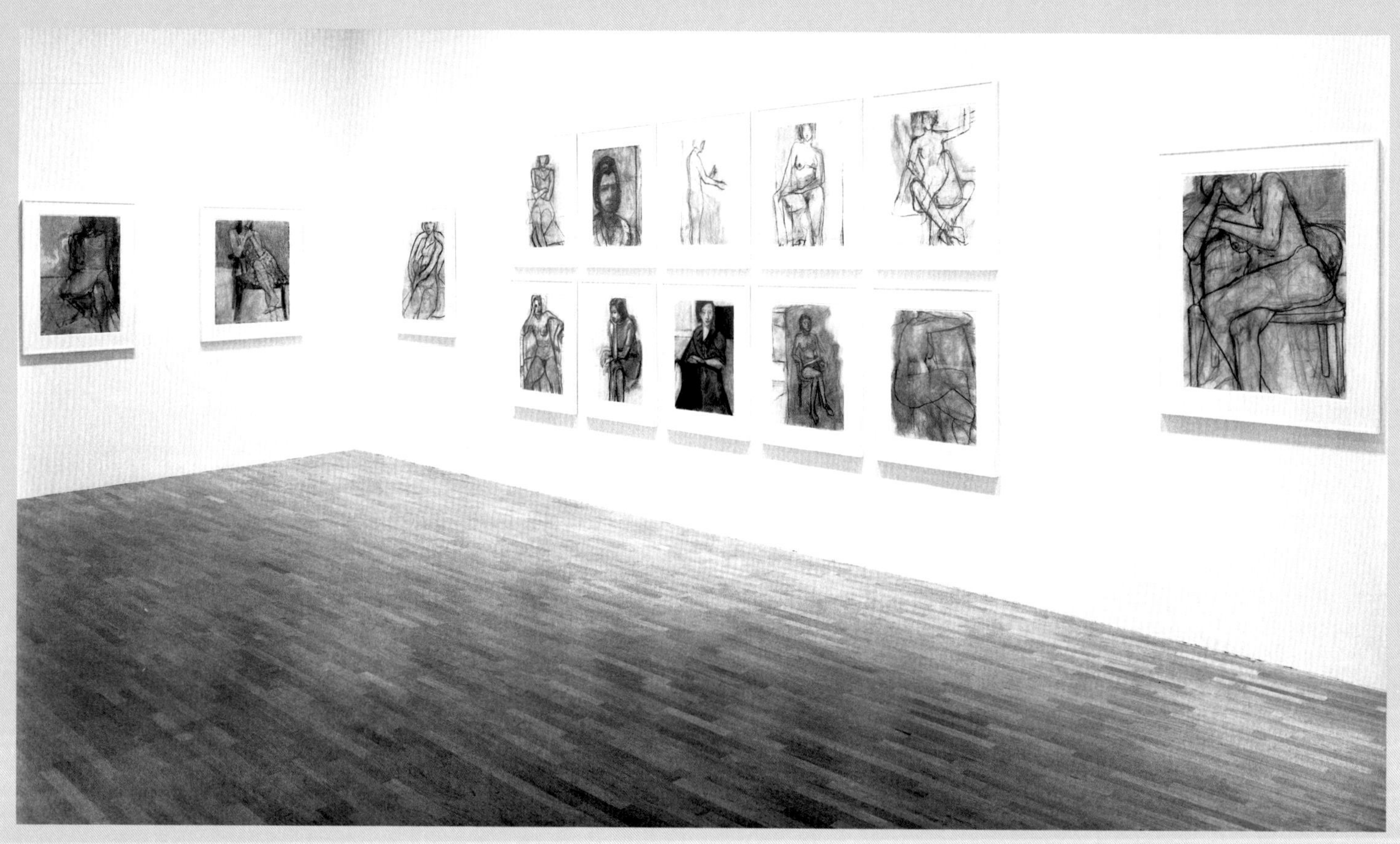

Imagining into Another

John Elderfield

One of the most mysterious semi-speculations is, one would suppose, that of one Mind's imagining into another.

—John Keats, Marginalia to *Paradise Lost*, 1.53–75[1]

Both of them began, as many artists do, with the wish to record something close at hand, to make an image of something that rang true to their experience of it. Then, in their different ways at their distant moments, Henri Matisse and Richard Diebenkorn came to the realization that to make a true statement in painting—something that spoke credibly of its subject in their own, individual voices—would require attending very carefully to the language of their art: this obliged them to both *pay* attention and *call* attention to the means that they used. It is reasonable that critics have concentrated mostly on the stylistic affinities between the two artists, but their most important practical commonality may be a quality of alertness, a mixture of judgment and vigilance, about what happens in the process of making a painting.

For some modern painters, the process of making has been intrinsically important, effectively the replacement for an external subject. This obviously was not the case for Matisse; and, even in Diebenkorn's abstract compositions, not for him either. True, the marks of the making—of erasure and revision as well as of assertion—were valued by both artists and continue to be by their audiences. However, these marks were and are (or should be) valued not only for their materiality but also for their experientiality, for their evocation of external elements, subjectively understood, be they tangible objects or intangibles like space, mood, and light. In holding this dual affiliation to the material and the experiential, the two artists were, in their different ways at their distant moments, disciples of Paul Cézanne. But the question for the present is: what was Diebenkorn's lineage from Matisse?

The critic Waldemar George's introduction to a book on Matisse's drawings, published by Éditions des quatre chemins in 1925, opens with the words "Morphologie ou Idéographie?" and suggests that drawing can aim either at the creation of form or at registering personal emotion.[2] Sometime in late 1983 Diebenkorn pulled out this book when I was writing an essay for a catalogue of an exhibition of Matisse's drawings, saying I now had a greater use for it than he did. We agreed that George was wrong: it wasn't a matter of either/or but

Installation view of *The Drawings of Richard Diebenkorn*, curated by John Elderfield at The Museum of Modern Art, New York, November 17, 1988–January 10, 1989. On wall, at far right: *Untitled (Seated Nude)* (1966, plate 68)

of both. This led to talk about the either/or of abstraction and representation, and he said that while they had different methodologies, both clearly could aim at the creation of form and register personal emotion. Then, looking at the drawings illustrated in that book, some awkward, many extremely fluent, he observed that, despite Matisse's reputation as a superb draftsman, neither kind of drawing gave the impression of the artist making (or perhaps he said displaying) a performance.

In 1948 Matisse had worried that "the impression of apparent facility" may be produced by "a rapid, even superficial, viewing" of recent paintings from which he had removed all signs of revision by wiping off from his canvas all traces of one state after another, until he had produced a seemingly effortless final result.[3] But his, and Diebenkorn's, visibly revised compositions pose the no less worrying problem that anything short of careful attention to them may give the erroneous impression of emendation displayed, even contrived, for effect. This is what I think Diebenkorn was referring to when he said what he said about Matisse's drawings: that the impression neither of difficulty nor of ease was offered as a spectacle, even if a rapid and superficial viewing may enjoy it as such.

This was hardly a problem in England in the 1960s, when I was a fine art student there: any kind of viewing of Diebenkorn's paintings was impossible, none being in any European public collection, nor shown in any exhibition save the Tate Gallery's 1964 *Painting and Sculpture of a Decade*. And precious few works by Matisse could be seen in London—or, in fact, in Paris, the French national collections having long neglected their greatest modern painter. However, the accessibility of Matisse's work suddenly improved on the centenary of his birth, with major retrospective exhibitions in those cities in 1969 and 1970, respectively. These stunned their audiences—certainly me—with breathtaking paintings previously unknown, other than in reproduction, except by those who had visited museums in the Soviet Union or the United States, or who had seen the earlier exhibitions that had appeared with some regularity in America, most recently the great Los Angeles show of 1966.

As explained elsewhere in this publication, Diebenkorn had visited the Soviet Union in 1964; had seen that Los Angeles exhibition in 1966; and had previously become familiar with works by Matisse in U.S. museums, including The Phillips Collection in Washington, D.C., and The Museum of Modern Art (MoMA) in New York. While the Soviet experience was obviously critical for him, so were his encounters with the artist's work within the United States. And, in considering the present exhibition, it is important to remember that an artist living in America, or a critic or art historian, for that matter, could achieve a greater familiarity with Matisse's work than one in England or France who had not visited this country—*could*, but no other artist of his time *did* to the extent that Diebenkorn did.[4] Certainly, when I first met him, in 1972, he had far, far more appreciation of Matisse's art than I had, even with the experience of the European centenary exhibitions just behind me.

I had moved to the United States on a two-year fellowship in 1970 and had begun to publish exhibition reviews. One day in late 1971, out of the blue, I received a telegram from James Fitzsimmons, the editor of the then-vibrant *Art International*, saying that Clement Greenberg had told him he should ask me to write a piece on Diebenkorn's paintings, and that Gilbert Lloyd would show them to me at Marlborough Gallery in New York. I hardly knew Greenberg; had never met Fitzsimmons or Lloyd; and had never seen a painting by Diebenkorn. Indeed, I am not sure that I even knew Diebenkorn's name then. I therefore walked unprepared into Marlborough Gallery on Fifty-Seventh Street to see *Ocean Park* paintings on the walls.

The article I wrote prompted an invitation from the artist to visit him the next time I found myself on the West Coast.[5] I had never been there and made it a point to get there soon. Following that first visit to Dick and Phyllis Diebenkorn, I would see them many times after I returned to the United States in 1975 and opened the first of what would be five exhibitions featuring Matisse that I curated at MoMA during Diebenkorn's lifetime.

It may be of interest in considering his indebtedness to Matisse to know that Diebenkorn saw all of these exhibitions except the last, and largest—the winter

1992–93 retrospective of more than four hundred works—owing to the illness preceding his death the next spring. But we looked together at the catalogue of that show the last time I saw him, just as we had looked together at the catalogues of all the previous shows, as well as at all but the first of the exhibitions themselves. For the record, then, this is what Diebenkorn saw.[6]

He saw the first exhibition, on Matisse and his Fauvist colleagues, when it was shown in San Francisco in summer 1976: so I learned when I reconnected with him late in that year, on the occasion of the first major retrospective of his work. By then I was also beginning to meet with two of Matisse's children, Marguerite Duthuit and Pierre Matisse, doing research for a 1978–79 exhibition of works by Matisse in the MoMA collection, which Diebenkorn would also see. However, it was in the decade from the early 1980s to the early 1990s that I spent the most time curating and writing about both Matisse's and Diebenkorn's art and, therefore, talking about Matisse with Diebenkorn. The 1985 exhibition of Matisse's drawings, which I mentioned earlier, was soon followed by the lengthy process of preparing an exhibition on Diebenkorn's drawings, which opened in 1988 (page 12). Two years later came an exhibition of Matisse's Moroccan paintings, to which I contributed a catalogue essay. A year later, in 1991, I did the same for a Diebenkorn show at Whitechapel Art Gallery (now the Whitechapel Gallery) in London, while preparing my large Matisse retrospective. Claude Duthuit, who following his mother's death had assumed the leadership of his grandfather's estate and archives, was very interested in my working simultaneously on the two artists. It turned out that he too was a great admirer of Diebenkorn's paintings. Still, I was surprised and delighted when one day he said: "Wouldn't it be wonderful to see a Matisse/Diebenkorn exhibition?" That must have been in 1992.

My first take on Diebenkorn's work, twenty years earlier, in 1972, seems very stilted to me now. I know that it didn't reflect a "rapid, even superficial, viewing" of the *Ocean Park* paintings. Rereading it, though, I realize that it was the dramatic presence of these grand compositions that mattered most—as it did with Matisse's radical paintings of the teens, which had emboldened Diebenkorn, and with which I was then becoming familiar on visits to MoMA. As time passed, though, what grew in importance for me in the work of both artists was consciousness of the resistance through which their visual thoughts had passed in order to gain their grandeur. Or, equally affecting in its own way, to find a more modest circumstance: both artists were mistrustful of occasions when, as the poet Elizabeth Bishop nicely put it, "emotion too far exceeds its cause."[7]

This is why, for Diebenkorn as well as for Matisse, *gratuitous* revision was as much to be avoided as the exercise of facility: both practices produced unacceptably ingratiating results, signs of emotion unearned. The difficulty was that, while painting had to be about something other than the act of painting, that "something," if it were to seem credible, could only be defined as it was discovered in the act. This is why, I think, both of these artists enjoyed (or, more likely, suffered through) keeping a painting in a state of flux: to resist finalizing statement while registering the forming of statement. To do so left room, even as each was willing the surface into shape, for something unexpected and unplanned: "something given to him" and "scarcely his own" precisely because it couldn't be willed, as John Keats described his own experience of inspiration.[8]

Keats also said that an inspired thought "seemed rather the production of another person than his own." Implicit in these statements is the recognition that inspiration of this kind, which comprises "one Mind's imagining into another," finds a deeper root than any conscious borrowing. To that point, the announced derivation of Diebenkorn's *Recollections of a Visit to Leningrad* (1965, plate 72) from *Red Room (Harmony in Red)* (1908, plate 71) may be better described as an imagining *after*, rather than *into*, another's practice. In contrast, many *Ocean Park* paintings do show that Diebenkorn had imagined himself deeply *into* Matisse's imagining, into the processes of making works like *View of Notre Dame* (1914, plate 96) and *French Window at Collioure* (1914, plate 100).[9]

In this respect, it is very much to the point that these two canvases look not only almost abstract but also, in the former case, unfinished, and in the latter, unelaborated. They represent a side of Matisse so extreme that he himself must have thought it "scarcely his own," for he neither signed nor exhibited them.[10] And, if recognized to be scarcely his own, then they were all the more readily available for appropriation—at least by an artist as alert as Diebenkorn was where Matisse was concerned—and especially so because their unfinish and unelaboration made them inviting of further development. Reviewing the first New York showing of *Ocean Park* paintings, in 1968, the art critic John Canaday had therefore been prompted to observe, "Structurally, it is as if Matisse . . . had developed as an abstract painter in the person of his protégé-by-example."[11]

This is too strong, though. While Matisse's name must top the list of the artists to whom Diebenkorn was indebted, others should not be forgotten, ranging from the cartoonist George Herriman to Paul Cézanne, Piet Mondrian, and Willem de Kooning. "A poet cannot help being influenced," T. S. Eliot wrote, "therefore he should subject himself to as many influences as possible, in order to escape from any one influence."[12] However, the catalogue of Diebenkorn's first retrospective exhibition may innocently have left the wrong impression by listing some thirty artists in whose work he is said to have been interested.[13] As one of Diebenkorn's favorite poets, Wallace Stevens, once observed, "There is a kind of critic who spends his time dissecting what he reads for echoes, imitations, influences, as if no one was ever simply himself but is always compounded of a lot of other people."[14]

No one was ever more simply—and sometimes not so simply—himself than Diebenkorn was. Not despite but because of the deepness of his imagining into the processes of others, most prominently Matisse, he was able to make them new.[15] As such, his Matisse was his own, and every affinity between his and Matisse's art is also a mark of his singularity.

Notes

1. John Keats, *The Complete Poems* (London: Penguin, 2006), 518.
2. Waldemar George, *Henri-Matisse: Dessins* (Paris: Éditions des quatre chemins, 1925), 5.
3. Henri Matisse, "Letter to Henry Clifford" (1948), in *Matisse on Art: Revised Edition*, ed. Jack Flam (Berkeley: University of California Press, 1995), 182.
4. Many of the American artists indebted to Matisse, from 1907 into the present century, comprise the subject of the exhibition *Matisse and American Art* at the Montclair Art Museum, New Jersey, February 4–June 18, 2017.
5. John Elderfield, "Diebenkorn at Ocean Park," *Art International* 16, no. 2 (February 1972): 20–25.
6. I refer in the following paragraph to these exhibitions and catalogues: *The "Wild Beasts": Fauvism and Its Affinities*, 1976; *Matisse in the Collection of The Museum of Modern Art*, 1978–79; *The Drawings of Henri Matisse*, 1985; *The Drawings of Richard Diebenkorn*, 1988–89; John Elderfield, "Matisse in Morocco: An Interpretive Guide," in *Matisse in Morocco: The Paintings and Drawings, 1912–1913*, exh. cat., by Jack Cowart, Pierre Schneider, John Elderfield, et al. (Washington, D.C.: National Gallery of Art, 1990), 201–39; John Elderfield, "Figure and Field," in *Richard Diebenkorn*, exh. cat., ed. Paul Bonaventura and Catherine Lampert (London: Whitechapel, 1991), 13–33; and *Henri Matisse: A Retrospective*, 1992.
7. Elizabeth Bishop, "The Map" (*North & South*, 1946), in *Poems* (New York: Farrar, Straus and Giroux, 2011), 5.
8. John Keats, "Letter to Richard Woodhouse" (1820), quoted in Christopher Ricks, "Keats's sources, Keats's allusions," in *The Cambridge Companion to Keats*, ed. Susan J. Wolfson (Cambridge, UK: Cambridge University Press, 2011), 155.
9. I discuss this comparison and broader issues in Diebenkorn's relationship to the tradition of modern painting in greater detail in "Allusions to Ocean Park," in *Richard Diebenkorn: The Catalogue Raisonné*, ed. Jane Livingston and Andrea Liguori, vol. 1 (New Haven: Yale University Press, 2016), 89–113.
10. Matisse's signature on *View of Notre Dame* is an estate stamp. This is not noticed in the otherwise very full discussions of these two works in Stephanie D'Alessandro and John Elderfield, *Matisse: Radical Invention, 1913–1917*, exh. cat. (Chicago: The Art Institute of Chicago, 2010), 192–95, 232–35.
11. John Canaday, "Richard Diebenkorn: Still Out of Step," *New York Times*, May 26, 1968, D37.
12. T. S. Eliot, "Tradition and the Practice of Poetry" (1936), in *T. S. Eliot: Essays from the "Southern Review,"* ed. James Olney (Oxford, UK: Clarendon Press, 1988), 13.
13. Maurice Tuchman, "Diebenkorn's Early Years," in *Richard Diebenkorn: Paintings and Drawings, 1943–1976*, exh. cat., by Robert T. Buck Jr., Linda L. Cathcart, Gerald Nordland, et al. (Buffalo: Albright-Knox Art Gallery, 1976), 5–24.
14. Wallace Stevens quoted in Harold Bloom, *The Anxiety of Influence: A Theory of Poetry* (London: Oxford University Press, 1975), 6–7.
15. "The perpetual task of poetry is to *make all things new*. Not necessarily to make new things." T. S. Eliot, "Tradition and the Practice of Poetry," 13 (emphasis in original).

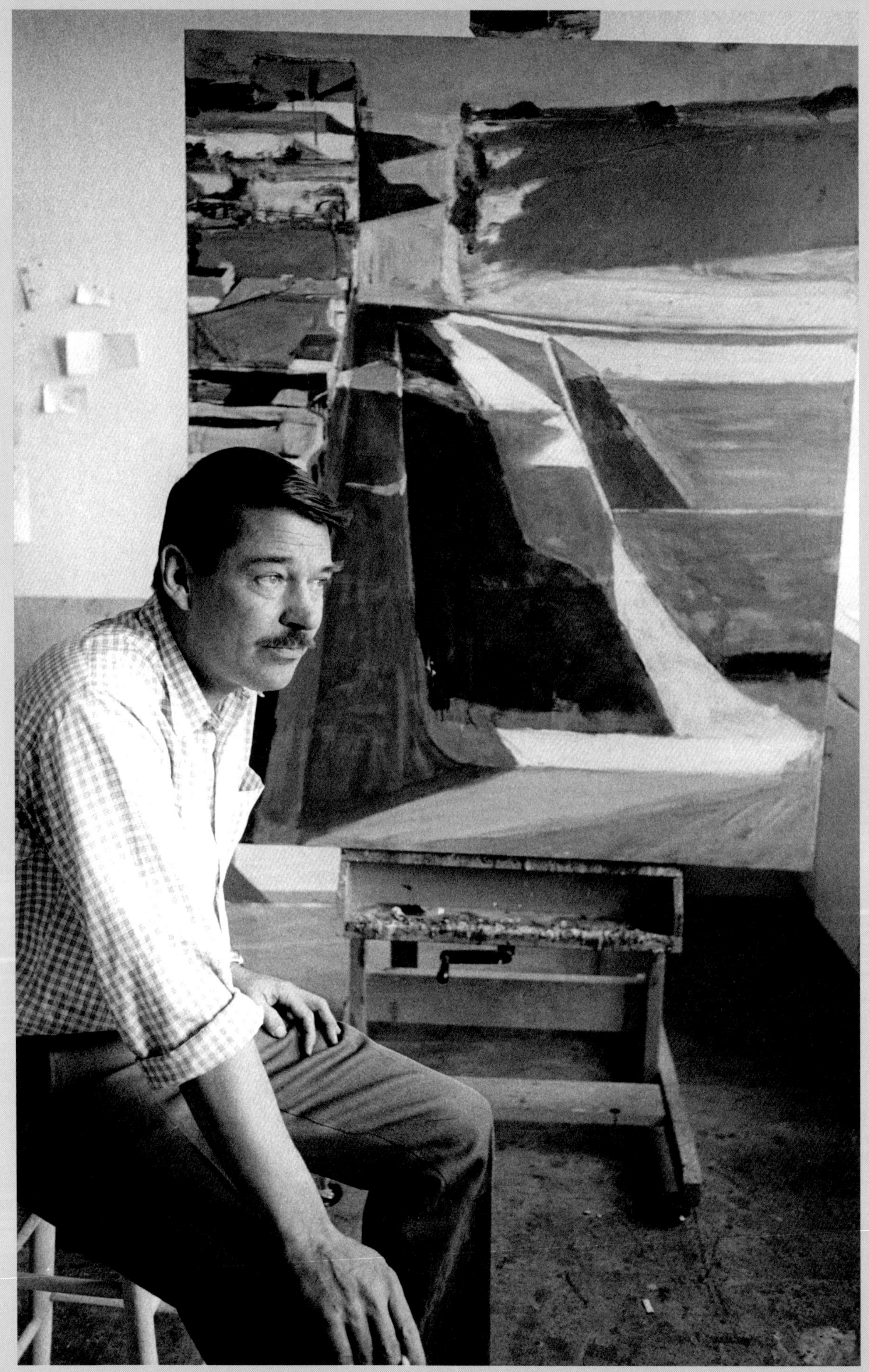

Making Matisse His Own: Richard Diebenkorn's Early Abstractions and Figurative Paintings

Janet Bishop

Two seemingly unrelated bits of art news appeared in the July 20, 1952, edition of the *Los Angeles Times*: an announcement that a big Henri Matisse show was about to open on Wilshire Boulevard and a notice that "Mr. and Mrs. R.C. Diebenkorn and children" were visiting relatives in the San Fernando Valley.[1] For Matisse, the last stop of his American retrospective, organized by the legendary director of The Museum of Modern Art (MoMA), New York, Alfred H. Barr Jr., only further cemented an already colossal reputation. The eighty-two-year-old artist was touted in the Los Angeles press as "the foremost colorist of our century" and "the greatest living French painter."[2] Mounted in ground-floor offices that had been converted into a temporary gallery space, the exhibition drew tens of thousands of visitors over the course of its brief run,[3] as well as the attention of the local industry, with movie actress Arlene Dahl helping with publicity by posing with *The Girl with Green Eyes* (1908, plate 102).[4] For thirty-year-old Richard Diebenkorn, an accomplished abstract painter who had just received his master of fine arts degree from the University of New Mexico, Albuquerque, the coincidence of the exhibition's arrival in Los Angeles and his Southern California stay with his in-laws allowed for his first truly immersive experience of Matisse's work. The show consisted of sixty-six objects—among them paintings as commanding as *The Blue Window* (1913, plate 25), *The Red Studio* (1911), and *The Piano Lesson* (1916, plate 98). Diebenkorn later recalled: "It absolutely turned my head around."[5]

Although Diebenkorn had already been looking at Matisse for almost a decade, until the 1952 exhibition his growing interest was not especially evident in his own work. It was after seeing the show in Los Angeles that he began to fully absorb Matisse's approach to painting and internalize ways of looking, seeing, and translating the experience of the physical world onto canvas that would give the French artist's example primary relevance to his own practice for the rest of his life. In 1954 Diebenkorn bought Barr's book *Matisse: His Art and His Public* (1951),[6] the first of dozens of volumes on the artist he would amass over the years and one of particular value to him.[7] Whether in person or through images, Diebenkorn's engagement with Matisse—the artist of whom he spoke most frequently and freely and whose approach resonated with him most deeply—is among the most productive instances of one painter looking at another's paintings in the history of twentieth-century art.

Raised in San Francisco, Diebenkorn was first exposed to Matisse during his undergraduate years at Stanford University, where he enrolled in 1940. He

Richard Diebenkorn in his studio at Stanford University, Stanford, California, 1963. On easel: *Cityscape #1* (1963, plate 49). Photograph by Leo Holub

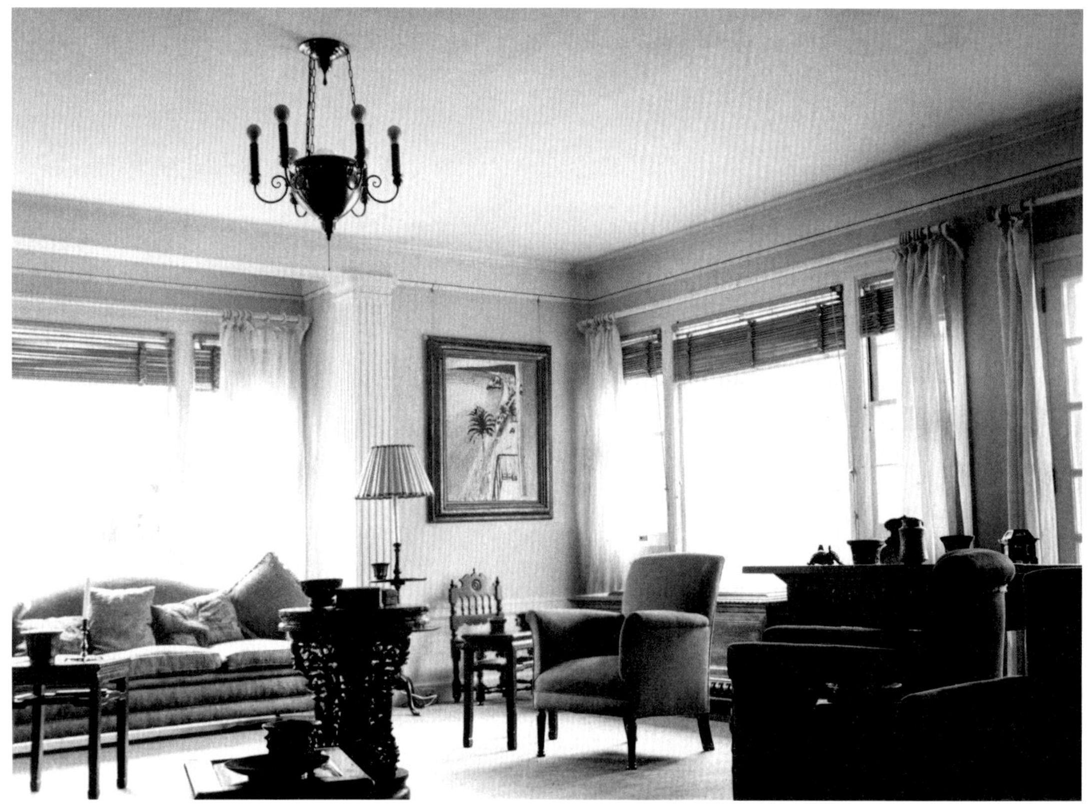

Fig. 1. Sarah Stein's living room, Kingsley Avenue, Palo Alto, California, ca. 1940s. On wall: Henri Matisse, *The Bay of Nice* (1918)

made the most of the few art classes he took there—watercolor and art history with Daniel Mendelowitz and painting with Victor Arnautoff. He connected especially with Mendelowitz, a committed Americanist and Edward Hopper enthusiast. According to Diebenkorn, "European Modernism was really kind of a thorn in Dan's side."[8] Mendelowitz covered the material in his own way, as Diebenkorn affectionately remembered: "He did marvelous lectures . . . so astute, but then he'd come to Modernism and show Picasso or Matisse . . . and he couldn't resist making comments that would bring down the house in the little theater there. . . . In such a sincere way, he would defend Matisse. . . . 'And you know, there's nothing really, nothing wrong with this. It's like a nice necktie. [*laughter*] A nicely patterned necktie.'"[9]

Impressed with his student's seriousness of purpose, Mendelowitz arranged for the two of them to have lunch at the Palo Alto home of Sarah Stein (figs. 1 and 2), who, with her husband, Michael, and his siblings Gertrude and Leo, had been one of the most daring and important collectors of the Parisian avant-garde in the early years of the century. At the time of their visit, in spring 1943, the collection Sarah and Michael Stein had built over three decades of living in France included a few works each by Pablo Picasso and Paul Cézanne, and more than a hundred by Matisse: thirty paintings, sixteen drawings, seventy lithographs, seven etchings, eight bronzes, four ceramics, and at least one illustrated book.[10] Art appeared throughout the ground floor, with paintings and drawings on every wall, sculpture integrated with Renaissance furniture, and prints stored in chests.[11] Matisse's monumental garden scene *Tea* (1919), which Diebenkorn came to appreciate for its unresolved details,[12] dominated the dining room. His quintessential fauve masterpiece, *Woman with a Hat* (1905, plate 79), and *The Bay of Nice* (1918), both hung in the living room, were likewise memorable to the young artist.[13] Diebenkorn would also have seen early examples of Matisse's work such as *Open Door, Brittany* (1896) and *Still Life with Blue Jug* (ca. 1900–1903, plate 35); his

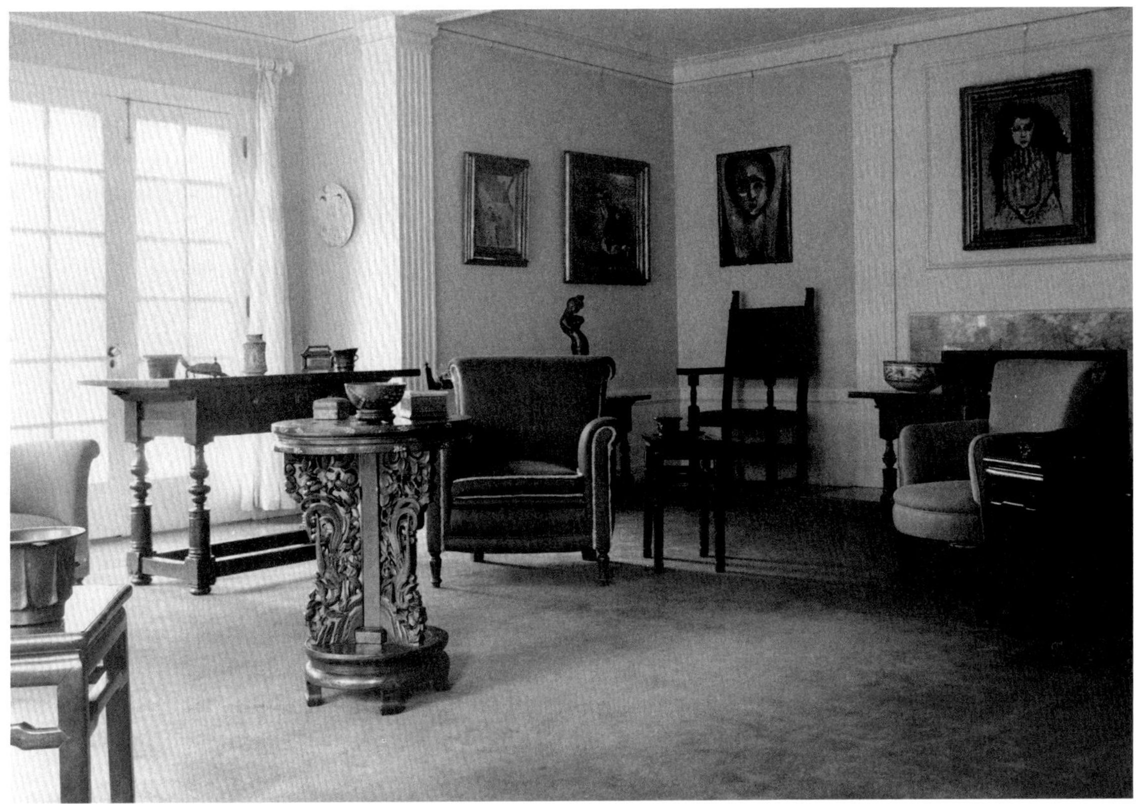

Fig. 2. Sarah Stein's living room, Kingsley Avenue, Palo Alto, California, ca. 1940s. On walls, from left: Henri Matisse, *La Pudeur (L'Italienne)* (1906); *Still Life with Blue Jug* (ca. 1900–1903, plate 35); *Sarah Stein* (1916, plate 37); and *Marguerite* (1901)

fauve *Landscape: Broom* (1906, plate 8) and the oil sketch for *The Joy of Life* (1905–6); and his companion portraits of Sarah (plate 37) and Michael Stein (both 1916), all of which were prominently displayed. Sarah clearly enjoyed hosting Diebenkorn—so much so that she gave him a mounted reproduction of a Matisse drawing of a standing nude woman seen from behind.[14] In describing this initial encounter, Diebenkorn later recalled: "Right there I made contact with Matisse, and it has just stuck with me all the way."[15] He would take every opportunity to seek out Matisse's work from that point forward.

Diebenkorn enlisted in the Marine Corps with the expectation that he would be able to complete his studies at Stanford through the V-12 program, but he was able to stay only through his junior year before being called into service. Over the summer of 1943 he and fellow Stanford student Phyllis Gilman married, and he was transferred for one semester to the University of California, Berkeley, where he was the only art student in uniform. In early 1944 he was assigned to a base in Quantico, Virginia. Phyllis accompanied her new husband to the mid-Atlantic, and the two put his weekend furloughs to use frequenting East Coast museums. He made his first visits to MoMA, which already had such exemplary Matisse paintings as *The Blue Window*, and the Philadelphia Museum of Art, where he eventually developed a special regard for a Nice interior, *Interior at Nice (Room at the Hôtel Beau-Rivage)* (1918).[16] Closer to the base, Diebenkorn "just feasted"[17] on the museums in the nation's capital: the National Gallery of Art, the Corcoran Gallery of Art, and, especially, The Phillips Collection (then The Phillips Memorial Art Gallery, figs. 3 and 4). He later reflected: "It was certainly a key point in my life when I was in Washington, or rather in Quantico. Here's a painter in the armed services during wartime. Here was Duncan Phillips's magnificent house which he opened to all comers, and the marvelous thing about it was . . . that it wasn't like a museum . . . you could smoke, there were concerts. . . . It was a refuge . . . a kind of sanctuary

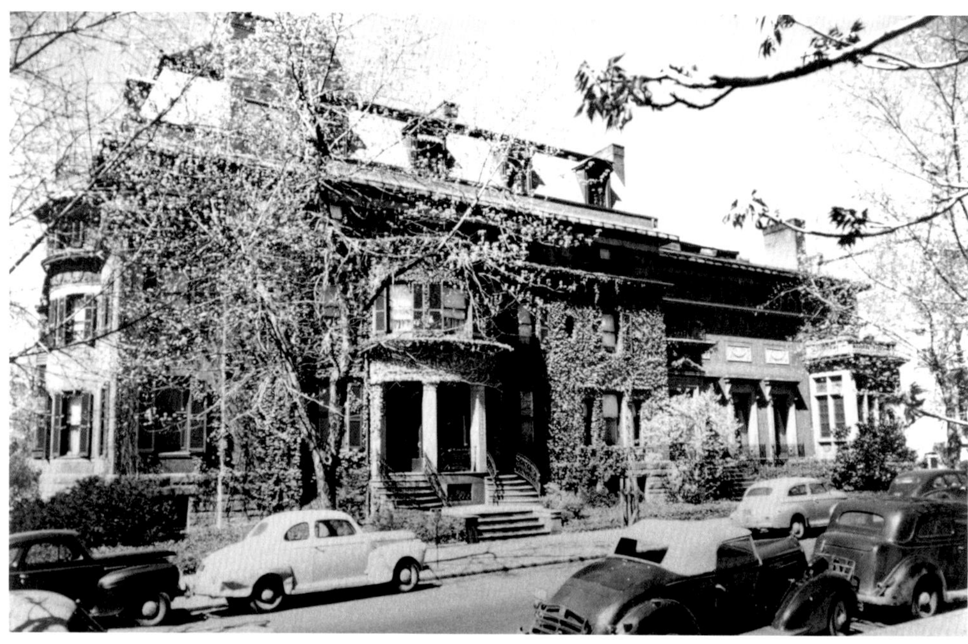

Fig. 3. The Phillips Collection, Washington, D.C., ca. 1940s

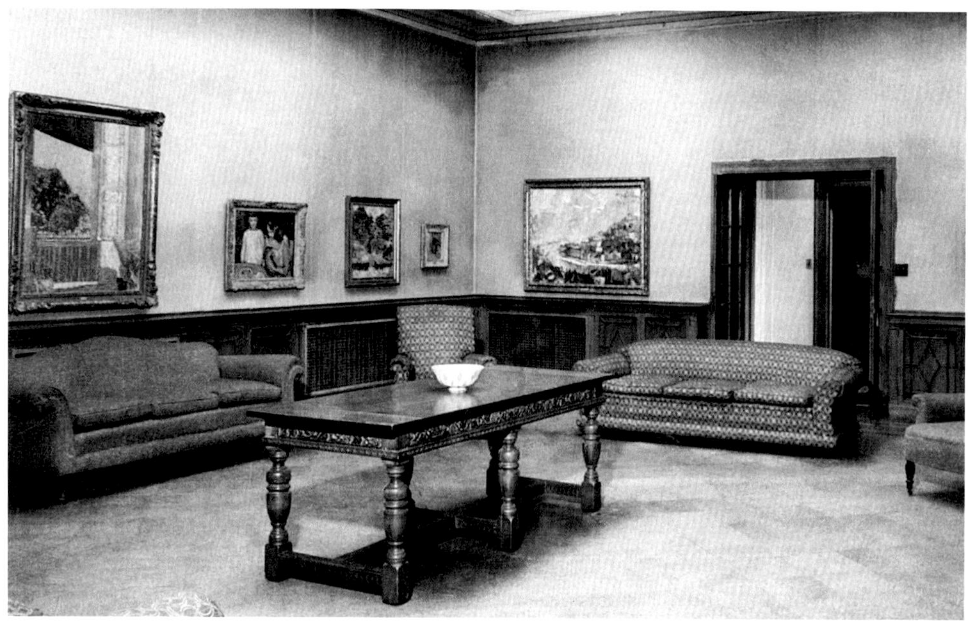

Fig. 4. Main gallery of The Phillips Collection, Washington, D.C., ca. 1940s. On wall, at far left: Pierre Bonnard, *The Open Window* (1921)

for me, and I just absorbed everything on those walls."[18] For her part, Phyllis later recalled, "'Going' doesn't even explain it. We'd stay all day."[19]

Among the great European paintings in The Phillips Collection, Diebenkorn was especially drawn to Pierre Bonnard's *The Open Window* (1921) and Matisse's *Studio, Quai Saint-Michel* (1916, plate 1), which became "the big one" for him.[20] He was fascinated with Matisse's treatment of indoors and outdoors, his way of structuring his canvases, the subject of the artist's studio, and his open declaration of process. Though it would be several years before the impact of *Studio, Quai Saint-Michel* would reverberate in Diebenkorn's own work, he later recalled that Matisse hit him hard in Washington, priming him, in a sense, for the revelatory experience of Matisse's 1952 American retrospective.

By the time Diebenkorn got to Los Angeles that summer, the war had ended. He had spent four years studying and then teaching at the Abstract Expressionist–dominated California School of Fine Arts (CSFA, now the San Francisco Art Institute)—a place where nonobjective painting was the only acceptable mode of expression—and he had continued to develop his painting in the same vein during his two and a half years in Albuquerque. Teaching positions for newly minted MFAs were scarce, so with two children in tow he accepted the one he was offered and headed in fall 1952 to Urbana, Illinois. In most respects Diebenkorn felt out of sorts there—unhappy with his assignment in the architecture department and so uninspired by the landscape that he blacked out his studio windows. If not moved by his immediate surroundings, he was definitely galvanized by his recent experience of Matisse's exhibition: it was as though his first decade of looking at the other artist's work had been a prolonged gestation whose effects were about to erupt onto his canvases.

Two of the great pictures in the show were *Goldfish and Palette* (1914, plate 6) and *Interior at Nice* (1919 or 1920, plate 4). Each, although distinct—the former bold and reductive, the latter gentler in palette and mood—possesses much of what Diebenkorn admired in Matisse's way of approaching a canvas and that he could apply to his own, largely nonobjective works. Conjuring the abstracted hint of a painter holding a palette above bent knees in *Goldfish and Palette*, Diebenkorn's quasi-abstract sportsman in *Urbana #2 (The Archer)* (1953, plate 3) emerges from the right, partially cut off, within a composition dominated by blocks of saturated color. Diebenkorn's *Urbana #6* (1953, plate 7) makes use of the blue, black, and white of *Goldfish and Palette*. Looking at the two side by side, the blue square at the upper right of *Urbana #6* evokes a clear sky seen through a window, with the red flecks at the painting's center taking on the life of Matisse's fish.

The influence of *Interior at Nice* is especially evident in *Urbana #5 (Beach Town)* (1953, plate 5), with which it shares a seaside theme, palette, and division of space. Urbana is, of course, not a beach town at all, but as Diebenkorn explained: "Here I was in the Midwest, and I was pretty unhappy there because of all this ground and hay and stuff around, and then this painting occurred. . . . I've always numbered pictures; I did this for some years afterwards, but this one I guess I identified because of the special feelings I had about it, and it was to me like a town near an ocean and just to remember it, I referred to it as 'Beach Town.'"[21] Matisse's *Studio, Quai Saint-Michel* did not travel to Los Angeles for the 1952 show. Yet it clearly remained seared in Diebenkorn's mind during his fruitful school year in Urbana. For *Urbana #4* (1953, plate 2) the young painter appears to have repurposed the blocks of color that make up the Parisian studio interior to create a composition seemingly devoid of familiar points of reference. Later in the year, after Diebenkorn returned to the San Francisco Bay Area, the impact of the Matisse canvas continued to be felt. In *Berkeley #7* (1953, plate 10), for instance, the vertical form at the right bridges our world with the one depicted in much the same way that the curtain in *Studio, Quai Saint-Michel* does. Both feature dark spaces, with the field of fleshy pink in Diebenkorn's painting finding precedent in the red couch and the pentimenti—areas of visible reworking—seen throughout Matisse's. As Matisse and, in turn, Diebenkorn understood, shapes that might correspond with objects in a representational painting could function just as demonstratively in formal terms.

When the Diebenkorns got to Berkeley in fall 1953, they were back on familiar terrain, physically and culturally. The paintings the artist made there over the next two years are robust achievements: vigorously executed canvases with roots in CSFA action painting. In the main, the connection to Matisse is less overt in these works than in what directly preceded and what would follow. In titling them after a place, Diebenkorn invited associations with landscape. And indeed many of them include elements that reinforce the connection. The forms of the brilliantly colored *Berkeley #5* (1953, plate 9), for instance, fit together like patches of farmland seen from above. Others are built up with horizontal strata and incorporate horizon lines, as in *Berkeley #22* (1954, plate 11). Both canvases call to mind Matisse views such as *Landscape: Broom*, the earlier canvas structurally and coloristically, the later one in its suggestion of sky.

The Matisse referent for Diebenkorn's *Berkeley #47* (1955, plate 16) registers with startling specificity. In a summary of important encounters with Matisse, Diebenkorn pointed to a visit to the Cone Collection at The Baltimore Museum of Art in 1947.[22] That year's presentation of the works assembled by sisters Claribel and Etta Cone included nine drawings and twenty-two paintings by Matisse, among them *Yellow Pottery from Provence* (1905, plate 15), a somewhat raw still life including elements that Diebenkorn seems to have adapted for *Berkeley #47*, which bears an almost identical, very unusual color scheme. The vertical bands at the top of *Yellow Pottery* effectively tip over ninety degrees and expand into horizontals to make up the composition of Diebenkorn's canvas. And Matisse's ochre jug might have morphed into a ghost of a coffee cup at the foot of *Berkeley #47*.

Diebenkorn reused some of the dominant colors in *Berkeley #47* for *Berkeley #57* (1955, plate 14). A few of the geometric forms that appear at the bottom of the canvas emerge again in *Berkeley #58* (1955, plate 18), which takes a more decorative turn. Matisse's interests stretched from the austere to the ornate, a level of opulence that Diebenkorn would never attempt. In *Berkeley #58*, however, he filled some of his blocks with polka dots. A black heart appears at the left, and the very Matisse-like blue, which made its way onto Diebenkorn's palette for the first time in Urbana, reappears here in a place where one might expect to find a window. Though distinct in their overall impact, Matisse's pattern-rich interiors such as *Seated Odalisque, Left Knee Bent, Ornamental Background and Checkerboard* (1928, plate 12), from the Cone Collection, offer precedent for building a composition through interlocking shapes, as in Diebenkorn's *Berkeley #23* (1955, plate 13), #57, and #58.

Diebenkorn's *Berkeley* series reflects enormous momentum, comprising more than sixty canvases, as well as works on paper, by a talent who garnered interest and respect on both coasts. So when he began explicitly incorporating elements of the world around him into his painting, some were baffled. Phyllis, even, who had been fully indoctrinated in the merits of abstraction and thus resisted the urge to "look for things" in her husband's canvases, found the new figurative work "a little square."[23] Part of the change in course had to do with the fact that his closest friends, artists David Park and Elmer Bischoff, with whom he drew from models regularly, were finding their own figurative pursuits so productive. It wasn't so much about the specifics of what they were doing. Diebenkorn even recalled asking himself, "My God, what's happened to David?"[24] upon first seeing an image of Park's *Kids on Bikes* (1950), with its wildly exaggerated perspective. Yet the example his peers provided of painting with a connection to the real world was compelling. As Diebenkorn later remembered, "For someone who was intending to continue as an abstract painter I was clearly consorting with the wrong company."[25] Matisse took on an enhanced relevance for his painting, now by offering precedent for not only *how* but also *what* to paint.

Beginning in late 1955, and for the next dozen or so years, Diebenkorn focused on a handful of subjects connected to his daily life: still lifes, figures, interiors, and views. Abstract Expressionism had become, in his words, a "stylistic straightjacket."[26] So he got in his car and drove around in search of something to paint. The small-format *Chabot Valley* (1955, plate 20) was among the first of his new representational works. Like Matisse, who sometimes took his paint box outdoors to work *en plein air* on compositions such as *Landscape: Broom*, Diebenkorn made *Chabot Valley* outside. Rendered as lushly as Matisse's *Corsican Landscape* (1898, plate 19), *Chabot Valley* meant a lot to the artist—he hung it on the walls of various studios and elaborated upon the basic subject and structure many times, as in *View from the Porch* (1959, plate 28).

Still Life with Orange Peel (1955, plate 22) was another early representational effort. The quirky tabletop scene takes on a bird's-eye view. The elements of the composition are pulled almost into plane with the canvas, an effect that is accentuated by the aqua green and white striped fabric, which Diebenkorn had salvaged from a childhood bedspread.[27] Artist Wayne Thiebaud has openly admired Diebenkorn's gift for making the ordinary so special,[28] whether a piece of fruit, matchsticks, open scissors, or a bottle of turpentine. And Diebenkorn was emphatic about the importance of the things he painted, maintaining that if they survived until a canvas was complete, they were never just information or places to hang his "conceptions of painting."[29] They mattered to him. (Both *Still Life with Orange Peel* and the related *Still Life with Orange Peel II*

[1955/1956, plate 24], curiously, include a rotten lemon.) Through Matisse paintings such as the Steins' *Still Life with Blue Jug and Lemons on a Pewter Plate* (1926, reworked 1929, plate 21), which had been in the 1952 show, Diebenkorn could find abundant precedent for a focus on color, form, and pattern.

As he moved to a larger scale, Diebenkorn's compositions regularly incorporated figures—generally women in quiet moments, posed or candid. Matisse provided a vast array of productive examples. Every time Diebenkorn opened the Barr book, for instance, he would have seen the color reproduction of *Woman with a Hat*—Matisse's portrait of his wife, Amélie—on its frontispiece (page 168). Similarly, seated women appear throughout Diebenkorn's figurative period, from *Woman on a Porch* (1958, plate 26) and *Coffee* (1959, plate 29) to *Seated Figure with Hat* (1967, plate 80), a portrait of Phyllis sporting a wide-brimmed hat. When asked specifically about Matisse's fauve paintings, however, Diebenkorn observed that for Matisse, circa 1905, Fauvism was in some ways a move toward Abstract Expressionism, whereas for the Bay Area painters, fifty years later, "the new figuration was precisely the reverse."[30] Diebenkorn and his peers were coming off everything they had learned from Abstract Expressionism and were applying it to representation. Figures had to be situated solidly in environments. Surfaces had to be "responsibly" realized. Color could not be arbitrary.

Matisse and Diebenkorn shared an interest in non-Western art, the latter noting that his attraction to Indian miniatures, in particular, "probably came out of what Matisse did with them."[31] Shortly before his transition to figuration, Diebenkorn purchased a group of Rajput paintings from Ray Lewis, a San Francisco print dealer, which he noted having displayed "wherever I've lived ever since, and which are specifically the miniatures that have gotten into my work."[32] While the flatness of an eighteenth-century watercolor with three figures in a landscape (fig. 5) resonates most strongly in Diebenkorn's later work (plates 103 and 105, for example), one sees the swift impact of an eighteenth-century gouache (fig. 6) in *Man and Woman in a Large Room* (1957, plate 31), one of the relatively few of his paintings that depict more than one person.[33] Both the Indian composition and Diebenkorn's feature a pair of figures at the left, a triad of apertures behind them,

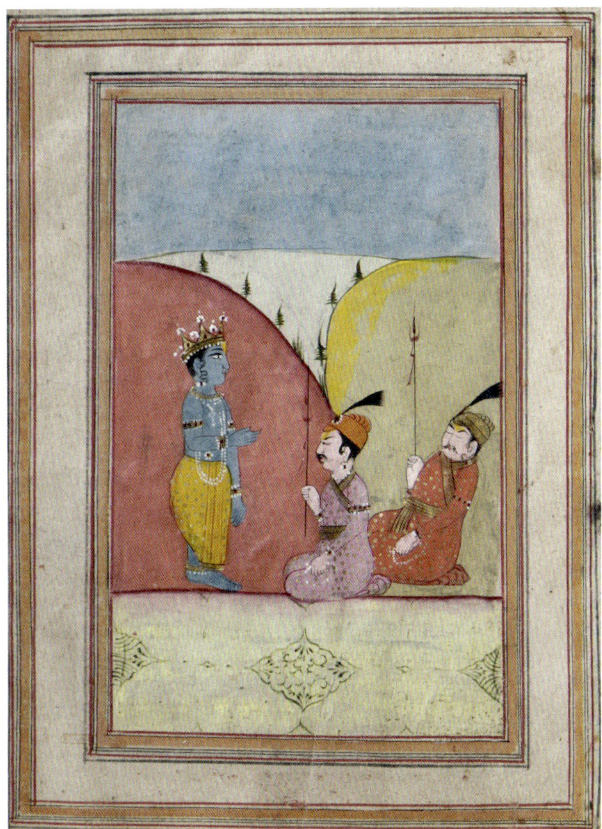

Fig. 5. Indian miniature, 18th century. Watercolor, ink, and metallic paint on paper, 18 x 13 in. (45.7 x 33 cm). Acquired by Phyllis and Richard Diebenkorn, 1954

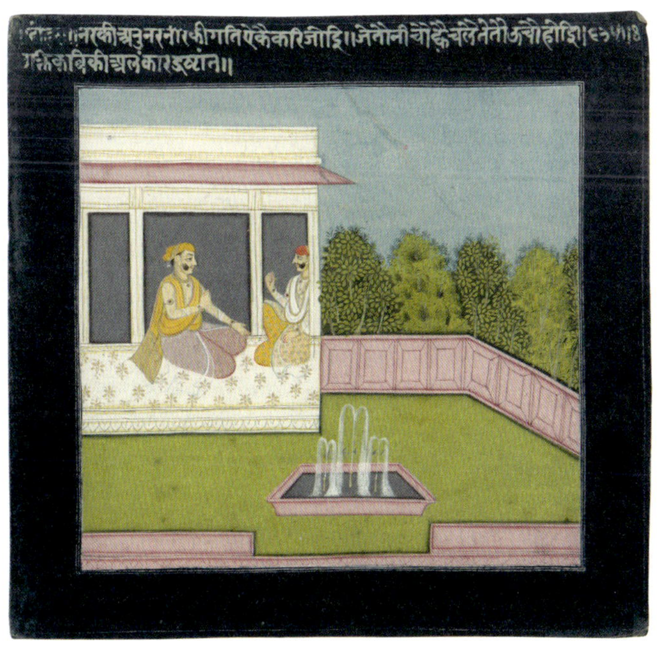

Fig. 6. Indian miniature, 18th century. Gouache, ink, and metallic paint on paper, 8¾ x 9⅜ in. (22.2 x 28.3 cm). Acquired by Phyllis and Richard Diebenkorn, 1954

and an expansive parallelogram defining the lower zone of the painting. And they both rely on dark envelopes, as does Matisse's *Studio, Quai Saint-Michel*.

Notable in *Man and Woman in a Large Room*, as well as in a number of Diebenkorn's other representational canvases, are the stripes of the woman's skirt—an inversion of who gets to wear them in Matisse's *The Conversation* (1908–12, page 125), which Diebenkorn knew in reproduction. The figure in *Woman by the Ocean* (1956, plate 27) also wears a blue and white striped skirt, though the bands are horizontal, like those on the model's shirt in Matisse's intimate, contemplative *The Blue Eyes* (1935, plate 32). Matisse was obsessed with stripes and patterns in general. (In 1930, during Matisse's second trip to the United States, curator René d'Harnoncourt took him to a baseball game in Philadelphia. Apparently the French artist found the activity on the field totally incomprehensible, but he admired the players' uniforms, with their crisp blue and white striped detailing.)[34] For Diebenkorn, clothing was typically more generalized: all blue for the women in *Coffee* and *Sleeping Woman* (1961, plate 38), for example. One notable exception appears in *Girl with Flowered Background* (1962, plate 42). Diebenkorn pays homage to Matisse in the arabesques of the setting, also seen in *Cane Chair—Outside* (1959, plate 41), and surely to Edvard Munch, too, in the treatment of the shadow.[35] The sitter's quiet composure echoes that of Matisse's models in paintings such as *Laurette in a Green Robe, Black Background* (1916, plate 30), which Diebenkorn knew from the 1952 Los Angeles show, and *The Blue Eyes*. But he acknowledged that the girl's tennis sweater was "a kind of outrageous [*chuckles*] thing for the attitude of the figure."[36]

One question, for Diebenkorn, was how to handle faces. As he explained of his transition to figurative painting: "I had just put over ten years of abstract painting behind me. . . . I wanted it both ways—a figure with a credible face—but also a painting wherein the shapes, including the face shape, worked with the allover power that I'd come to feel was a requirement of a total work. Clearly there was an inherent trap here and when I first got caught in it, I knew why Matisse sometimes left his faces blank. Matisse was relaxed in his centuries-old tradition of figure painting whereas I was *not* and it would have been a first day cop-out not to deal with the complete figure image—face and all."[37]

The examples of faces Matisse provided were vast: some blank, some masklike, some dabbed in with a few quick brushstrokes, and some clearly labored over. The sensitivity with which Matisse approached the face of the woman in *The Blue Eyes*, for instance, or the care that he took in coming to a resolution with his depiction of his friend Sarah Stein, offered perhaps more daunting examples to Diebenkorn, who wouldn't allow himself to leave facial features unarticulated, as in *Man and Woman in a Large Room*, or generalized, as in *Woman by the Ocean*, without a clear artistic rationale.

In spring 1960 Diebenkorn visited the Barnes Foundation in Merion, Pennsylvania. Until 1991 none of the works collected by Albert C. Barnes could appear in color reproduction, and they never traveled for exhibitions, making the pilgrimage a particular necessity in order to experience them in a meaningful way. After exchanging several letters with Violette de Mazia, a longtime Barnes Foundation educator and

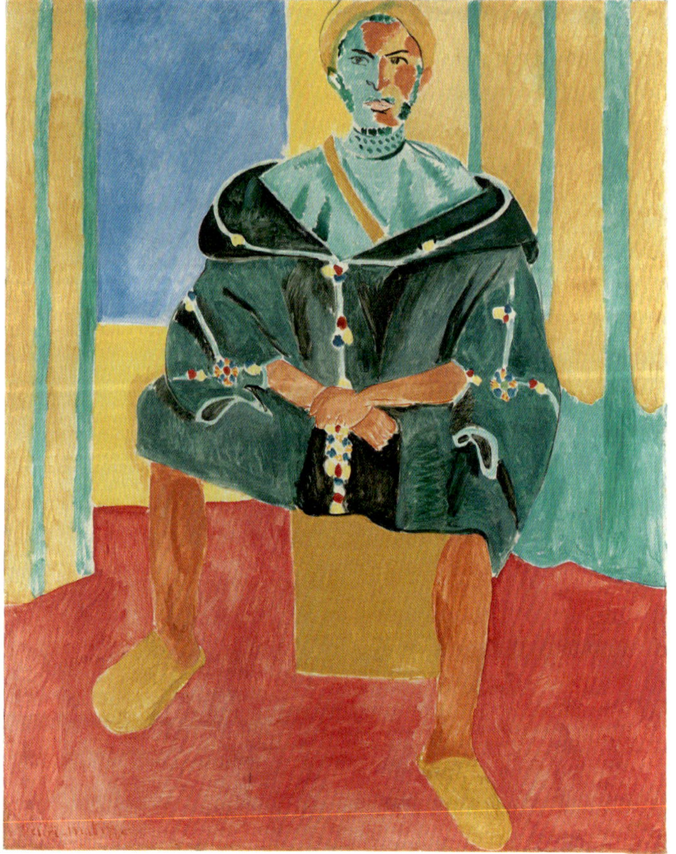

Fig. 7. Henri Matisse, *Seated Riffian*, 1912. Oil on canvas, 78⅞ x 63¼ in. (200.3 x 167.7 cm). The Barnes Foundation, Philadelphia

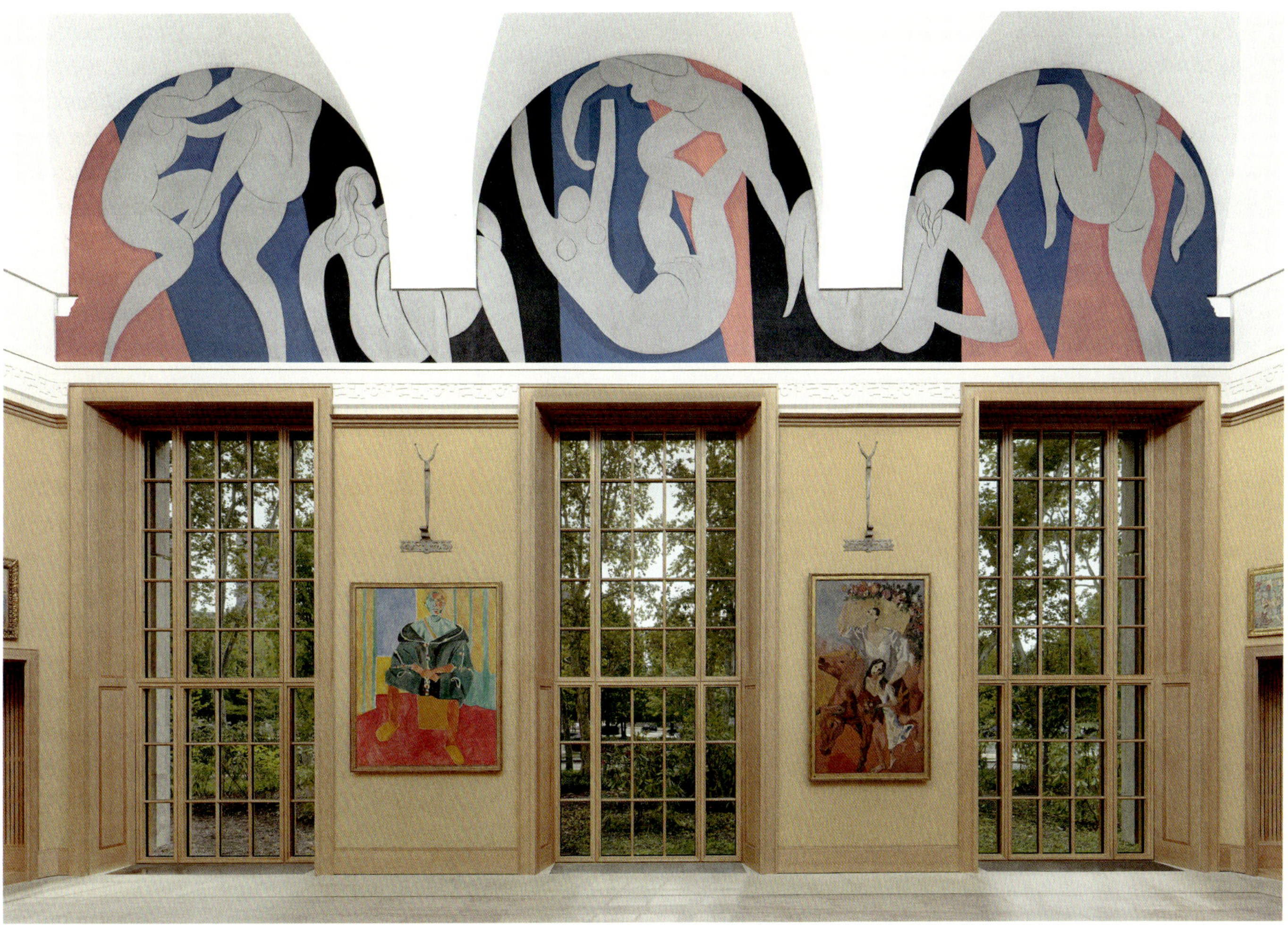

Fig. 8. Main gallery, south wall, of the Barnes Foundation in its original location, Merion, Pennsylvania. On wall, left: Matisse, *Seated Riffian* (1912); above: Matisse, *The Dance* (1932–33)

gatekeeper, the artist and Phyllis were sent admission cards allowing for a two-hour visit on Tuesday, May 10.[38] If the day was typical, there would have been fifty-nine Matisses on view, including such celebrated masterworks as *The Joy of Life* (1906) and *Red Madras Headdress* (1907). *Seated Riffian* (1912, fig. 7), a larger-than-life-size canvas dominated by a traditionally clad Moroccan man, was not a Barnes favorite. In the 1920s Barnes had considered trading it for "two French primitives" until finally deciding he had found a good spot for it.[39] In later Barnes Foundation literature it was described by de Mazia as "too expansive for what the contents warrant."[40] Diebenkorn, however, who would have found *Seated Riffian* in the main gallery (fig. 8) between two south-facing windows, singled it out as especially memorable.[41] And indeed the piece had a dramatic impact on his painting later that year. *Girl with Plant* (1960, plate 34), for instance, seems to fuse aspects of the general structure and material detail of Matisse paintings like *Interior, Flowers and Parakeets* (1924, plate 33) with the specific planes of bright color seen in *Seated Riffian*. It is almost as though Diebenkorn took some of *Seated Riffian*'s key parts—a striped mustard wall with an intense blue block for a window—and shifted them around to his own ends.

Interiors with windows were such a favorite subject of Matisse's that he was once asked to address their "charm." His response, transcribed in the Barr book and hence known to Diebenkorn, was that it probably stemmed "from the fact that for me the space from the horizon to the inside of the room is continuous and that the boat which passes lives in the same space as the familiar objects around me: the wall around the window does not create two worlds."[42] And throughout his figurative years, too, Diebenkorn was nonhierarchical about foreground and background, inside and out. The little building, perhaps a gas station, across the street in *Interior with Doorway* (1962, plate 40) has the same reality within the painting as the unoccupied chair in the foreground. The plant just outside the window of Matisse's *Interior with a Violin* (1918, plate 39) is of the same world as the violin case in front of it.

Diebenkorn and Matisse also shared a deep interest in capturing something of the experience of the working artist. Diebenkorn likely saw Matisse's *Carmelina* (1903, plate 50) at the Museum of Fine Arts, Boston, around 1960.[43] In the bold early canvas, Matisse situates the model in the private space of his studio, and the artist himself is seen in a reflection. Diebenkorn's studio, too, offered abundant inspiration for what to paint. There is something especially personal in Diebenkorn's choice to depict the cigarette butts that would accumulate every day in *Ashtray and Doors* (1962, plate 44), which is set in the triangular Berkeley studio where he worked from 1958 to 1965. *Studio Wall* (1963, plate 51) includes a hint of the distinctive Triangle Building studio floor, a vacant chair, and an allover field of darkness filled with figure drawings—light rectangles on a dark plane as seen in *Studio, Quai Saint-Michel. Seated Nude, Hands behind Head* (1961, plate 36) and *Sleeping Woman* are among the most ambitious of Diebenkorn's figures in interiors from the early 1960s. His languid women stand in contrast with Matisse's confrontational *Carmelina*, though Matisse's canvas, also known to Diebenkorn through the Barr book, must have drawn his interest for its inclusion of art within art and the device of the mirror.

At Boston's Isabella Stewart Gardner Museum, Diebenkorn would have found *The Terrace, Saint-Tropez* (1904, fig. 9), which he remembered specifically, in the corner of a former cloakroom. Since a color picture did not appear in any of the Matisse books Diebenkorn then owned, he glued one onto a blank page between plates 20 and 21 of his copy of Gaston Diehl's 1958 Matisse monograph. *The Terrace, Saint-Tropez* bears a strong central perspective, with an elaboration of foliage at the left and geometric planes at the right, all of which would reverberate in Diebenkorn's ambitious *Cityscape #1* (1963, plate 49), described by Thiebaud as an instance of Diebenkorn "anthologizing [the] process of painting."[44] San Francisco–based views constitute some of the last canvases Diebenkorn made in the Bay Area. *Ingleside* (1963, plate 46) features the tidy, master-planned neighborhood on the southern side of the city where he grew up. The painter's perspective is from the middle of the street, which snakes back through vertical rows of houses on the hill in the background, not unlike the dynamic view of the Seine from Matisse's studio window in *Notre Dame, a Late Afternoon* (1902, plate 45), leading the eye to the towers of the cathedral.

Diebenkorn's output from 1964 is relatively modest. He made works on paper such as *Untitled* (plate 48), a pared-down, almost elegiac still life for which Matisse's *Pansies* (ca. 1903, plate 47) may have served as a model. But he completed no major canvases. As Katherine Rothkopf notes in her essay in this publication, it was a transitional year during which his travels with Phyllis to the Soviet Union to see the great Matisse collections of the State Hermitage Museum, Leningrad (now Saint Petersburg), and the Pushkin State Museum of Fine Arts, Moscow, precipitated a shift in direction. The experience had a dramatic impact on the last of his Northern California figurative paintings and fueled the next big chapter of his career—his *Ocean Park* series—after he moved south. Diebenkorn's understanding of Matisse across decades of his practice was profound, and the manifestation of this interest could not have been more distinctly his alone. "For a painter," he once said, "I think there is nothing better than that his works are really looked at—and seen."[45] No one can say that Richard Diebenkorn wasn't really looking, or didn't really see.

Notes

1. A.[rthur] M.[illier], "Matisse Exhibit Adds Stature to Local Culture," *Los Angeles Times*, July 20, 1952, D4. "People and What They're Doing in the Valley," *Los Angeles Times*, July 20, 1952, F8.
2. A.M., "Matisse Exhibit Adds Stature to Local Culture." The show had originally been scheduled to end after its tour to New York, Cleveland, Chicago, and San Francisco.
3. Arthur Millier, "22,000 Prove People Will Pay to See Art," *Los Angeles Times*, September 7, 1952, E6. The exhibition ran for twenty-five days.
4. Art Ryon, "One Moment, Please," *Los Angeles Times*, July 24, 1952, A5.
5. Richard Diebenkorn quoted in John Gruen, "Richard Diebenkorn: The Idea Is to Get Everything Right," *Art News* 85, no. 9 (November 1986): 84.
6. Richard Diebenkorn, letter to Bruce Grenville, November 8, 1981. In conducting research for his master's thesis, "Henri Matisse in America, 1900–1955: A Study of the Dissemination of His Art and Ideas in the United States with Particular Reference to His Influence on Abstract Expressionist Painting in New York" (Queen's University, Kingston, Ontario, 1983), Grenville queried Diebenkorn about his interest in Matisse. Diebenkorn's

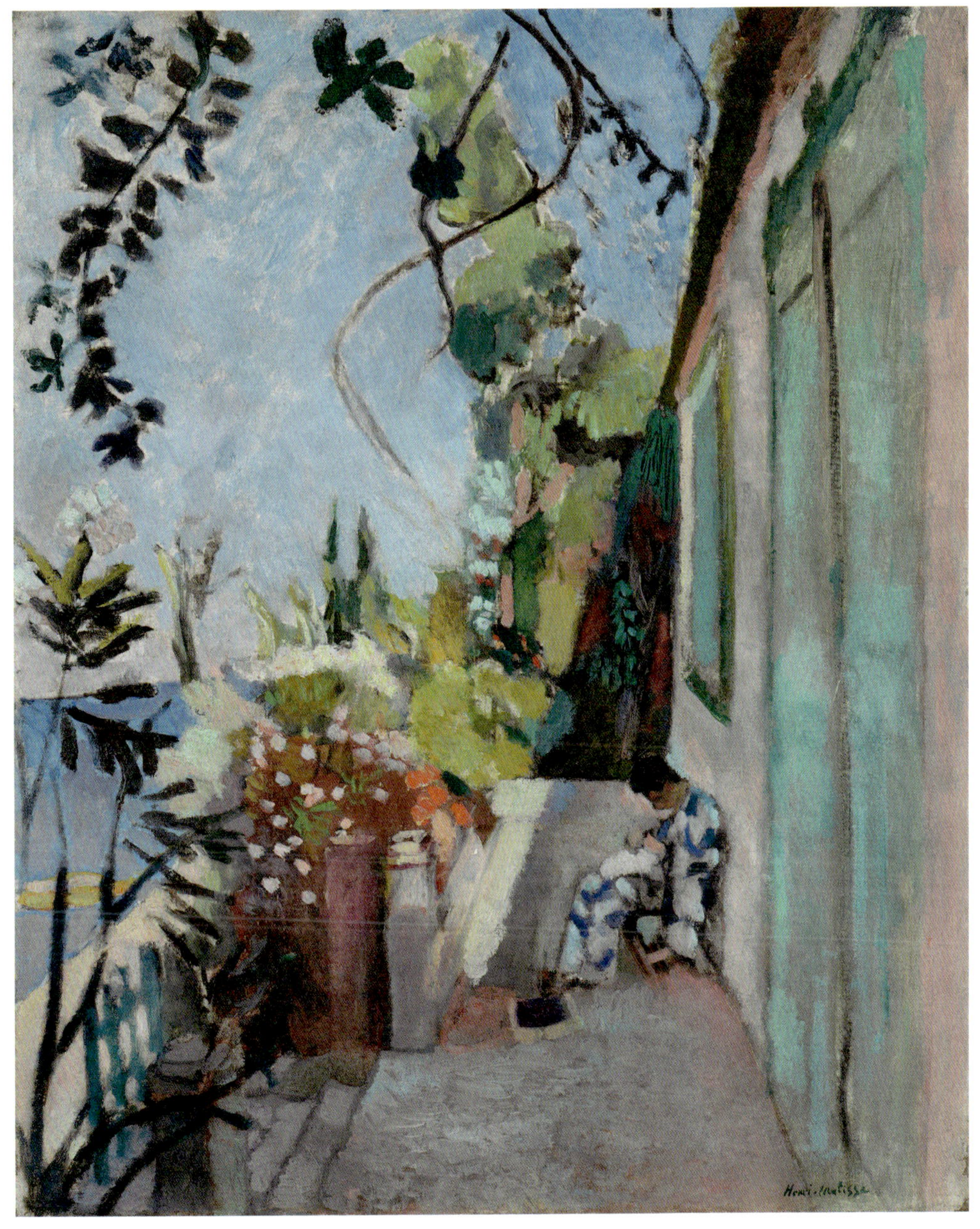

Fig. 9. Henri Matisse, *The Terrace, Saint-Tropez,* 1904. Oil on canvas, 28⅜ x 22⅞ in. (72 x 58 cm). Isabella Stewart Gardner Museum, Boston

written response constitutes a very useful chronological summary of his encounters with Matisse's art in private and public collections, as well as an expression of his ongoing interest in Matisse publications. Grateful thanks to Gail Stavitsky for generously sharing this letter with Katherine Rothkopf via email, January 29, 2015.
7. See the section on Diebenkorn's library on pages 167–72 in this publication.
8. Richard Diebenkorn in "Oral history interview with Richard Diebenkorn, May 1, 1985–December 15, 1987," conducted by Susan Larsen. Archives of American Art, Smithsonian Institution, Washington, D.C. See session 1, May 1, 1985.
9. Diebenkorn, "Oral history interview," conducted by Larsen, May 1, 1985.
10. Information about the contents of Sarah Stein's collection comes from an inventory in a letter from Grace McCann Morley, director of the San Francisco Museum of Art (now San Francisco Museum of Modern Art [SFMOMA]) to Mr. J. J. O'Brien of Messrs. Cosgrove and Company, San Francisco, July 7, 1937, SFMOMA Archives. The partially itemized list also includes fifty Japanese prints. All Matisse works known by the author to have been owned by Sarah and Michael Stein are cataloged in Janet Bishop, Cécile Debray, and Rebecca Rabinow, eds., *The Steins Collect: Matisse, Picasso, and the Parisian Avant-Garde*, exh. cat. (San Francisco: San Francisco Museum of Modern Art in association with Yale University Press, 2011).
11. Information about the installation of the art comes from photographs of the home's interior, as well as a floor plan provided by Dr. Stanley Steinberg, a regular visitor to the house between 1942 and 1948, in an email to Carrie Pilto, former SFMOMA project assistant curator, November 23, 2009. Exhibition files for *The Steins Collect*, SFMOMA Department of Painting and Sculpture.
12. Jane Livingston, "Matisse's 'Tea,'" *Los Angeles County Museum of Art Bulletin* 20, no. 2 (1974): 54. The article quotes Diebenkorn: "Sometimes a painter gets to the end of a painting and something seems wrong or weak. You'll try to fix it and find out it was the key to the whole thing, and you've ruined it. Matisse learned one lesson early—to forego the temptation of fixing that one more place."
13. These three paintings (with *Tea* identified as *Easter*) are noted as having been memorable for the artist in Gerald Nordland, *Richard Diebenkorn* (New York: Rizzoli, 1987), 12. In a conversation with the author, March 18, 2009, Nordland indicated that it was only after Diebenkorn went away and visited East Coast museums that he could put what he had seen at the Stein home in context.
14. An image was provided by Carl Schmitz, visual resources and art research librarian, Richard Diebenkorn Foundation, in an email to the author, January 21, 2016. The mount is inscribed in Diebenkorn's hand: "Gift of Mrs. Stein—Palo Alto—1943?"
15. Richard Diebenkorn quoted in Jan Butterfield, "Pentimenti: Seeing and Then Seeing Again," in *Resource/Response/Reservoir—Richard Diebenkorn: Paintings 1948–1983*, exh. brochure (San Francisco: San Francisco Museum of Modern Art, 1983), n.p.
16. Diebenkorn defended his interest in the painting: "There's a simplicity that it has and it's terribly rich in the way it's painted, but . . . [it is a] fairly austere one in other ways." Diebenkorn, "Oral history interview," conducted by Larsen, May 1, 1985.
17. Diebenkorn, "Oral history interview," conducted by Larsen, May 1, 1985.
18. Richard Diebenkorn in "Transcript of 1982 Interview with Richard Diebenkorn by Fritz Jellinghouse," The Phillips Collection Library and Archives, Washington, D.C.
19. Phyllis Diebenkorn, letter to Nancy Boas, March 15, 2007, quoted in Nancy Boas, *David Park: A Painter's Life* (Berkeley: University of California Press, 2012), 95.
20. Diebenkorn, "Oral history interview," conducted by Larsen, May 1, 1985.
21. Richard Diebenkorn quoted in Frederick Wight, "The Phillips Collection—Diebenkorn, Woelffer, Mullican: A Discussion," *Artforum* 1, no. 10 (April 1963): 27.
22. Diebenkorn to Grenville, 1981.
23. Phyllis Diebenkorn quoted in Dan Hofstadter, "Profiles: Almost Free of the Mirror," *New Yorker*, September 7, 1987, 54.
24. Richard Diebenkorn quoted in Paul Mills, *The New Figurative Art of David Park* (Santa Barbara, CA: Capra Press, 1988), 70.
25. Richard Diebenkorn in response to a questionnaire by Dan Tooker, April 3, 1973, quoted in Nordland, *Richard Diebenkorn*, 88.
26. Diebenkorn quoted in Butterfield, "Pentimenti," n.p.
27. Recollection of Phyllis Diebenkorn noted in Ruth E. Fine, "Reality: Digested, Transmuted, and Twisted," in *The Art of Richard Diebenkorn*, exh. cat., ed. Jane Livingston (New York: Whitney Museum of American Art, 1997), 105, fn14.
28. Jori Finkel, "Wayne Thiebaud Examines a Still Life," *Los Angeles Times*, June 30, 2013.
29. Diebenkorn quoted in Butterfield, "Pentimenti," n.p.
30. Ibid.
31. Diebenkorn quoted in Hofstadter, "Profiles," 55.
32. Richard Diebenkorn, letter to Dore Ashton, March 13, 1985. Dore Ashton papers, Archives of American Art, Smithsonian Institution, Washington, D.C. He later recalled of Lewis, "His Persian and Mogul paintings were already expensive, but the Rajput ones, which I like the best, were still affordable; I never paid more than a hundred dollars for anything, and at the same time even that seemed a bit expensive." Diebenkorn quoted in Hofstadter, "Profiles," 55.
33. "I often began with two, rarely three, figures. And I think I could count on my hand, one hand probably, the paintings where both figures survived." Diebenkorn, "Oral history interview," conducted by Larsen, May 2, 1985.
34. John Elderfield shared Anne d'Harnoncourt's story of her father's outing with Matisse in a conversation with the author and Katherine Rothkopf, July 25, 2014. Joseph Rishel added additional detail in a conversation with the author, April 13, 2016. In all likelihood, the game Matisse attended was an end-of-season matchup between the Philadelphia Athletics and the New York Yankees.
35. "Munch has interested me particularly only since I changed to representation. I was in Albuquerque when the Munch exhibition was shown in Denver and I can remember deciding that this would be too great a trip to look at pictures. I'm sure I would have made it for the Matisse show." Richard Diebenkorn, letter to Ellen Johnson, July 20, 1958. Allen Memorial Art Museum archives, Oberlin College, Ohio.
36. Diebenkorn, "Oral history interview," conducted by Larsen, May 2, 1985.
37. Diebenkorn quoted in Butterfield, "Pentimenti," n.p.
38. Barnes Foundation Archives, Merion, Pennsylvania.
39. Barnes Foundation secretary, letter to the Ehrich Galleries, New York, June 15, 1928. Object file, Barnes Foundation, Philadelphia.
40. Violette de Mazia, "E Pluribus Unum—Cont'd: Part III," *Journal of the Art Department* 8, no. 1 (Merion Station, PA: The Barnes Foundation Press, Spring 1977): 35.
41. Diebenkorn to Grenville, 1981. "1959, Barnes Foundation (Riffian, etc.)" appears in the artist's list of encounters with Matisse. The actual date of his visit has since been confirmed as 1960.
42. Henri Matisse in a 1942 broadcast, transcribed in Alfred H. Barr Jr., *Matisse: His Art and His Public* (New York: The Museum of Modern Art, 1951), 562.
43. In Diebenkorn to Grenville, 1981, the artist noted a visit to Boston and the Isabella Stewart Gardner Museum in 1960. He would not have passed up the chance to visit the Museum of Fine Arts, Boston, which has had *Carmelina* in its holdings since 1931.
44. Wayne Thiebaud quoted in Richard Wollheim, "On Thiebaud and Diebenkorn: Richard Wollheim Talks to Wayne Thiebaud," *Modern Painters: A Quarterly Journal of the Fine Arts* 4, no. 2 (Autumn 1991): 68.
45. Diebenkorn to Johnson, 1958.

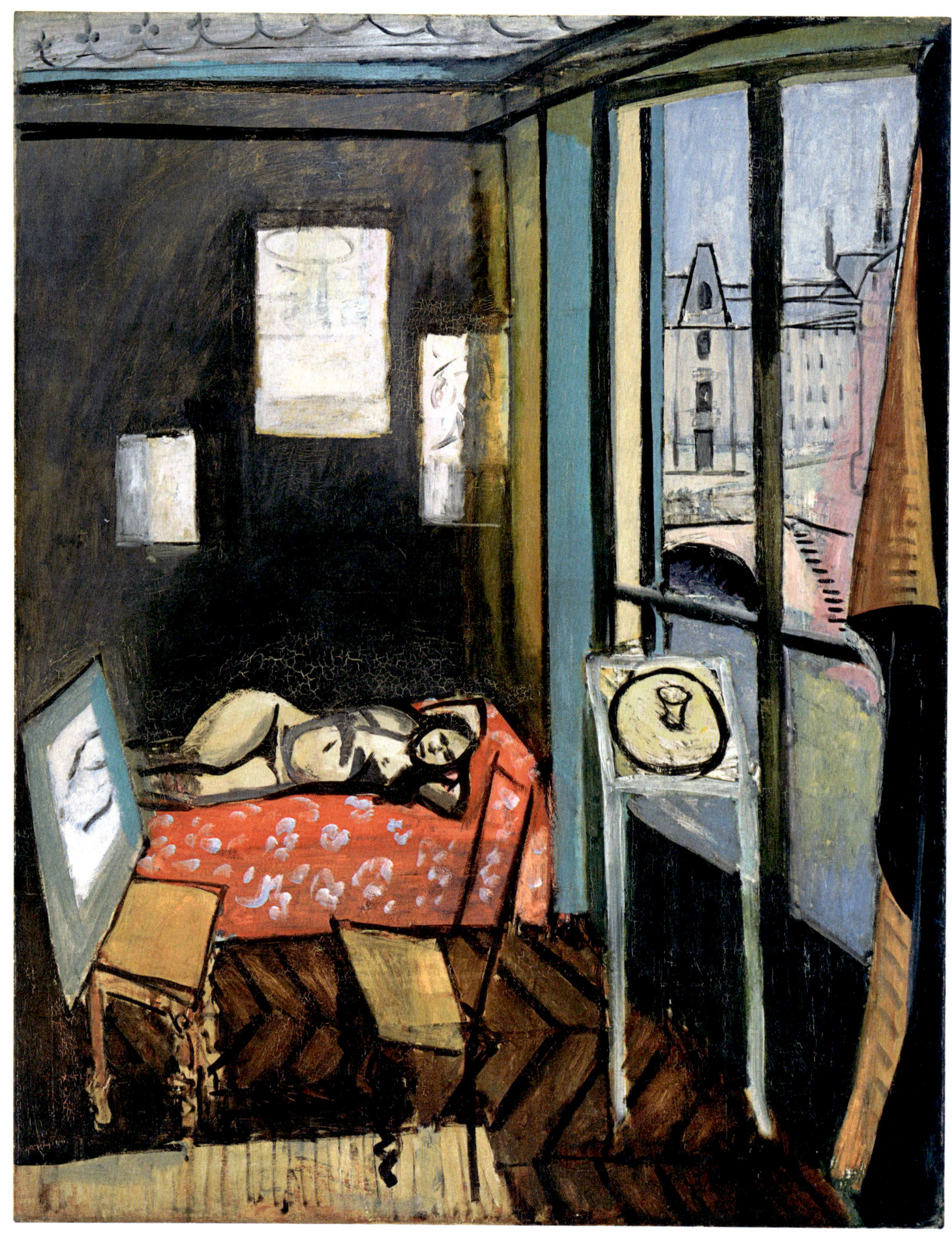

Plate 1. Henri Matisse, *Studio, Quai Saint-Michel,* 1916. Oil on canvas, 58¼ x 46 in. (148 x 116.8 cm). The Phillips Collection, Washington, D.C.

OPPOSITE
Plate 2. Richard Diebenkorn, *Urbana #4,* 1953. Oil on canvas, 66 x 49 in. (167.6 x 124.5 cm). Colorado Springs Fine Arts Center, gift of Julianne Kemper Gilliam

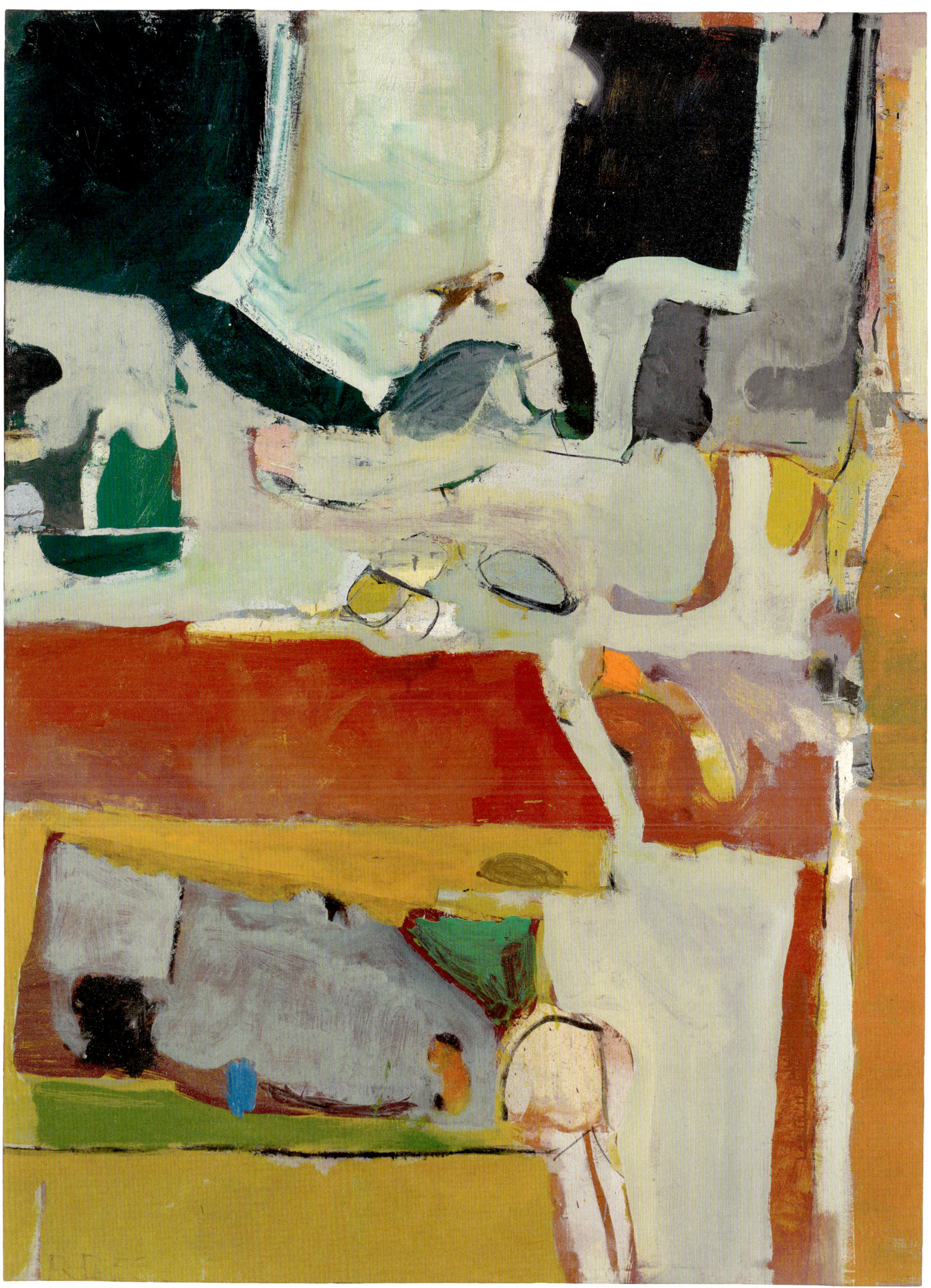

Plate 3. Richard Diebenkorn, *Urbana #2 (The Archer)*, 1953. Oil on canvas, 64½ x 47½ in. (163.8 x 120.7 cm). Estate of the artist

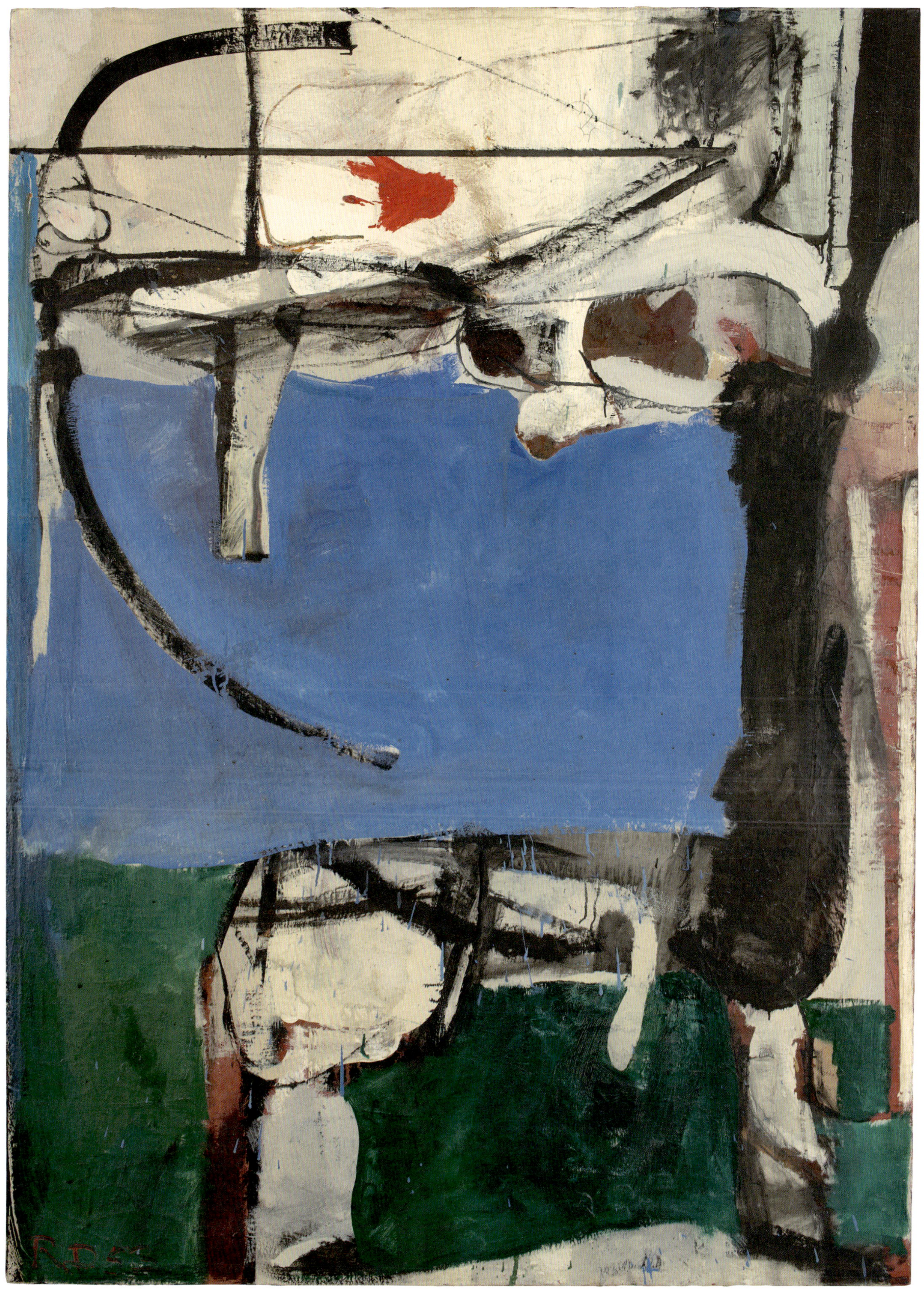

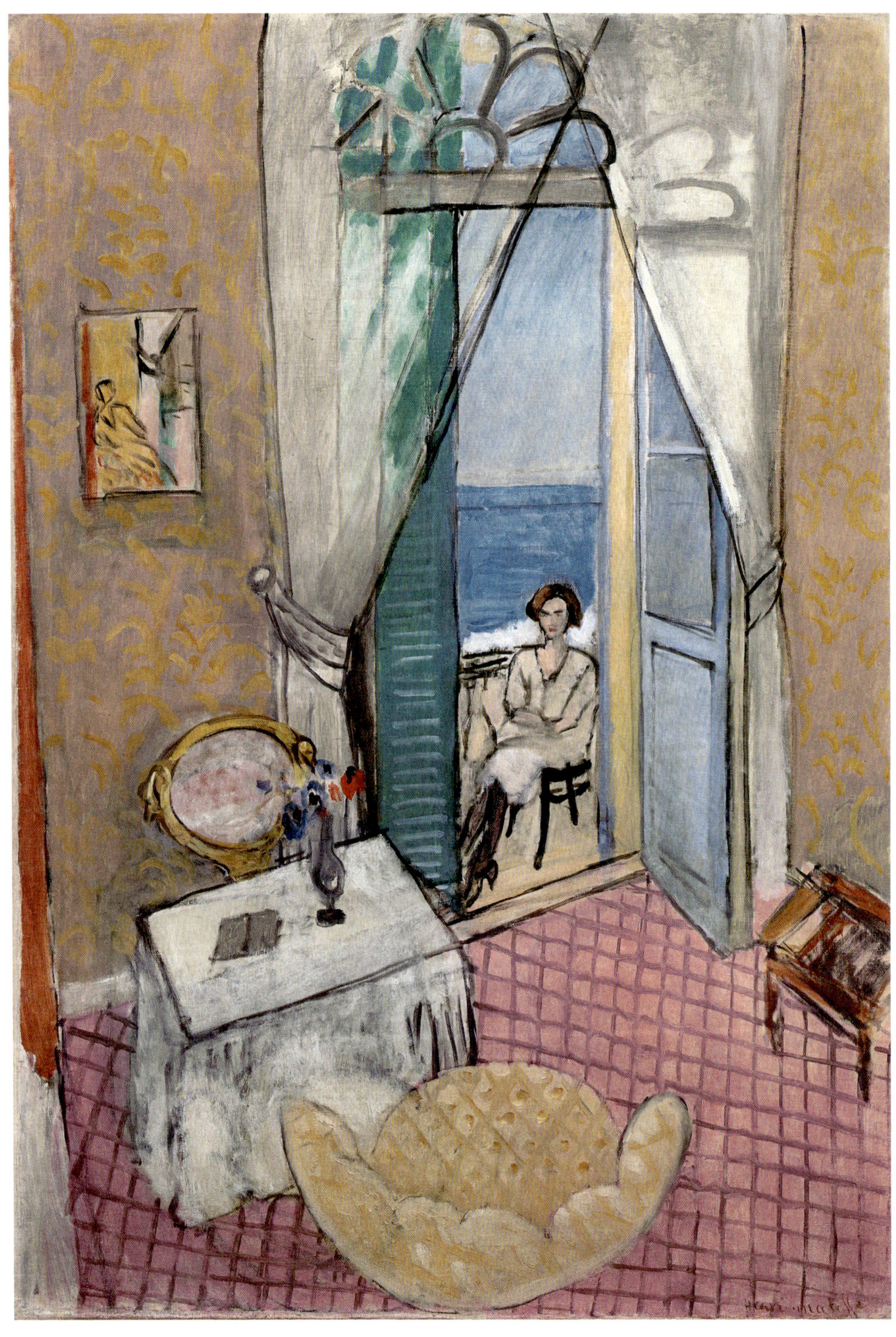

Plate 4. Henri Matisse, *Interior at Nice,* 1919 or 1920. Oil on canvas, 52 x 35 in. (132.1 x 88.9 cm). The Art Institute of Chicago, gift of Mrs. Gilbert W. Chapman

OPPOSITE
Plate 5. Richard Diebenkorn, *Urbana #5 (Beach Town),* 1953. Oil on canvas, 68 x 53½ in. (172.7 x 135.9 cm). Collection of Joann K. Phillips

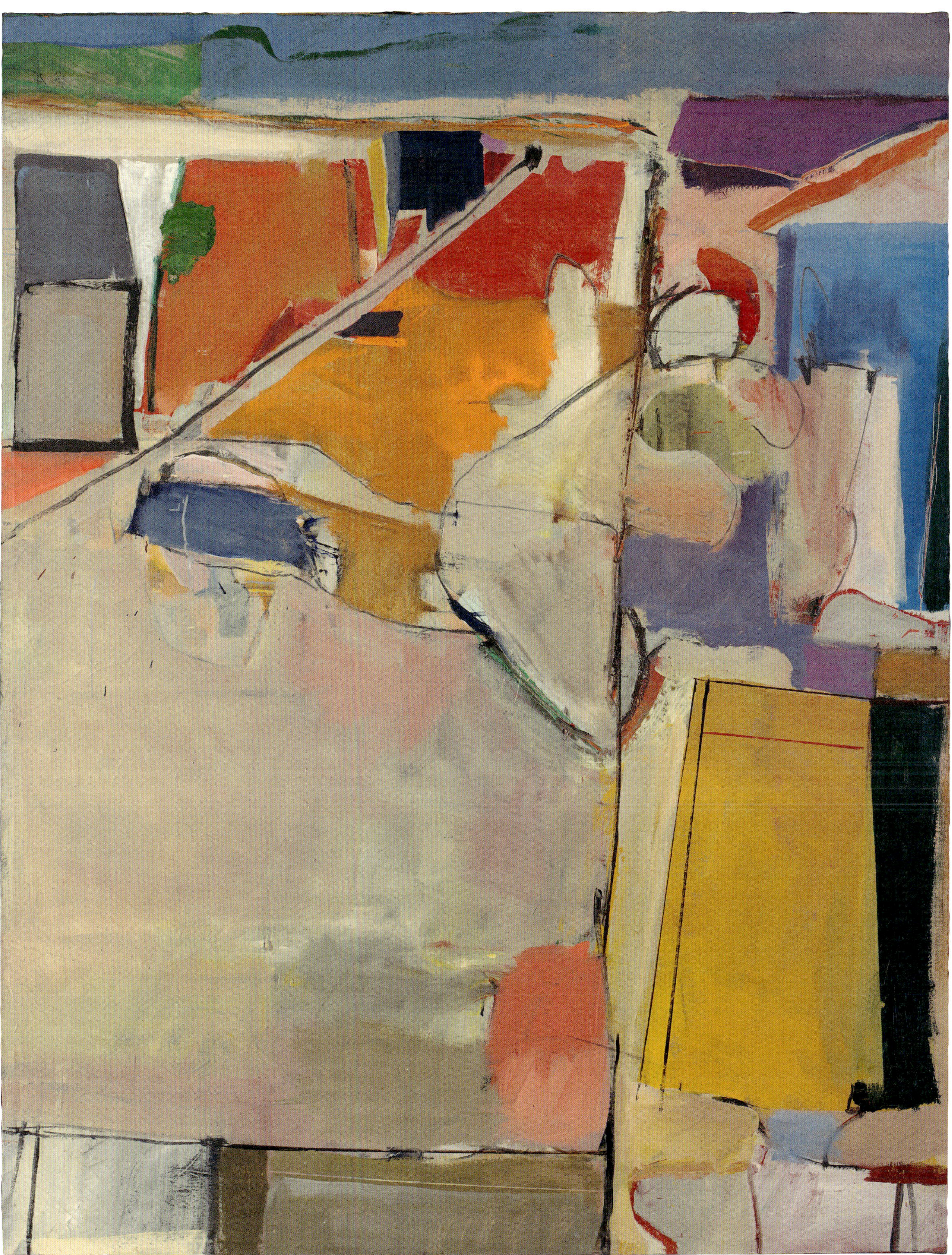

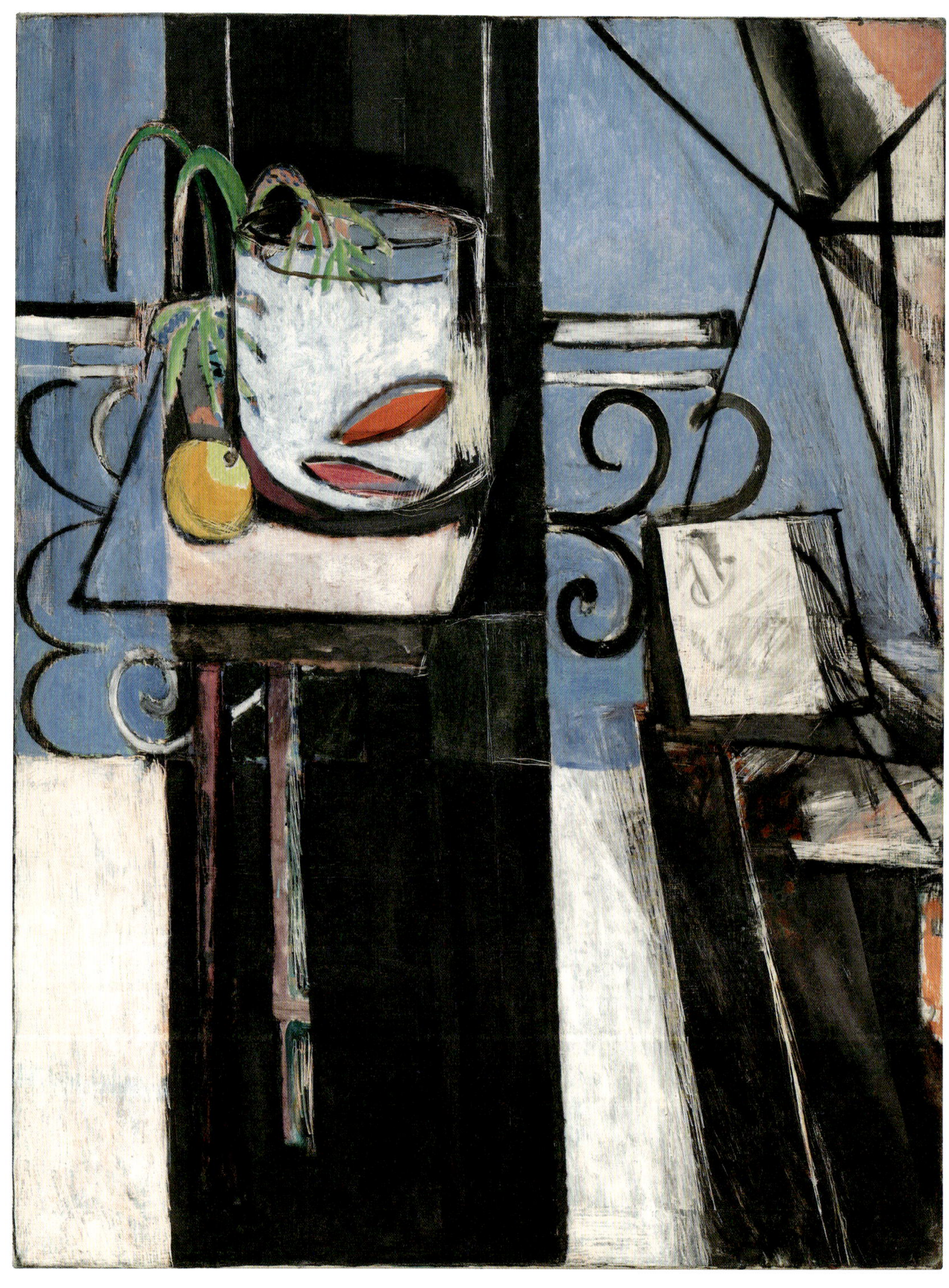

Plate 6. Henri Matisse, *Goldfish and Palette,* 1914. Oil on canvas, 57¾ x 44¼ in. (146.7 x 112.4 cm). The Museum of Modern Art, New York, gift and bequest of Florene M. Schoenborn and Samuel A. Marx

OPPOSITE
Plate 7. Richard Diebenkorn, *Urbana #6,* 1953. Oil on canvas, 69¼ x 58 in. (175.9 x 147.3 cm). Modern Art Museum of Fort Worth, museum purchase, Sid W. Richardson Foundation Endowment Fund

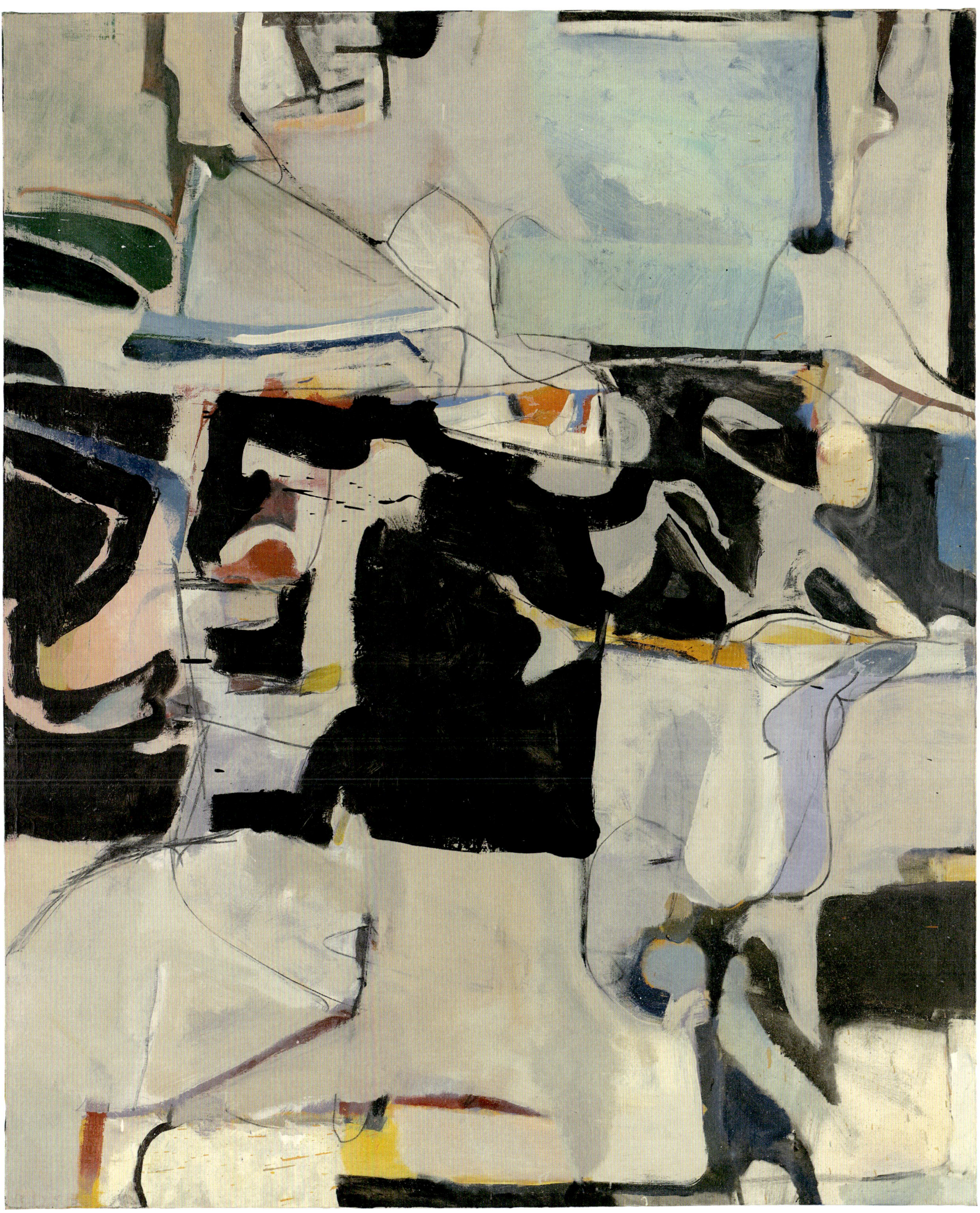

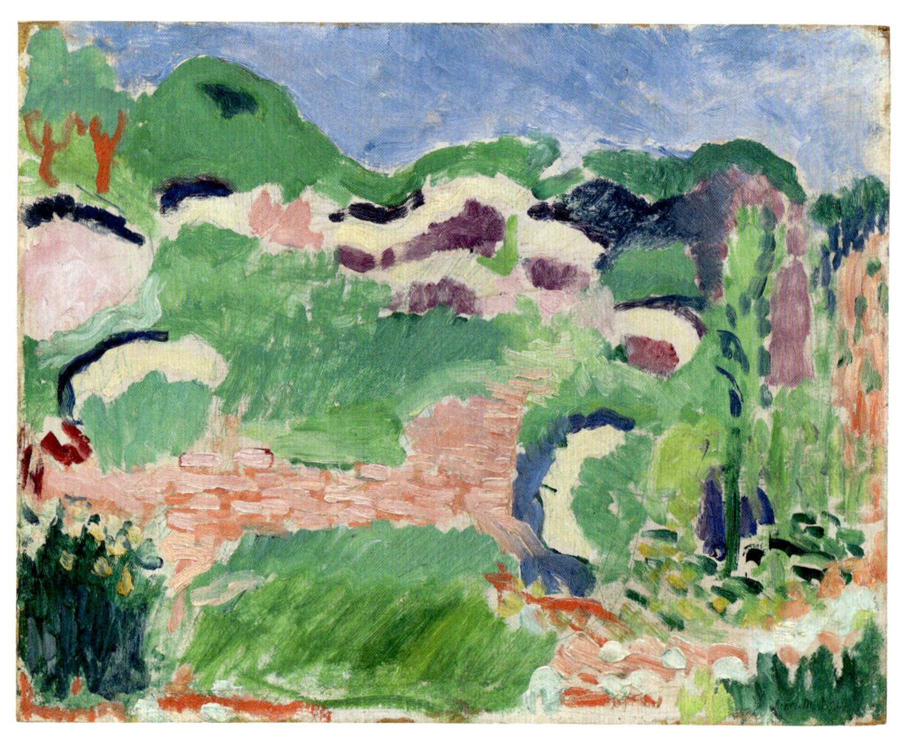

Plate 8. Henri Matisse, *Landscape: Broom,* 1906. Oil on panel, 12 x 15⅝ in. (30.5 x 39.7 cm). San Francisco Museum of Modern Art, bequest of Elise S. Haas

OPPOSITE
Plate 9. Richard Diebenkorn, *Berkeley #5,* 1953. Oil on canvas, 53 x 53 in. (134.6 x 134.6 cm). Private collection

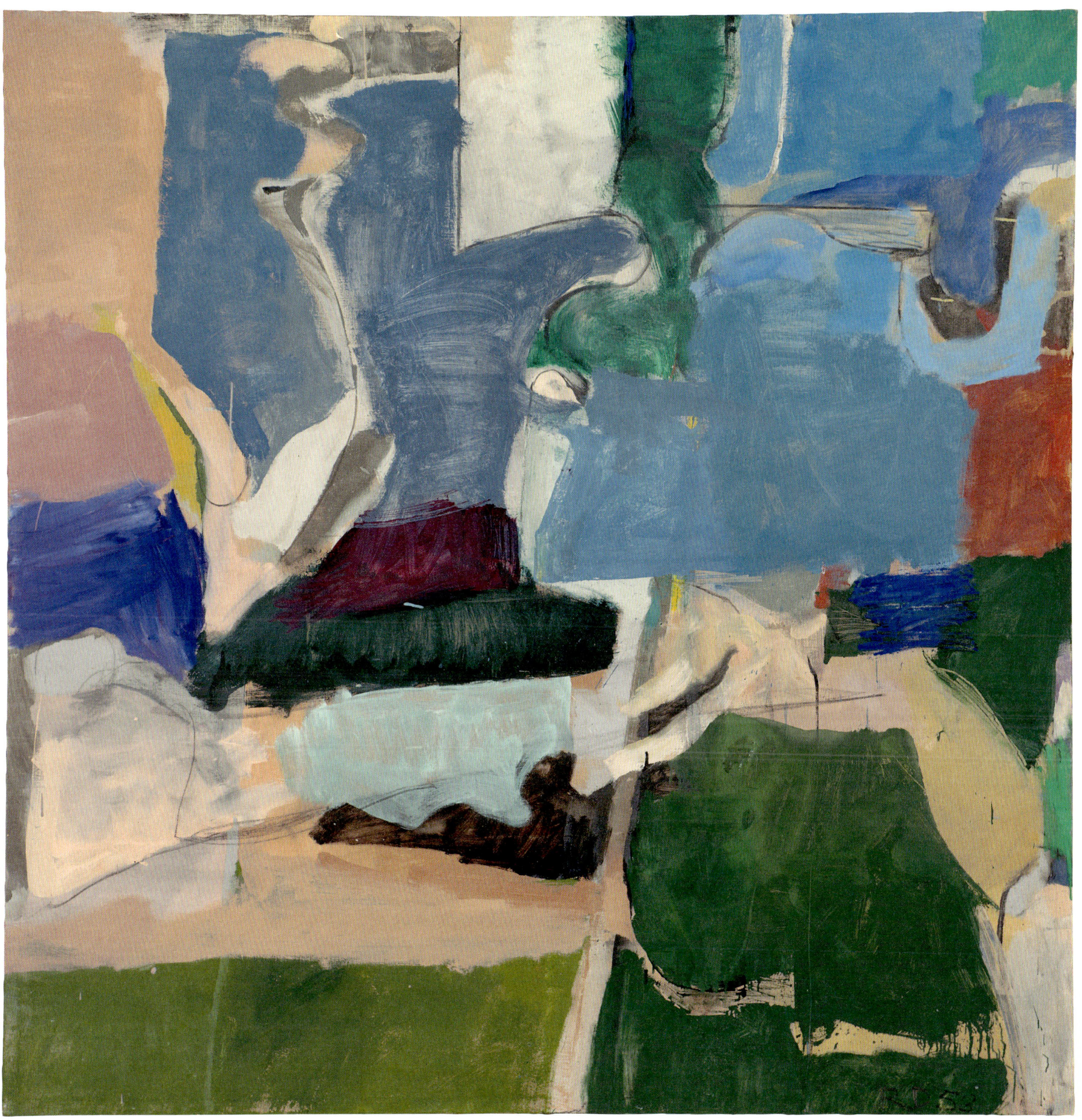

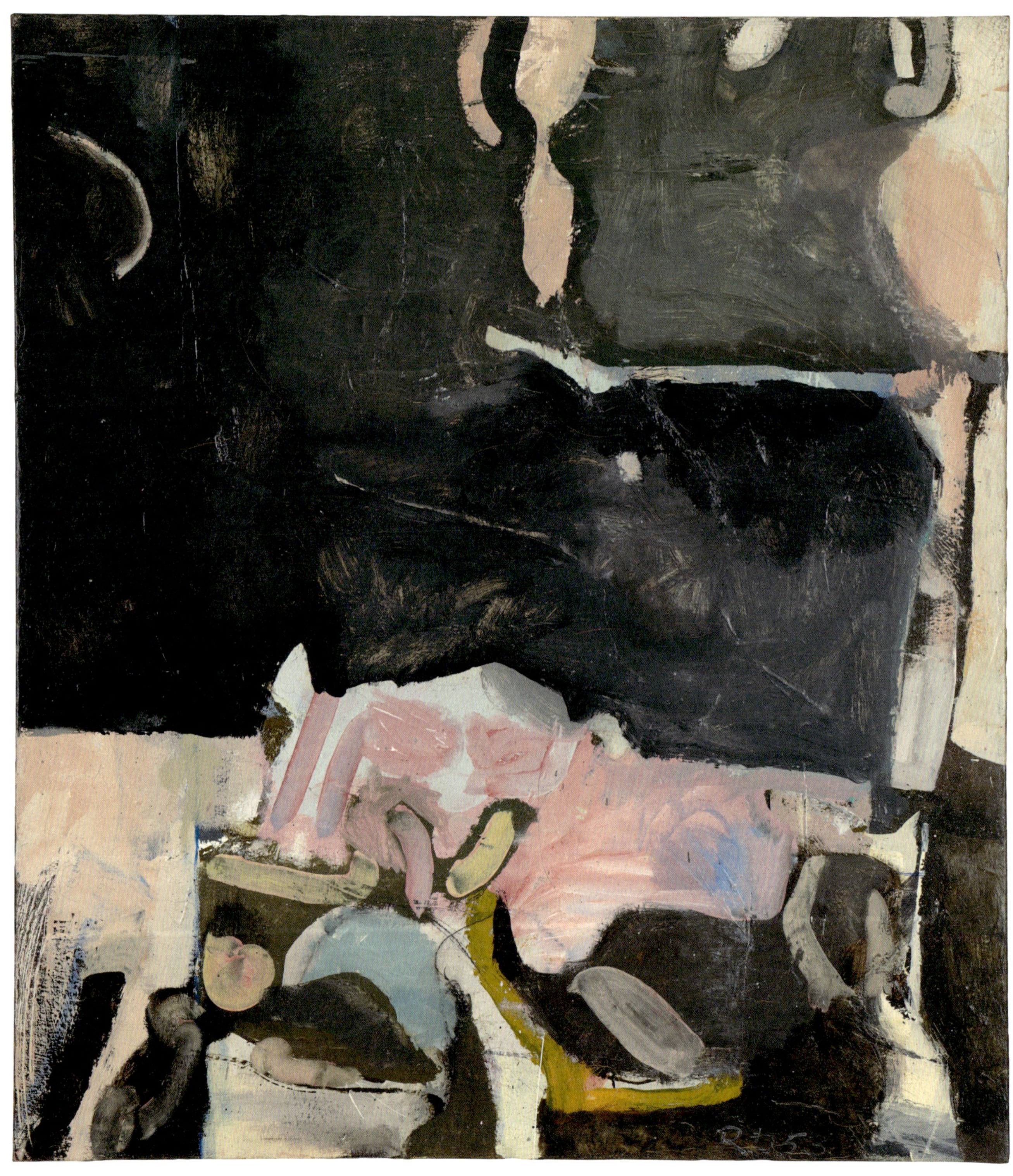

Plate 10. Richard Diebenkorn, *Berkeley #7,* 1953. Oil on canvas, 47¾ x 43 in. (121.3 x 109.2 cm). Mildred Lane Kemper Art Museum, Washington University in St. Louis, gift of Joseph Pulitzer Jr.

OPPOSITE
Plate 11. Richard Diebenkorn, *Berkeley #22,* 1954. Oil on canvas, 59 x 57 in. (149.9 x 144.8 cm). Hirshhorn Museum and Sculpture Garden, Smithsonian Institution, Washington, D.C., Regents Collections Acquisition Program

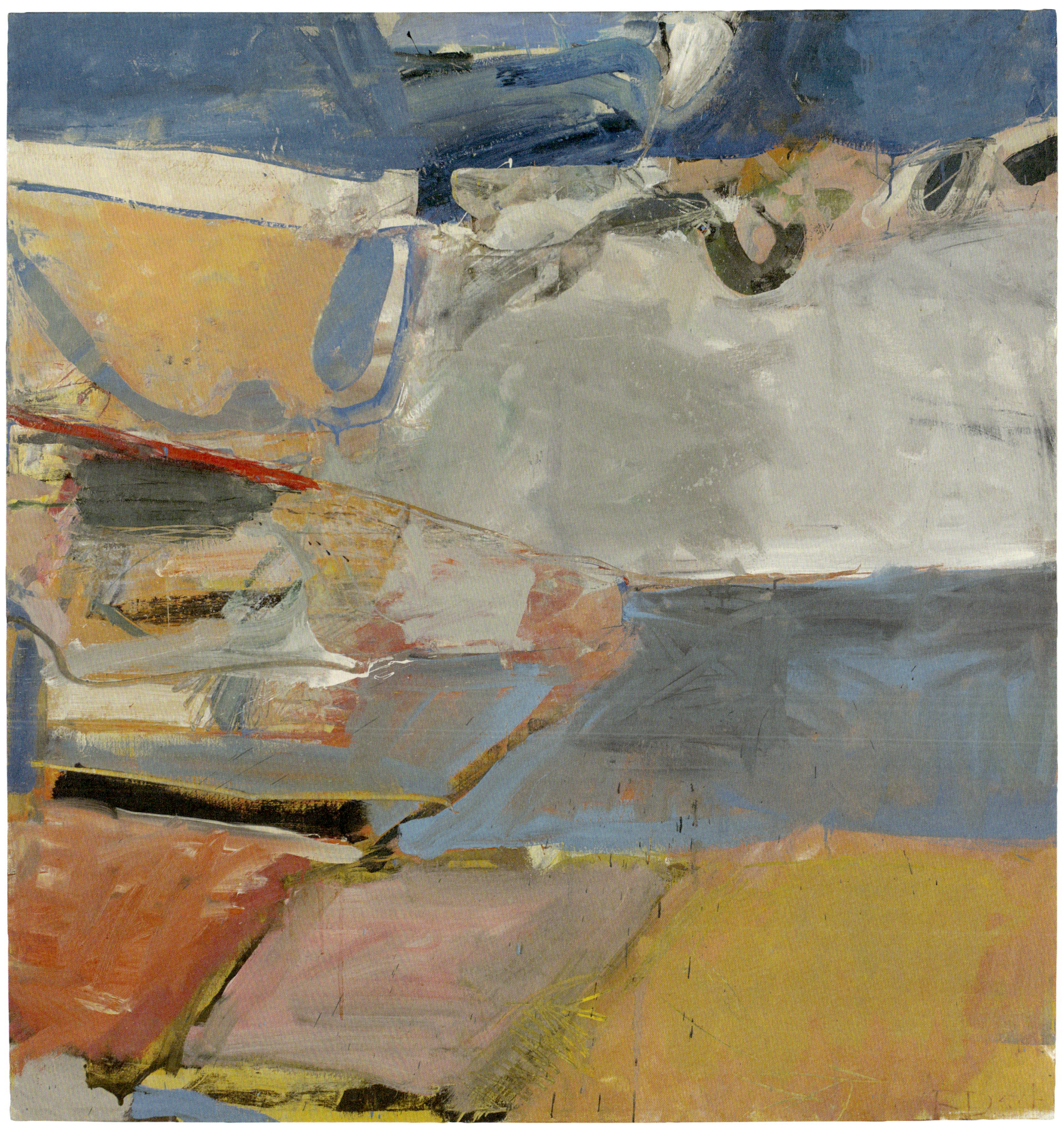

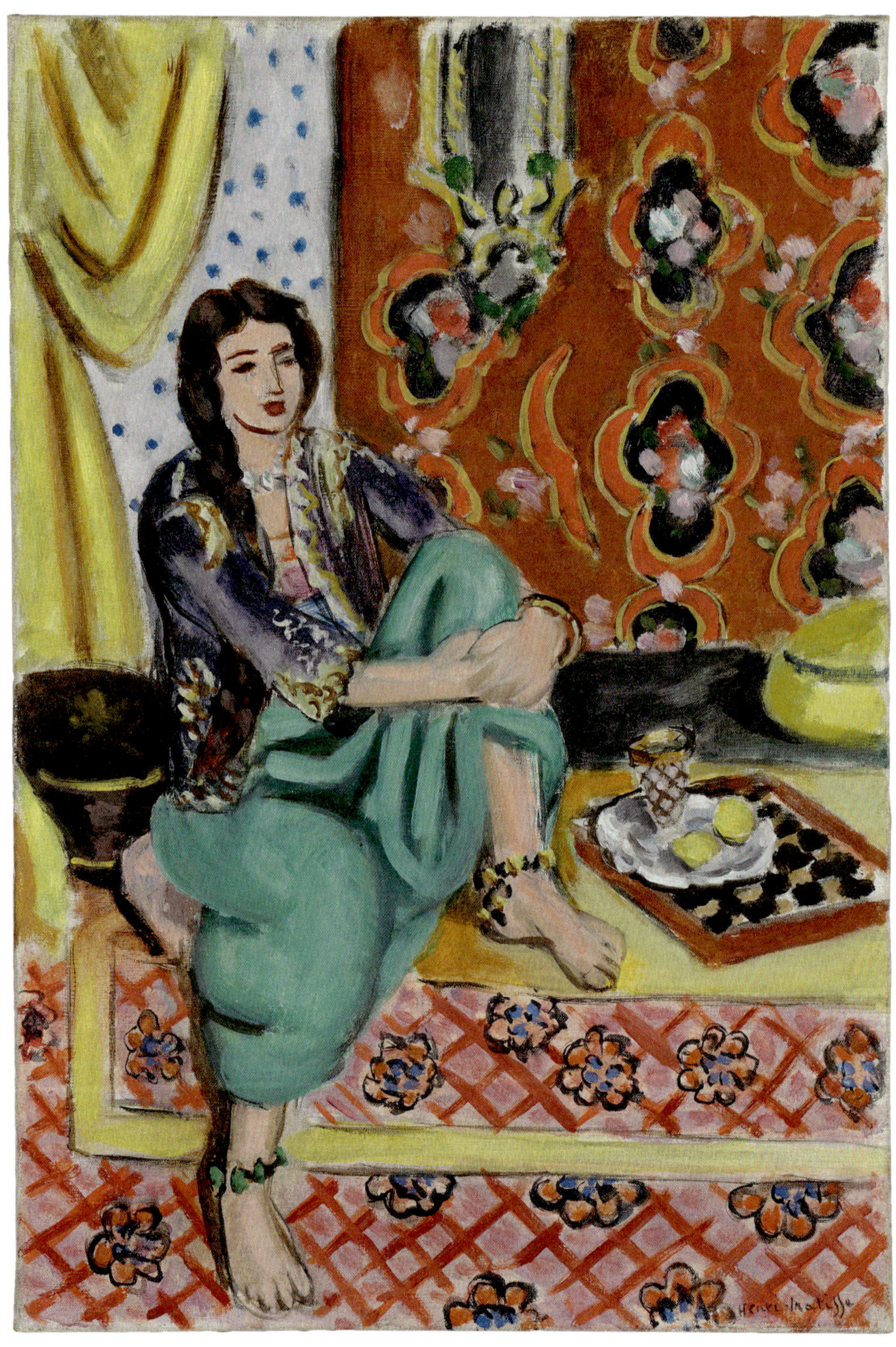

Plate 12. Henri Matisse, *Seated Odalisque, Left Knee Bent, Ornamental Background and Checkerboard,* 1928. Oil on canvas, 21⅝ x 14⅞ in. (54.9 x 37.8 cm). The Baltimore Museum of Art: The Cone Collection, formed by Dr. Claribel Cone and Miss Etta Cone of Baltimore, Maryland

OPPOSITE
Plate 13. Richard Diebenkorn, *Berkeley #23,* 1955. Oil on canvas, 62 x 54¾ in. (157.5 x 139 cm). San Francisco Museum of Modern Art, gift of the Women's Board

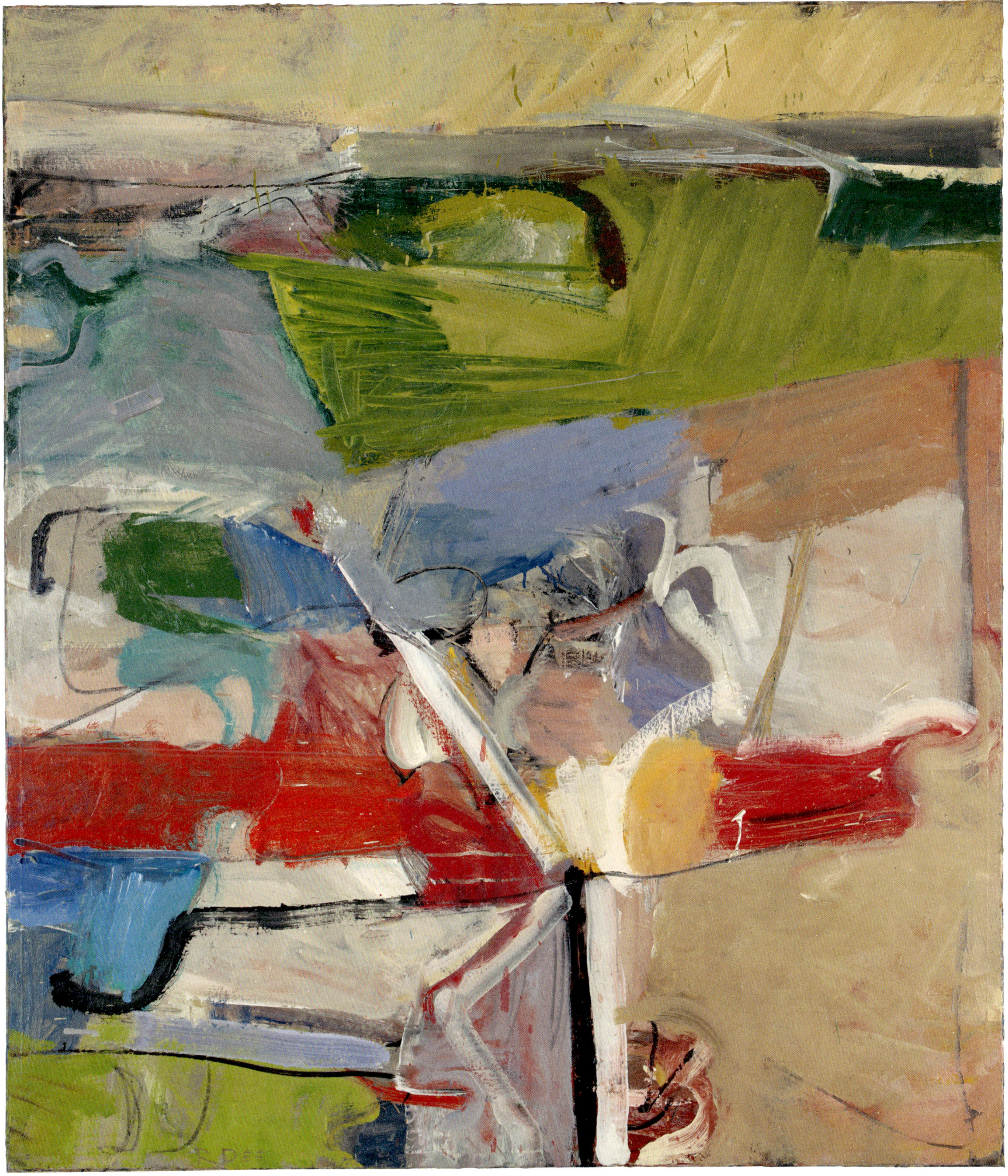

Plate 14. Richard Diebenkorn, *Berkeley #57,* 1955. Oil on canvas, 58¾ x 58¾ in. (149.2 x 149.2 cm). San Francisco Museum of Modern Art, bequest of Joseph M. Bransten in memory of Ellen Hart Bransten

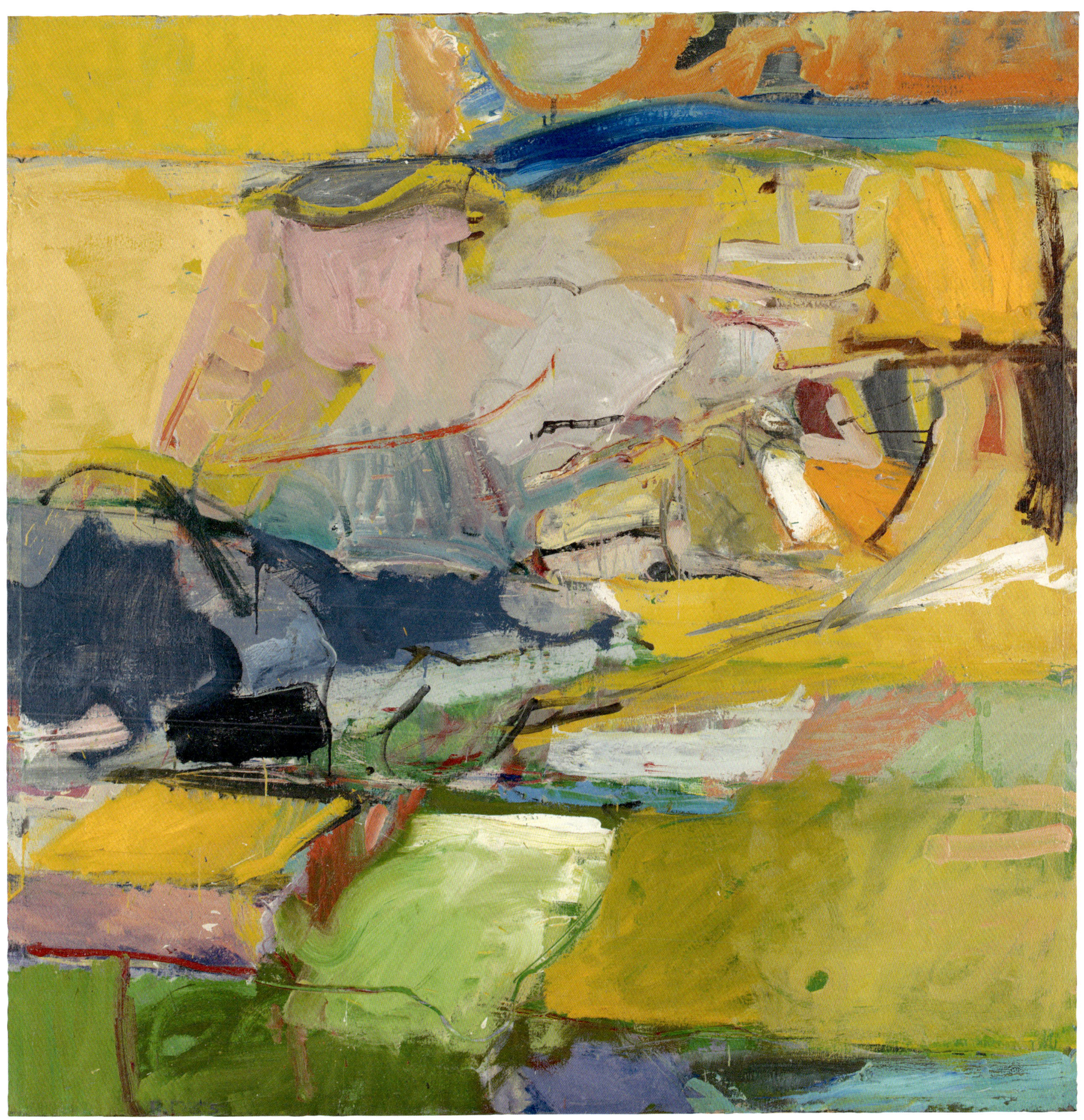

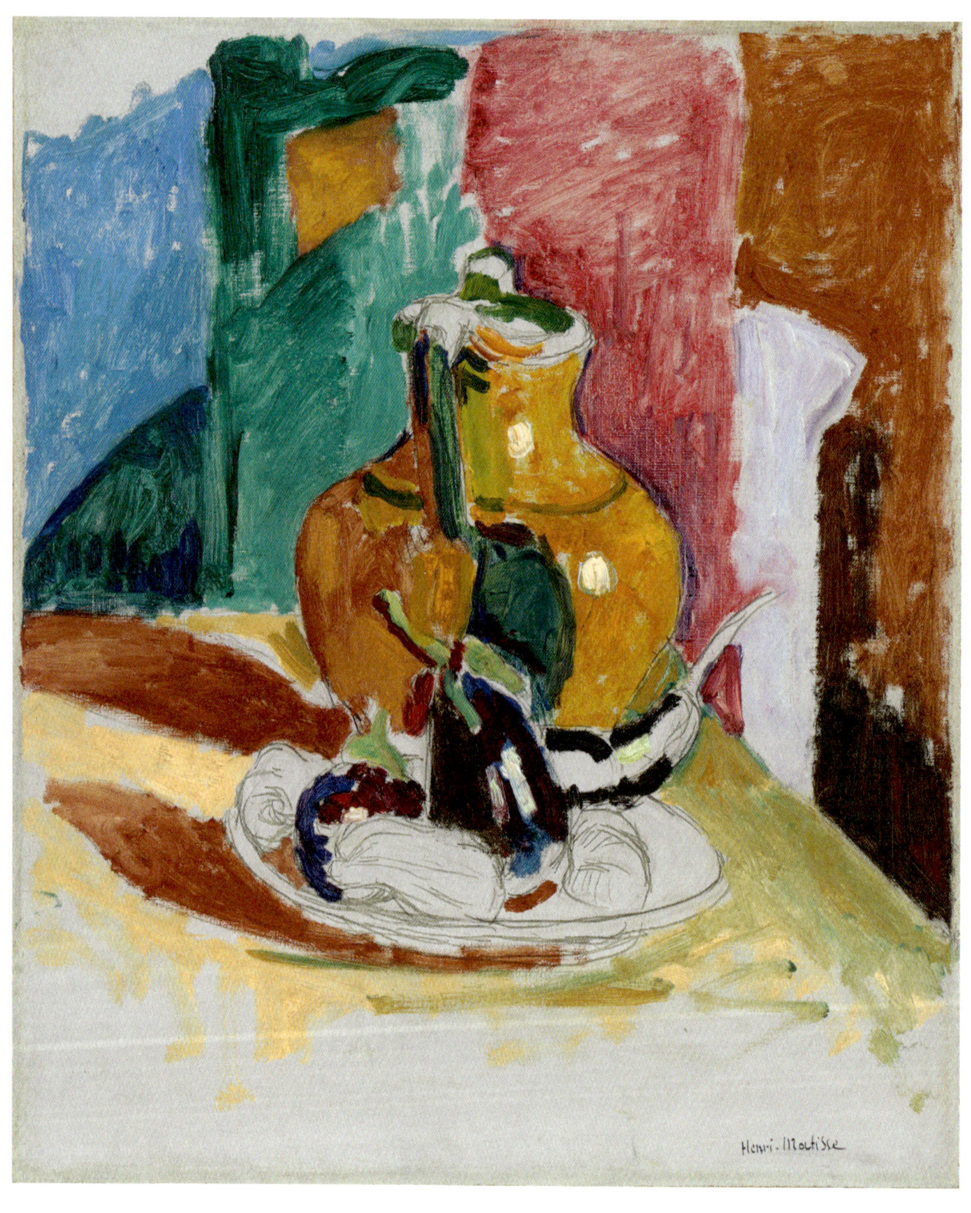

Plate 15. Henri Matisse, *Yellow Pottery from Provence,* 1905. Oil on canvas, 21⅞ x 18⅜ in. (55.6 x 46.7 cm). The Baltimore Museum of Art: The Cone Collection, formed by Dr. Claribel Cone and Miss Etta Cone of Baltimore, Maryland

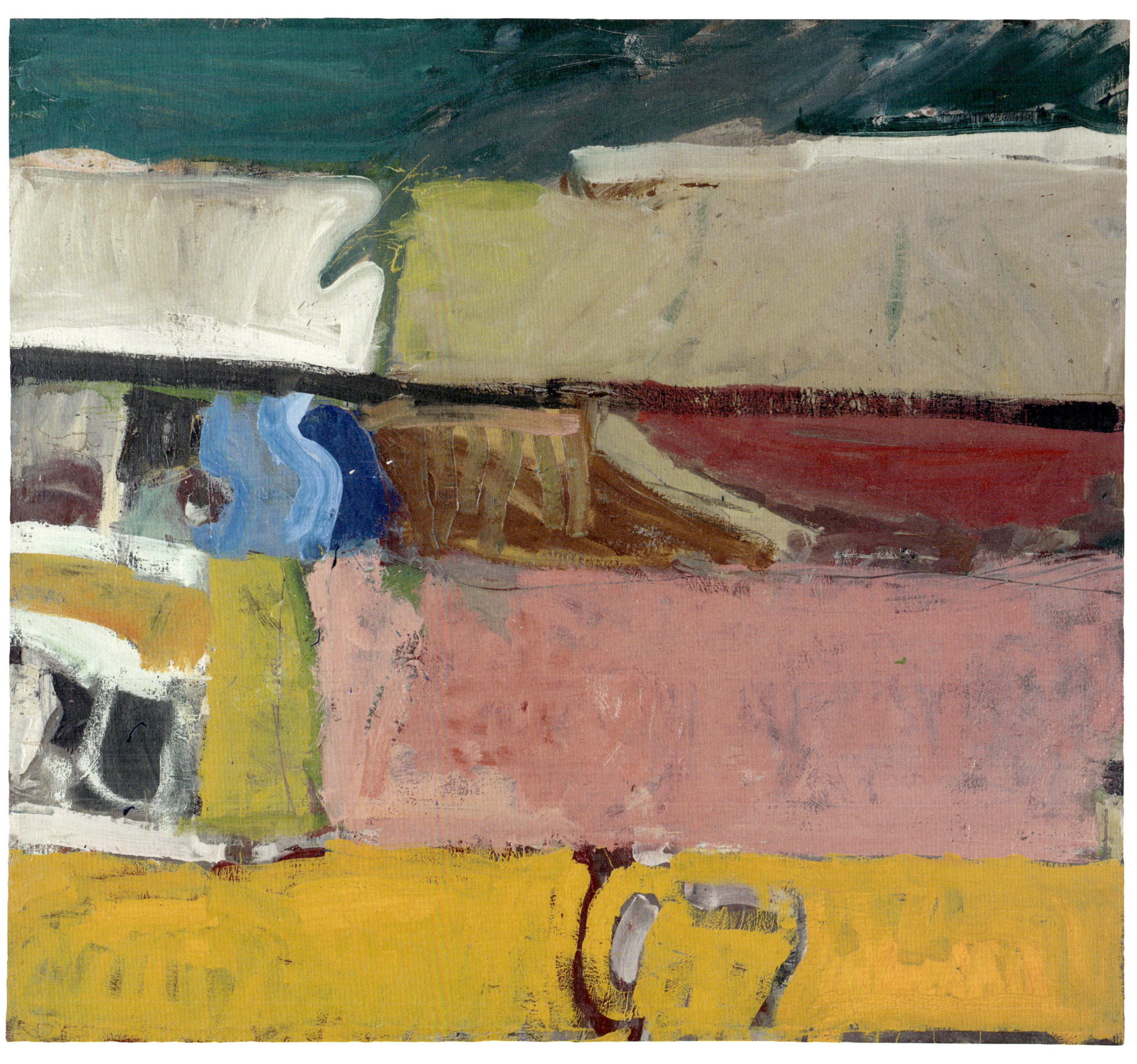

Plate 16. Richard Diebenkorn, *Berkeley #47*, 1955. Oil on canvas, 58⅞ x 65⅞ in. (149.5 x 167.3 cm).
The Doris and Donald Fisher Collection at the San Francisco Museum of Modern Art

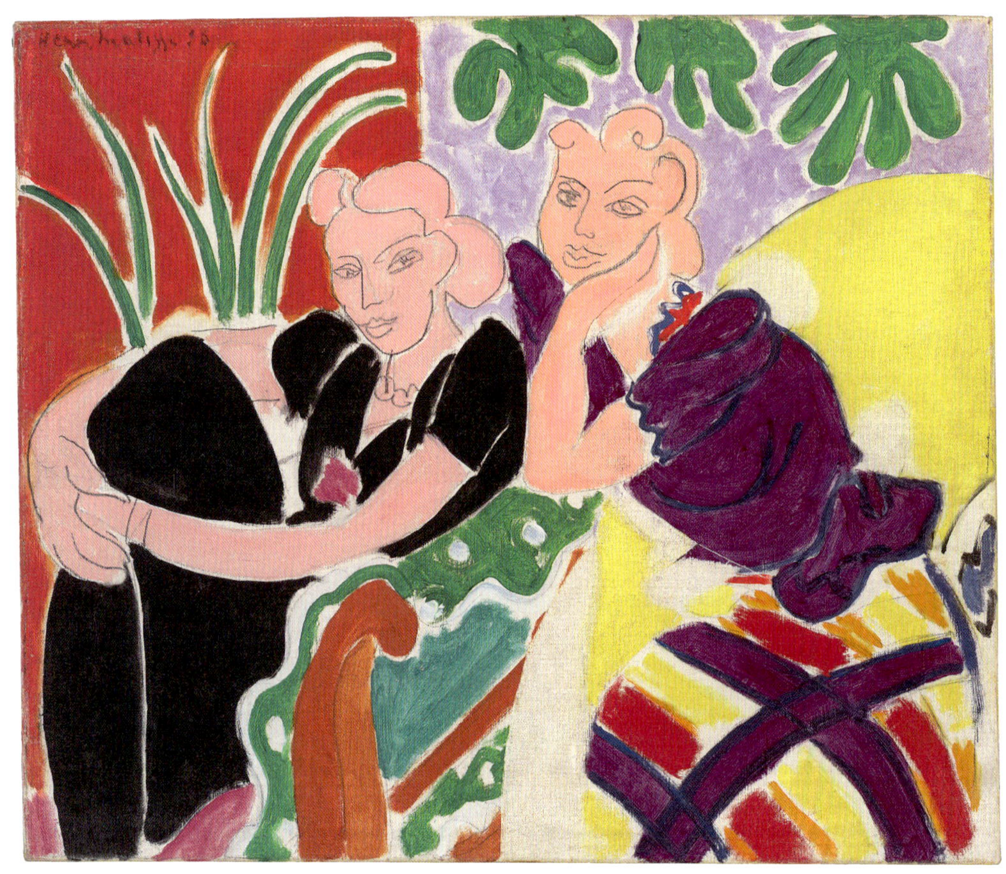

Plate 17. Henri Matisse, *The Conversation,* 1938. Oil on canvas, 18⅜ x 21¾ in. (46.7 x 55.3 cm). San Francisco Museum of Modern Art, bequest of Mr. James D. Zellerbach

OPPOSITE
Plate 18. Richard Diebenkorn, *Berkeley #58,* 1955. Oil on canvas, 64 x 58¾ in. (162.6 x 149.2 cm). Private collection

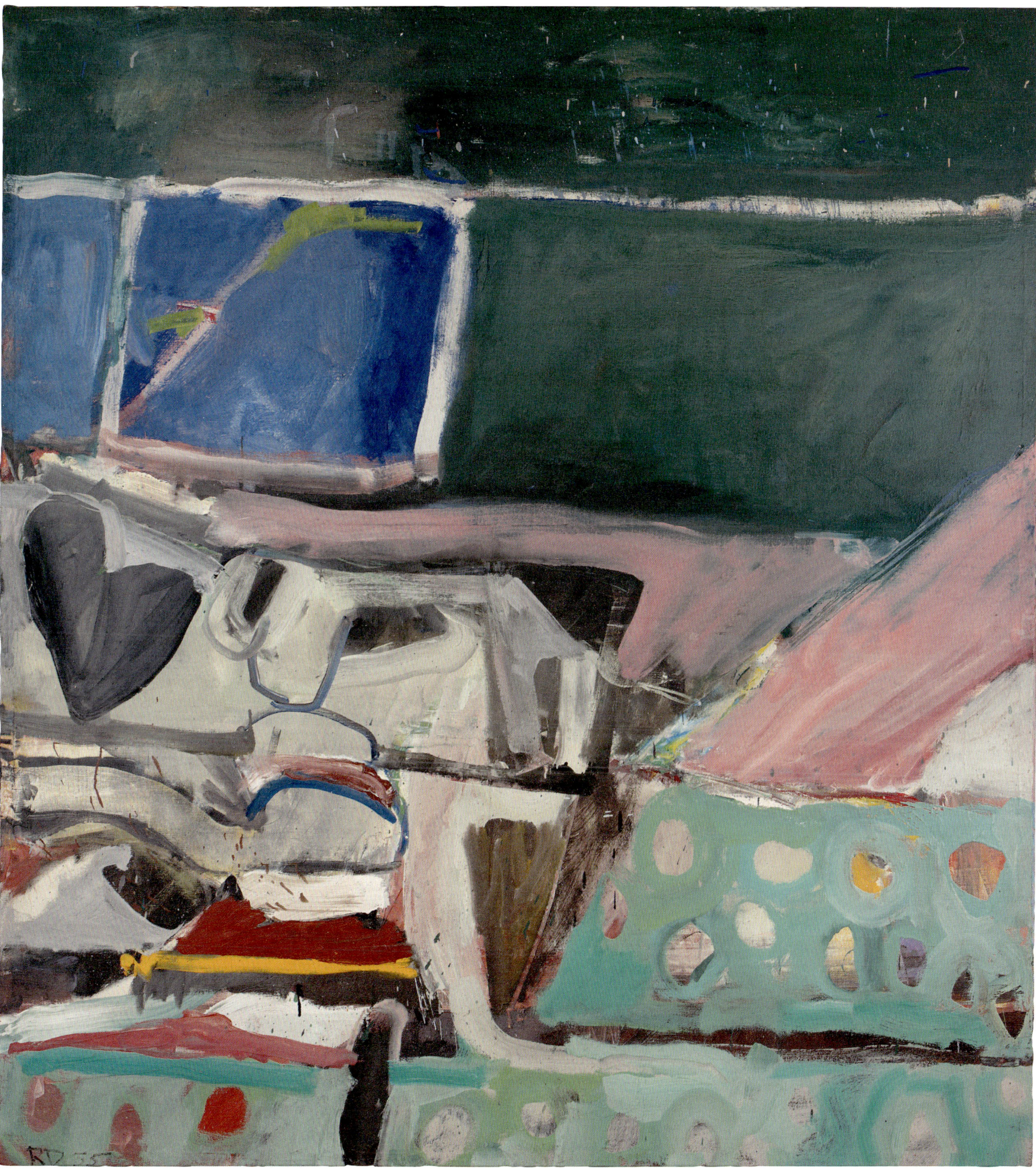

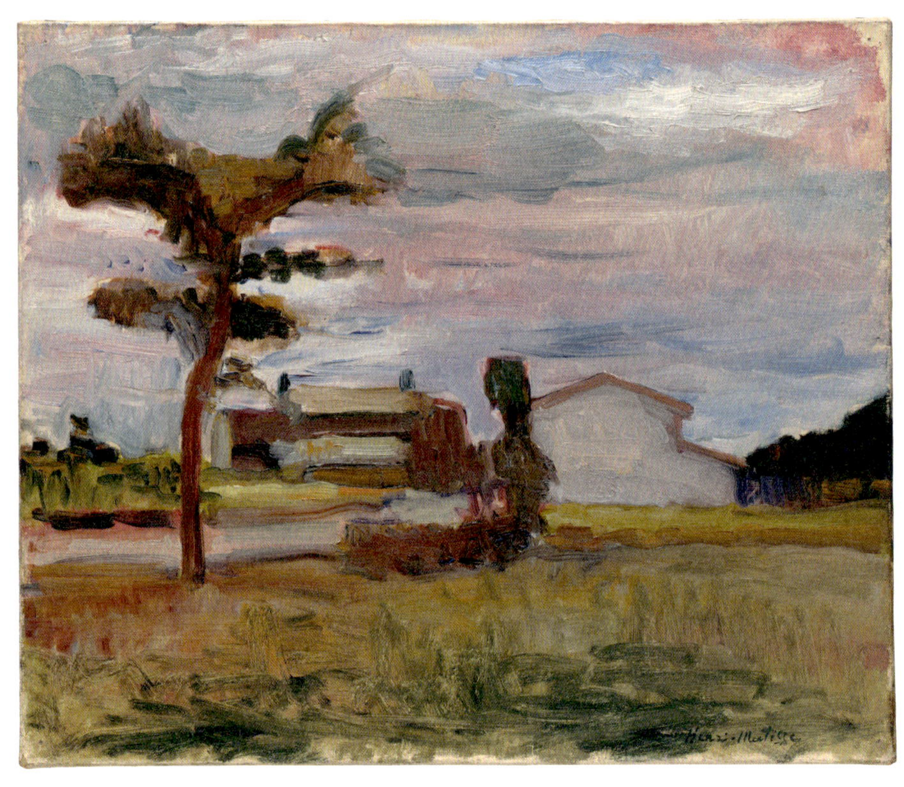

Plate 19. Henri Matisse, *Corsican Landscape,* 1898. Oil on canvas, 15⅛ x 18¼ in. (38.4 x 46.4 cm). San Francisco Museum of Modern Art, bequest of Harriet Lane Levy

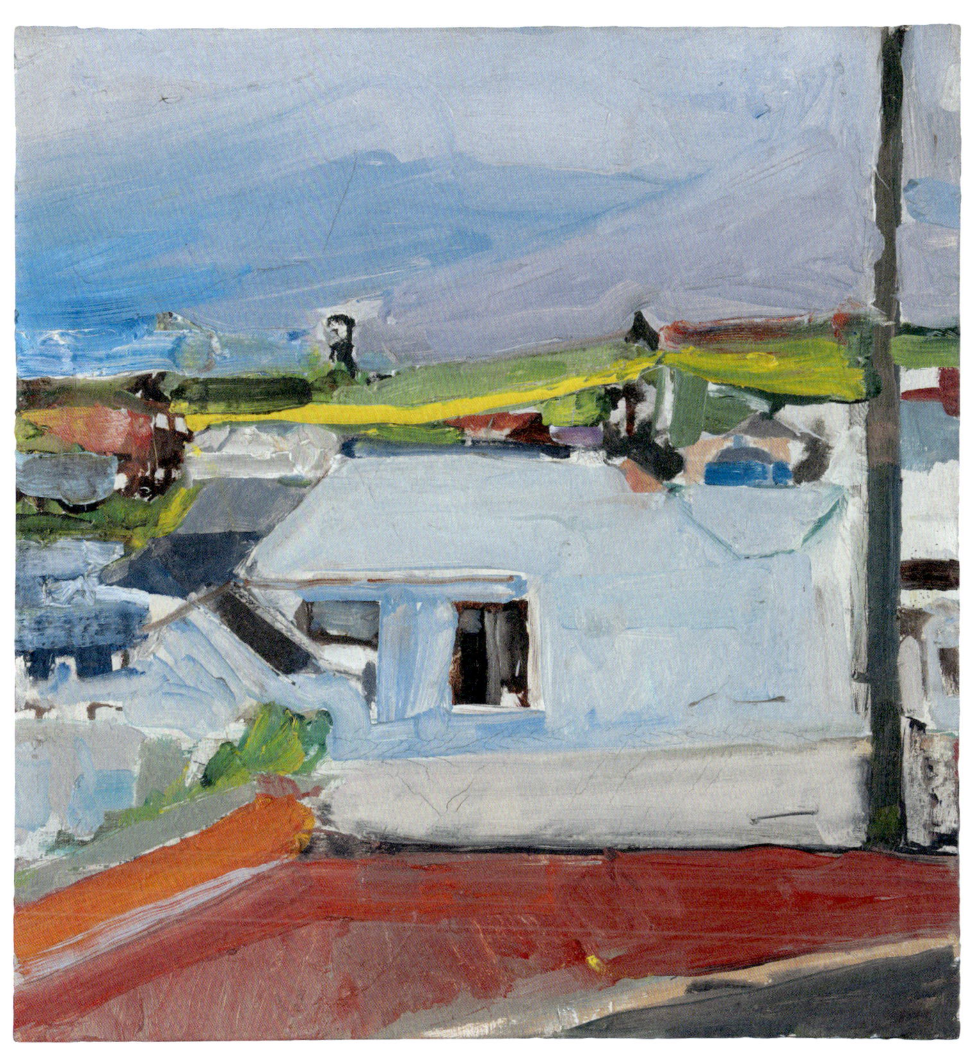

Plate 20. Richard Diebenkorn, *Chabot Valley,* 1955. Oil on canvas, 19½ x 18¾ in. (49.5 x 47.6 cm). Collection of Christopher Diebenkorn

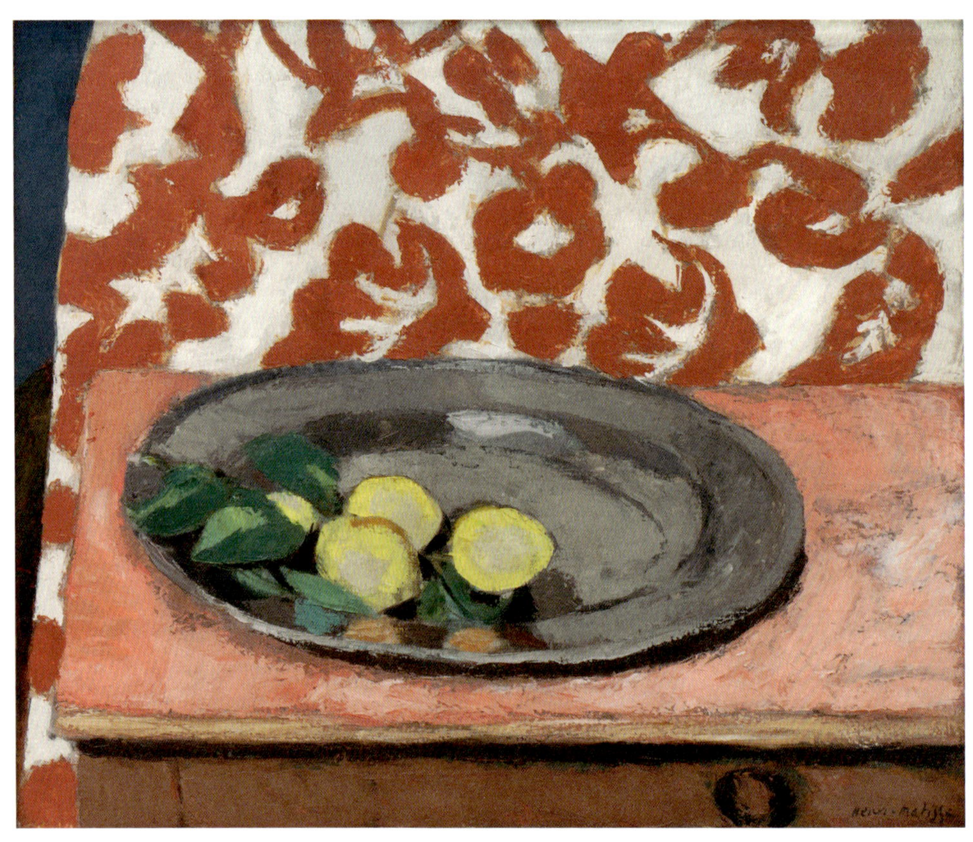

Plate 21. Henri Matisse, *Lemons on a Pewter Plate,* 1926, reworked 1929.
Oil on canvas, 21⅝ x 26⅛ in. (55 x 66.4 cm). The Art Institute of Chicago, a Millennium Gift of the Sara Lee Corporation

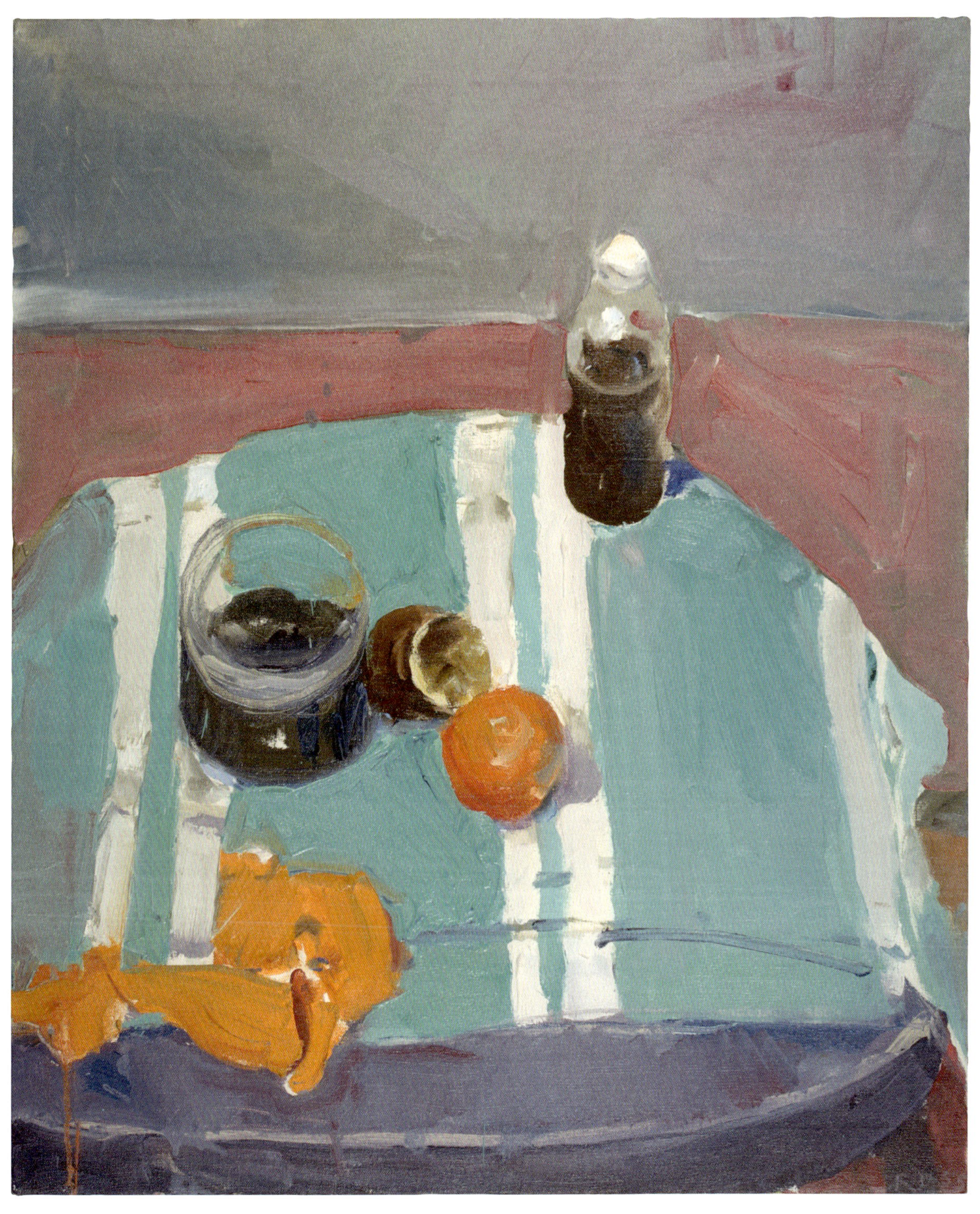

Plate 22. Richard Diebenkorn, *Still Life with Orange Peel,* 1955. Oil on canvas, 29¼ x 24½ in. (74.3 x 62.2 cm). San Francisco Museum of Modern Art, bequest of Barbara E. Foster

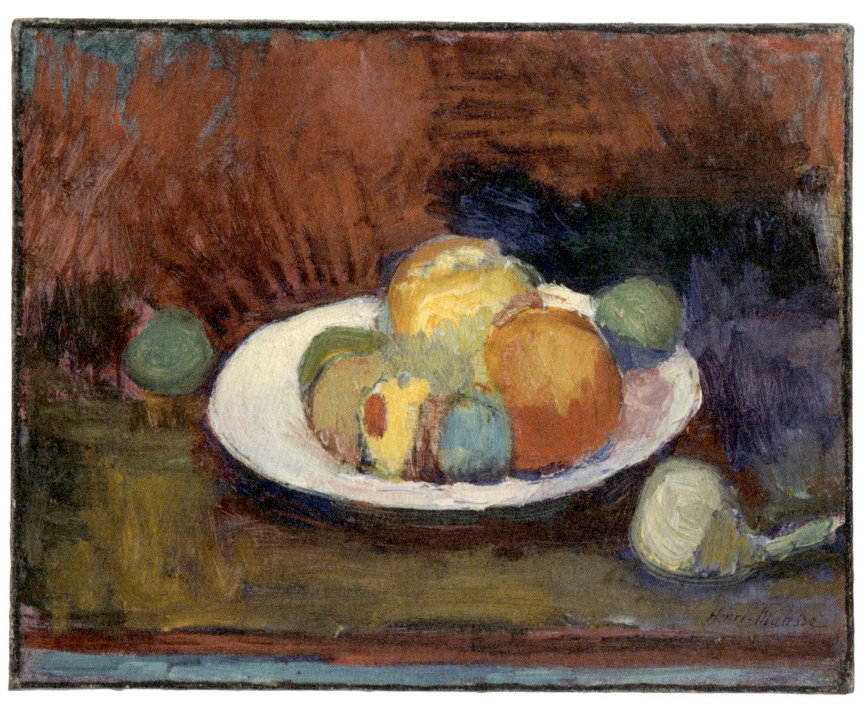

Plate 23. Henri Matisse, *Fruit Dish,* 1902–3. Oil on canvas, 10⅝ x 13⅞ in. (27 x 35.3 cm). San Francisco Museum of Modern Art, bequest of Harriet Lane Levy

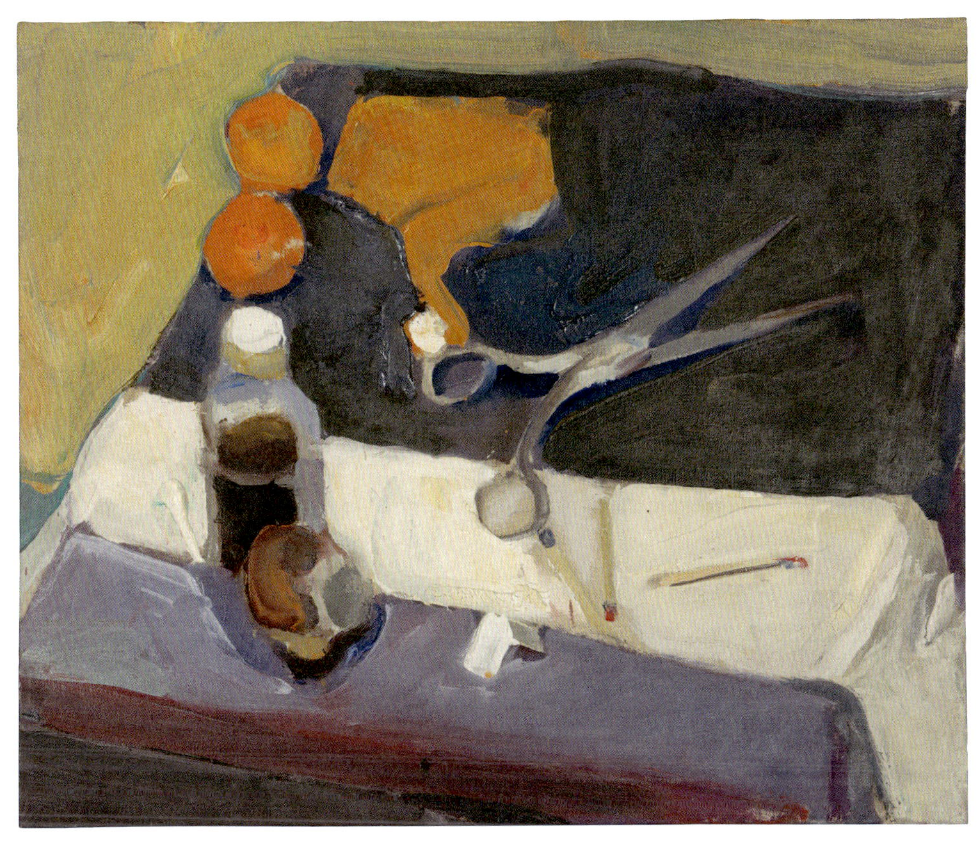

Plate 24. Richard Diebenkorn, *Still Life with Orange Peel II,* 1955/1956.
Oil on canvas, 15⅛ x 18⅜ in. (38.4 x 46.7 cm). Private collection

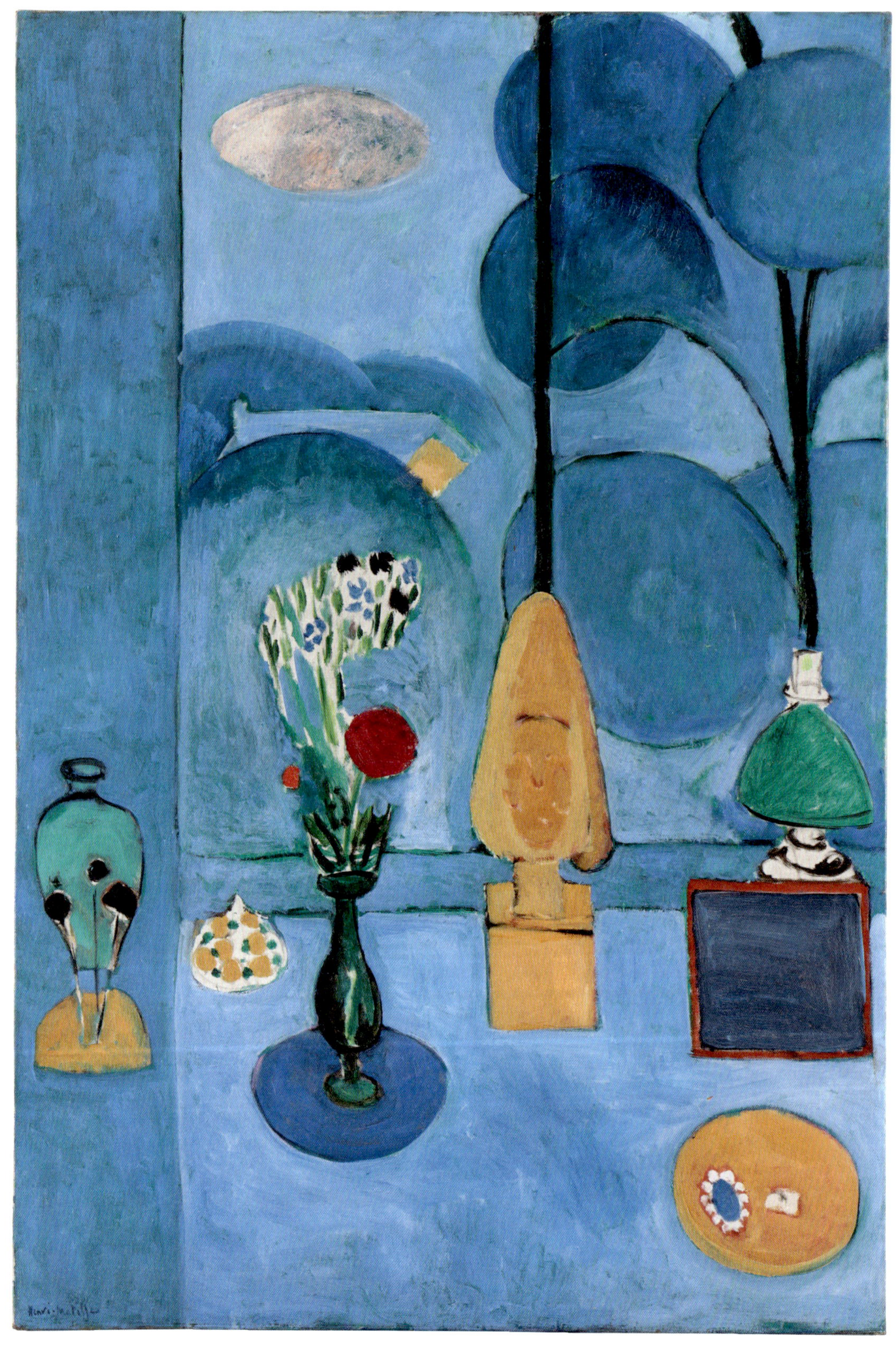

Plate 25. Henri Matisse, *The Blue Window,* 1913. Oil on canvas, 51½ x 35⅝ in. (130.8 x 90.5 cm).
The Museum of Modern Art, New York, Abby Aldrich Rockefeller Fund

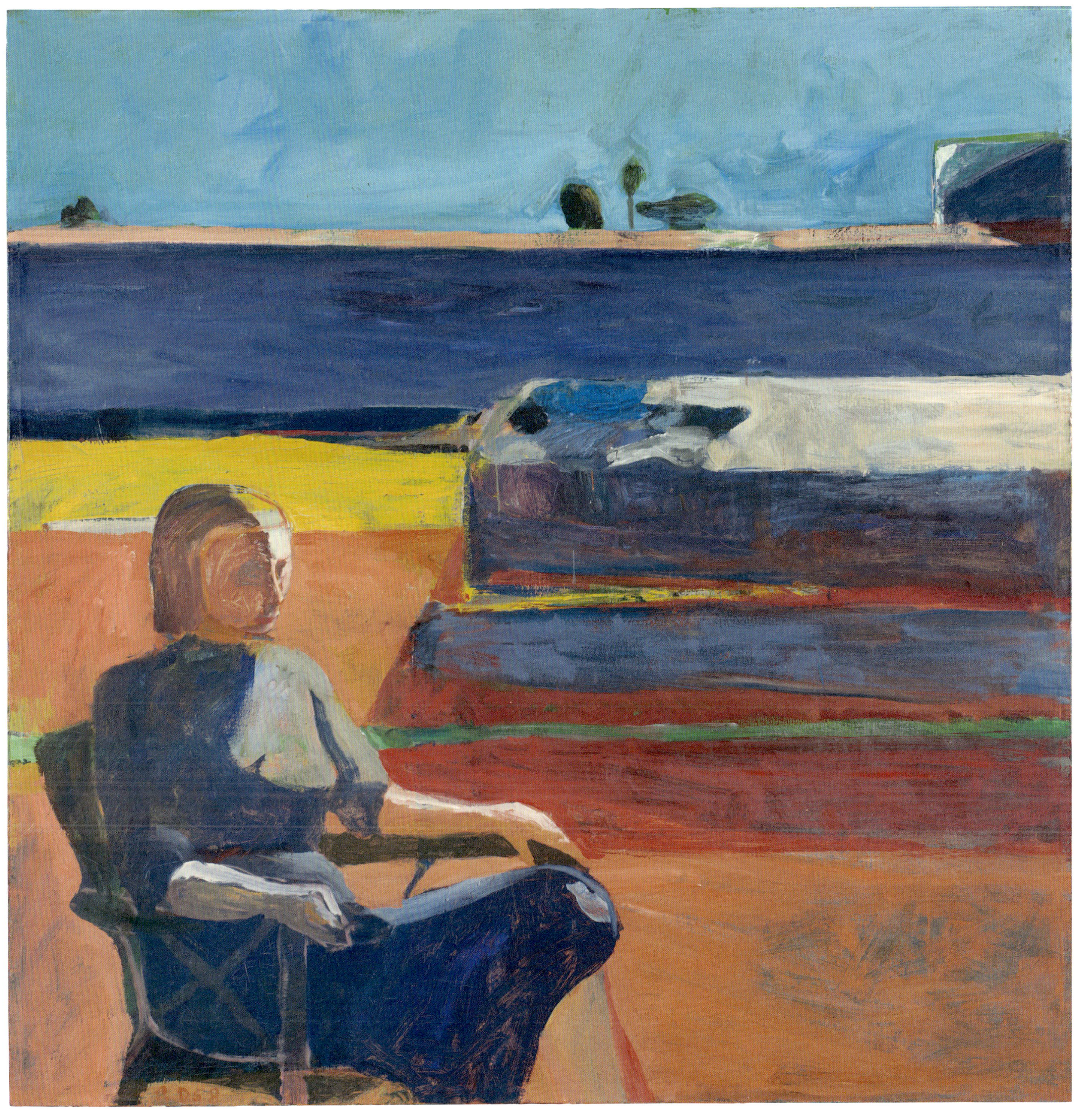

Plate 26. Richard Diebenkorn, *Woman on a Porch,* 1958. Oil on canvas, 72 x 72 in. (182.9 x 182.9 cm).
New Orleans Museum of Art, museum purchase through the National Endowment for the Arts Matching Grant

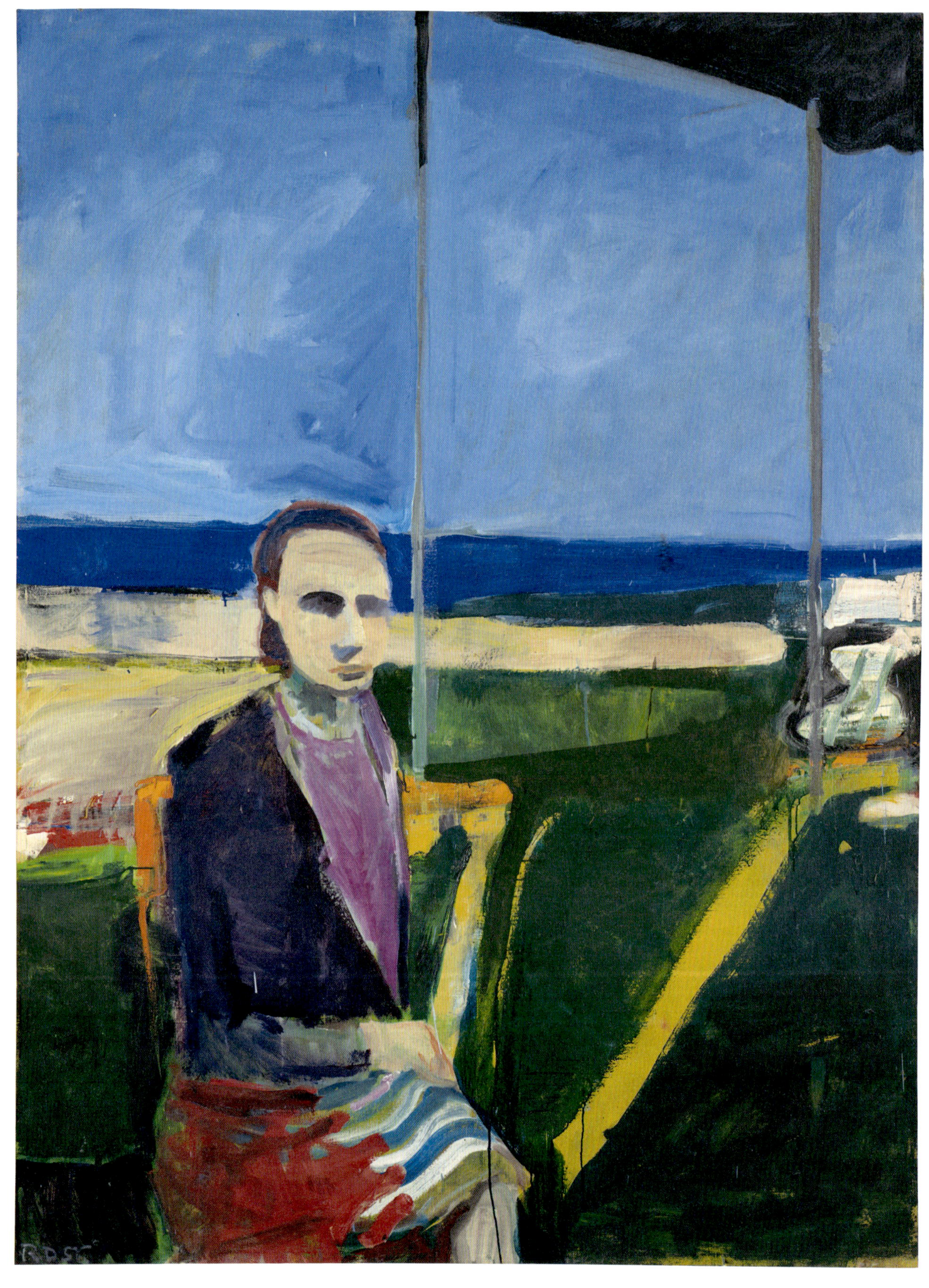

Plate 27. Richard Diebenkorn, *Woman by the Ocean,* 1956. Oil on canvas, 79 x 59 in. (200.7 x 149.9 cm). Collection of the Lisa and Douglas E. Goldman family

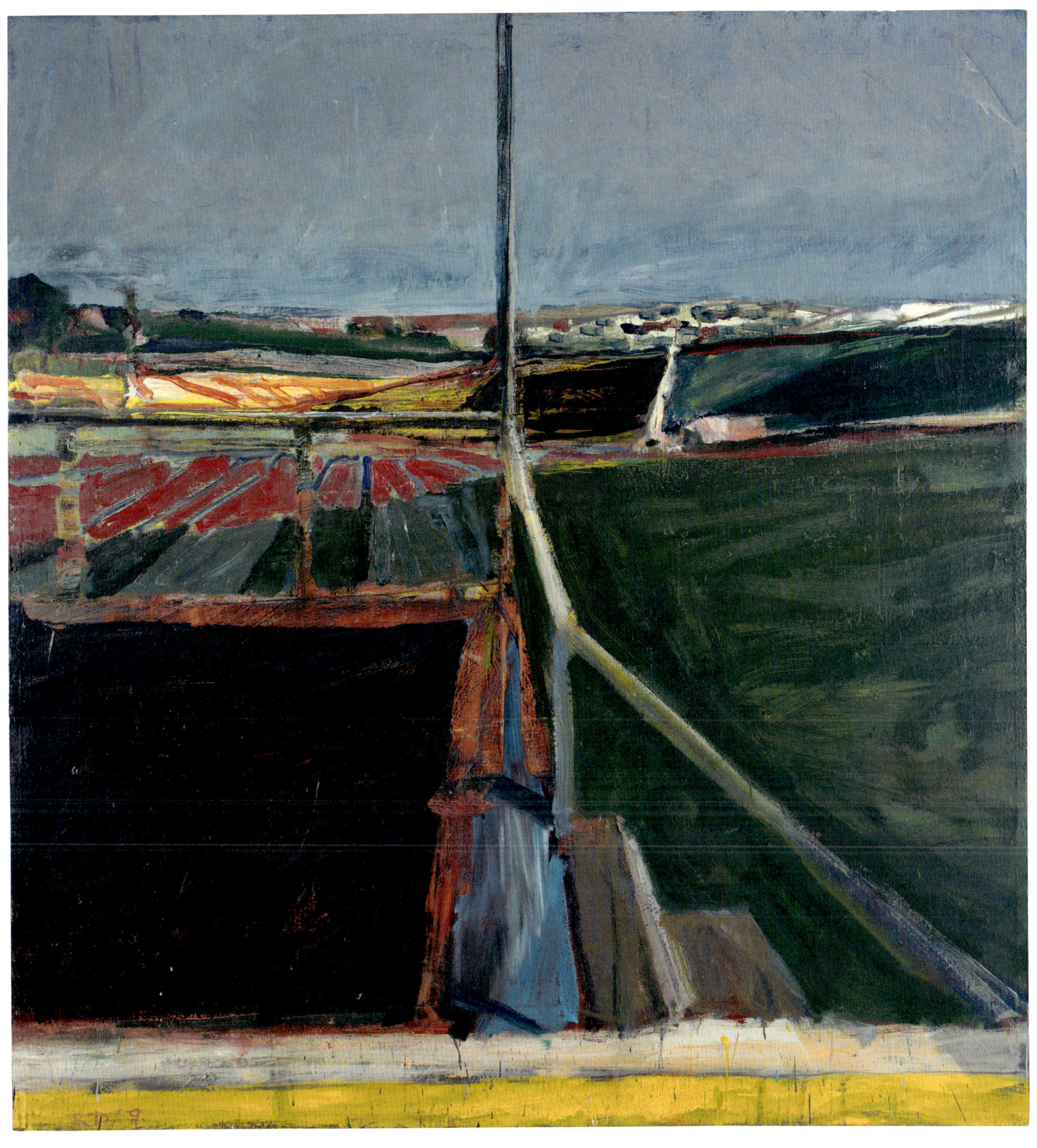

Plate 28. Richard Diebenkorn, *View from the Porch,* 1959. Oil on canvas, 70 x 66 in. (177.8 x 167.6 cm).
Collection of Harry W. and Mary Margaret Anderson

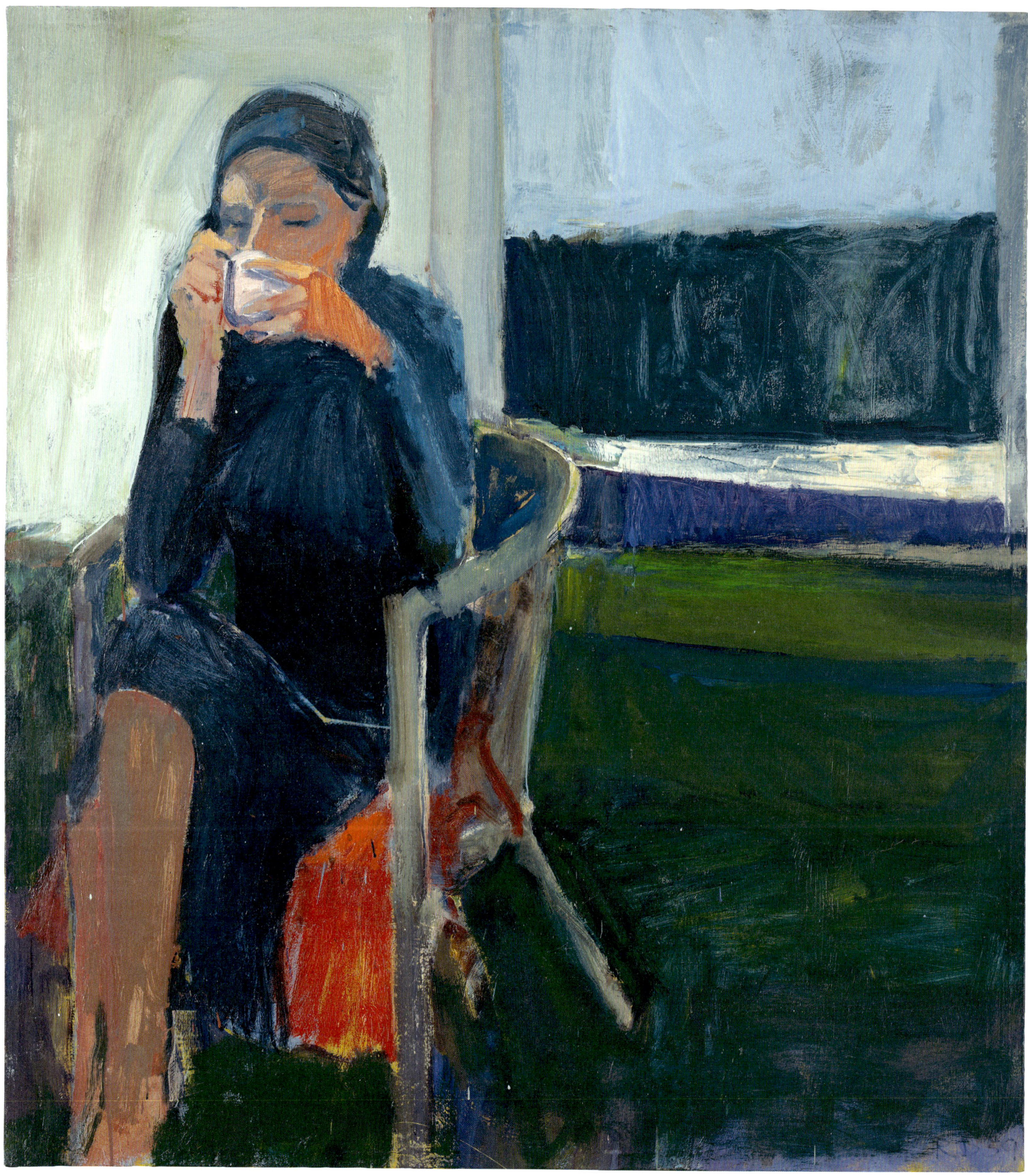

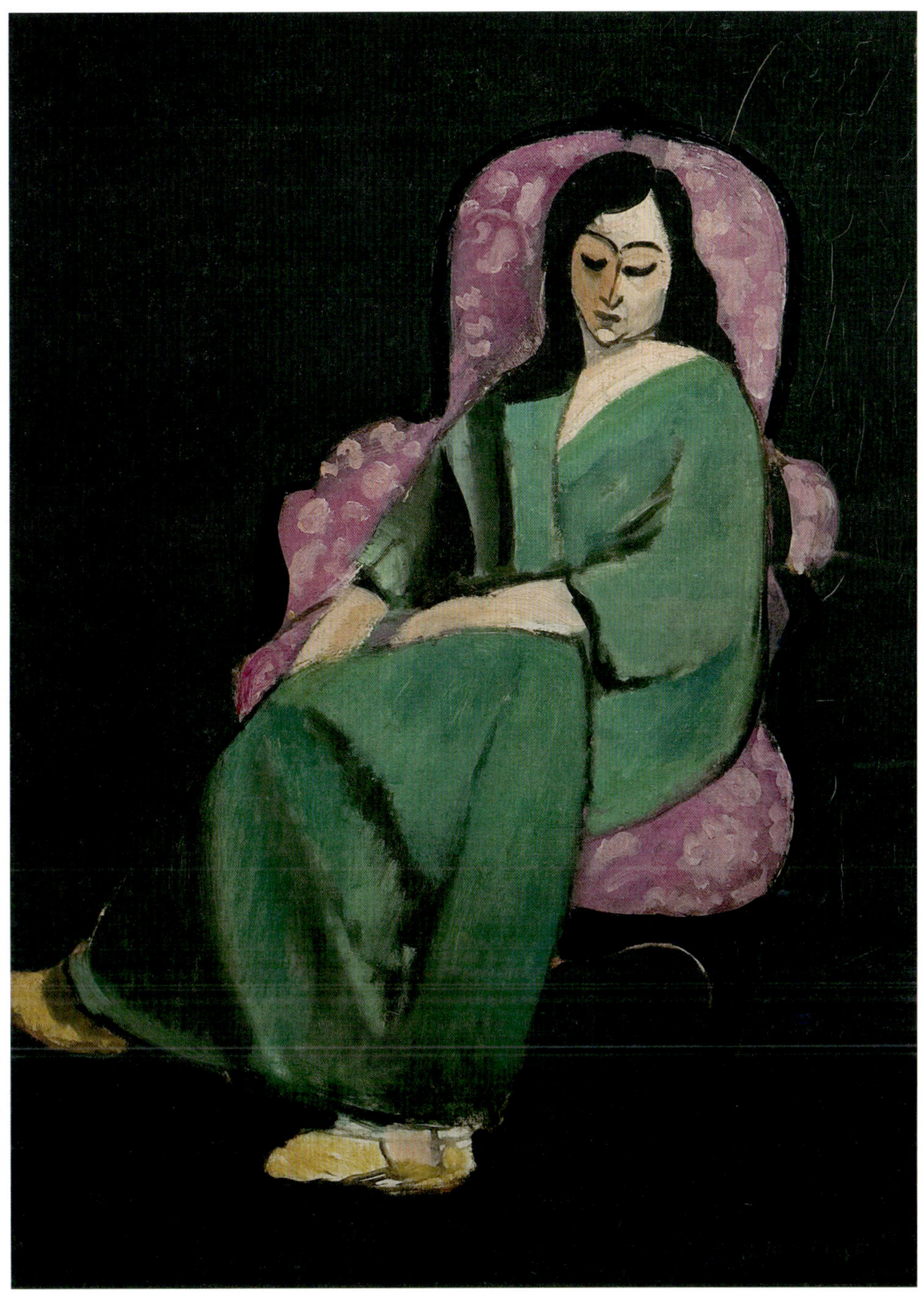

OPPOSITE

Plate 29. Richard Diebenkorn, *Coffee,* 1959. Oil on canvas, 57½ x 52¼ in. (146.1 x 132.7 cm). San Francisco Museum of Modern Art, fractional and promised gift of Barbara and Gerson Bakar

Plate 30. Henri Matisse, *Laurette in a Green Robe, Black Background,* 1916. Oil on canvas, 28¾ x 21⅜ in. (73 x 54.3 cm). The Metropolitan Museum of Art, New York, Jacques and Natasha Gelman Collection

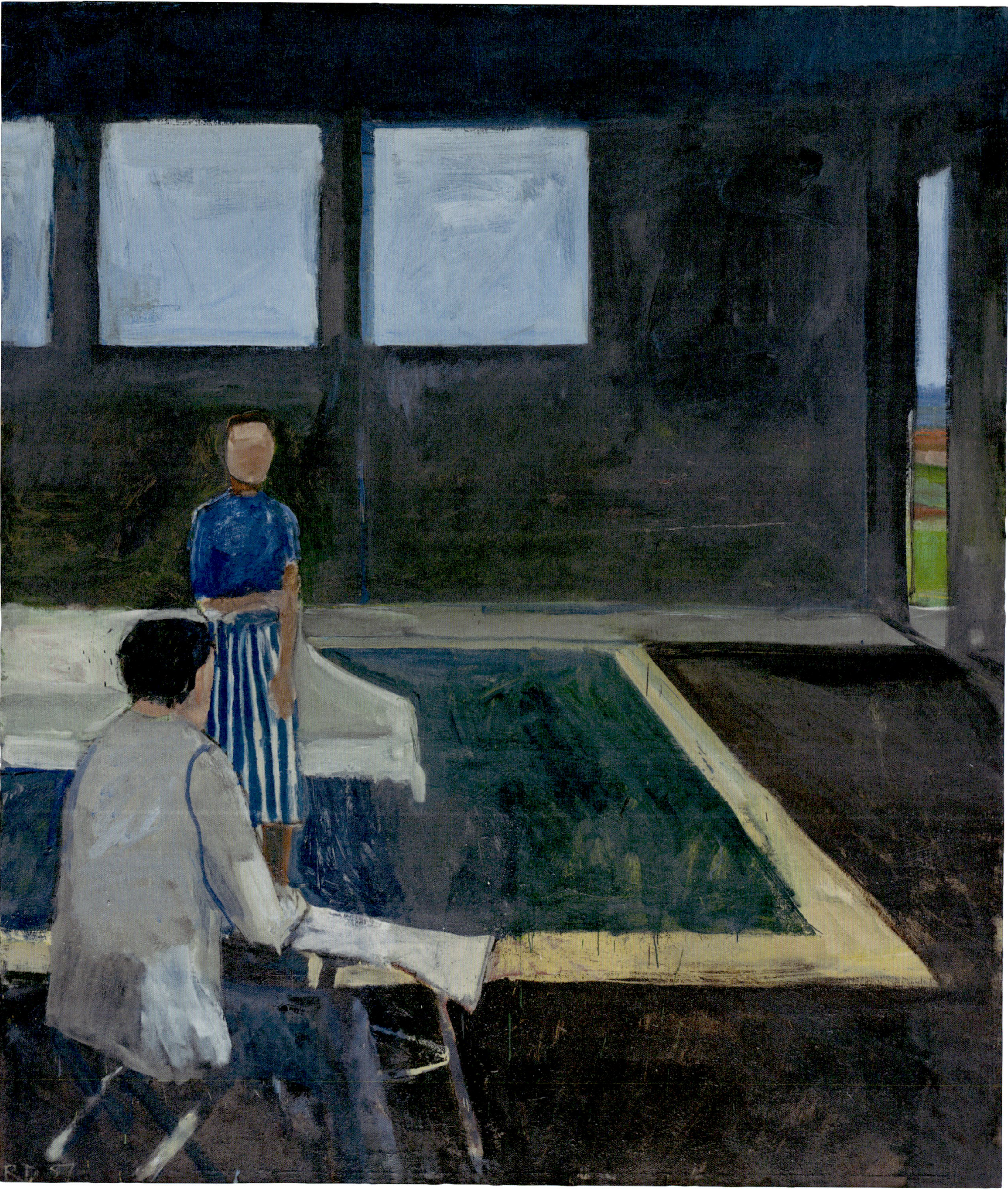

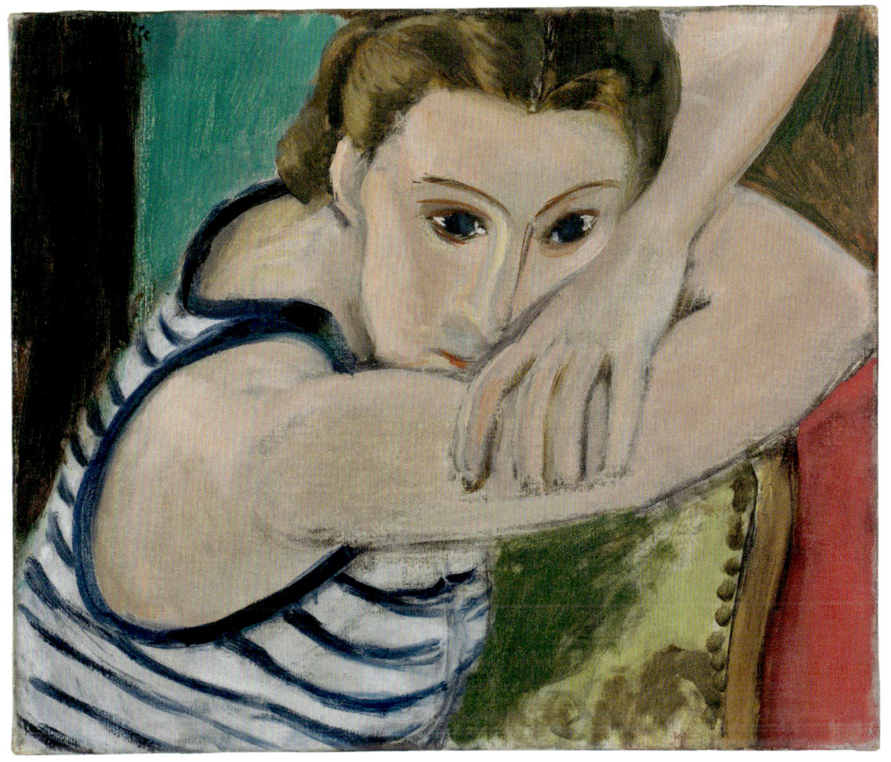

OPPOSITE

Plate 31. Richard Diebenkorn, *Man and Woman in a Large Room,* 1957. Oil on canvas, 71⅛ x 62½ in. (180.7 x 158.8 cm). Hirshhorn Museum and Sculpture Garden, Smithsonian Institution, Washington, D.C., gift of the Joseph H. Hirshhorn Foundation

Plate 32. Henri Matisse, *The Blue Eyes,* 1935. Oil on canvas, 15 x 18 in. (38.1 x 45.7 cm). The Baltimore Museum of Art: The Cone Collection, formed by Dr. Claribel Cone and Miss Etta Cone of Baltimore, Maryland

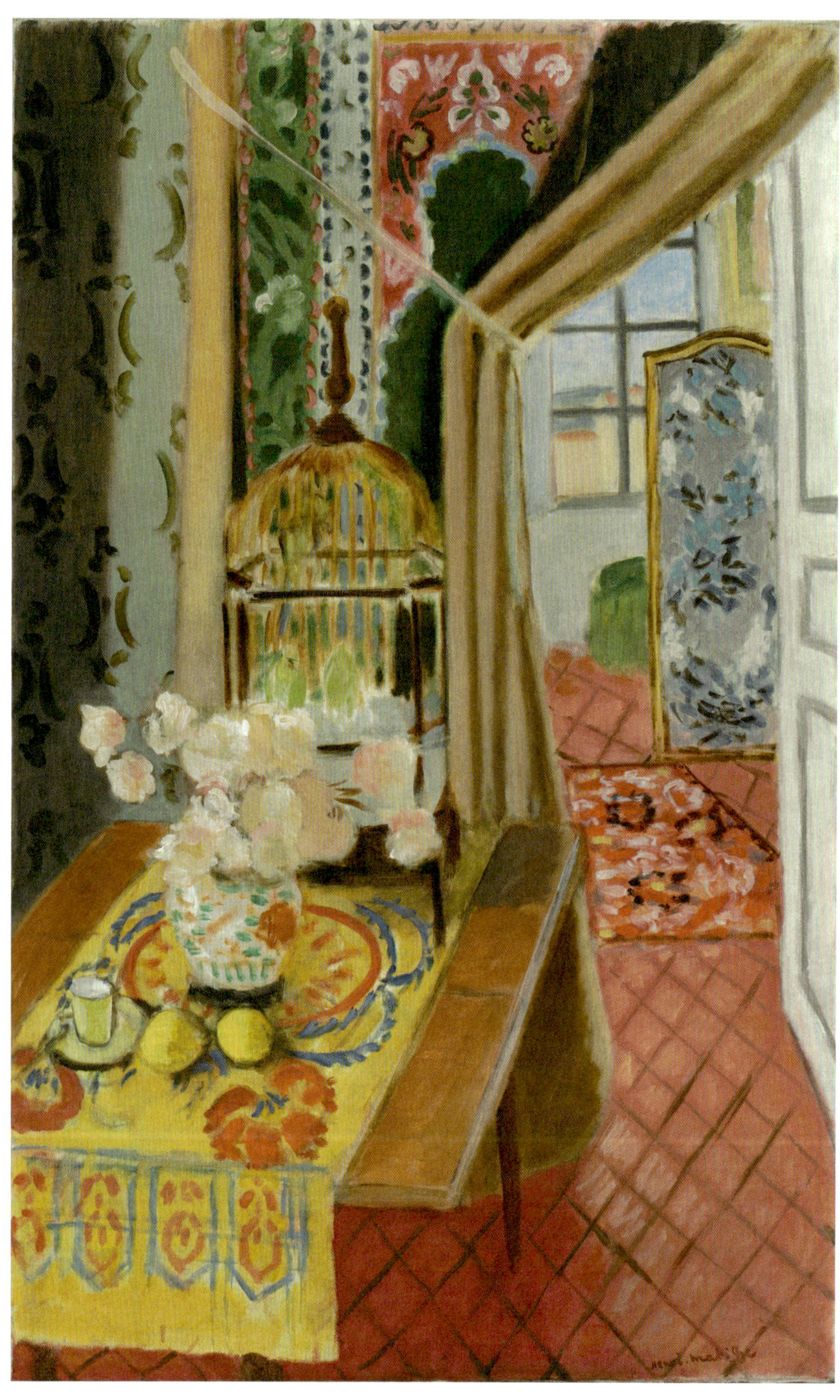

Plate 33. Henri Matisse, *Interior, Flowers and Parakeets,* 1924.
Oil on canvas, 46¼ x 29 in. (117.5 x 73.7 cm). The Baltimore Museum of Art: The Cone Collection, formed by Dr. Claribel Cone and Miss Etta Cone of Baltimore, Maryland

OPPOSITE
Plate 34. Richard Diebenkorn, *Girl with Plant,* 1960. Oil on canvas, 80 x 69½ in. (203.2 x 176.5 cm). The Phillips Collection, Washington, D.C.

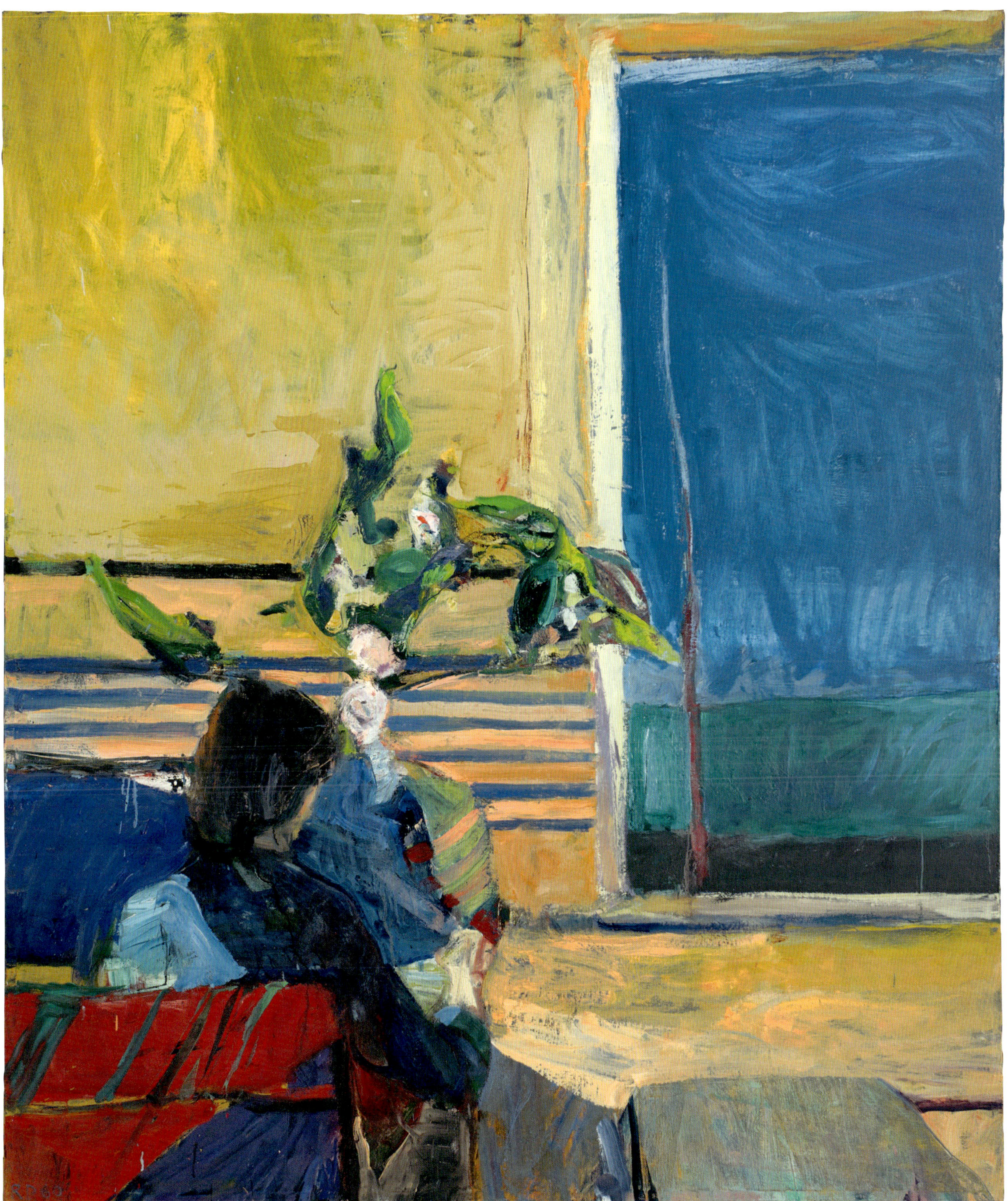

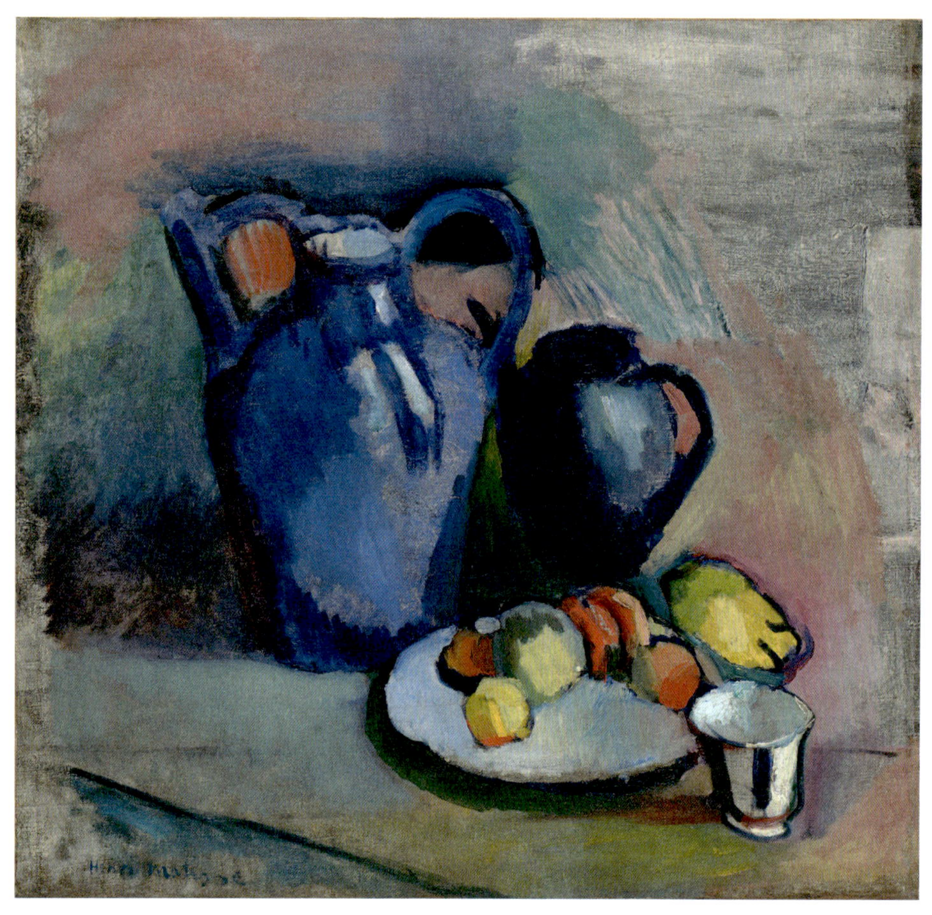

Plate 35. Henri Matisse, *Still Life with Blue Jug,* ca. 1900–1903. Oil on canvas, 23 x 25 in. (58.4 x 63.5 cm). San Francisco Museum of Modern Art, bequest of Matilda B. Wilbur in honor of her daughter, Mary W. Thacher

OPPOSITE
Plate 36. Richard Diebenkorn, *Seated Nude, Hands behind Head,* 1961. Oil on canvas, 84 x 69 in. (213.4 x 175.3 cm). Collection of Jane Wenner

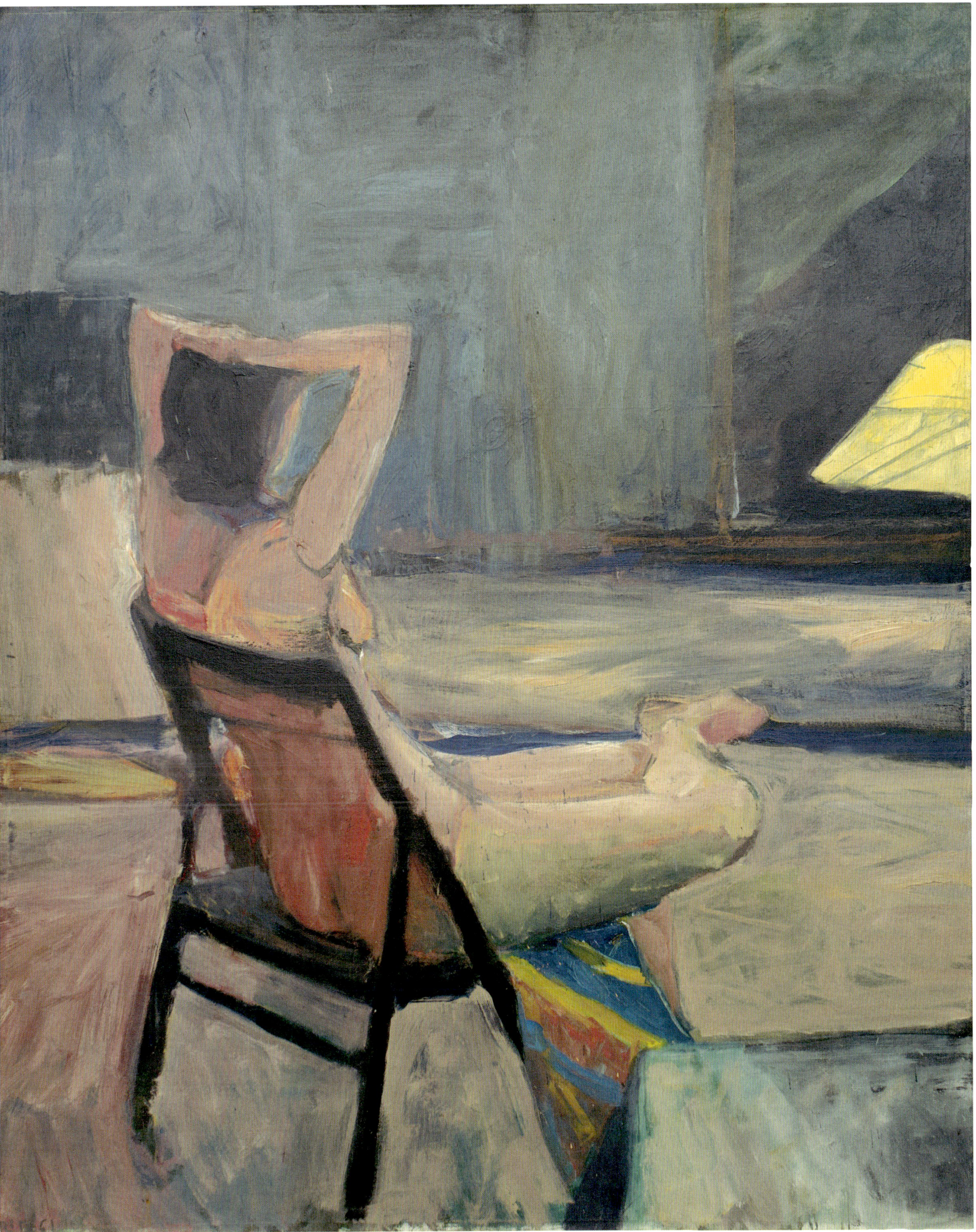

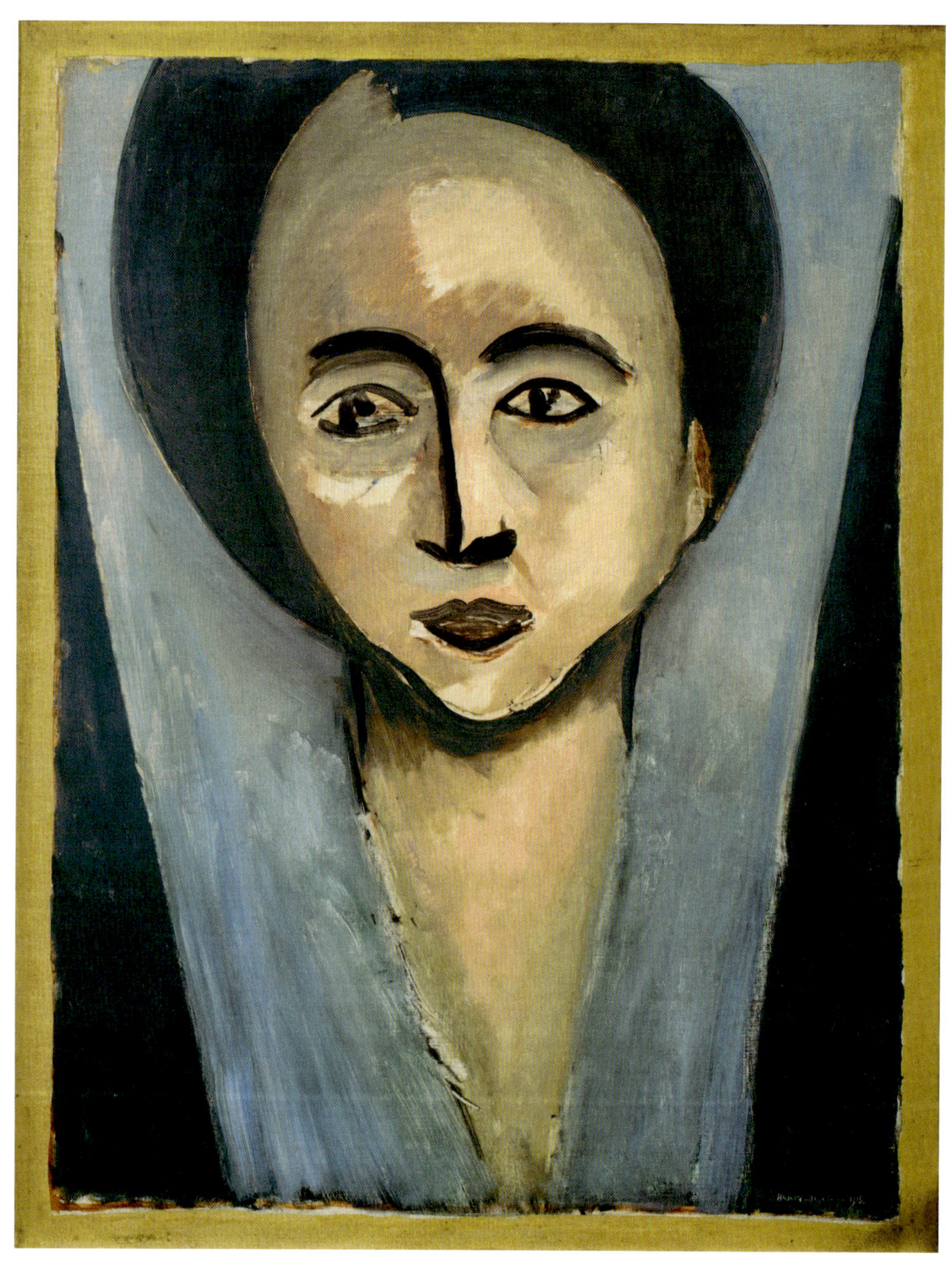

Plate 37. Henri Matisse, *Sarah Stein,* 1916. Oil on canvas, 28½ x 22¼ in. (72.4 x 56.5 cm). San Francisco Museum of Modern Art, Sarah and Michael Stein Memorial Collection, gift of Elise S. Haas

OPPOSITE
Plate 38. Richard Diebenkorn, *Sleeping Woman,* 1961. Oil on canvas, 70 x 58 in. (177.8 x 147.3 cm). Kalamazoo Institute of Arts, Michigan, Director's Fund Purchase

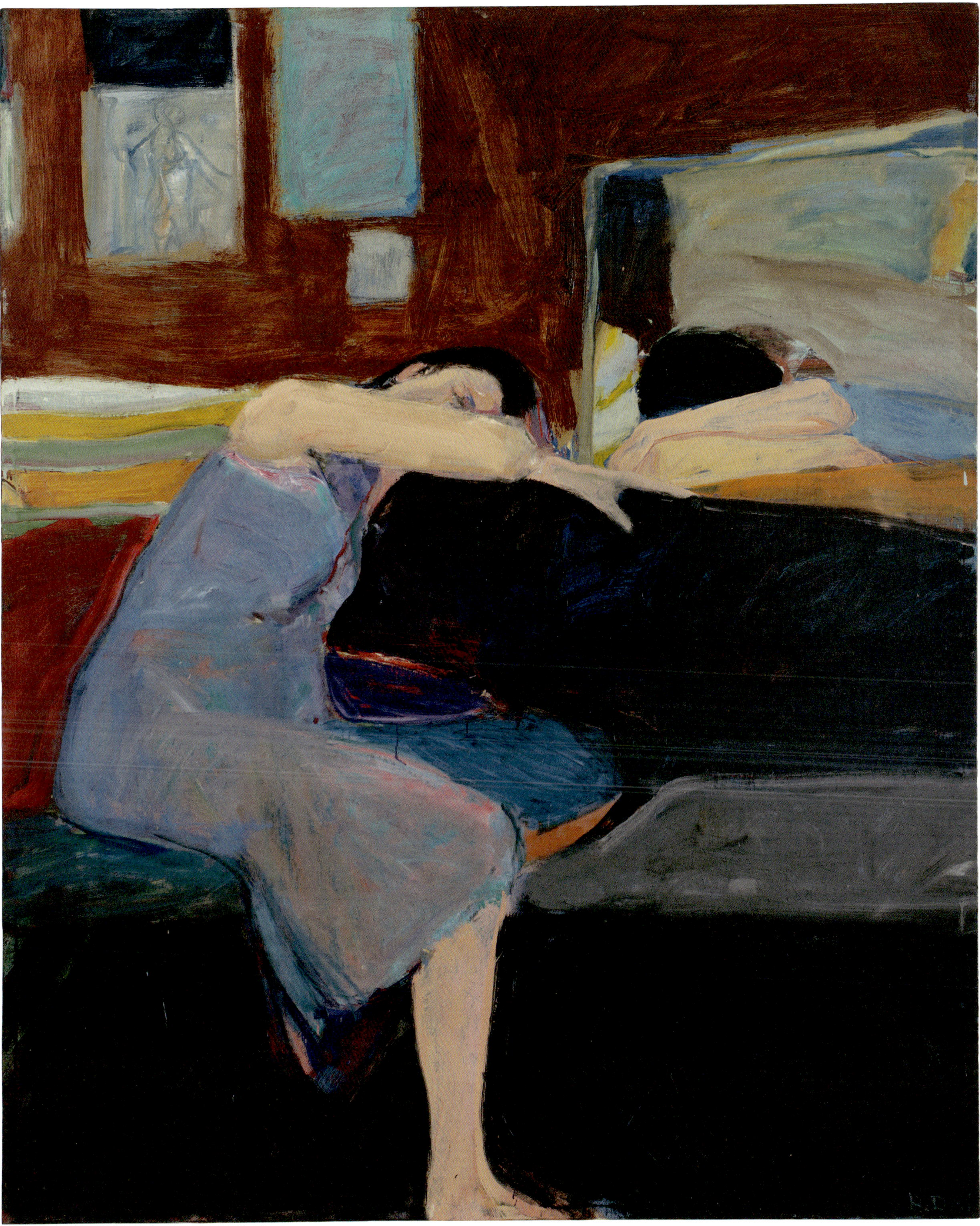

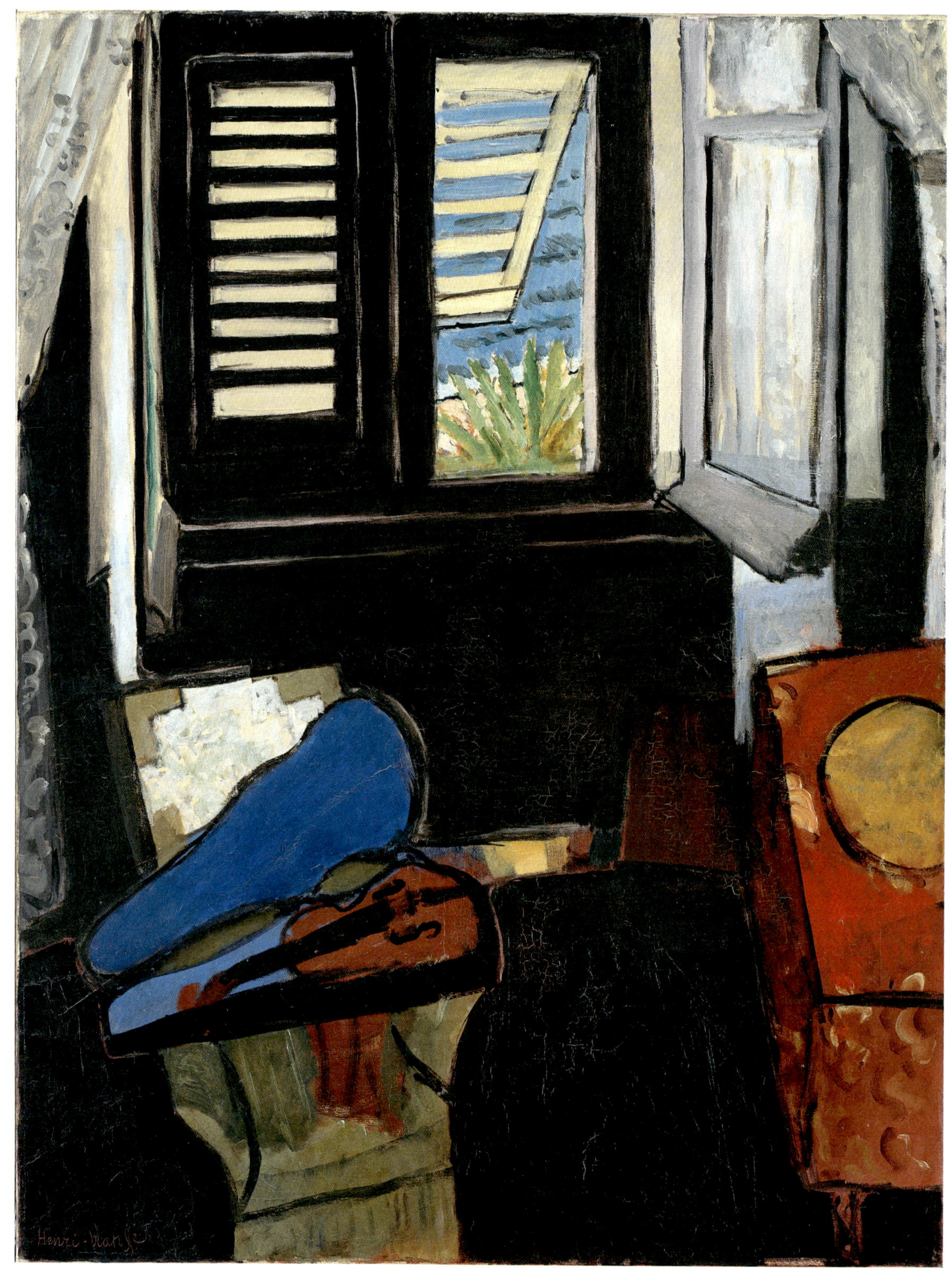

Plate 39. Henri Matisse, *Interior with a Violin,* 1918. Oil on canvas, 45⅝ x 35 in. (115.9 x 88.9 cm). Statens Museum for Kunst, Copenhagen

OPPOSITE
Plate 40. Richard Diebenkorn, *Interior with Doorway,* 1962. Oil on canvas, 70⅜ x 59½ in. (178.8 x 151.1 cm). Pennsylvania Academy of the Fine Arts, Philadelphia, Henry D. Gilpin Fund

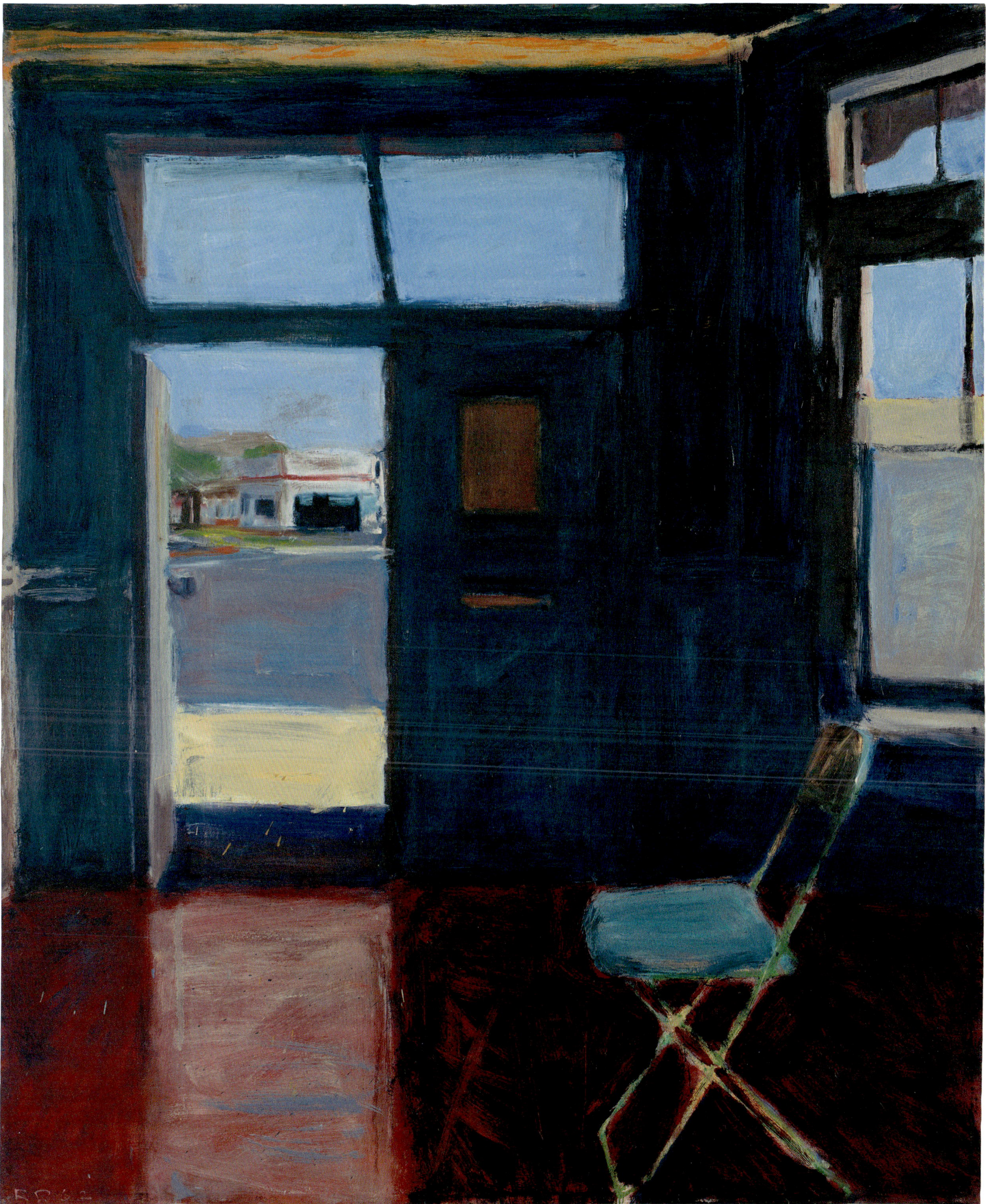

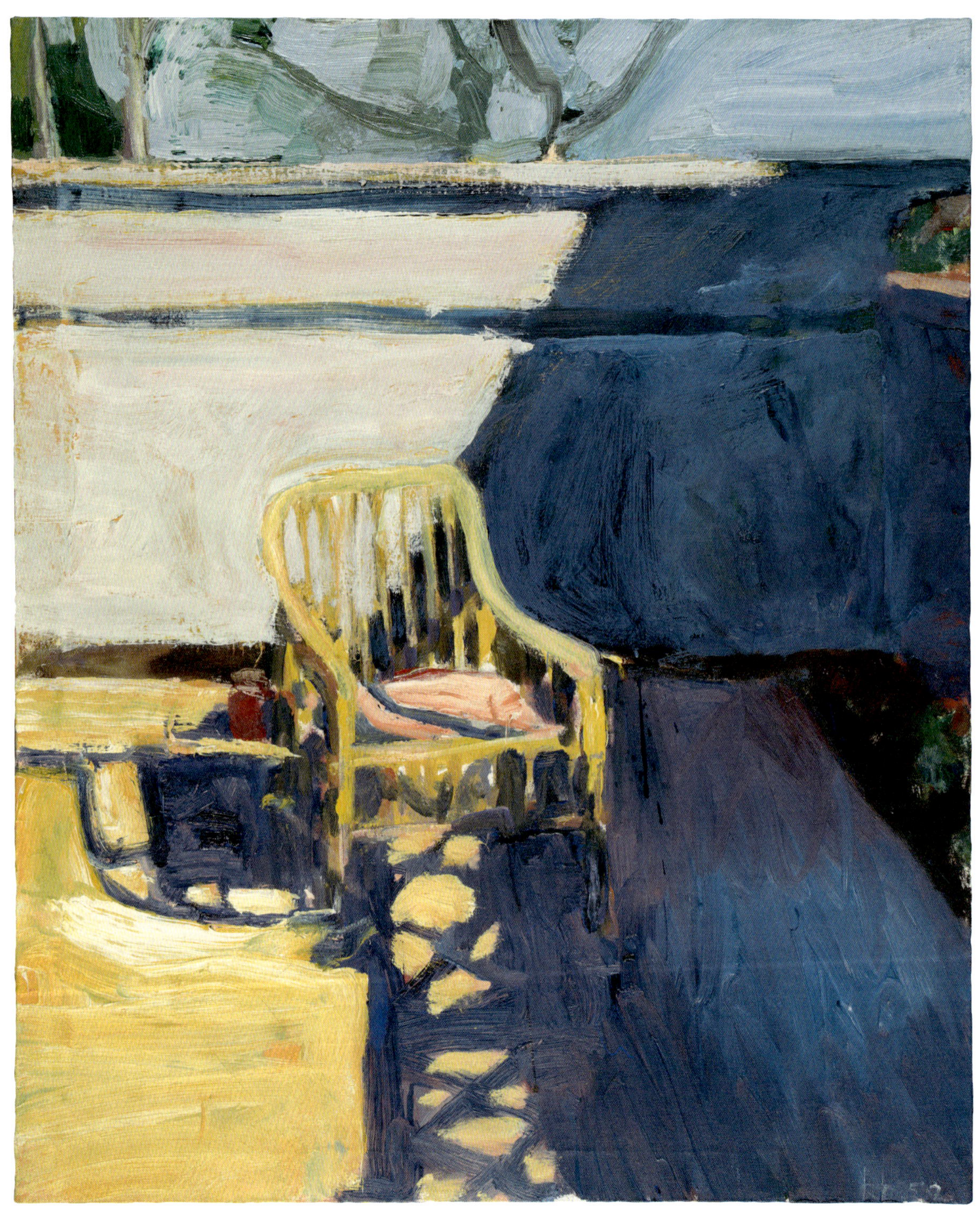

Plate 41. Richard Diebenkorn, *Cane Chair—Outside,* 1959. Oil on canvas, 32 x 27 in. (81.3 x 68.6 cm). Promised gift of a private collection to the San Francisco Museum of Modern Art

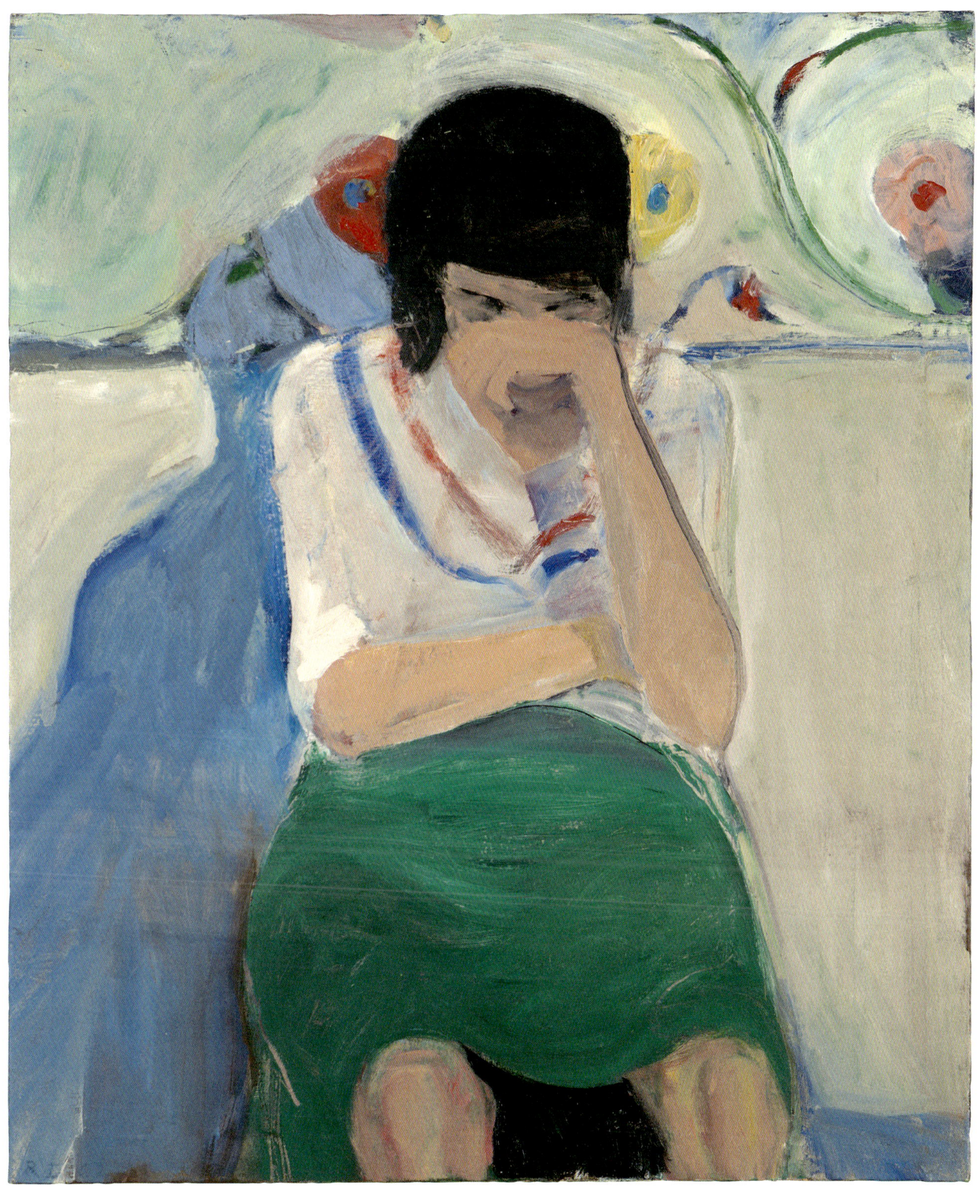

Plate 42. Richard Diebenkorn, *Girl with Flowered Background,* 1962. Oil on canvas, 40 x 34 in. (101.6 x 86.4 cm). Modern Art Museum of Fort Worth, museum purchase, Sid W. Richardson Foundation Endowment Fund

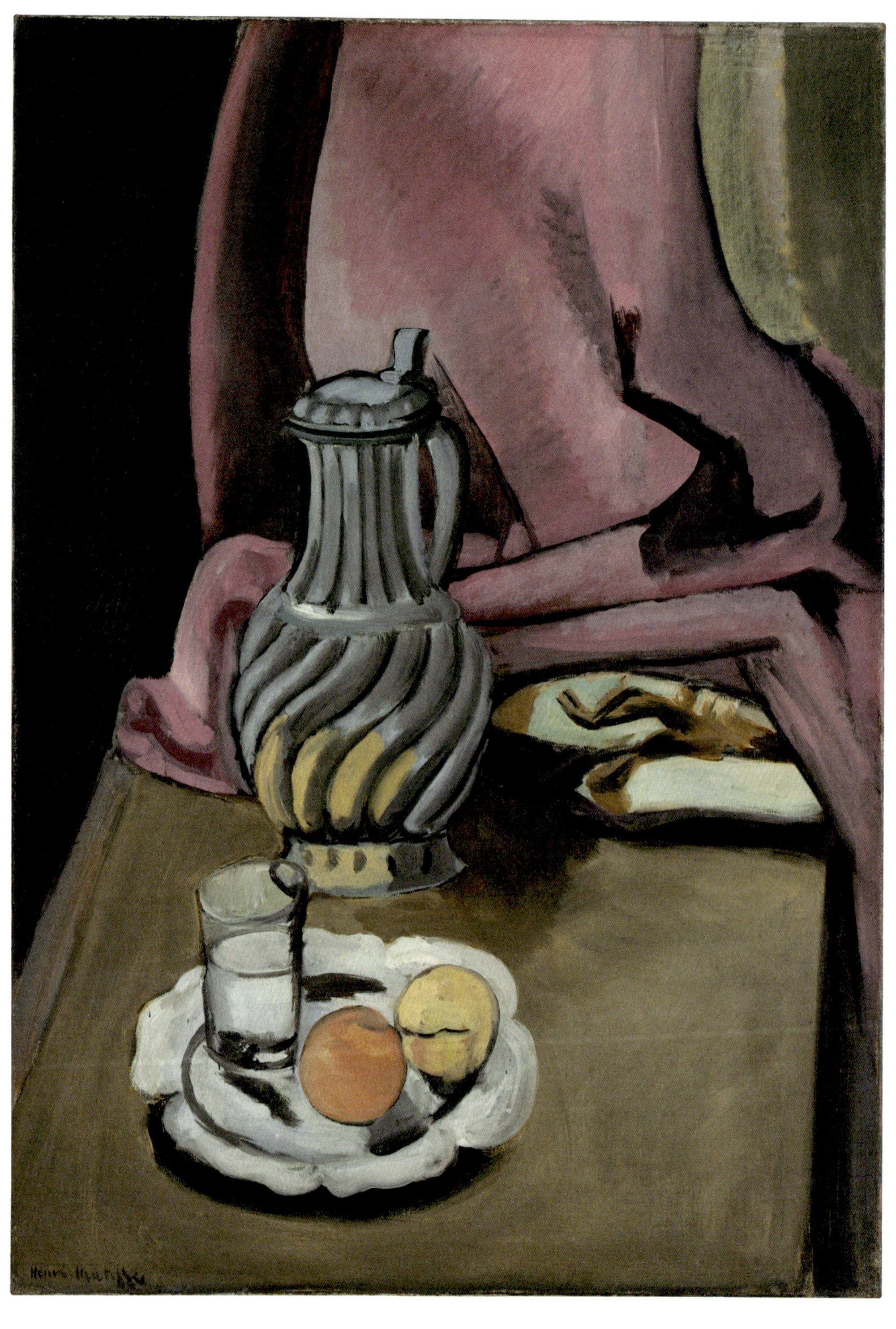

Plate 43. Henri Matisse, *The Pewter Jug,* 1917. Oil on canvas, 36⅜ x 25½ in. (92.4 x 64.8 cm). The Baltimore Museum of Art: The Cone Collection, formed by Dr. Claribel Cone and Miss Etta Cone of Baltimore, Maryland

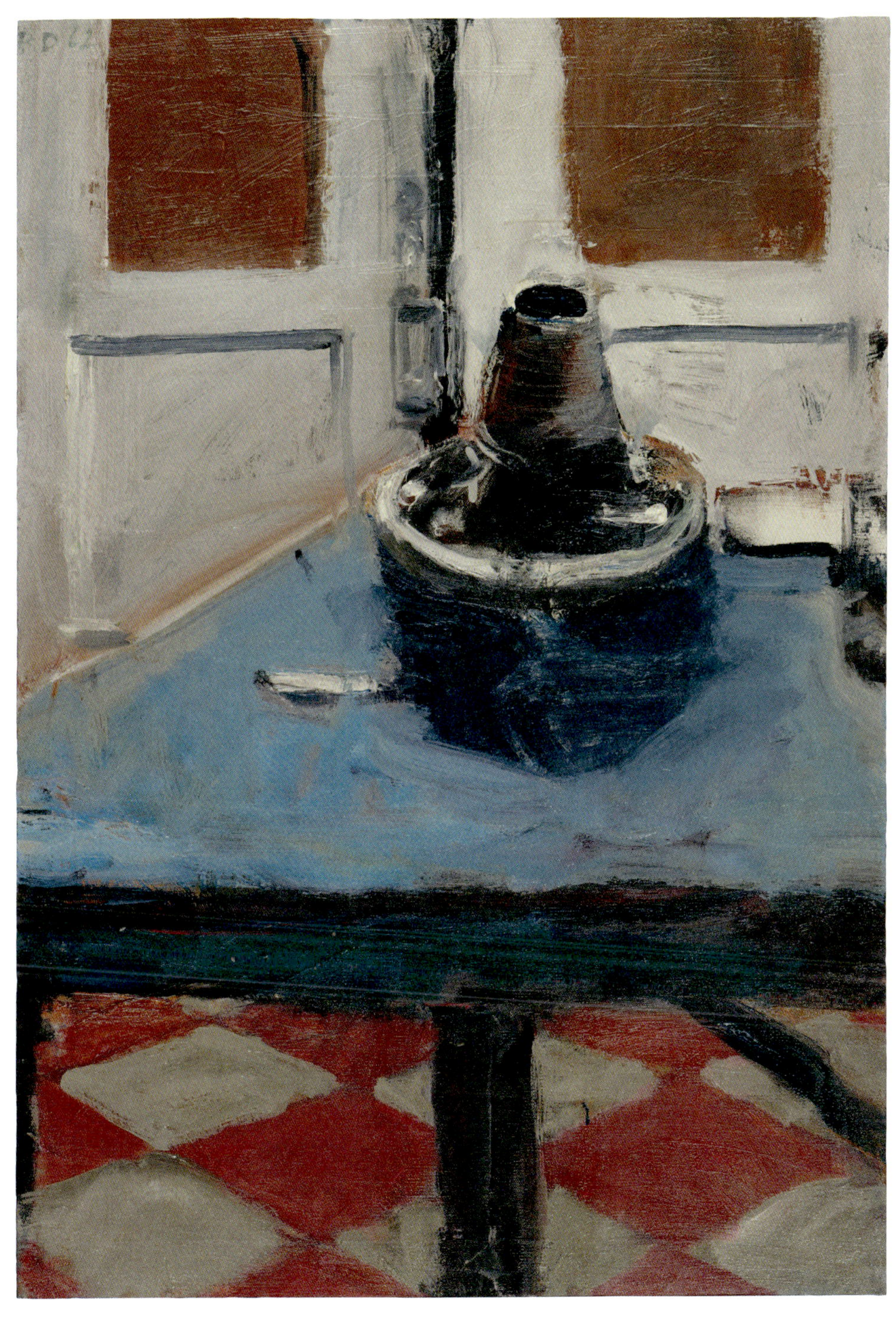

Plate 44. Richard Diebenkorn, *Ashtray and Doors,* 1962. Oil on canvas, 29 x 20⅜ in. (73.7 x 51.8 cm). Estate of the artist

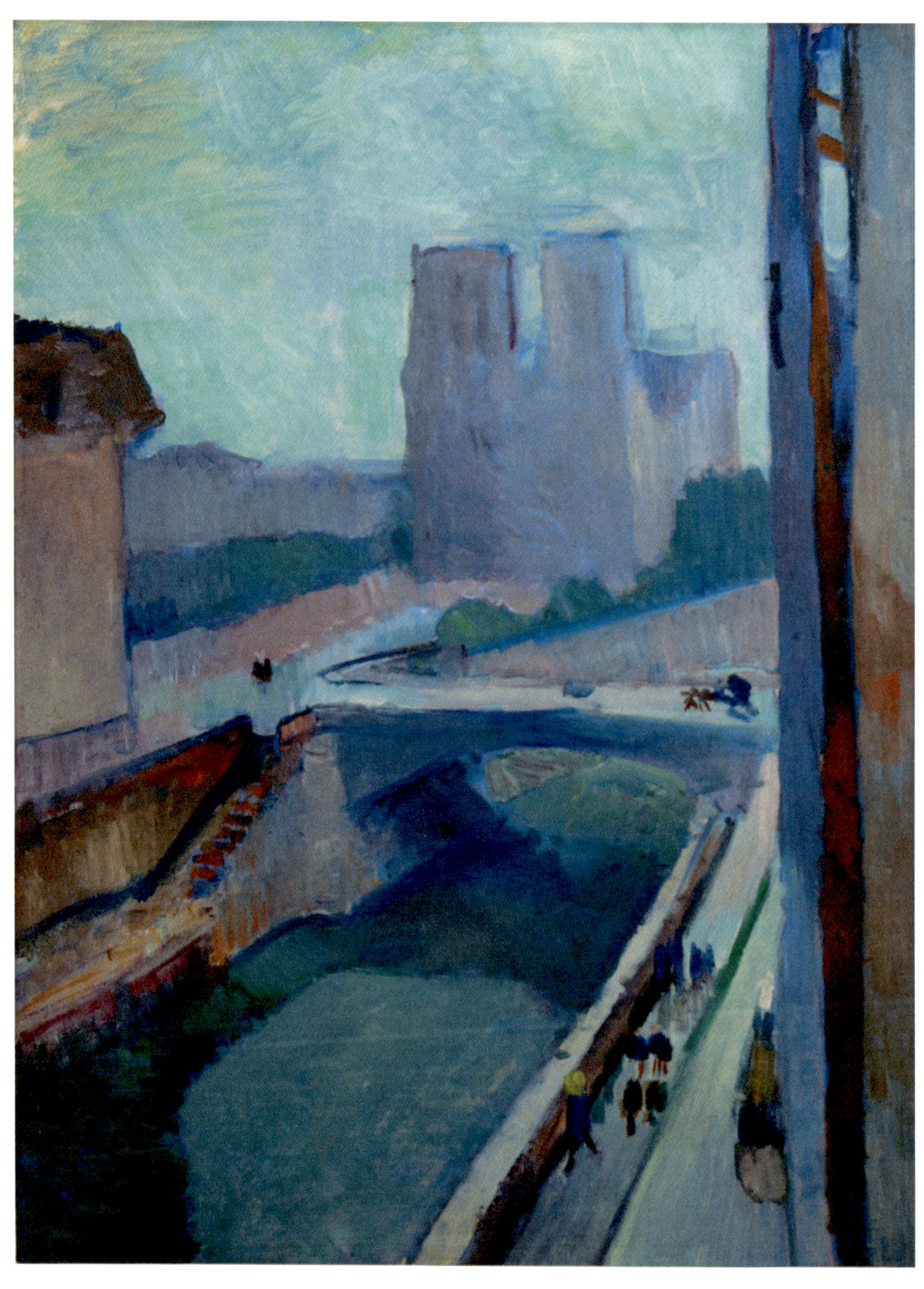

Plate 45. Henri Matisse, *Notre Dame, a Late Afternoon,* 1902. Oil on paper mounted on canvas, 28½ x 21½ in. (72.4 x 54.6 cm). Albright-Knox Art Gallery, Buffalo, gift of Seymour H. Knox Jr.

OPPOSITE
Plate 46. Richard Diebenkorn, *Ingleside,* 1963. Oil on canvas, 81¾ x 69½ in. (207.6 x 176.5 cm). Grand Rapids Art Museum, museum purchase

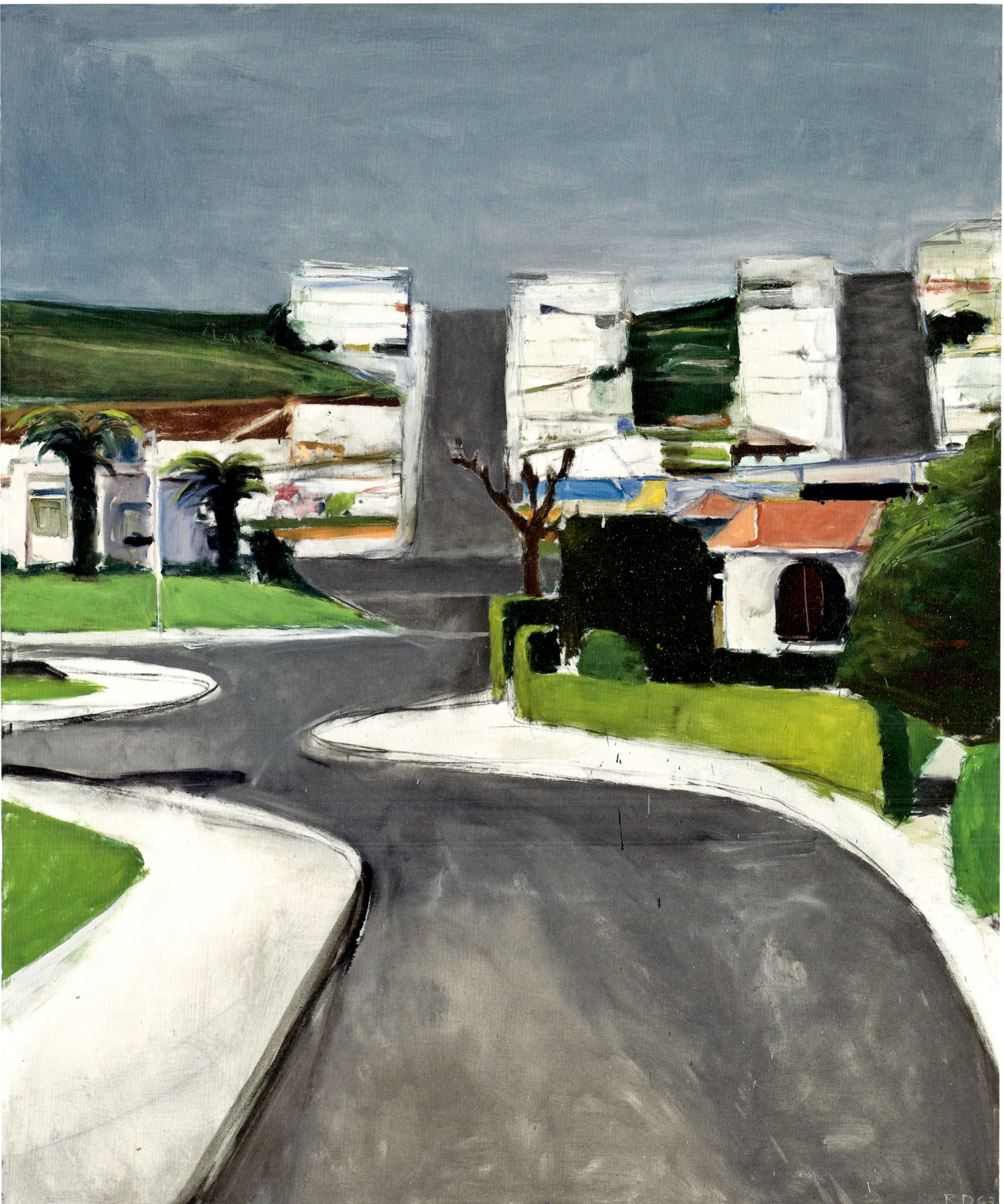

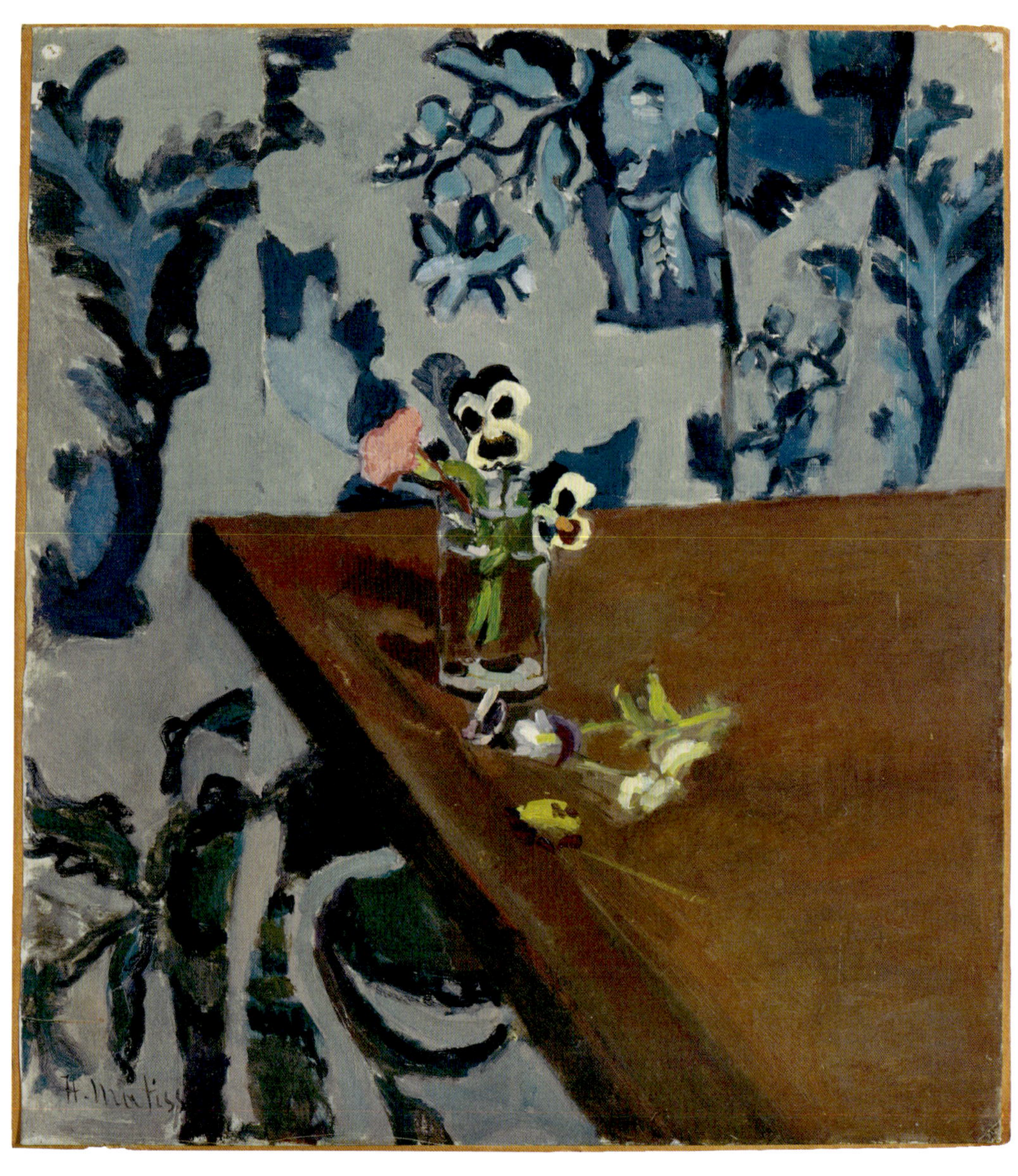

Plate 47. Henri Matisse, *Pansies,* ca. 1903. Oil on paper mounted on paperboard, 19¼ x 17¾ in. (48.9 x 45.1 cm). The Metropolitan Museum of Art, New York, bequest of Joan Whitney Payson

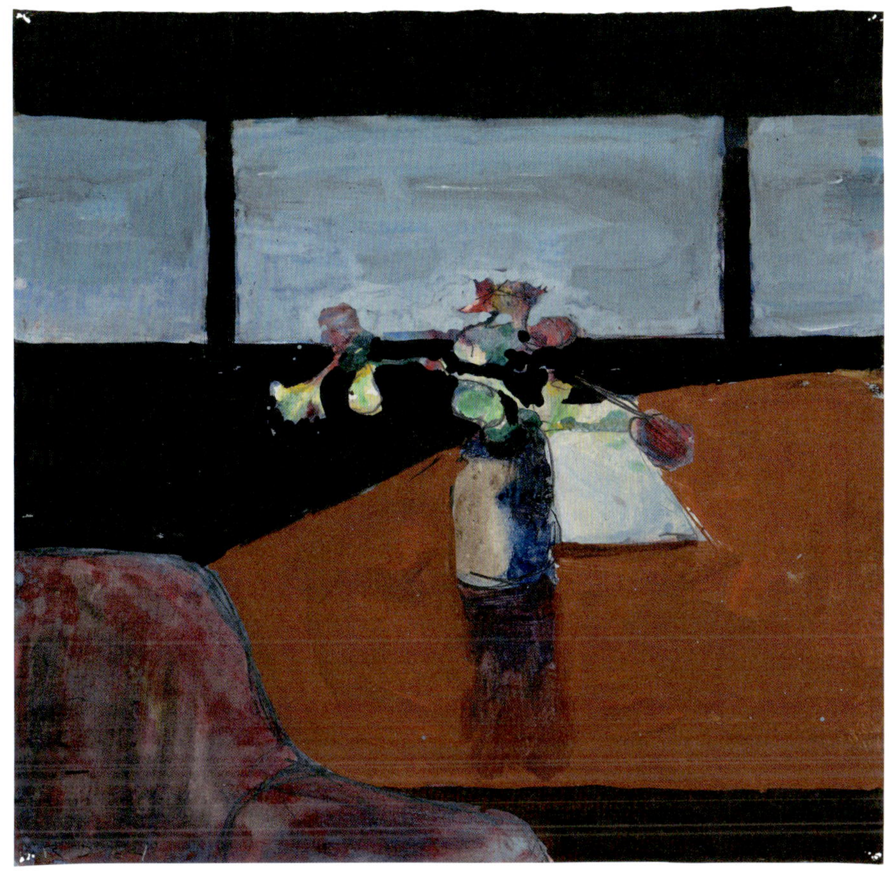

Plate 48. Richard Diebenkorn, *Untitled,* 1964. Gouache and graphite on paper, 13⅜ x 13⅞ in. (34 x 35.2 cm). Collection of John and Sally Van Doren, courtesy Van Doren Waxter

Plate 49. Richard Diebenkorn, *Cityscape #1,* 1963. Oil on canvas, 60¼ x 50½ in. (153 x 128.3 cm). San Francisco Museum of Modern Art, purchase with funds from Trustees and friends in memory of Hector Escobosa, Brayton Wilbur, and J. D. Zellerbach

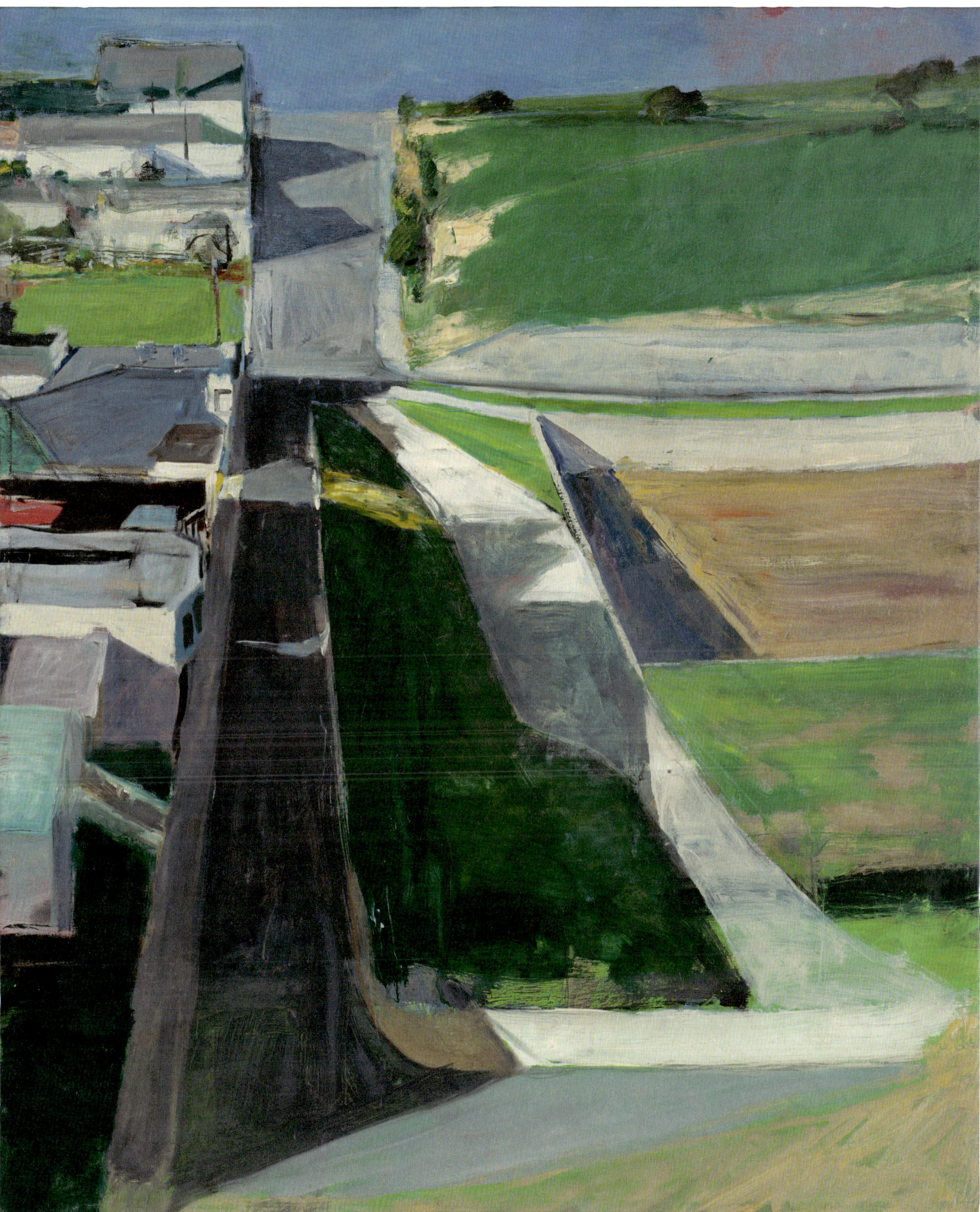

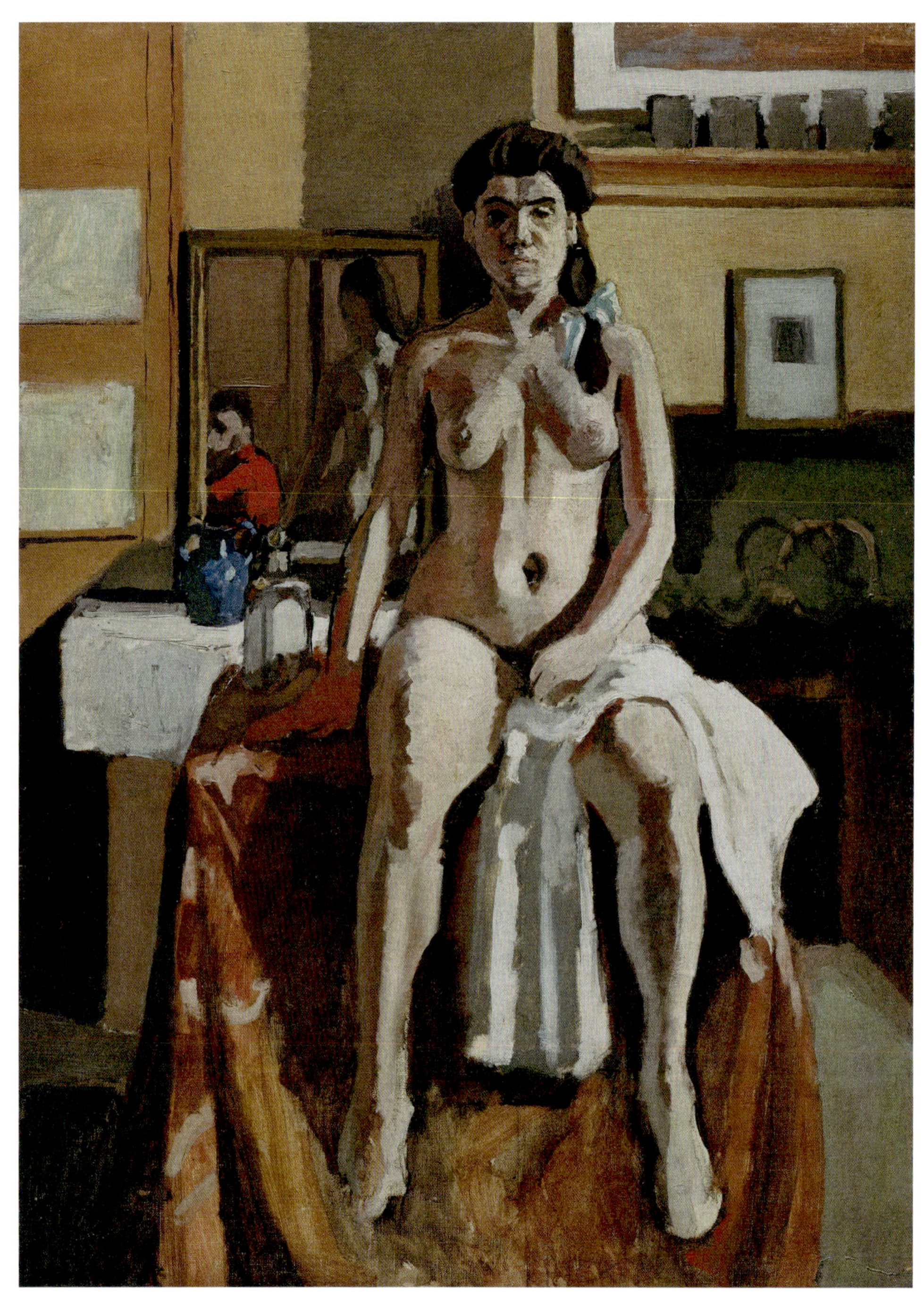

Plate 50. Henri Matisse, *Carmelina,* 1903. Oil on canvas, 32 x 23¼ in. (81.3 x 59 cm).
Museum of Fine Arts, Boston, Tompkins Collection—Arthur Gordon Tompkins Fund

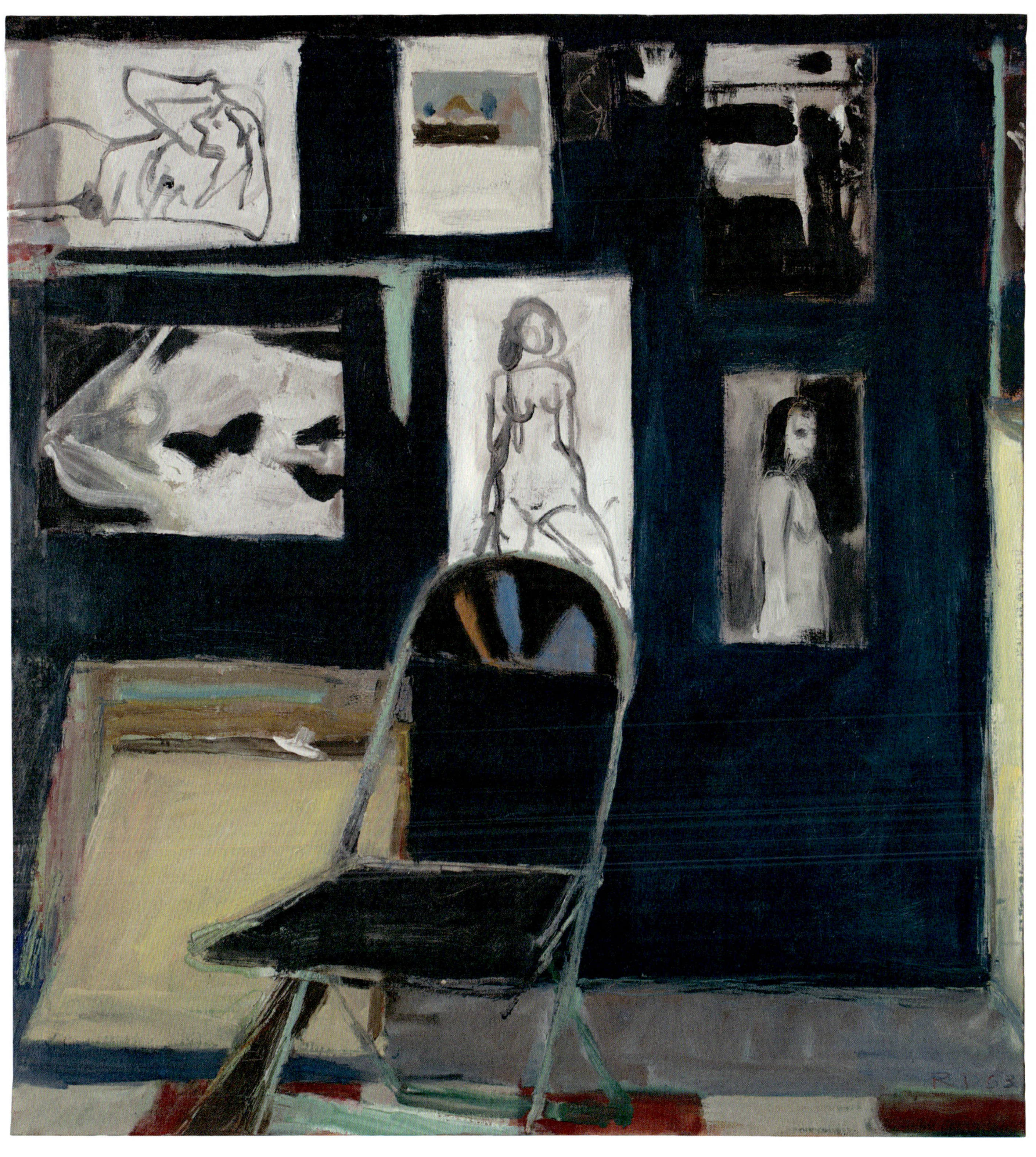

Plate 51. Richard Diebenkorn, *Studio Wall,* 1963. Oil on canvas, 45⅜ x 42½ in. (115.3 x 108 cm).
U.C. Berkeley Art Museum and Pacific Film Archive, gift of Richard and Phyllis Diebenkorn

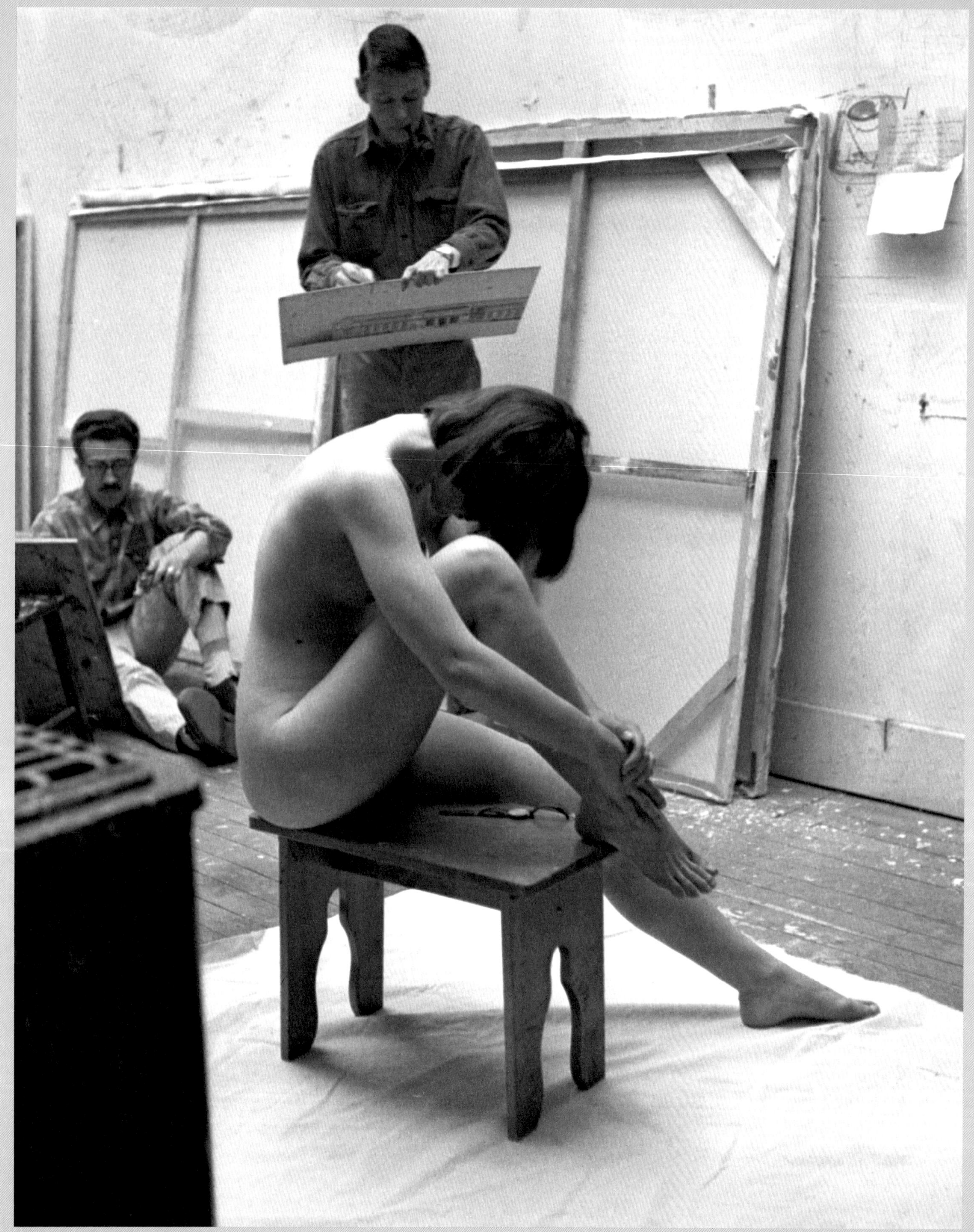

Breaking All the Rules: The Drawings of Richard Diebenkorn and Henri Matisse

Jodi Roberts

Richard Diebenkorn was a shrewd student of art history. His private sketchbooks—filled with hundreds of impromptu drawings, notes, and ephemera cut out from books, magazines, and newspapers—reveal a curious mind drawn to a wide variety of past art: quick sketches of ancient Greek kylixes hint at an attraction to the vessels' curvaceous contours; a clipping with a portrait by Rembrandt suggests deep admiration for the Dutch artist's facility with paint; compositions built from contrasting light and dark geometric shapes reveal an eager interest in Cubism and the early development of abstraction.[1] Quick to discuss his personal pantheon of artist heroes, Diebenkorn often highlighted the late nineteenth- and early twentieth-century figures who left their mark on him: Jean Arp, Paul Cézanne, Edward Hopper, Joan Miró, Piet Mondrian, Pablo Picasso, and Kurt Schwitters, among others. Yet the name that appears most frequently in discussions of Diebenkorn's work is Henri Matisse. He too figures prominently in Diebenkorn's sketchbooks, in which dozens of quickly dashed-off still lifes, studio interiors, and images of women chime with Matisse's treatments of similar themes. One volume even contains a small souvenir homage to the French artist—a postcard reproduction of his *Grande liseuse* (Woman Reading) (1923, fig. 1) stashed between its pages.

Diebenkorn's firsthand encounters with Matisse's pictures are often described as moments of recurring epiphany. First there was his eye-opening visit to Sarah Stein's home in Palo Alto in 1943, when he was a student

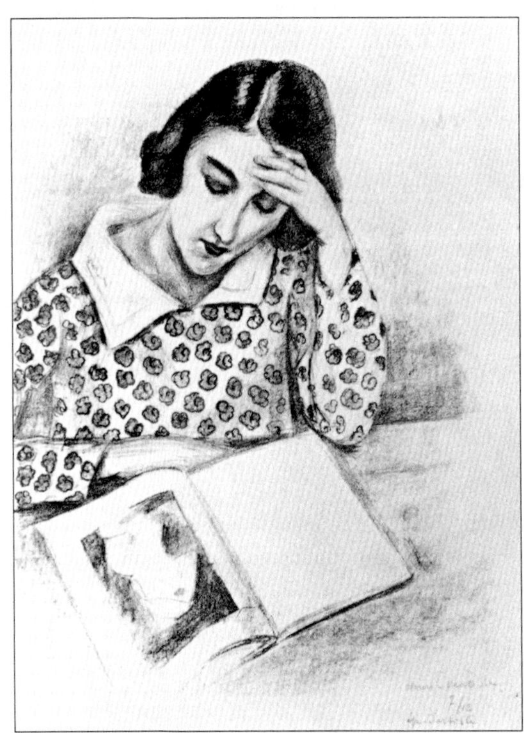

Fig. 1. Postcard with Henri Matisse's *Grande liseuse* (Woman Reading) (1923) inserted into Richard Diebenkorn's *Sketchbook #16*. Iris & B. Gerald Cantor Center for Visual Arts at Stanford University, Stanford, California

Richard Diebenkorn and Nathan Oliveira sketching at the studio of Theophilus "Bill" Brown and Paul Wonner, Berkeley, 1955. Photograph by Lincoln (Linc) Yamaguchi at Stanford University. Then there were his regular trips to The Phillips Collection in Washington, D.C., and the treks he made to New York's Museum of Modern Art and the Philadelphia Museum of Art in 1944, while he was stationed in Virginia for military duty. In 1952 Diebenkorn visited a major retrospective of Matisse's work at the Los Angeles Municipal Art Department. More than a decade after that, in 1964, he spent time with impressive examples of the French painter's work from the collections of Sergei Shchukin and Ivan Morozov, which had been divided between the Pushkin State Museum of Fine Arts in Moscow and the State Hermitage Museum in Leningrad (now Saint Petersburg). A close look at the Matisse paintings in these collections offers entry into the exercise of mapping a genealogy for Diebenkorn's breakthroughs as a painter.[2] What is rarely noted about Diebenkorn's long, productive dialogue with Matisse's work, however, is that it played out on paper as much as on canvas. Pilgrimages to the above-mentioned collections—many of which include numerous works on paper by Matisse—furnished lessons about the French artist's dynamic drawing techniques as well as his innovative painting style.[3] Diebenkorn's studies of Matisse as a draftsman also continued at home through a personal library that, over time, accumulated multiple exhibition catalogues and major books on the older artist's graphic work.[4]

The strongest evidence of Diebenkorn's preoccupation with Matisse's works on paper resides, of course, in the thousands of drawings he produced over the course of a long career that plumbed the possibilities of abstraction and figuration, as well as the fruitful spaces in between. Both artists sketched daily and defined the medium of drawing expansively, experimenting with techniques and materials traditional and new. Matisse used pens, reeds, and brushes to lay down fluid lines of ink. He blended and smudged charcoal edges with a stumping tool to create subtle variations in tone. Ever inventive, he mastered "drawing with scissors" late in life, creating room-size compositions with cut-out, painted paper. Diebenkorn, in turn, worked with graphite and charcoal, watercolor washes and conté crayon, gouache and oilstick, liquid ink and cheap ballpoint pen. Notwithstanding key disparities in their approaches to art making—natural departures given their fifty-three-year age difference, not to mention the distinct cultural milieus of early twentieth-century France and midcentury California—their drawings, seen side by side, shine a light on Diebenkorn's reasons for returning to Matisse, his favorite creative interlocutor, again and again. In Matisse, Diebenkorn found a way of thinking through art history, of metabolizing its lessons and values and pushing through its established rules. And in drawings that often hold to subject matter with deep roots in tradition, both artists found ways of laying down dark lines and swaths of shadowy gray that nonetheless upended convention.

Matisse and Diebenkorn dutifully put themselves through the paces of rigorous academic training, which included ample lessons in illusionistic drawing. The former endured early-morning drawing classes at the École Maurice Quentin de La Tour in Saint-Quentin before moving on to the Académie Julian in Paris and then becoming an unofficial student at the esteemed École des Beaux-Arts. His academic regimen included drawing plaster casts, sketching in city streets, and copying masterworks at the Musée du Louvre. The few extant drawings from Matisse's student days, such as a study of an old man completed in the 1890s (fig. 2), reveal his painstaking efforts to render the look and texture of flesh and muscle bound to the body's skeleton. The schools Diebenkorn attended lacked the weighty history of Matisse's French institutions, but through high school art classes, courses with Daniel Mendelowitz and Victor Arnautoff at Stanford, and instruction with Erle Loran and Worth Ryder at the University of California, Berkeley, he honed his descriptive skill, often unleashing it full force on the humblest of objects (fig. 3).

Mimesis, however, was only a starting point. Late in life Matisse confessed his career-long struggle against the pressures he had felt as a young artist to depict "observations made from nature" and to "copy nature stupidly."[5] He determined instead to find "possibilities of expression beyond the literal copy."[6] In works like *Marguerite in Three Poses* (1906, plate 53), this attempt to capture an identity that surpasses outward appearance resulted in compellingly summary descriptions of a sitter's salient traits, both physical and psychological. Diebenkorn, in contrast, came of age artistically in the wake of Modernists like Matisse, whose radical experiments with composition, color, and art making materials

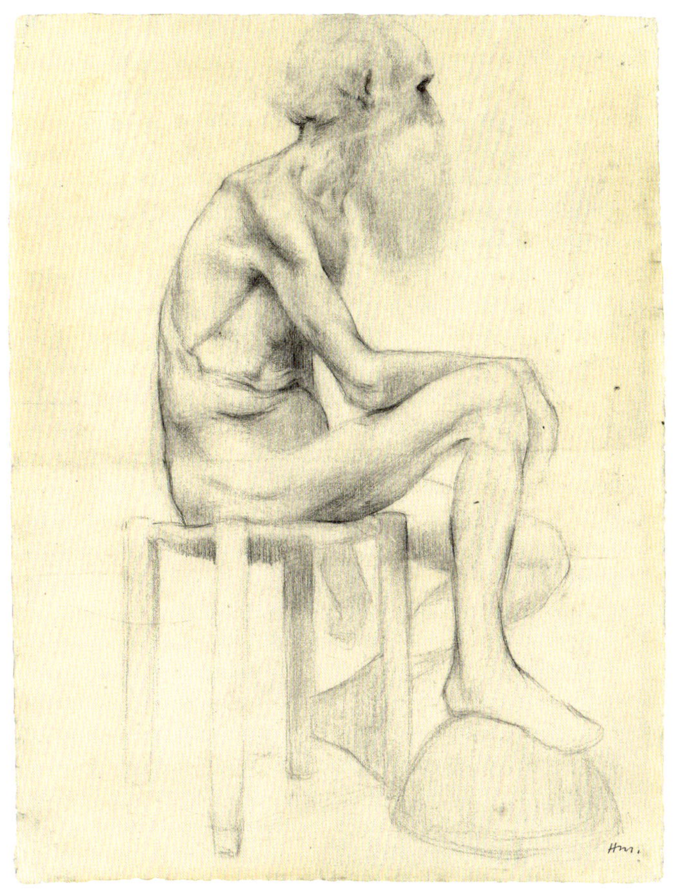

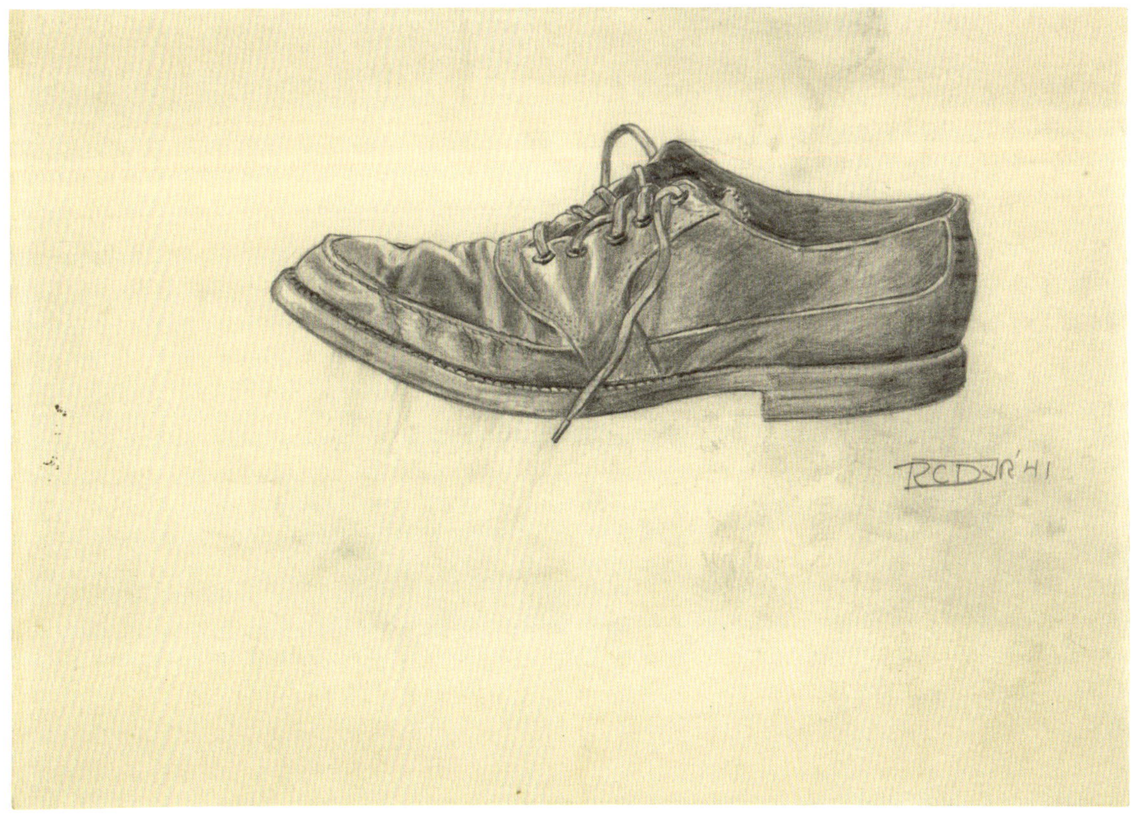

Fig. 2. Henri Matisse, *Study of a Seated Old Man*, ca. 1893–95. Charcoal on paper, 24⅞ x 18⅞ in. (63 x 48 cm). Musée Matisse, Nice, France, bequest of Madame Henri Matisse, 1960

Fig. 3. Richard Diebenkorn, *Untitled*, 1941. Graphite on paper, 7⅝ x 11 in. (19.4 x 27.9 cm). The Grant Family Collection gave birth to wholly new modes of figuration and opened pathways to abstraction. For the younger artist the battle was not against tradition-bound teachers or peers but rather his own natural dexterity. Whether creating abstract or figurative works, he fought against what Jane Livingston has called a "preternatural 'wrist,'" an uncanny ability to summon a vast range of visual effects at will and, seemingly, without much effort.[7] Fellow California artist Elmer Bischoff remembered his friend Diebenkorn "cultivating a deliberate awkwardness" in his painting and drawing, a quest suggested in his intentionally ambiguous depictions of three-dimensional space and his frequent use of hasty scribbles and unsteady lines in drawings like *Untitled* (1958, plate 52).[8]

Matisse and Diebenkorn approached the vast majority of their drawings as independent experiments, conceived, they each insisted, without a finished painting or other composition in mind. In Matisse's time, as Yve-Alain Bois has noted, this declaration of drawing's autonomy was a meaningful departure from art historical norms. In refusing to prepare multiple small studies for larger painted works, Matisse overthrew the traditional notion of the cartoon or bozzetto, a drawn road map for a composition that can be scaled up or down to fit the dimensions of the final painting. In the process he also upset time-honored hierarchies of media, which since the Renaissance had classified drawing as the handmaiden to painting.[9] Matisse treated a work on paper as a whole unto itself, created with the exact proportions of its surface in mind, never to be enlarged or diminished. "If I take a sheet of paper of a given size, my drawing will have a necessary relationship to its format," he explained in 1908 in "Notes of a Painter," his most famous written statement. "I would not repeat this drawing on another sheet of different proportions, for example, rectangular instead of square. Nor should I be satisfied with a mere enlargement, had I to transfer the drawing to a sheet of the same shape."[10]

Diebenkorn, too, viewed drawing as a practice that complemented his painting while maintaining its own specificity. Already in 1965, in a book inspired by the first exhibition of his graphic work, which Diebenkorn helped organize at Stanford's art gallery, his drawings were described insistently as finished compositions, "complete in themselves."[11] Years later the artist elaborated on the parallel development of his work in different media. Drawings usually started as "sketch explorations of ideas," "a kind of tryout or rehearsal of general possibilities" that might provide food for thought for future canvases. But, once finished, a drawing formed "an independent work."[12] And like Matisse, Diebenkorn grounded his pursuit of drawing as an autonomous art form in questions of scale: "[I] need to do relatively small works, independent of others and complete in themselves," he explained. "But a small canvas usually becomes for me an unfeasible miniature. Paper, I find, is something else, lending itself to the different scale of the small size."[13] In figuring out the ideal proportions of composition to surface area for a given drawing, Diebenkorn matched Matisse's fastidiousness. He notoriously tortured his works' paper supports, covering up unsatisfactory passages, cutting down edges, and taping on additional materials until the desired relationships emerged (fig. 4).

The webs of partially erased lines present in so many drawings by Matisse and Diebenkorn disclose, with striking candor, this search for dynamic balance between the marks and materials on a page and the limits of its framing edges. Matisse's *Study of Sarah Stein* (1916, plate 67), for instance, reduces his patron's features to geometrically rigid lines and curves. Streaks of smudged graphite simultaneously betray his struggle to position the abstracted eyes, nose, and mouth and lend a sense of three-dimensionality to the figure's sunken undereyes and neck. In his *Reclining Nude with Arm behind Head* (1937, plate 65) the dark outlines that define the model's body imply quick execution, but the charcoal haze that coats the work's creamy paper support confesses the artist's arduous reworking of the figure. Diebenkorn pushed this aesthetic of unveiled labor to new extremes in *Untitled (Seated Nude)* of 1966 (plate 68). With its dense network of light and dark strokes that map the sitter's shifting positions on the chair, the finished work is a visual index of Diebenkorn's stop-and-start contact with the page, his movement around the model, and the time (no doubt lengthy) needed to locate and capture a satisfactory point of view.

Artistic ethics, as much as visual aesthetics, inspired these artists' willingness to lay bare their working processes. Matisse, for one, took special care to emphasize the effort he invested in creating a work of art, worrying openly that young artists might mistake the "apparent facility" of his compositions for a disregard of intellectual and manual discipline.[14] His "Notes of a Painter on his Drawing" of 1939 assures that his fluid, sparse ink drawings "are always preceded by studies in a less rigorous medium than pure line, such as charcoal or stump drawing." Despite the simplicity of some of his compositions, he vows: "It is only when I feel that I am drained by the work, which may go on for several sessions, that my mind is cleared and I have the confidence to give free rein to my pen."[15] Diebenkorn was less concerned with shoring up his reputation as an expert artist dedicated to a multistep process, but he similarly underscored the importance of work—of mental and physical exertion. Embedded early in his career in an art world awash in the creative ideologies of Abstract Expressionism, he devised working practices that were at once highly methodical and attuned to the current appetite for immediacy and "toughness" in visual art. As his teacher and friend David Park explained it, mid-twentieth-century painters rejected the idea that art should be "easily come by," believing instead that it "must be hard-bought," never "soft."[16] Vestiges of Diebenkorn's early belief that rewarding creative activity involved a charged encounter between artist and materials—a moment of heightened, existential self-awareness brought on by the labor of creation itself—shine through in works like the seated nude of 1966 discussed above. Completed years after Abstract Expressionism's influence had waned and in a figurative mode rebuffed by many of its key proponents, the drawing nonetheless registers the intensity of Diebenkorn's in-the-moment concentration and robust work ethic.

The bodies of women, more than any other subject, served as ground for both artists' drawing exercises—a thematic coincidence that again highlights their shared investment in the long history of Western art, as well as their acute awareness of their respective places within it. Matisse's abiding preoccupation with the female form resulted in hundreds of images of friends, family members, and, most often, models for hire: Loulou Brouty, Laurette (surname unknown), Antoinette Arnoud, Henriette Darricarrère, and Lydia Delectorskaya, to name the most famous. Together, these works expose Matisse's familiarity with time-honored feminine tropes—the mythological figure, the demure portrait sitter, the studio model, the seductive muse. In more recent years feminist scholars have pointed to the ways in which Matisse's presentations of women helped to entrench stereotypes about male and female roles in artistic creation (engaged, productive male versus passive, alluring female).[17] Yet if the artist's choice of female themes held to convention, his experiments in representing their appearance and surroundings marked a radical break. Matisse's enthrallment with color and pattern drove his pictures of women. Even in relatively unassuming, monochromatic drawings such as *Reclining Model with a Flowered Robe* (ca. 1923–24, plate 59), sharp shifts in decorative

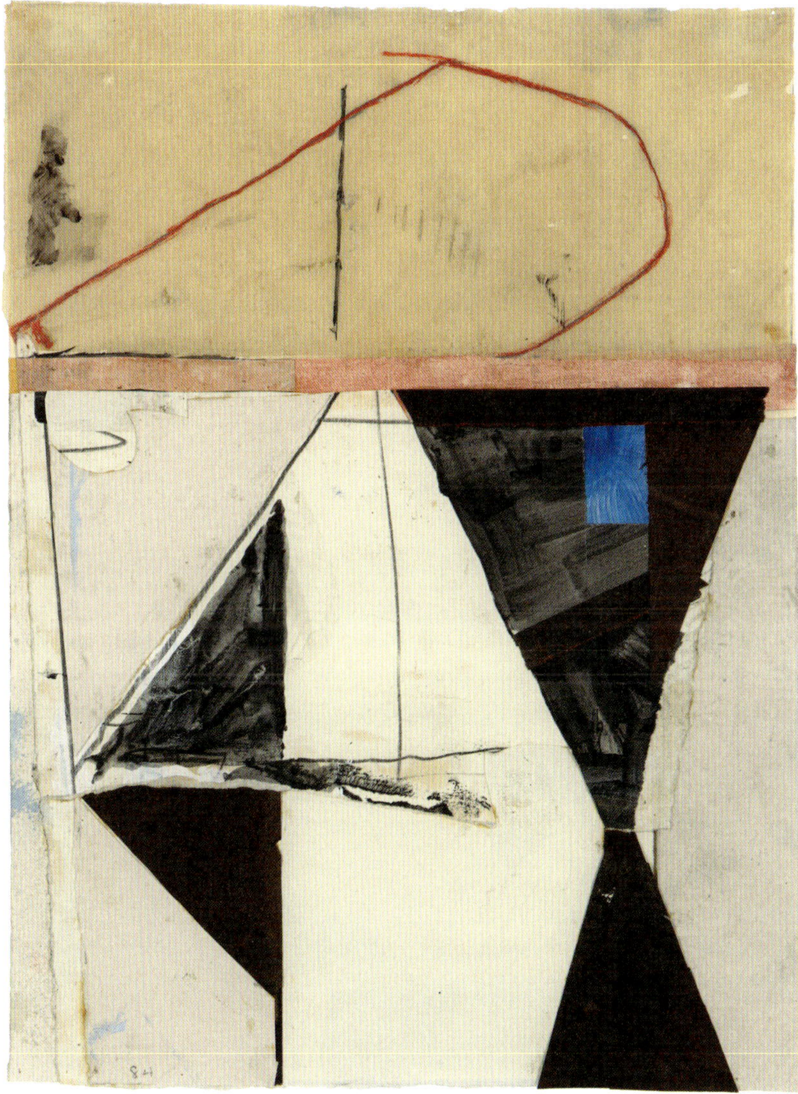

Fig. 4. Richard Diebenkorn, *Untitled,* 1984. Gouache, crayon, charcoal, and pasted paper on paper, 18⅛ x 13⅞ in. (46 x 35.2 cm). Museum of Fine Arts, Houston, Museum Purchase with funds provided by the Alice Pratt Brown Museum Fund and gift of an anonymous donor, 1994

design and tonal value guide a viewer's eye across the entire expanse of the page. Matisse's feminine subjects, thematically bound up in tradition, became the sites of groundbreaking investigations into composition, pattern, line, and color. The artist himself recognized the combination of visual, emotional, and psychological forces at play in these works. "The emotional interest [my models] inspire in me is not especially visible in the representation of their bodies, but more often in the lines or special values distributed over the whole canvas," he explained, adding, "It is perhaps sublimated voluptuousness, something that may not yet be perceptible to everyone."[18]

The sensual force of Matisse's drawings certainly registered with Diebenkorn, who classified several of the French artist's images of reclining women as among the most erotic of the modern era.[19] This said, Diebenkorn's own drawings address the reality of the female body with a directness unmatched by Matisse. At key moments in his career, Diebenkorn participated in group drawing sessions with hired models, but just as often he turned to women he knew personally (fig. 5). In his hundreds of drawings, representations of primly dressed and posed subjects are balanced with sketches that delve frankly into the facts of flesh and the feel of desire. In studio corners and domestic settings, nude and partially dressed women sit unselfconsciously, their breasts bared and their legs spread to expose their genitals (fig. 6 and plate 64); they lounge together in intimate scenes that suggest moments of postcoital repose (plate 56). Throughout, Diebenkorn refuses recourse to mythology or fantasy, the excuse so many artists before him (including, often, Matisse) had contrived to justify their renditions of enticing female bodies. Instead, through details of dress, decor, hairstyles, and an occasional casually placed cigarette, Diebenkorn asserts the reality of the moments in which his images were made.

This is not to say that Diebenkorn's drawings of women are wholly unfettered. He, like Matisse, found in the process of depicting women and their immediate environs a means of meditation on the materials and techniques of art making and the visual pleasures they precipitate. The eye's awareness continually shifts between the subjects Diebenkorn portrays and his particular way of laying down the ink, graphite, and wash that render them recognizable. In *Untitled*, a drawing from 1962 (plate 58), the thick, uneven crease between a model's thighs and buttocks is simultaneously, and undeniably, a feathery line of pigment put down with an extremely moist brush. In *Untitled (Standing Nude)* (plate 61), a composition from the same year, the dark pubic hair of a standing model also declares itself to be, in reality, a mass of overlapping diagonals and triangles. In *Untitled* (plate 54), a third work from that period, the white highlights on a woman's body and the pale chair on which she sits function, at the same time, as brazen acknowledgments of the paper support's milky surface.

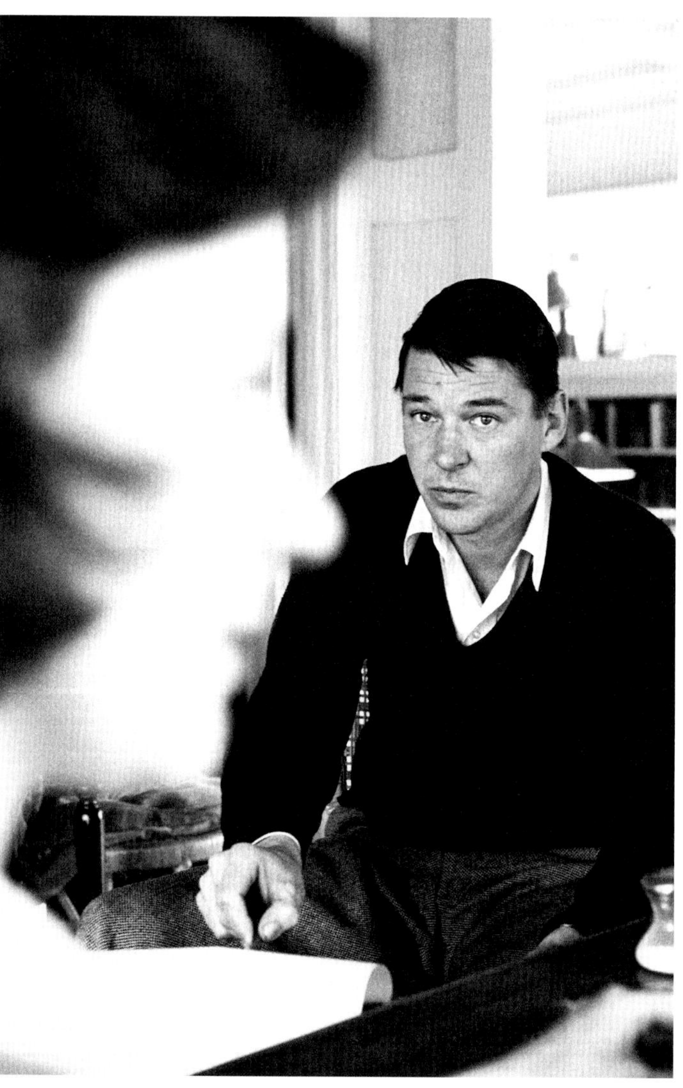

Fig. 5. Richard Diebenkorn drawing his wife, Phyllis, in their living room, Hillcrest Road, Berkeley, 1958. Photograph by Hans Namuth

Diebenkorn was clear about the significance of figure drawing to his overall development. Recalling his drawing sessions with models in the early 1950s, a moment when his painting remained mostly abstract, the artist described his recourse to figuration as a contemplative move forward. "I was drawing figuratively all of the time that I was doing abstract painting," he stated. "I would draw the figure at night . . . as a sort of *exercise in seeing*."[20] Diebenkorn, like Matisse before him, found in drawing the bodies of women a way to hone his skills as an artist attuned to the particular visual and tactile characteristics of his materials, ever mindful of past standards for art making and dedicated to breaking new ground as a draftsman and painter. It was a lesson in simultaneously looking backward and forward that Diebenkorn thought valuable enough to pass along to younger generations of artists. John Hultberg, one of his students, recalled that in Diebenkorn's classes "the idea was to break all the rules," a goal that, in practical terms, meant learning to draw "the nude à la Matisse."[21]

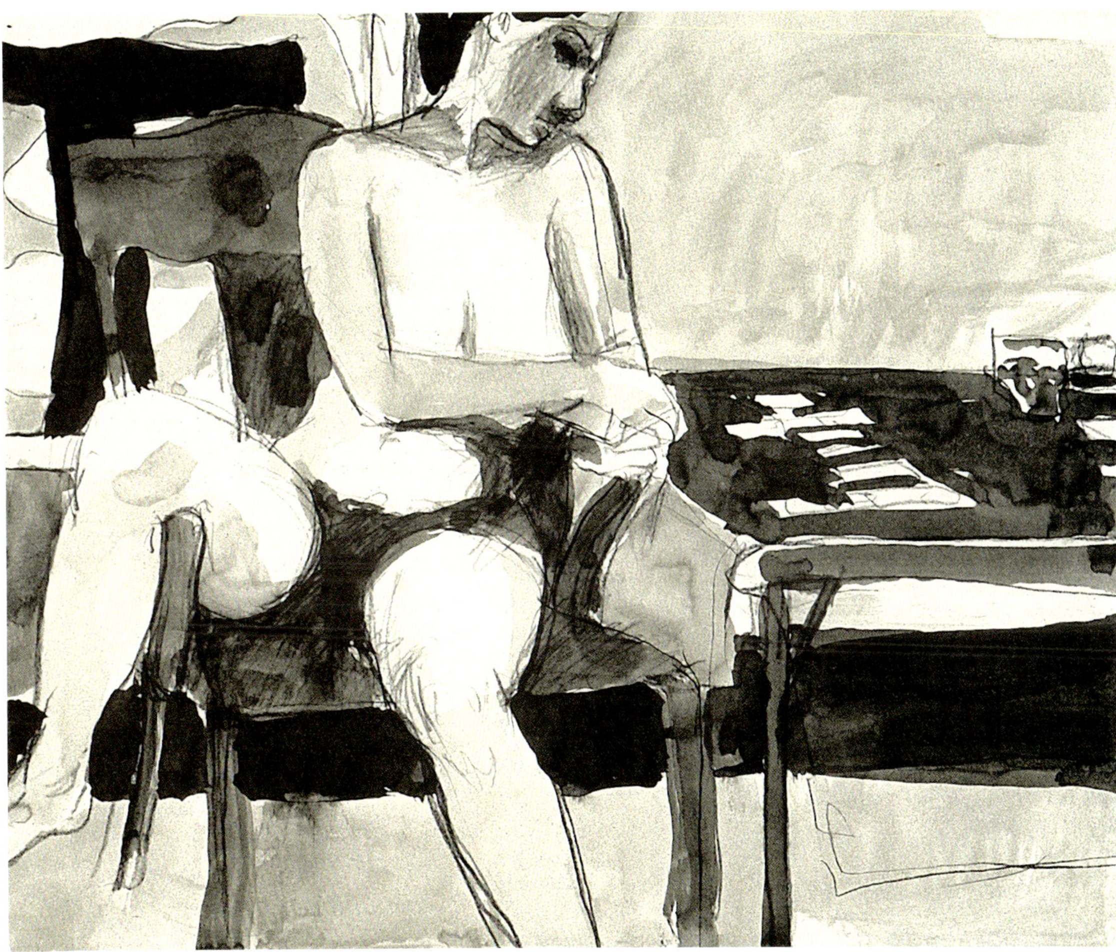

Fig. 6. Richard Diebenkorn, *Untitled,* ca. 1960–66. Ink wash and graphite on paper, 13¾ x 16¾ in. (34.9 x 42.6 cm). Collection of Vicki and Kent Logan, fractional and promised gift to the San Francisco Museum of Modern Art

Notes

1. In 2014 the Iris & B. Gerald Cantor Center for Visual Arts at Stanford University, Stanford, California, acquired Diebenkorn's sketchbooks as a gift from his widow, Phyllis Diebenkorn, and the Richard Diebenkorn Foundation. The next year the Cantor organized an exhibition of the twenty-nine books and published a major catalogue in conjunction with the show: *Richard Diebenkorn: The Sketchbooks Revealed* (Stanford, CA: Iris & B. Gerald Cantor Center for Visual Arts in association with Stanford University Press, 2015). The sketchbooks can be viewed in their entirety at http://museum.stanford.edu/diebenkornsketchbooks/.

2. For further discussion of the impact Diebenkorn's visit to the Soviet Union had on his painting practice, see the essay by Katherine Rothkopf on pages 116–28 in this publication.

3. An inventory of works at Sarah Stein's home in 1937, for example, lists "sixteen framed drawings by Matisse." Some of these works were likely still on the walls when Diebenkorn visited in 1943. I am grateful to Janet Bishop for sharing this information from her research on the Stein collection; for further discussion of the works Diebenkorn would have seen during this visit, see pages 20–21 of her essay in this publication. The Philadelphia Museum of Art began acquiring drawings and prints by Matisse in the early 1940s; by 1944 The Museum of Modern Art, New York, held more than two dozen Matisse works on paper, and it continued to actively collect his work for decades afterward. The 1952 Matisse retrospective exhibition in Los Angeles, organized by Alfred H. Barr Jr. of The Museum of Modern Art, included a total of twelve works on paper—drawings, watercolors, and prints.

4. For further discussion of Diebenkorn's collection of books on Matisse, see pages 167–72 in this publication. Sincere thanks to Janet Bishop and Jared Ledesma for providing this information.

5. Henri Matisse, "The Chapel of the Rosary" (1951), in *Matisse on Art: Revised Edition*, ed. Jack Flam (Berkeley: University of California Press, 1995), 196.

6. Ibid.

7. Jane Livingston, "The Art of Richard Diebenkorn," in *The Art of Richard Diebenkorn*, exh. cat., ed. Jane Livingston (New York: Whitney Museum of American Art, 1997), 34.

8. Elmer Bischoff quoted in ibid., 34.

9. Yve-Alain Bois, "Matisse and 'Arche-drawing,'" in *Painting as Model* (Cambridge, MA: MIT Press, 1990), 18–21.

10. Henri Matisse, "Notes of a Painter" (1908), in Flam, *Matisse on Art*, 38.

11. *Drawings by Richard Diebenkorn*, with an introduction by Lorenz Eitner (Stanford, CA: Department of Art and Architecture, Stanford University, 1965), n.p.

12. Richard Diebenkorn quoted in Edith Devaney, "Richard Diebenkorn's Drawings," in *Richard Diebenkorn*, exh. cat., by Sarah C. Bancroft and Edith Devaney (London: Royal Academy of Arts, 2015), 65.

13. Ibid., 62.

14. Bois, "Matisse and 'Arche-drawing,'" 50.

15. Henri Matisse, "Notes of a Painter on his Drawing" (1939), in Flam, *Matisse on Art*, 130–31.

16. David Park quoted in Maurice Tuchman, "Diebenkorn's Early Years," in *Richard Diebenkorn: Paintings and Drawings, 1943–1976*, exh. cat., by Robert T. Buck Jr., Linda L. Cathcart, Gerald Nordland, et al. (Buffalo: Albright-Knox Art Gallery, 1976), 10.

17. See, for example, Carol Duncan, "Virility and Domination in Early Twentieth-Century Vanguard Painting," in *Feminism and Art History*, ed. Norma Broude and Mary D. Gerrard (New York: Harper and Row, 1982), 292–313; and Marilynn Lincoln Board, "Constructing Myths and Ideologies in Matisse's Odalisques," *Genders*, no. 5 (Summer 1989): 21–49. For a compelling response to such feminist interpretations of Matisse's images, as well as formalist takes on his images of women, see John Elderfield, *Pleasuring Painting: Matisse's Feminine Representations* (London: Thames & Hudson, 1995).

18. Matisse, "Notes of a Painter on his Drawing," 132.

19. John Elderfield, *The Drawings of Richard Diebenkorn*, exh. cat. (New York: The Museum of Modern Art, 1988), 32.

20. Richard Diebenkorn quoted in Steven A. Nash, "Tension beneath Calm: Richard Diebenkorn's Figurative Work," in *Richard Diebenkorn: The Berkeley Years, 1953–1966*, exh. cat., by Timothy Anglin Burgard, Steven A. Nash, and Emma Acker (San Francisco: Fine Arts Museums of San Francisco, 2013), 44. Emphasis added.

21. John Hultberg quoted in Tuchman, "Diebenkorn's Early Years," 8.

Plate 52. Richard Diebenkorn, *Untitled,* 1958. Charcoal on paper, 12 x 8⅞ in. (30.5 x 22.5 cm).
Santa Cruz Island Foundation

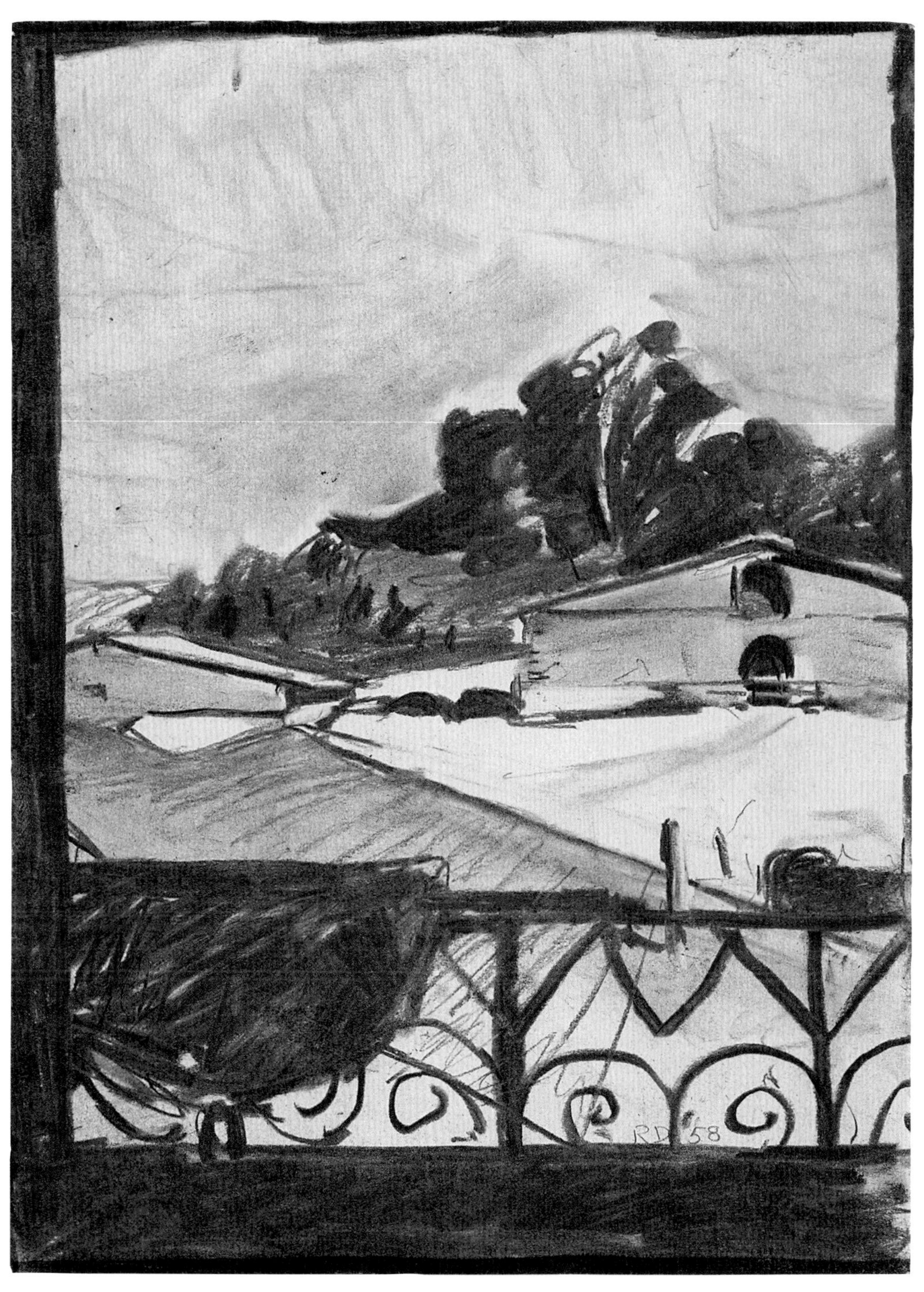
RD 58

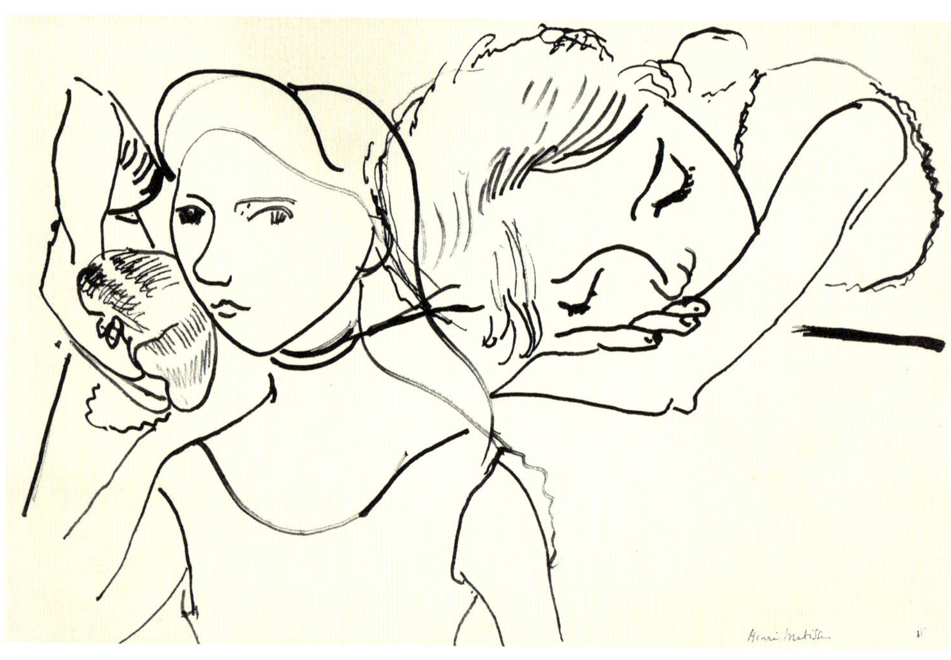

Plate 53. Henri Matisse, *Marguerite in Three Poses,* 1906. Ink on paper, 10 x 15⅝ in. (25.4 x 39.7 cm). San Francisco Museum of Modern Art, bequest of Elise S. Haas

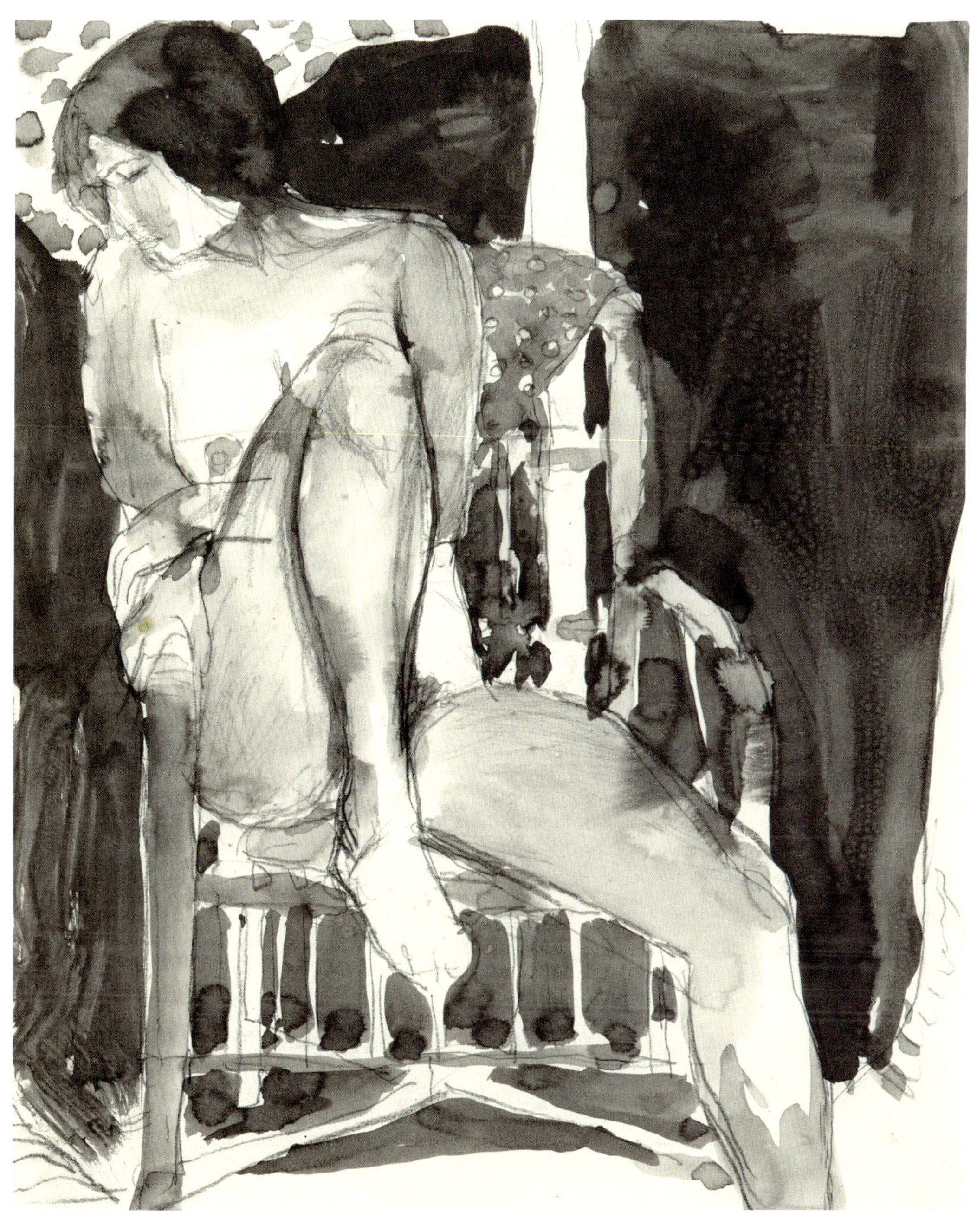

Plate 54. Richard Diebenkorn, *Untitled,* ca. 1960–66. Ink and charcoal on paper, 17 x 14 in. (43.2 x 35.6 cm). Private collection, courtesy Van Doren Waxter

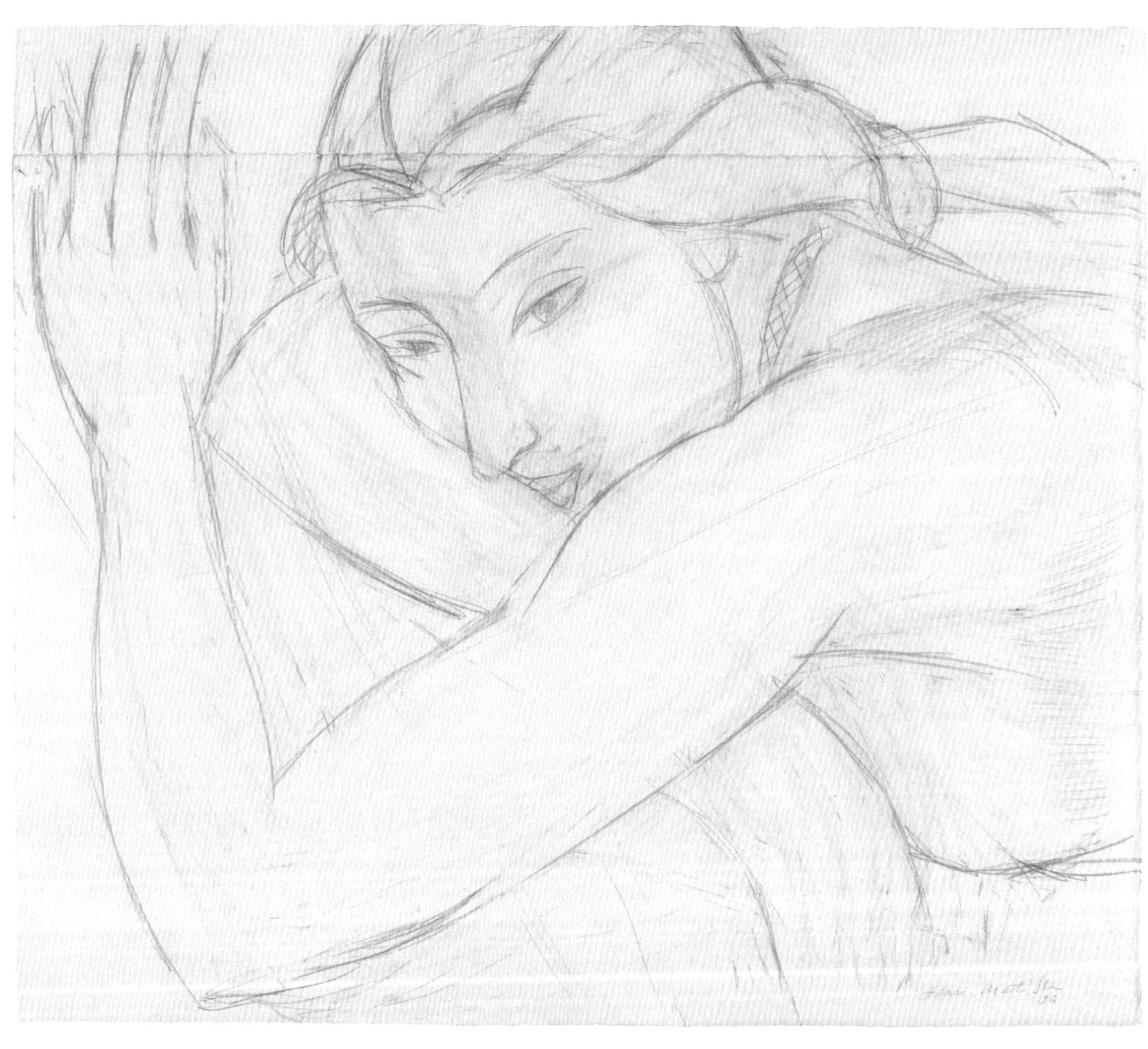

Plate 55. Henri Matisse, *Model Resting on Her Arms,* 1936. Graphite on paper, two joined sheets, overall: 17¼ x 20 in. (43.8 x 50.8 cm). The Baltimore Museum of Art: The Cone Collection, formed by Dr. Claribel Cone and Miss Etta Cone of Baltimore, Maryland

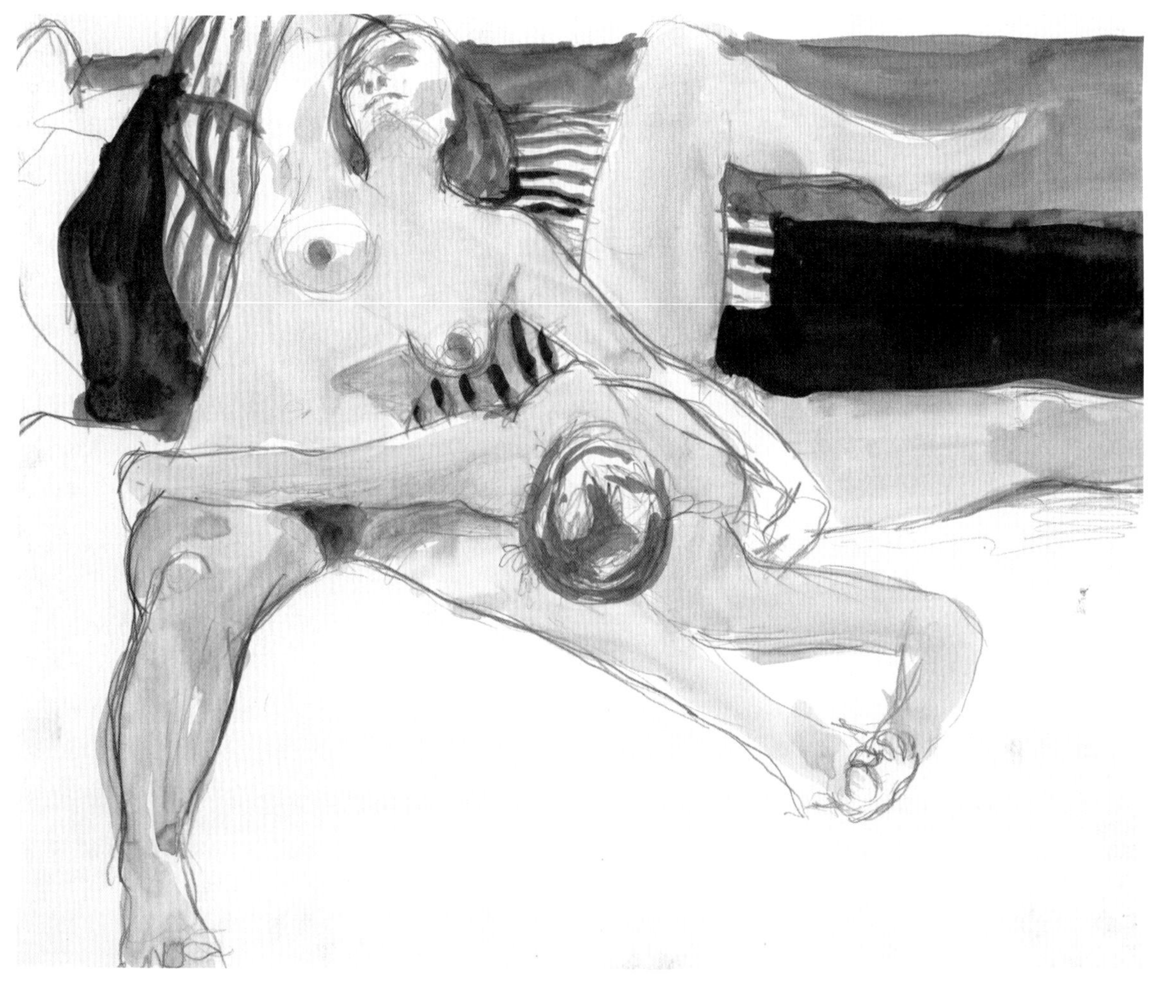

Plate 56. Richard Diebenkorn, *Untitled,* ca. 1961–62. Ink, charcoal, and graphite on paper, 13⅞ x 16⅞ in. (35.2 x 42.9 cm). Collection of John and Sally Van Doren, courtesy Van Doren Waxter

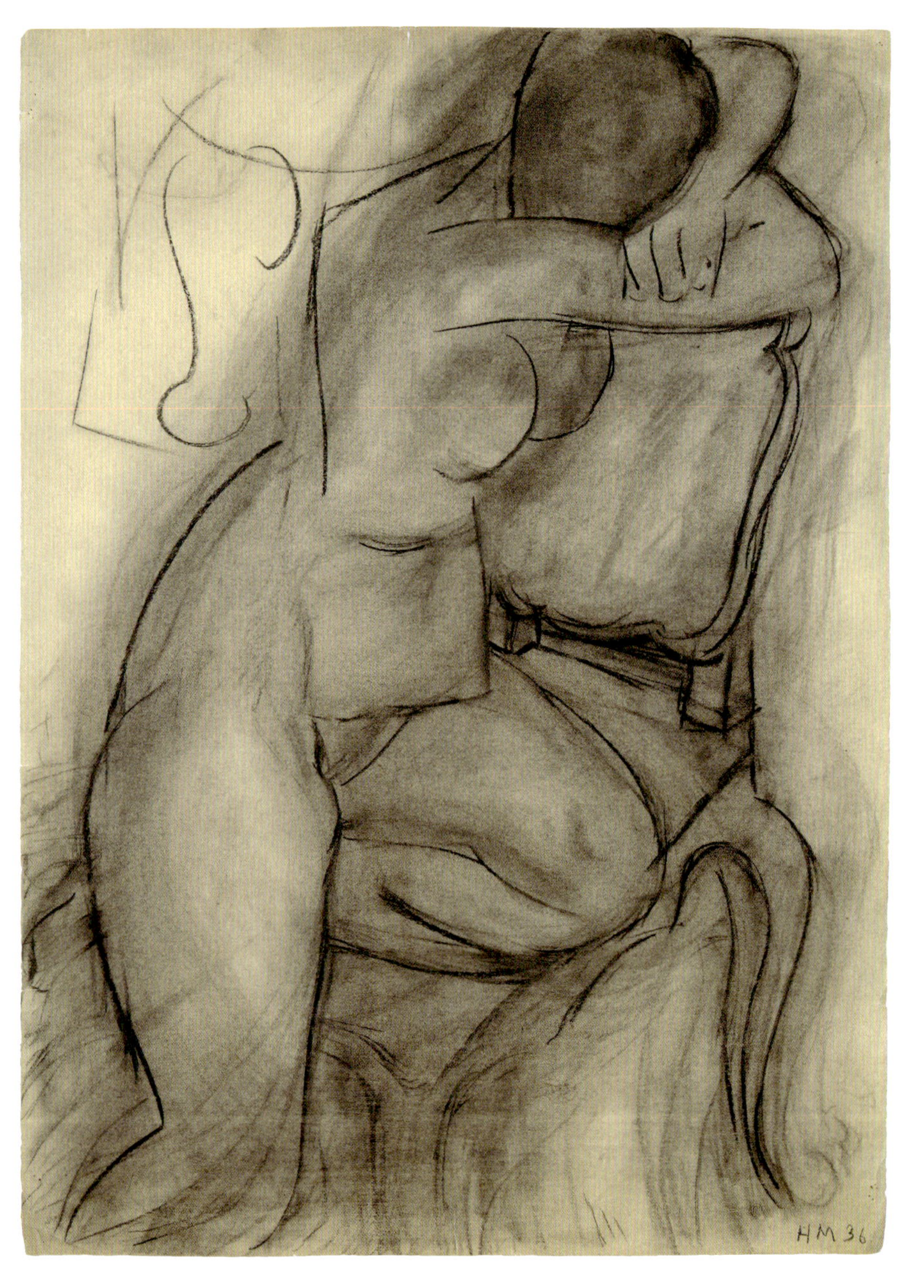

Plate 57. Henri Matisse, *Seated Nude, Head on Arms,* 1936.
Charcoal on paper, 28¾ x 21 in. (73 x 53.3 cm). Private collection

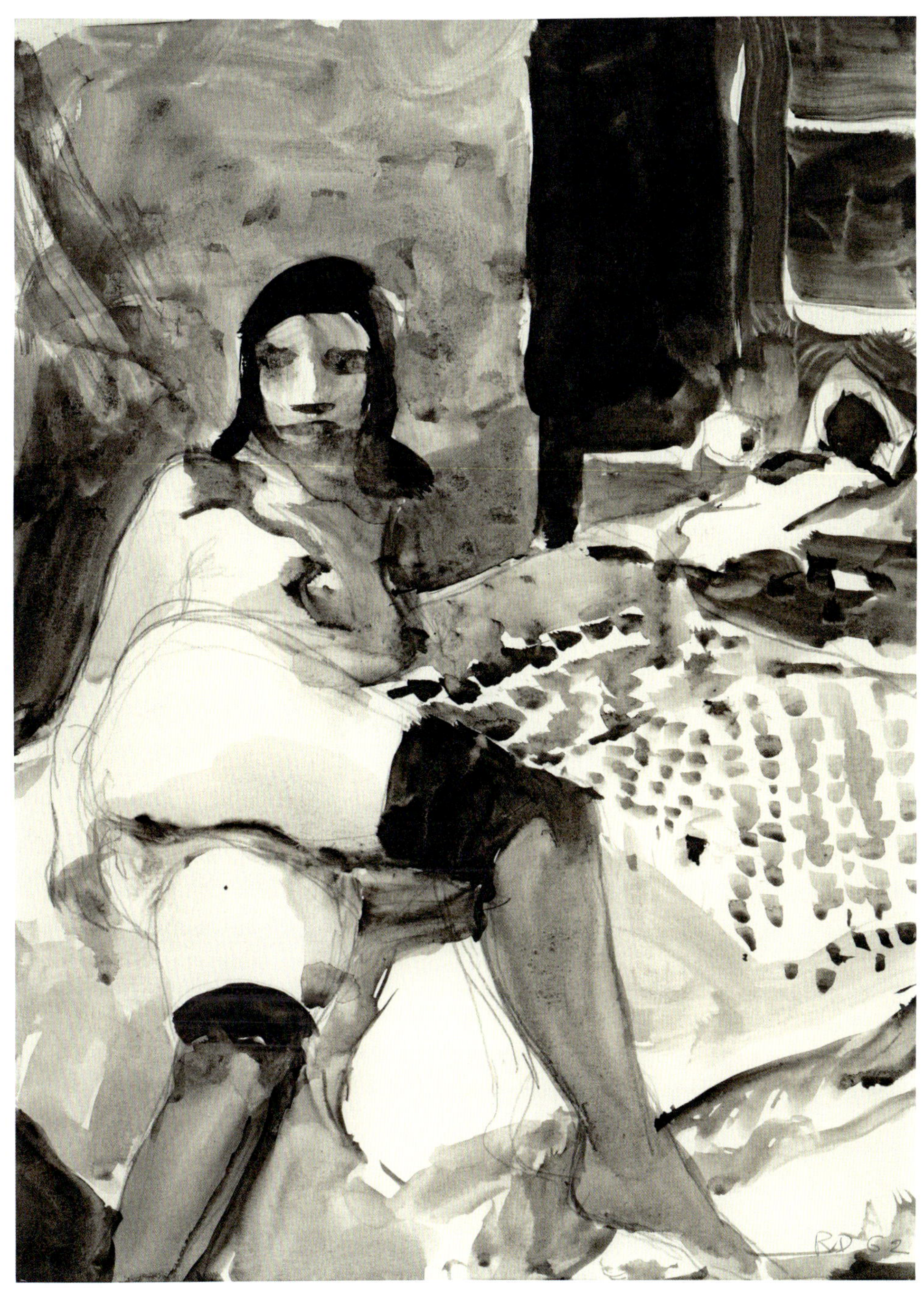

Plate 58. Richard Diebenkorn, *Untitled,* 1962. Ink and graphite on paper, 17 x 12½ in. (43.2 x 31.8 cm). San Francisco Museum of Modern Art, purchase through anonymous funds and the Albert M. Bender Bequest Fund

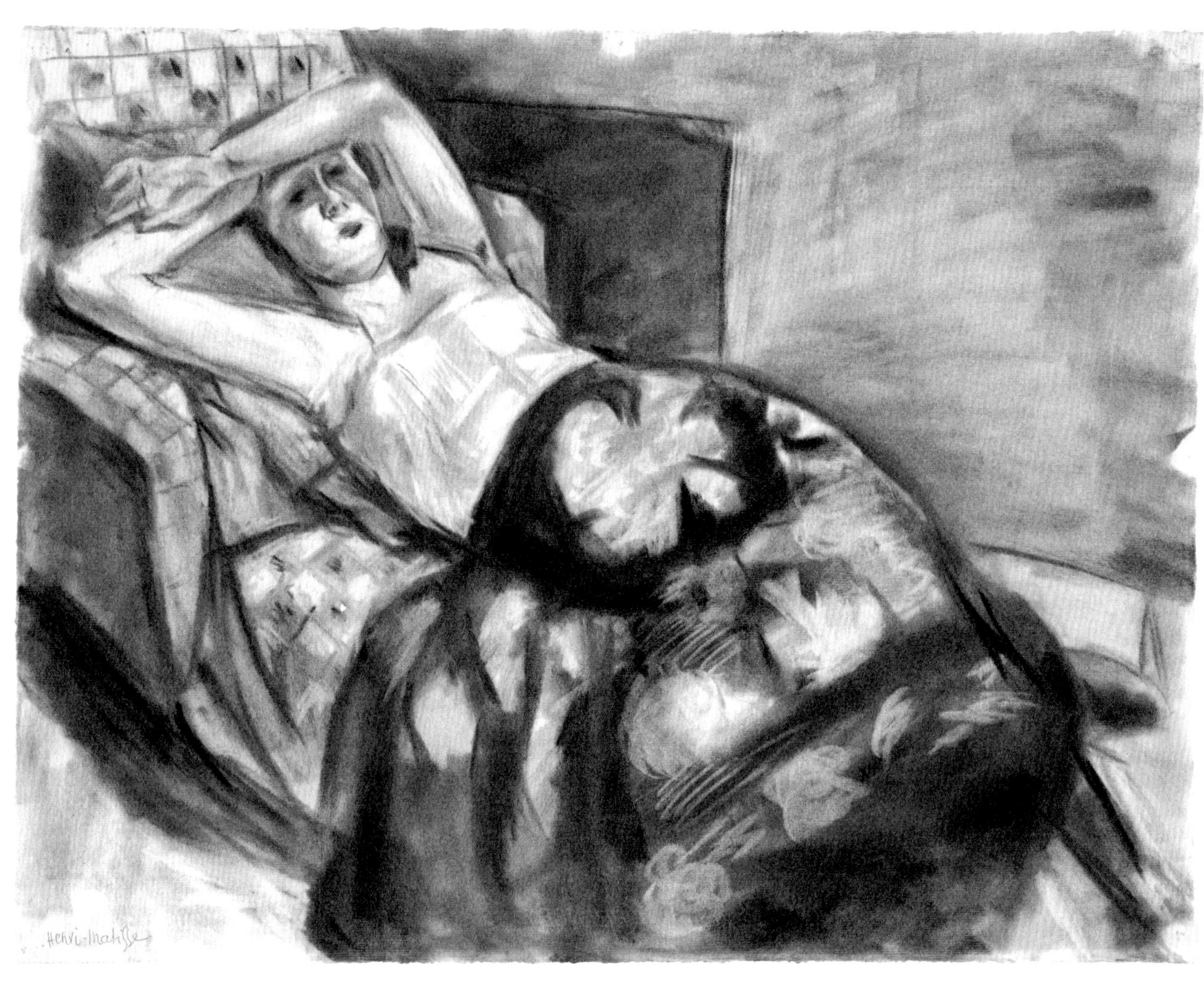

Plate 59. Henri Matisse, *Reclining Model with a Flowered Robe,* ca. 1923–24. Black chalk on paper, 18⅞ x 24¾ in. (47.9 x 62.9 cm). The Baltimore Museum of Art: The Cone Collection, formed by Dr. Claribel Cone and Miss Etta Cone of Baltimore, Maryland

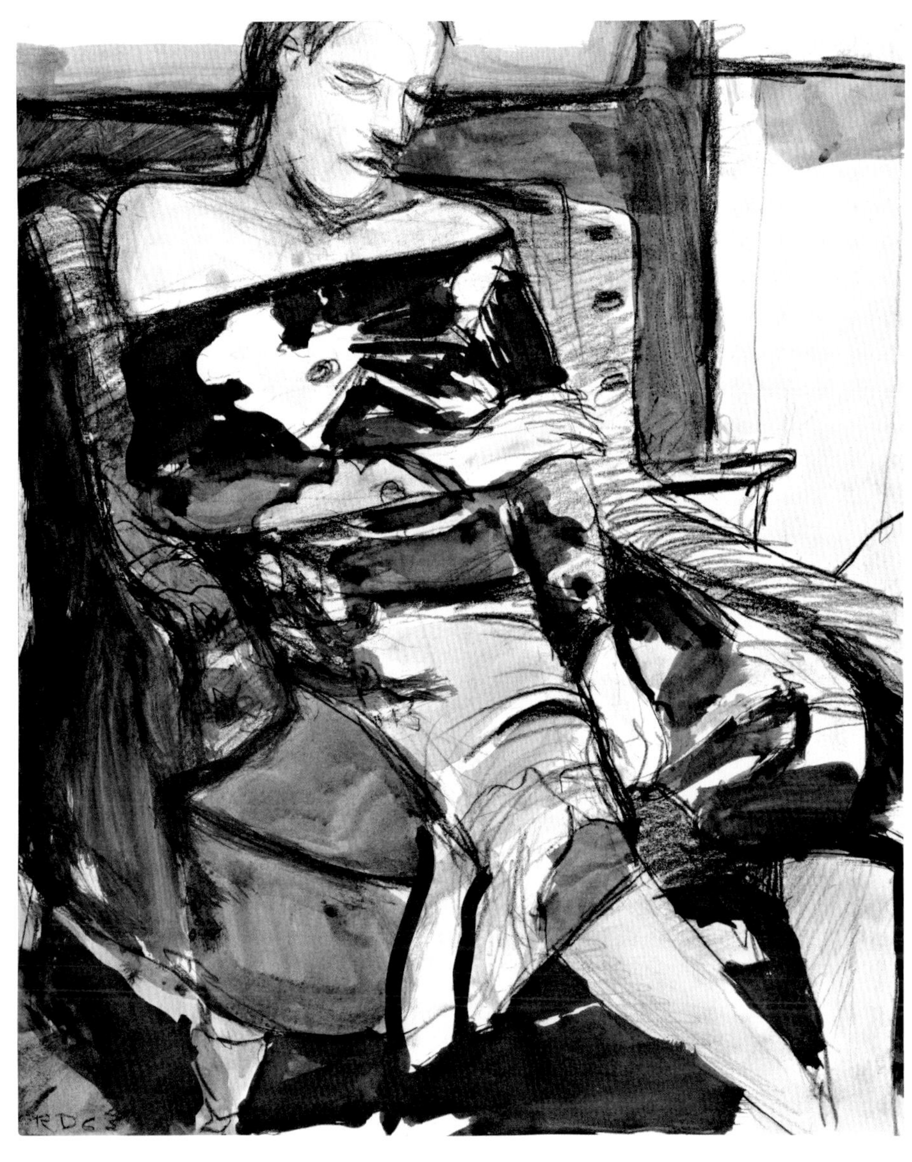

Plate 60. Richard Diebenkorn, *Untitled (Woman Seated in a Chair)*, 1963.
Ink, conté crayon, and charcoal on paper, 17 x 13⅞ in. (43.2 x 35.2 cm). The Baltimore Museum of Art: Thomas E. Benesch Memorial Collection

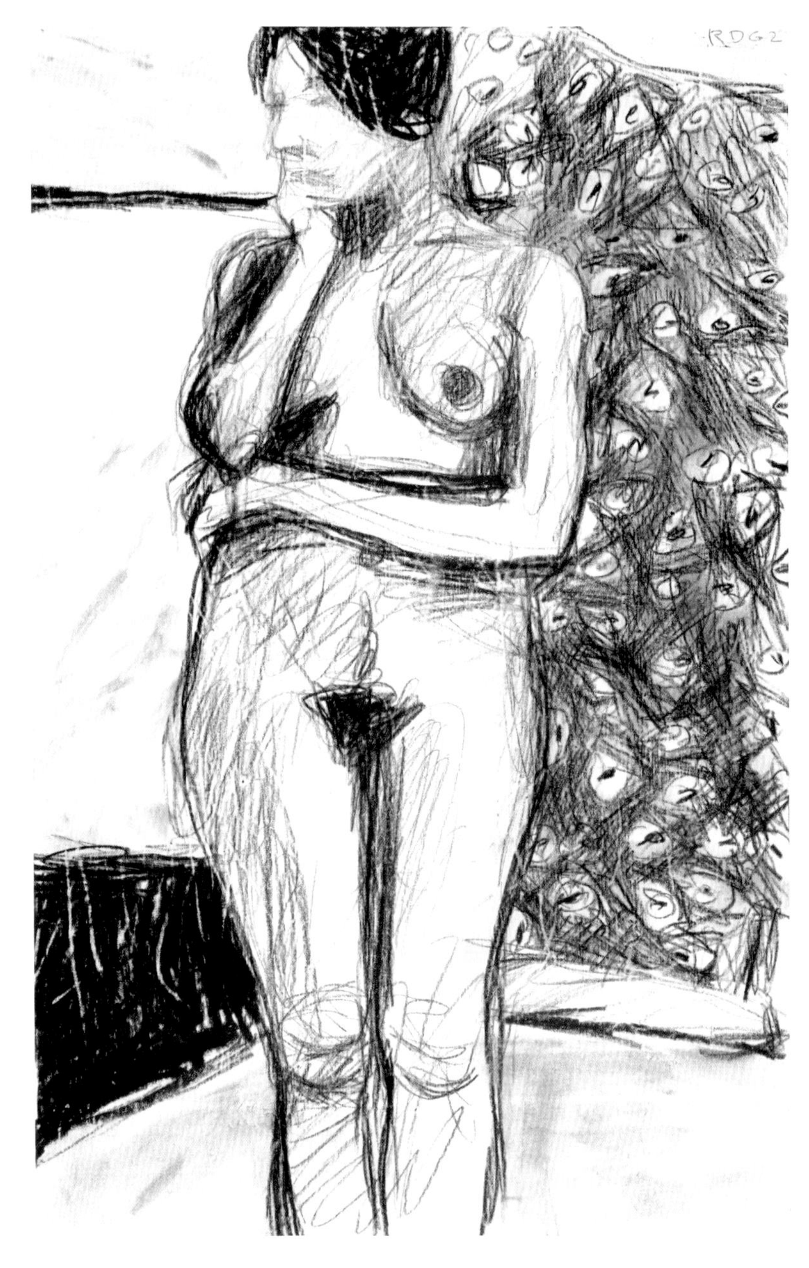

Plate 61. Richard Diebenkorn, *Untitled (Standing Nude),* 1962.
Conté crayon on paper, 17 x 11 in. (43.2 x 27.9 cm). The Baltimore Museum of Art: Thomas E. Benesch Memorial Collection

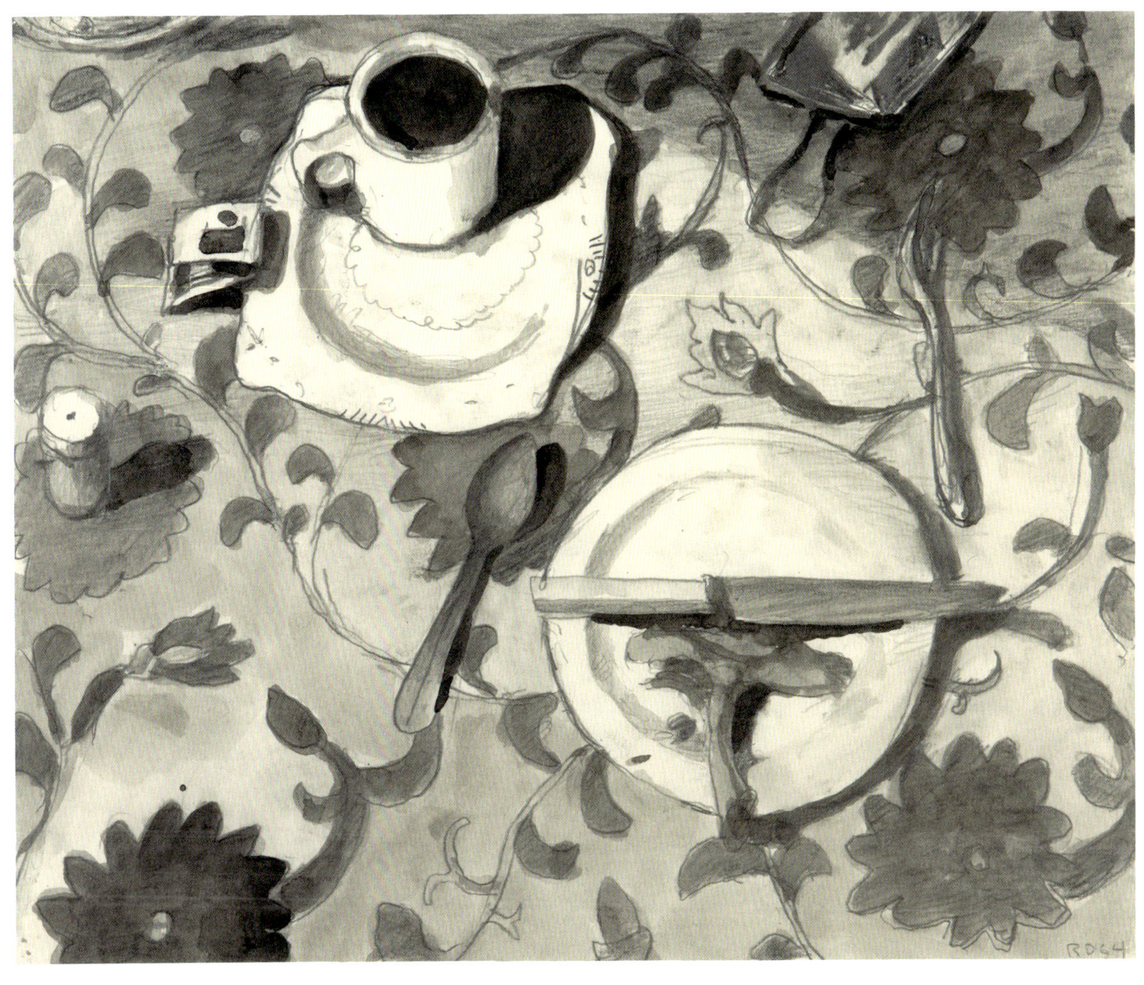

Plate 62. Richard Diebenkorn, *Untitled,* 1964. Graphite and ink on paper, 13⅞ x 16⅞ in. (35.2 x 42.9 cm). Collection of Leslie A. Feely, New York

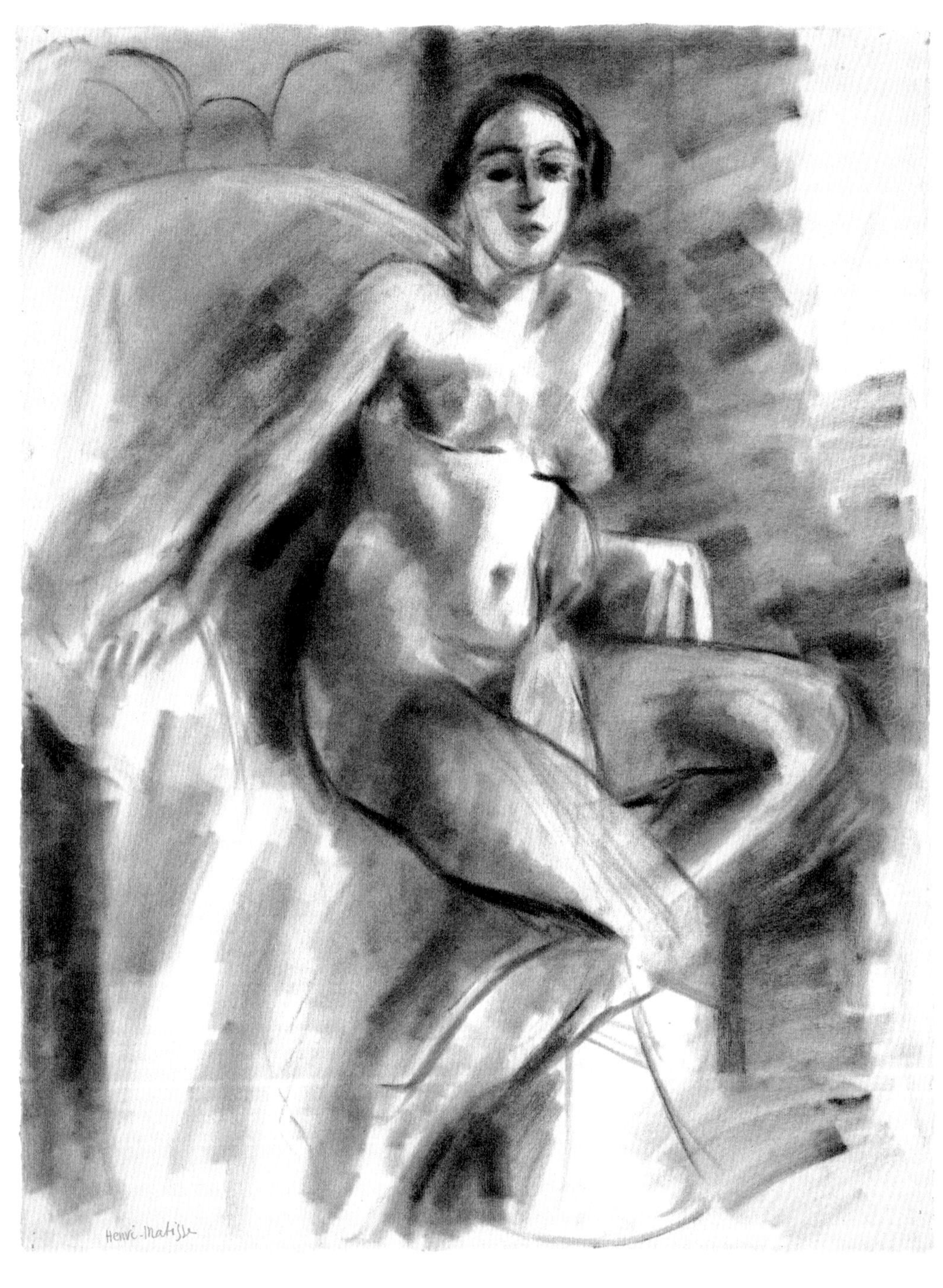

Plate 63. Henri Matisse, *Nude in Armchair,* ca. 1924. Charcoal on paper, 24⅞ x 19⅛ in. (63 x 48.6 cm). The Baltimore Museum of Art: Bequest of Blanche Adler

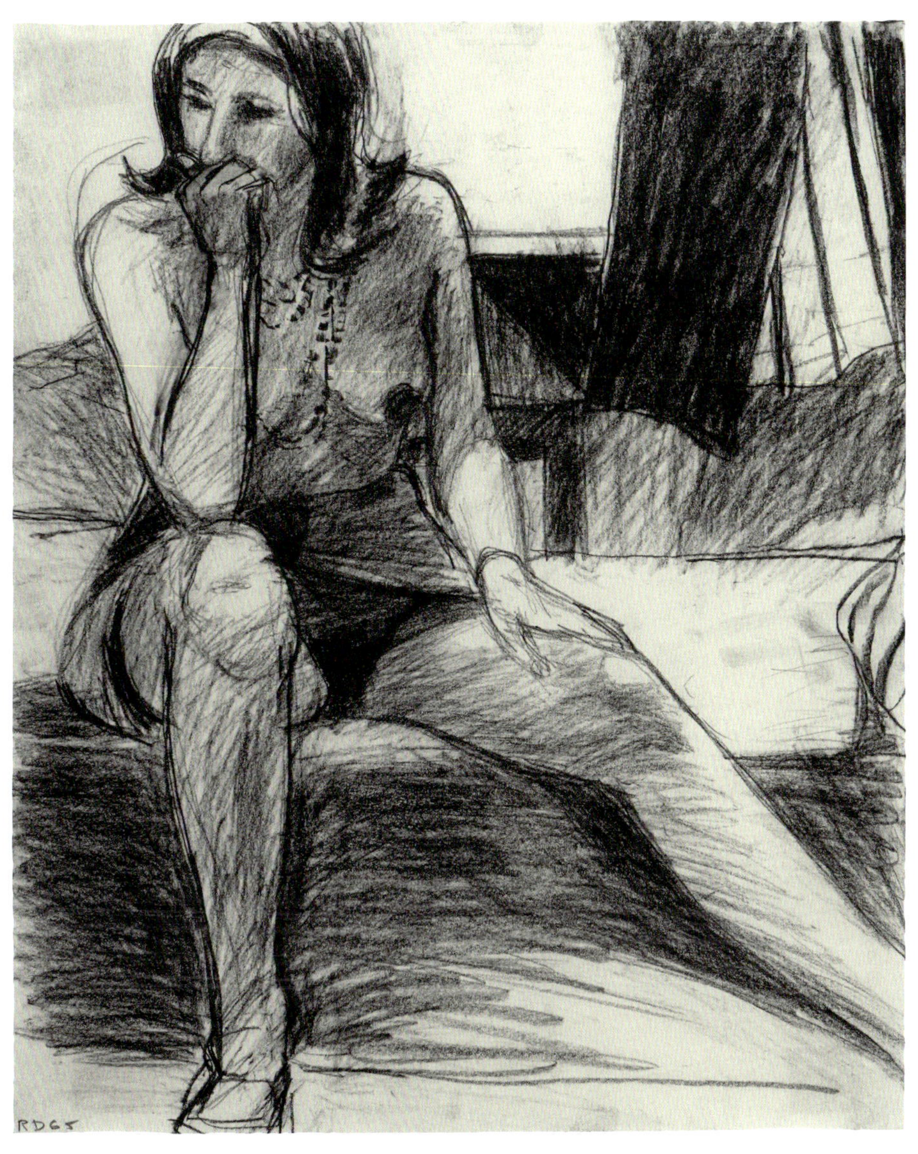

Plate 64. Richard Diebenkorn, *Untitled (Seated Woman)*, 1965. Conté crayon on paper, 16⅞ x 14 in. (42.9 x 35.6 cm). Collection of Eve Benesch-Goldschmidt

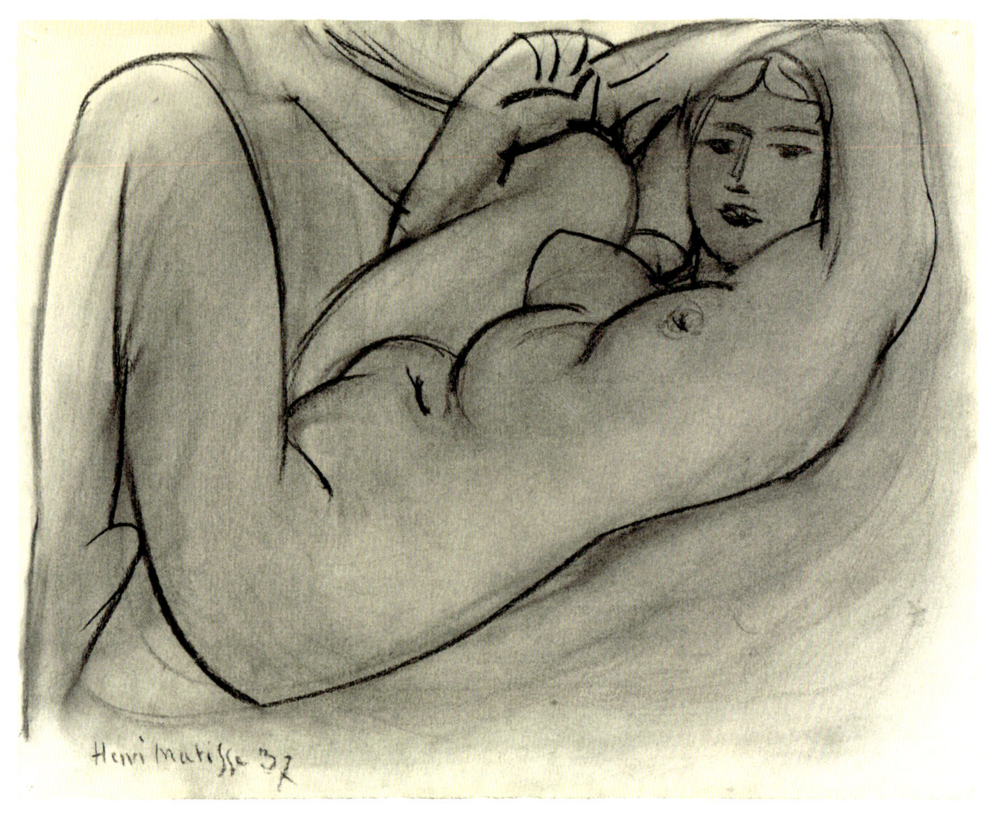

Plate 65. Henri Matisse, *Reclining Nude with Arm behind Head,* 1937. Charcoal on paper, 15 x 19 in. (37.9 x 48.3 cm). The Baltimore Museum of Art: The Cone Collection, formed by Dr. Claribel Cone and Miss Etta Cone of Baltimore, Maryland

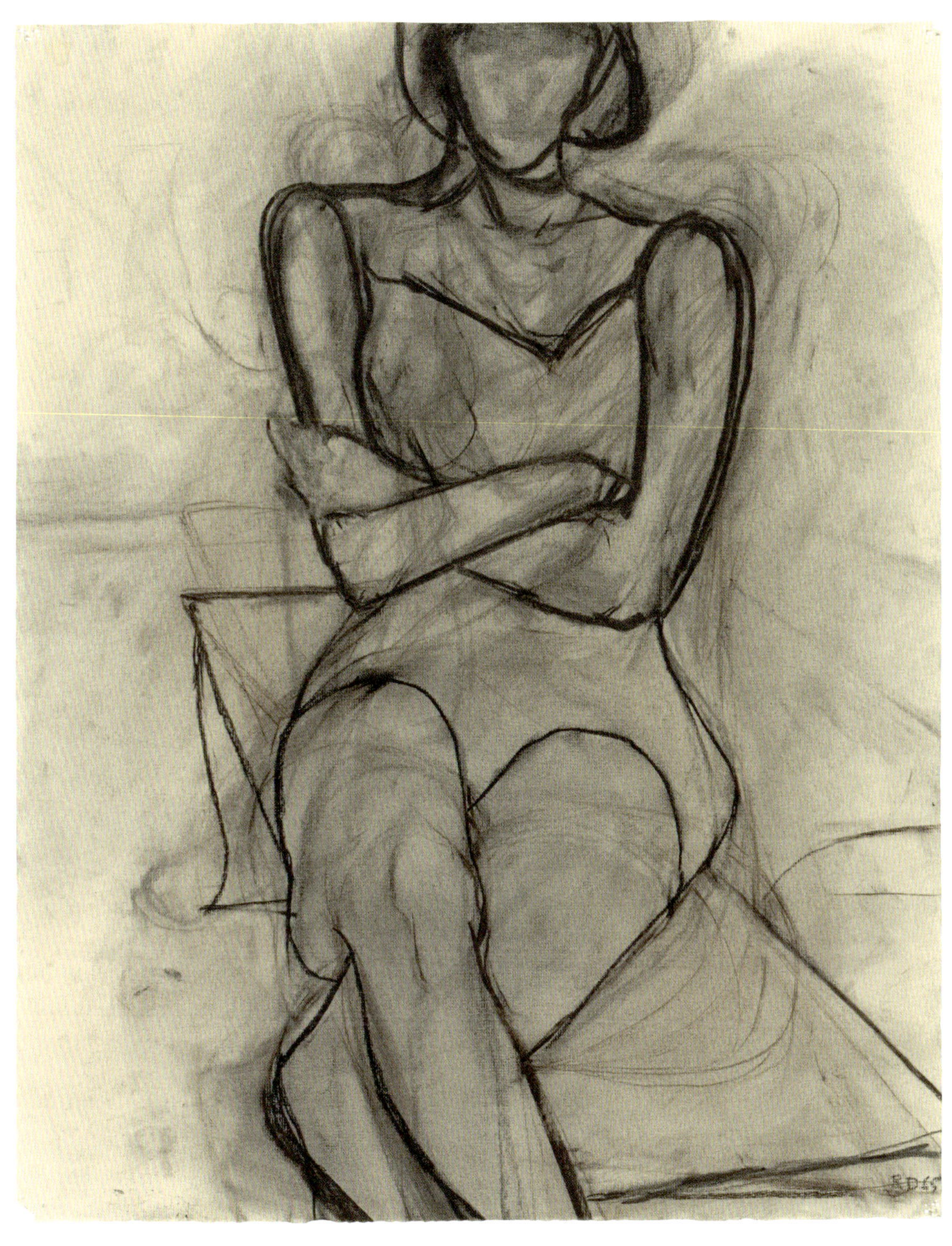

Plate 66. Richard Diebenkorn, *Untitled (Seated Woman)*, 1965. Charcoal on paper, 23¾ x 19 in. (60.3 x 48.3 cm). Collection of Susan and David Gersh, Los Angeles

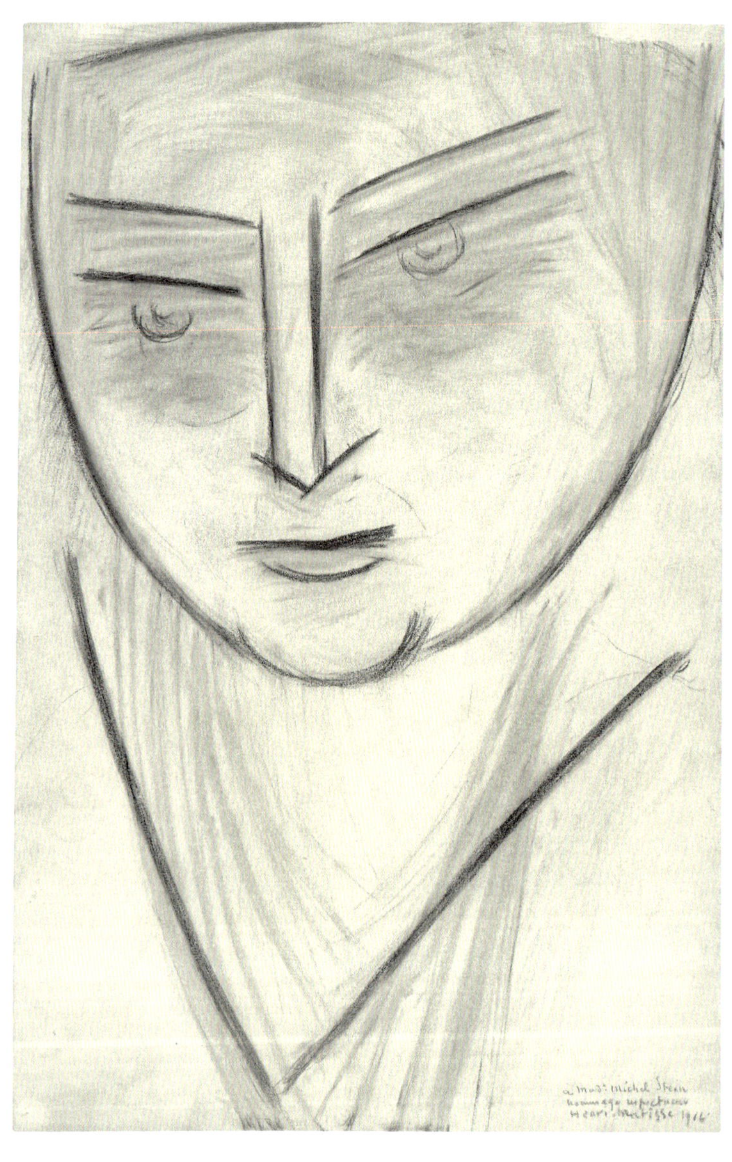

Plate 67. Henri Matisse, *Study of Sarah Stein,* 1916.
Graphite on paper, 19⅛ x 12⅝ in. (48.6 x 32.1 cm). San Francisco Museum of Modern Art, gift of Mr. and Mrs. Walter A. Haas

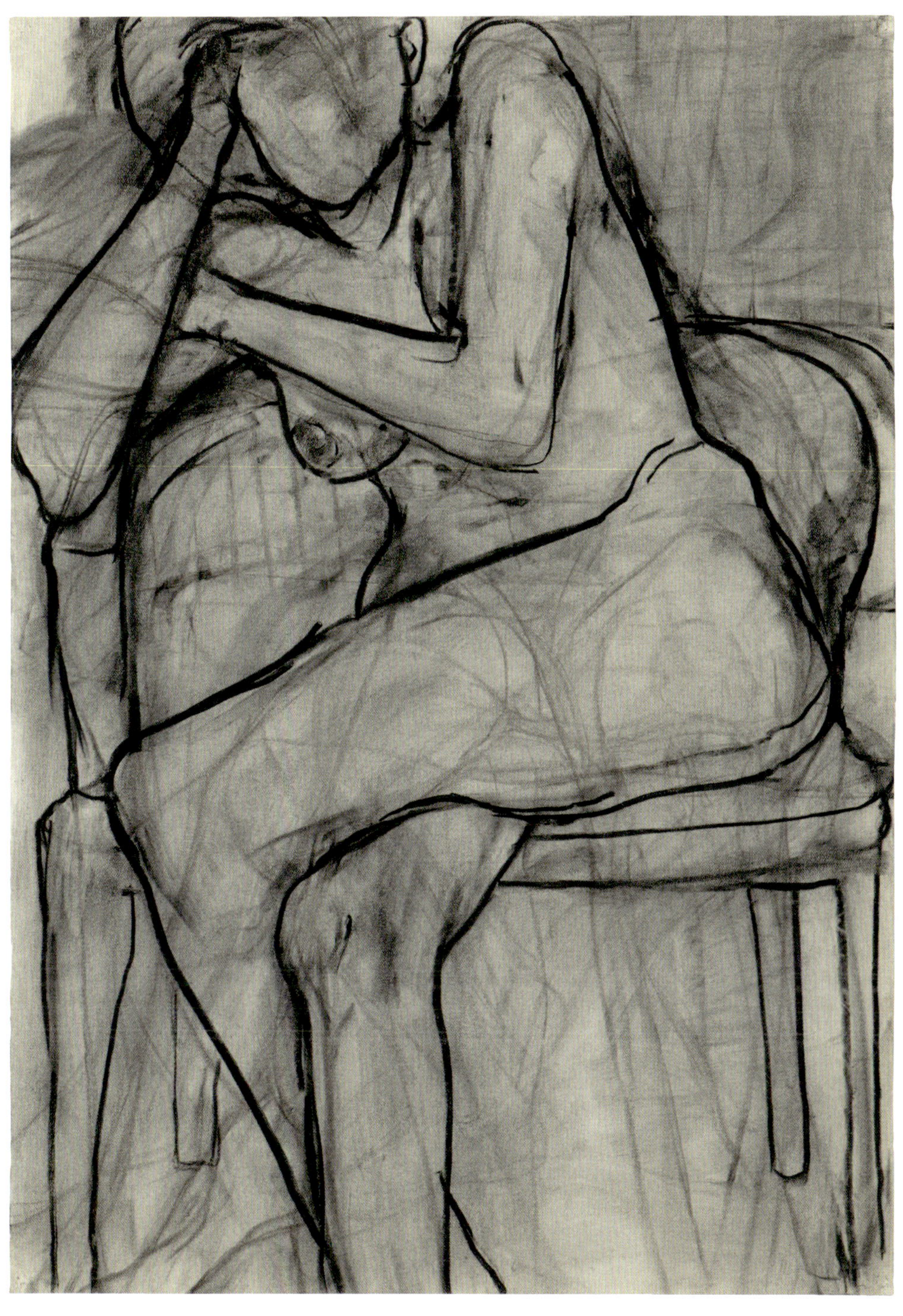

Plate 68. Richard Diebenkorn, *Untitled (Seated Nude),* 1966. Charcoal on paper, 33 x 23½ in. (83.8 x 59.7 cm). San Francisco Museum of Modern Art, gift of the Diebenkorn family and purchase through a gift of Leanne B. Roberts, Thomas W. Weisel, and the Mnuchin Foundation

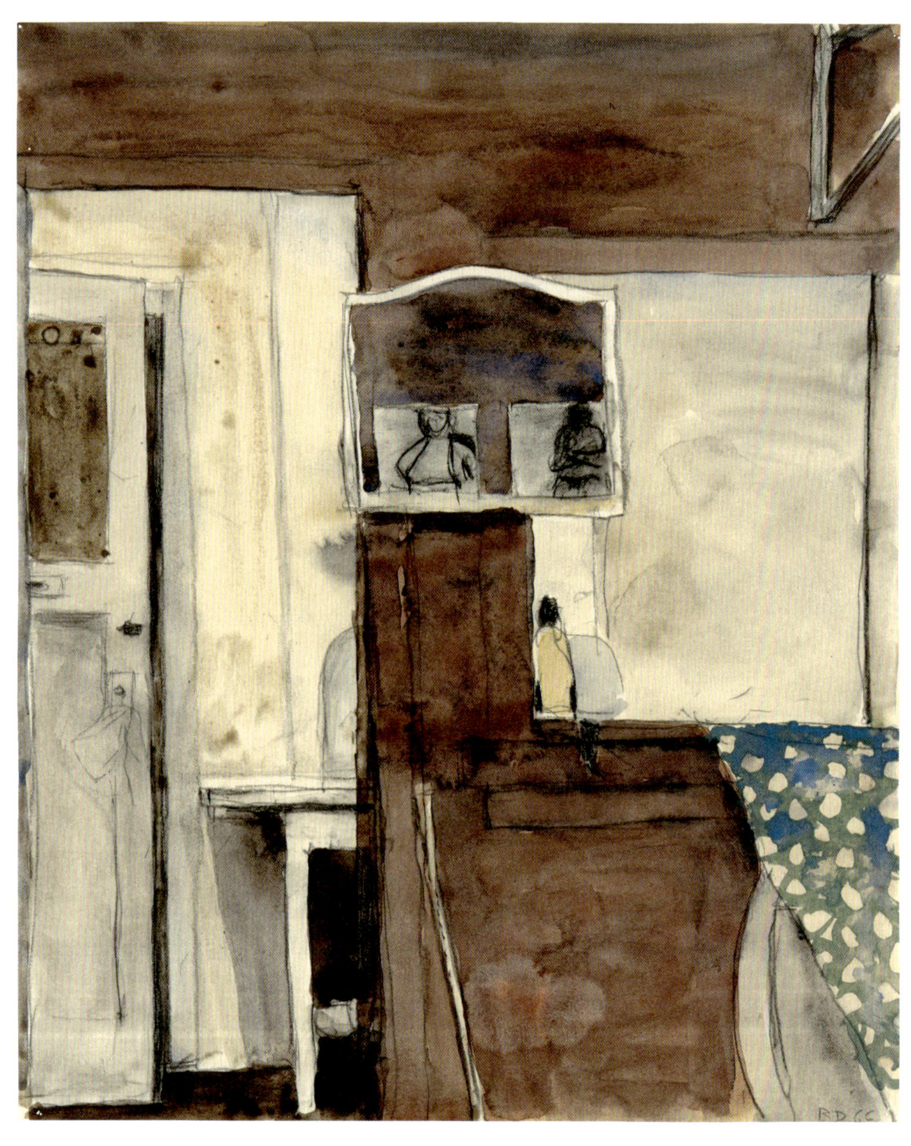

Plate 69. Richard Diebenkorn, *Untitled (Interior with Mirror),* 1966.
Watercolor, charcoal, and conté crayon on paper, 16⅞ x 14 in. (42.9 x 35.6 cm).
Private collection

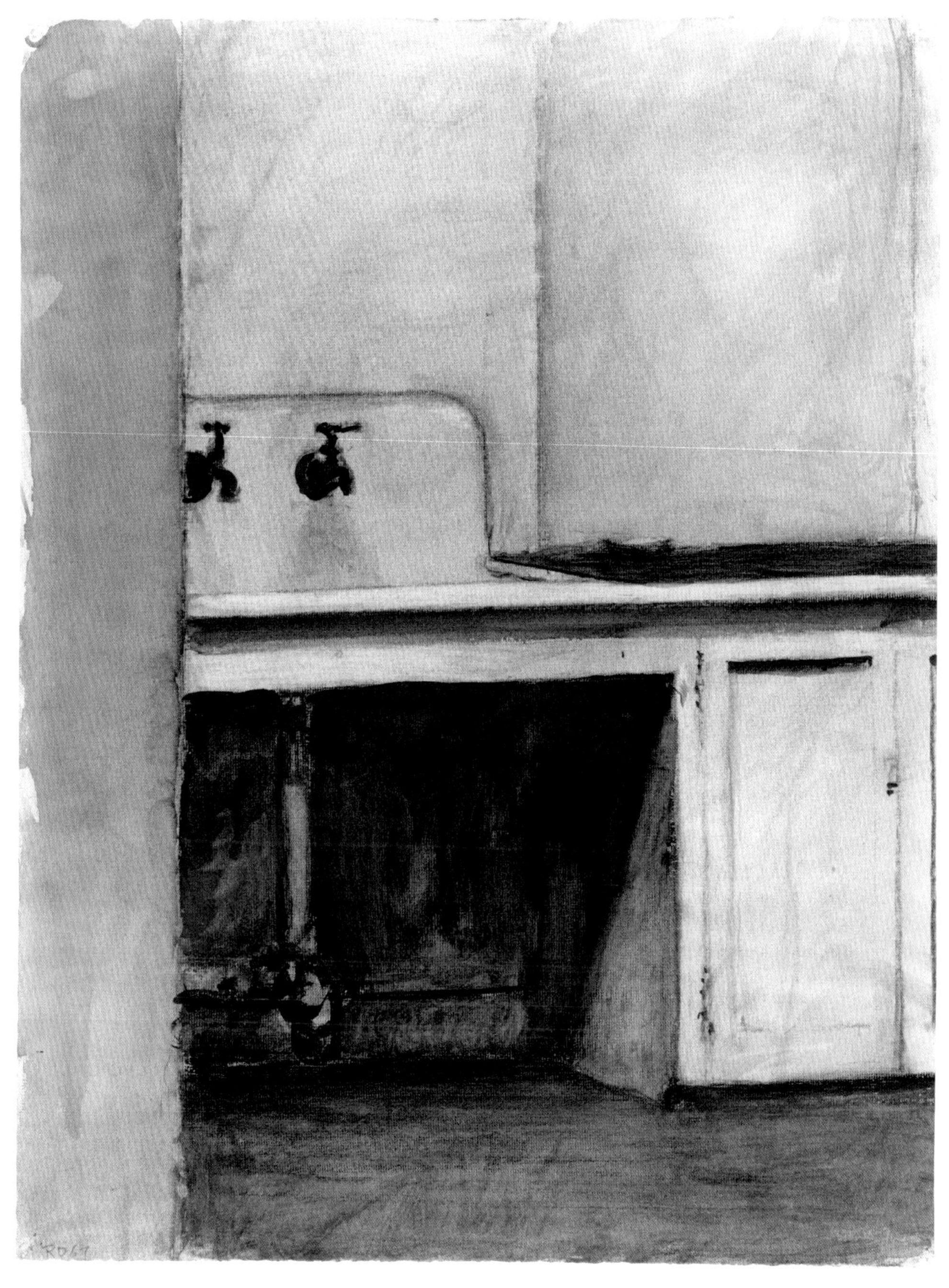

Plate 70. Richard Diebenkorn, *Sink,* 1967. Ink, charcoal, and watercolor on paper, 24¾ x 18¾ in. (62.9 x 47.6 cm). The Baltimore Museum of Art: Thomas E. Benesch Memorial Collection

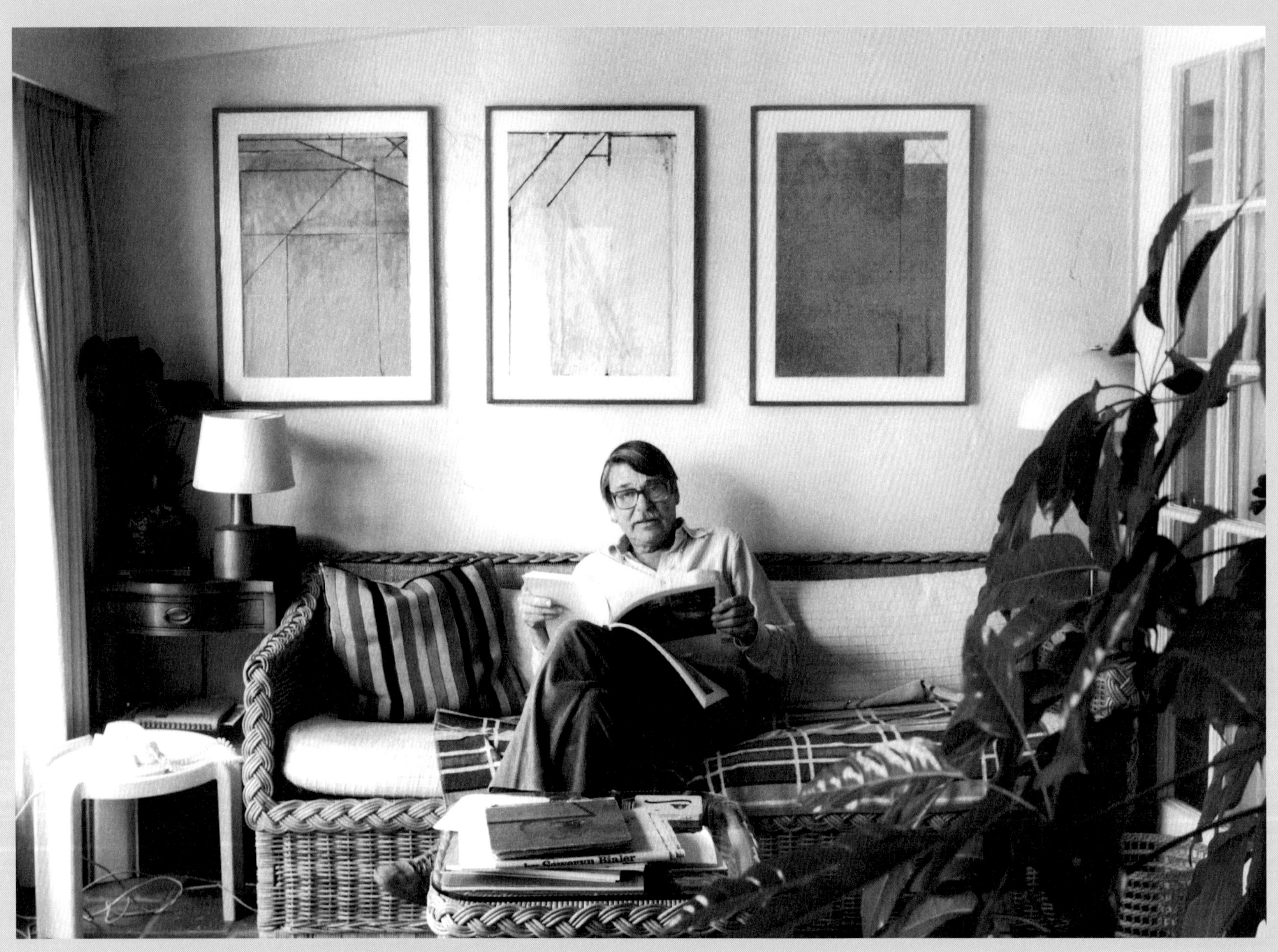

Richard Diebenkorn and Matisse, from Russia to Ocean Park

Katherine Rothkopf

I think such influence is natural when a young painter discovers an older one. I'm against the cult of originality, though I don't, of course, like copycats. But, after all, here's this tremendous experience, and what's the young painter supposed to do with it—stick it under the rug?

—Richard Diebenkorn[1]

Richard Diebenkorn was always searching for new ways to express himself. He seemed never to want to be categorized or considered too predictable. A commitment to exploration and shrugging off expectations was also a constant throughout Henri Matisse's career. Although the two never met, the similarities in their styles, working methods, and goals link them in a profound way. As much as Diebenkorn may have looked to Matisse's art for inspiration, he was also connected to the older artist through shared approaches and techniques. Both men had a deep love of color and structure and relied on a process of layering, scraping away, and adding paint to shape modern compositions that reflect their personal visions. Each of them turned to drawing to experiment and discover new possibilities and ideas for future work.[2] And for both artists, a sense of place played a major role in determining the style and focus of their paintings and drawings, with changes of scene often leading to abrupt transformations. Particularly profound were the shifts in Diebenkorn's work that developed following his pivotal trip to Russia in 1964 and continued to evolve after his move to Southern California two years later, when he began to create his renowned and resplendent *Ocean Park* paintings.

As Janet Bishop notes in her essay in this publication, when Diebenkorn turned from abstraction to representation in 1955, it was a seismic shift. In 1964, after almost a decade of producing figure paintings, interiors, still lifes, and landscapes in his Berkeley studio,[3] Diebenkorn and his wife accepted an invitation to visit the Union of Soviet Socialist Republics (USSR) as guests of the Soviet Artists' Union, an offer that would alter the course of his work yet again. The trip was organized by the U.S. State Department as part of a new cultural exchange initiative begun by President John F. Kennedy and Soviet Premier Nikita Khrushchev in 1963.[4] Abstraction was not of great interest to the Soviet government, and Diebenkorn (the first visual artist to participate in the exchange[5]) had been chosen by the United States Information Agency (USIA) to represent American contemporary art because he was well regarded for his figurative works.[6] It was an

Richard Diebenkorn in his living room, Amalfi Drive, Santa Monica, California, 1984. Photograph by Leo Holub opportunity to find inspiration at a time when he was searching for new possibilities in his art making.[7] Thanks to the ever-growing collection of publications in his library on Matisse, Diebenkorn was well aware of the wealth of paintings in museums in the Soviet Union, and his desire to see them in person likely contributed to his decision to make the trip. Alfred H. Barr Jr.'s Matisse monograph of 1951, which was a major source of inspiration for Diebenkorn for years, included black-and-white images of more than twenty such paintings.[8] Among them were still-life compositions whose playful forms already echoed in *Untitled* (1964, plate 62), a graphite and ink drawing Diebenkorn produced before the trip began. The elegant work incorporates everyday objects from the artist's home—including a coffee cup, matchbook, plate, lamb-chop bone, and utensils—on top of an ornate tablecloth that is tilted up dramatically, its patterned surface reminiscent of the vibrant textiles in so many paintings by Matisse.[9]

Prior to arriving in the USSR, Diebenkorn and his wife, Phyllis (fig. 1), visited Paris. According to Phyllis, the couple would go to the Soviet Embassy every morning to see if their visas had arrived; until their paperwork appeared they were free to sightsee in the French capital. It was their first visit to Europe, and they explored all that Paris had to offer.[10] Diebenkorn later recalled visiting works by Matisse at the Musée national d'art moderne[11] (fig. 2), which had a growing collection that included paintings such as *Le Luxe I* (1907), *The Painter in His Studio* (1916–17), *Decorative Figure on an Ornamental Ground* (1925–26), and *Still Life with Magnolia* (1941), all of which he would previously have seen as reproductions in the Barr monograph.

Once he arrived in the USSR Diebenkorn spent much of his time visiting with artists at art schools and studios. Although those he met worked in a socialist realist style quite unlike his own, he tried to connect with them as best he could, making an effort to understand their experiences as well as discuss his own work.[12] The trip was a challenge for Diebenkorn, as the Soviet Union was very different from the West both culturally and economically—not to mention in contrast to the open-minded world of the San Francisco Bay Area in the 1960s. As a respite from the bleak realities of Soviet life he spent time visiting the Pushkin State Museum of Fine Arts in Moscow and the State Hermitage Museum in Leningrad (now Saint Petersburg). Diebenkorn was most enthusiastic to see their holdings from the collections of modern art once owned by Sergei Shchukin and Ivan Morozov,[13] which had been seized by the government during the Revolution of 1917 and later divided between the two museums. Then, as now, the Shchukin and Morozov collections were considered to be two of the strongest concentrations of Matisse's works from the 1910s. Diebenkorn was eager to study them in person—and fully aware of the rarity of this opportunity.

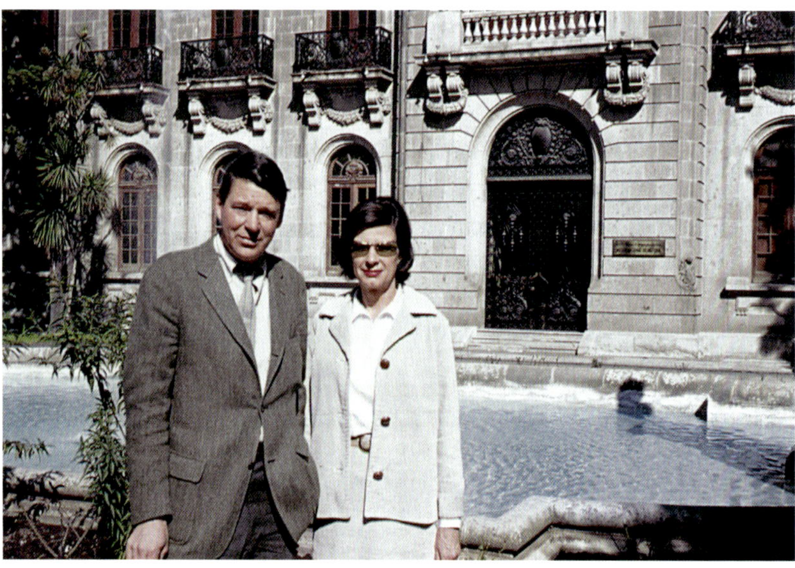

Fig. 1. Richard Diebenkorn and his wife, Phyllis, ca. 1964

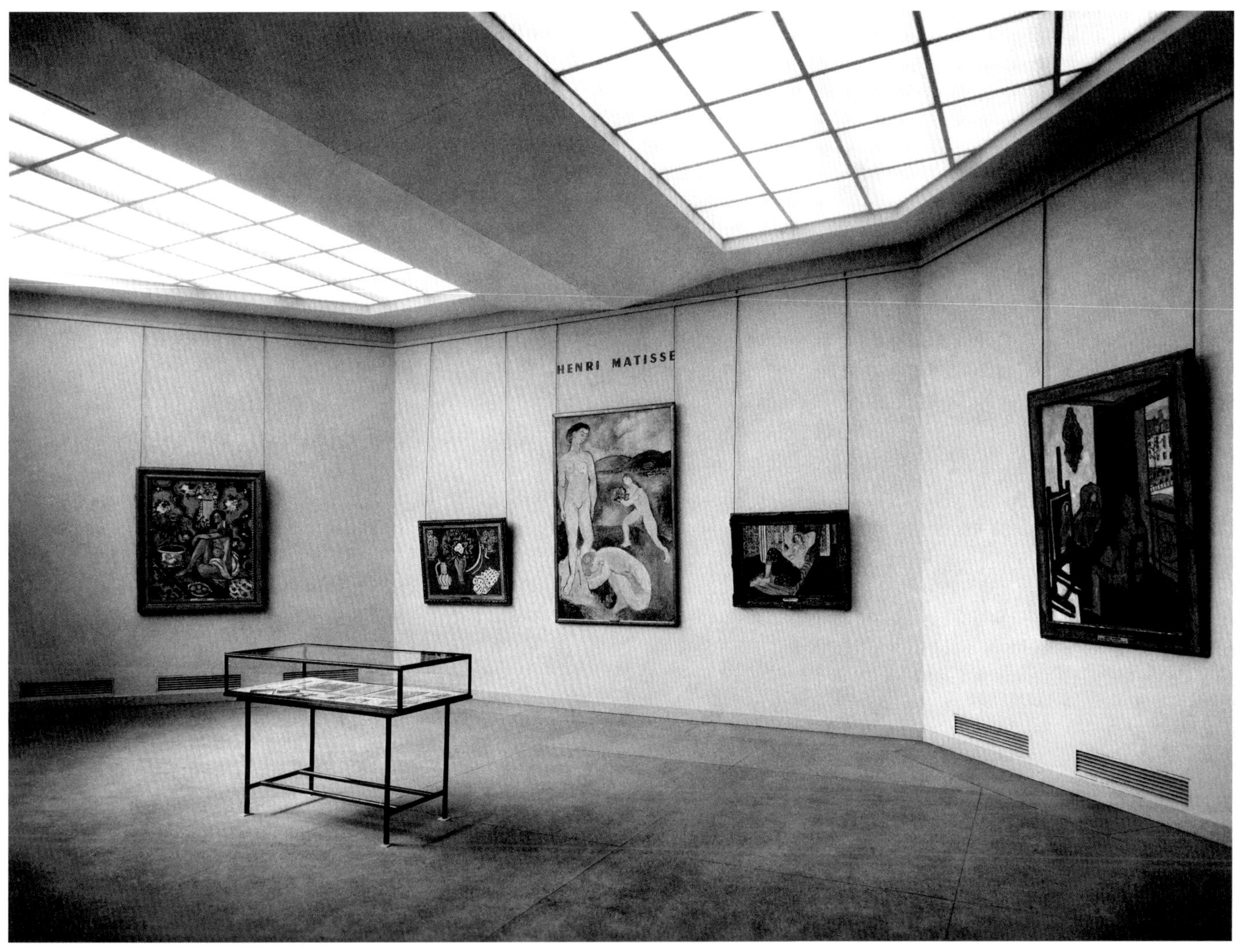

Fig. 2. Installation view of artworks by Henri Matisse at the Musée national d'art moderne, Palais de Tokyo, Paris, 1960. On walls, left to right: *Decorative Figure on an Ornamental Ground* (1925–26), *Still Life with Magnolia* (1941), *Le Luxe I* (1907), *Odalisque with Red Harem Pants* (1921), *The Painter in His Studio* (1916–17)

Accompanied by William Luers from the U.S. State Department, Diebenkorn and his wife twice visited the Pushkin Museum and were given a private tour through the State Hermitage Museum, where they were granted special access to Matisse works that were not on view in the galleries.[14] Although they saw compositions by many artists from different periods at the State Hermitage Museum, Luers recalls that Diebenkorn "lingered [over] and pondered longest the many Matisse paintings"[15] and was particularly intent on seeing works from his Moroccan period.[16] Diebenkorn later stated: "It was the high point of going through the Soviet Union—seeing the [Shchukin works]."[17] More than twenty years later he recounted his viewing of *The Moroccan Café* (1913, fig. 3) with particular fervor: "[It] must have been—oh, seven feet wide. It's in Alfred H. Barr's Matisse book. He says it's an oil—he's wrong there, it's a gouache—but the important thing is the way the paint's piled up. Unfortunately, it was in pretty bad shape. The museum people took me into a lab where it was on an easel, and asked if I had any helpful suggestions, but as far as my amateur eye could see there wasn't a thing they could do with it—that was the way it had to stay. It was . . . from around 1913, very 'decorative,' painted in flat, soft, matte colors. It was beautiful . . ."[18] In an interview for a *Connoisseur* magazine article published in 1986 he cited *The Moroccan Café* as the work seen during his trip to the USSR that was of the most importance to him, and he was still rhapsodic about the painting many years later.[19]

The artist's visual memory of the incredible collections he saw in the Soviet Union, along with the pictures he visited en route there, had a lasting impact. The many inspirations seen abroad were reflected in his own paintings and drawings soon after his return to California and would resonate in his work for years to come. Certainly the difficult journey and the effort required to see Matisse's works in person made them even more memorable. Diebenkorn later noted the significance of the entire experience, explaining: "It was a real marker in my . . . it was just a great trip, it just changed my head in—in a lot of ways, I think. . . . The

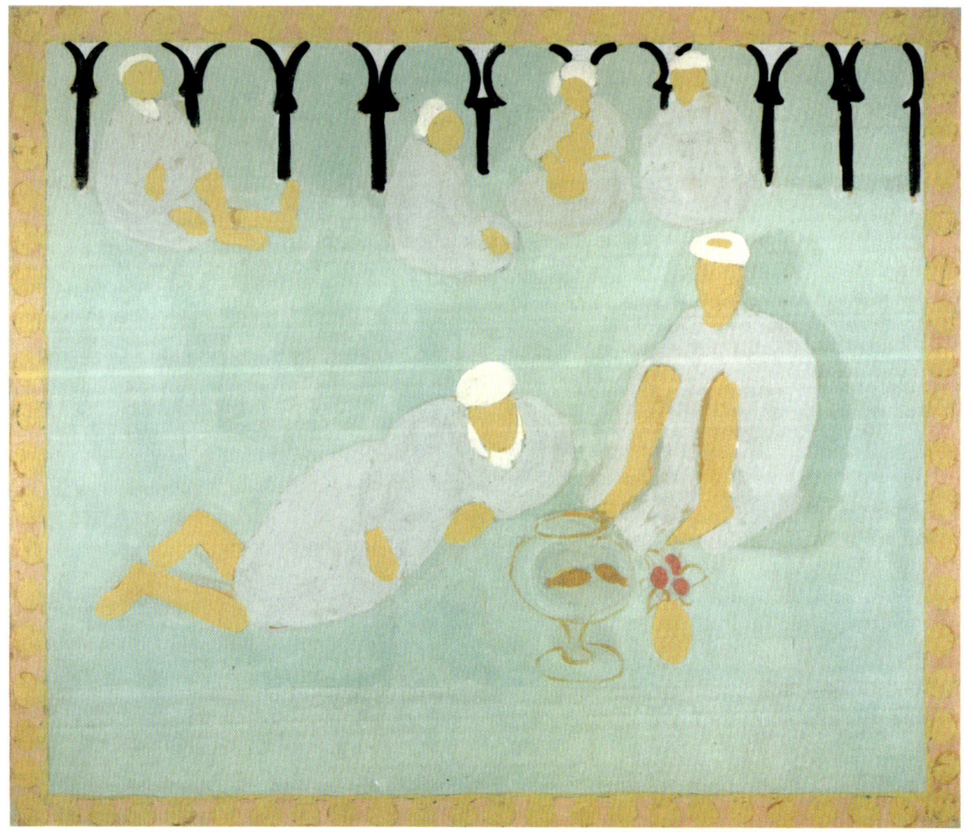

Fig. 3. Henri Matisse, *The Moroccan Café*, 1913. Distemper on canvas, 69⅜ x 82⅝ in. (176 x 210 cm). The State Hermitage Museum, Saint Petersburg

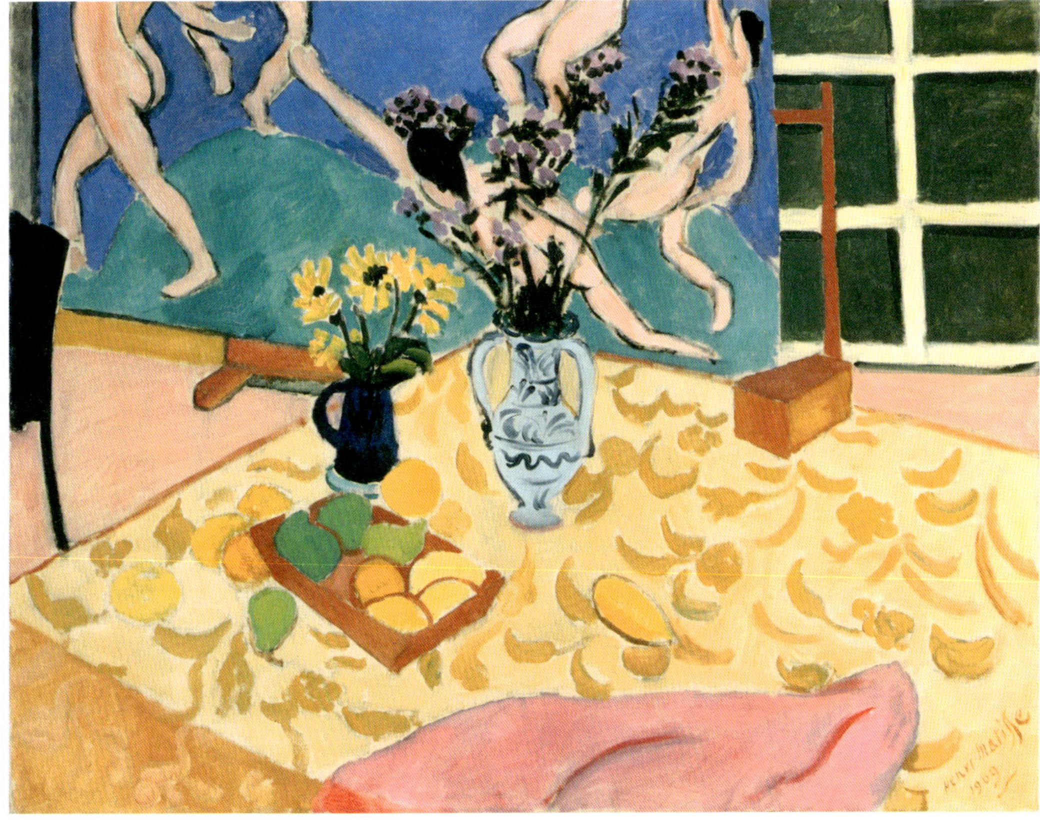

Fig. 4. Henri Matisse, *Still Life with "Dance,"* 1909. Oil on canvas, 35¼ x 46¼ in. (89.5 x 117.5 cm). The State Hermitage Museum, Saint Petersburg

representational thing, the figure thing, was kind of running its course. It was getting tougher and tougher, and at about the time of the trip—maybe it started before, or maybe it was right afterward—things really started to flatten out, in the representational. Five years earlier I was dealing with much more traditional depth, space." He continued, "At any rate, after I returned from Russia, then we came down here [to Los Angeles] almost immediately. And the painting I did here . . . really flattened out, and so it was like I was really preparing to go back to abstract painting, although I didn't know it."[20] His son has recalled that after the trip Diebenkorn was not only inspired by Matisse but also seemed to identify with the French artist, seeing his own practice as a continuation of Matisse's painterly tradition.[21]

The works produced in the years following Diebenkorn's return to the United States, a time known today as his late figurative period, are indeed much flatter and also more majestic in their compositional forms. One painting in particular stands apart for its striking resonance with Matisse's example in both form and title: *Recollections of a Visit to Leningrad* (1965, plate 72). Combining a number of recognizable elements from Matisse's bag of tricks—the floral wallpaper, the view through a window, the bright blocks of color—*Recollections* can be linked to several works by the older artist that Diebenkorn saw in the Soviet Union, including *Red Room (Harmony in Red)* (1908, plate 71), and stands as a tribute to his time there. Another composition from this period that seems closely tied to his experience abroad is *Large Still Life* (1966, plate 74). Here the tabletop is tipped up so it appears to merge with the wall, challenging our sense of space and perspective. The wallpaper, created with decorative arabesques that dance across the width of the painting, is juxtaposed with a more serious and somber group of familiar objects from Diebenkorn's studio. A similar focus on decorative patterning can

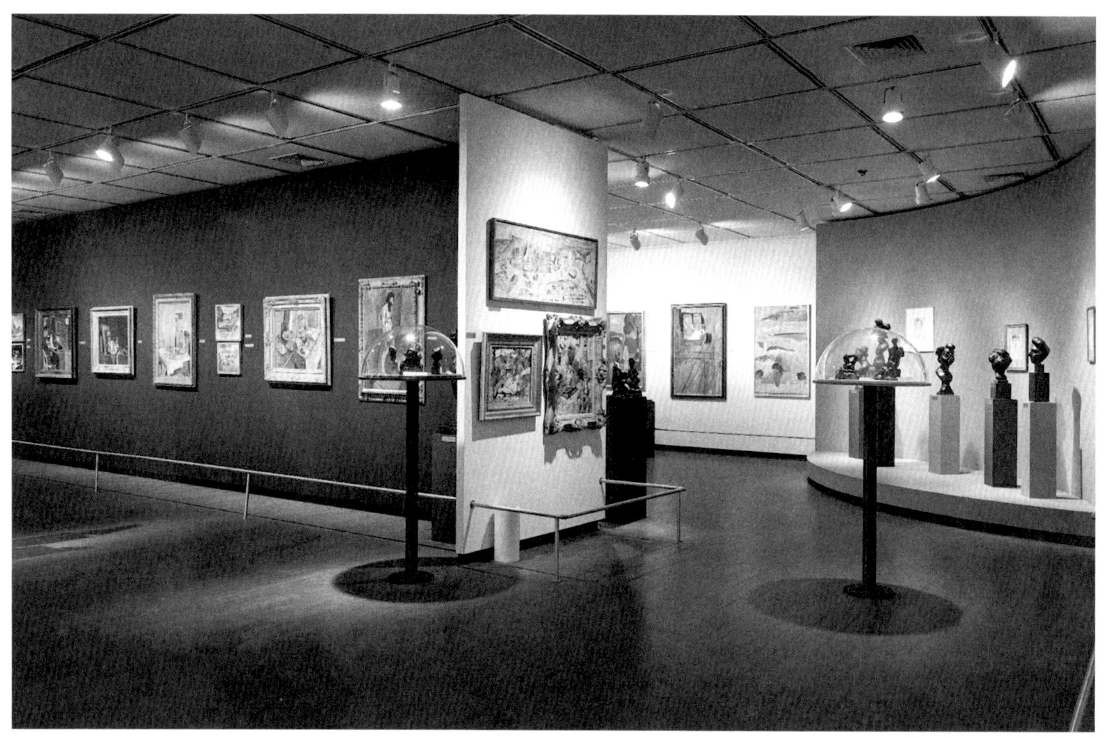

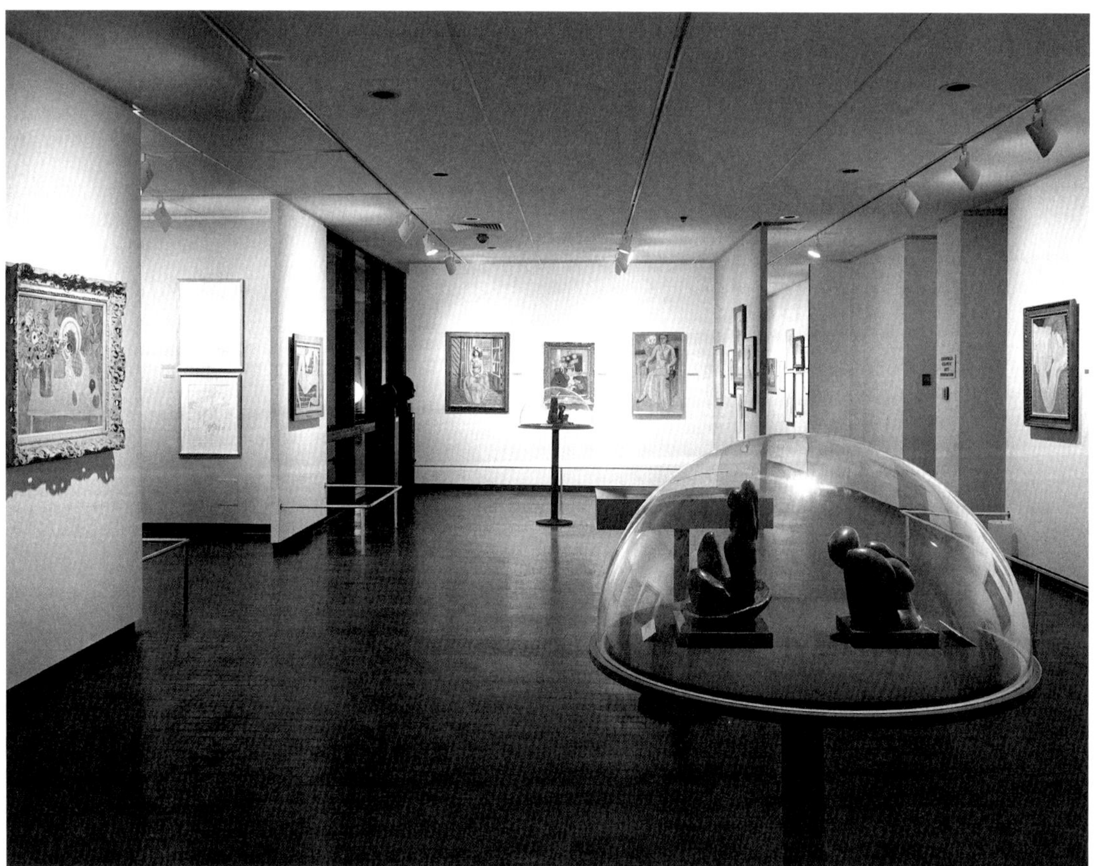

Figs. 5 and 6. Installation views of *Henri Matisse: Retrospective*, sponsored by the UCLA Art Council, University of California, Los Angeles, at the UCLA Art Galleries (now the New Wight Gallery), January 4–March 28, 1966

be found in several Matisse works that Diebenkorn would have seen in the USSR, including *Still Life with Blue Tablecloth* (1909, plate 73) and *Still Life with "Dance"* (1909, fig. 4).

In early 1966 Diebenkorn had another powerful encounter with Matisse's art when he visited *Henri Matisse: Retrospective*, sponsored by the UCLA Art Council, University of California, Los Angeles. Featuring 346 works including paintings, sculptures, drawings, prints, cut-outs, and illustrated books made over the course of the French master's long career, this massive exhibition encouraged a fresh assessment of Matisse's work; some of the more than ninety paintings were on loan from the artist's family and on view publicly in the United States for the first time (figs. 5 and 6). The exhibition received many positive reviews. Clement Greenberg put his finger on the color sense and painterly technique that had also caught Diebenkorn's eye, writing: "Matisse is a superb draftsman, but he is still a better painter, and as a painter he is an orchestrator of color areas before he is anything else."[22]

Diebenkorn later cited two paintings he first saw in the 1966 retrospective as having been of particular importance to him: *French Window at Collioure* (1914, plate 100) and *View of Notre Dame* (1914, plate 96).[23] One of Matisse's most abstract works, *French Window at Collioure* was described by one of the critics as "a striking anticipation of [Barnett] Newman done in 1914."[24] Its dark central form is framed by luminous planes of paint recognizable as abstracted elements of the open window; though the setting is very spare and somewhat foreboding, it nevertheless seems to encourage the viewer to look more closely. According to recent research, in raking light it is clear that Matisse at one time included a balcony and a landscape in the distance but later decided to conceal those details with a wash of black paint; it has been suggested that the artist may have considered this work unfinished.[25] Whatever Matisse may have intended, the modernity of *French Window at Collioure* had a tremendous impact on Diebenkorn when he saw it, modeling the expansive possibilities of abstraction at a time in his life when he was reexamining his own work. A similarly radical abstraction is present in *View of Notre Dame*, which offers an outlook from Matisse's studio on the quai Saint-Michel in Paris that is very different from his other window views. The physicality of his attack on the canvas is visible in his brushstrokes and in traces of scraping and repainting. Through this evidence of his hard work, the composition is seemingly constructed before the viewer's eyes. In a final sweep he covered most of the work's surface with a layer of blue paint, radically simplifying the scene to its most abstract elements of color, shape, and line, as he had done in *French Window at Collioure*. A third work that explores abstraction, *Large Reclining Nude* (1935, plate 83), must also have made an impression. Diebenkorn probably first saw the painting in 1947; he later recalled having visited the Cone Collection at The Baltimore Museum of Art that year.[26] It was featured on the cover of the 1966 exhibition catalogue, which Diebenkorn had a copy of in his library. Matisse worked on *Large Reclining Nude* for six months, and what began as a traditional depiction of a model reclining on a chaise longue with a vase of flowers on the chair behind her changed significantly in the final composition. The abstracted figure, which seems to grow up the trellis like a vine, along with the composition's pronounced focus on the two geometric grids, likely made the work of great interest to Diebenkorn when he saw it again in Los Angeles.

After two such intense engagements with Matisse's example in 1964 and 1966, it is not surprising that Diebenkorn's compositional choices began to change considerably. He later linked the shift in his work to his trip to the Soviet Union,[27] but the interaction with so many more Matisse works in Los Angeles must have had an indelible impact as well.[28] In his subsequent figure paintings, Diebenkorn's sense of space and form indeed became flattened, and the figures grew into larger, more powerful entities, as seen in the bold *Nude on Blue Ground* (1966, plate 82), which seems closely connected in pose and modeling to one of Matisse's great early paintings, *Nude Study in Blue* (ca. 1899–1900, plate 81), but mirrors some of the confidence seen in other early figurative works by the French master, such as *Nude with a White Scarf* (1909, plate 77).

Perhaps influenced by the more than ten cut-out compositions he saw in the Los Angeles retrospective, Diebenkorn also produced *Untitled (Yellow Collage)* (1966, plate 76), an assertive image of his wife created with cut and pasted paper in vivid tones of yellow, orange, blue, and purple. Diebenkorn also had an opportunity at the

Matisse retrospective to examine *The Yellow Dress* (1929–31, plate 75), a monumental figurative painting by the French artist that shows clear evidence of reworking and pentimenti. Matisse struggled over this painting on and off for two years, starting and stopping his process as he made the figure larger and more confident, increasing her stature until she came to dominate the composition.[29] Although less detailed, Diebenkorn's delicate 1966 gouache of a seated woman wearing a patterned dress and sandals (plate 78) showcases the younger artist's appreciation of distinctive textiles, an interest shared with Matisse and seen clearly in *The Yellow Dress*.

After more than a decade living and working in Northern California, in September 1966 Diebenkorn and his wife moved to the Los Angeles area, and he accepted a teaching position in the art department at UCLA. This significant change of location allowed the artist to open up to new possibilities and inspirations. Soon after the move he found a small studio in a Santa Monica neighborhood known as Ocean Park, where he worked for six months until a larger studio with windows became available in the same building. At first he mainly produced drawings.[30] After moving into the larger space, and with his trip to the USSR and the Los Angeles retrospective still fresh in his mind, he initially continued to create expansive figurative works that have a strong resonance with Matisse's example. With their large scale and grand forms, Diebenkorn's *Seated Figure with Hat* (1967, plate 80) and *Seated Woman* (1967, plate 86) can easily be associated with Matisse's *Portrait of the Artist's Wife* (1913, plate 85), a painting the younger artist saw in the Soviet Union in 1964 and still found fascinating more than twenty years later.[31] Matisse's daring portrait of his wife can also be linked with some of Diebenkorn's most commanding and inventive figure drawings from 1965 and 1966, which showcase a similar mood (plates 66 and 68).

Matisse's *The Conversation* (1908–12, fig. 7) had been of particular interest to Diebenkorn during his private tour of the State Hermitage Museum,[32] and one can see the connection between the stoic image of the French artist's wife seated on the right and the stately woman painted in profile in *Seated Figure with Hat*. For its part, Matisse's *Large Reclining Nude* can be tied to *Seated Woman*; in both works the ever-growing figure seems to overtake the composition. Diebenkorn's elegant and spare *Window* (1967, plate 84) clearly relates to *The Piano Lesson* (1916, plate 98), a painting the younger artist saw first in 1947[33] and again at the Matisse retrospective in Los Angeles in 1952, organized by The Museum of Modern Art. Diebenkorn's subject—an abstracted landscape seen through a window, complete with decorative wrought iron—and use of a relatively limited palette and broad areas of paint link the composition back to Matisse's masterpiece. The wrought-iron detail in *Window* can also be connected to the decorative element included in Matisse's *The Conversation*. Surprisingly, *The Piano Lesson* was not included in the 1966 Matisse retrospective that Diebenkorn had recently seen, but it was clearly on his mind, a connection perhaps reinforced by his new studio space, which featured a row of transom windows along one side.[34] He later wrote of how crucial the light they provided was to his work: "The only thin[g] I require in a studio is daylight, and coming from a direction where I don't get direct light, which really destroys things with the strong light that comes in. And also a light situation where I can somehow work without reflection on the surface of the canvas, and beyond that, I just accept the light [available]. . . . If it's a good painting space, well, the light that goes along with it."[35]

After Matisse's arrival in Nice in late 1917, his painting changed direction, adopting a brighter palette and mood prompted by the unique light and beauty of the coastland outside his studio window. Diebenkorn's move to his new Ocean Park studio (which had once been occupied by artist Sam Francis) had a similar impact, offering him an opportunity to rethink his work. At some point in 1967 he began to explore abstraction in his painting with much the same suddenness of his transition to representational work in 1955. He seemed surprised by his change in focus. "Maybe someone from the outside observing what I was doing would have known what was about to happen. But I didn't," he later recalled. "I didn't see the signs. Then, one day, I was thinking about abstract painting again. As soon as I moved into Sam's space, I did about four large canvases—still representational, but, again, much flatter. Then, suddenly, I abandoned the figure altogether."[36] Diebenkorn's increasing interest in abstraction in 1966 and 1967 was not limited to his paintings. The

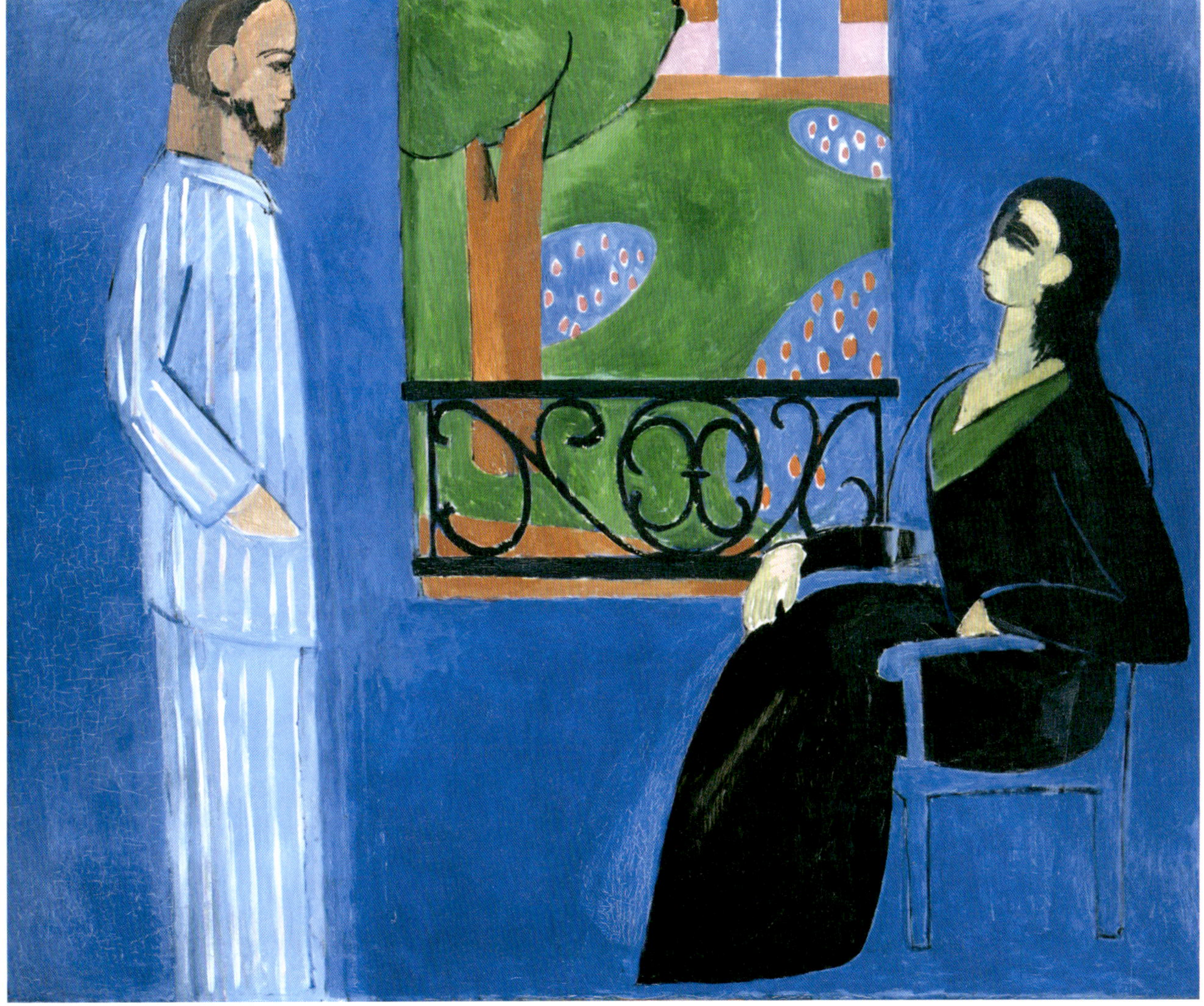

Fig. 7. Henri Matisse, *The Conversation*, 1908–12. Oil on canvas, 69⅝ x 71⅜ in. (177 x 217 cm). The State Hermitage Museum, Saint Petersburg

watercolor *Untitled (Interior with Mirror)* (1966, plate 69) is a spare and tonal view of his studio, the only decorative elements a vibrant blue bedspread and a mirror that reflects two of his drawings on the opposite wall. The interior in *Sink* (1967, plate 70) is pared down even further, focusing on one mundane element of his studio—his sink—in an abstracted composition featuring a series of geometric planes, with two faucets the only embellishments.

Diebenkorn's abstract paintings from this time became known as his *Ocean Park* series (1967–88), after his new studio location.[37] These works are united by an exploration of geometry, architectural elements, and structure in carefully worked and reworked compositions that bring to mind stripped-down views of the world, made complete with thin layers of luminous color. The *Ocean Park* paintings are very different from his *Berkeley* abstractions, which are full of organic shapes and gestural brushwork and convey a sense of speed. Here there is a new majesty, composure, and tension—all becoming visible only over time and with very close looking. For years some scholars have proposed that part of the impetus for the *Ocean Park* works was Diebenkorn's encounter with *French Window at Collioure* and *View of Notre Dame* at the 1966 retrospective.[38] But as this publication has established, the impact of Matisse's example cannot be isolated to a single moment and was in fact based on decades of careful study of many works by the French master. The immersive and transcendent experience of seeing so much of Matisse's art in person in Los Angeles built on Diebenkorn's visual memories of the paintings he had seen in the Soviet Union two years earlier and those he had studied in publications. It was the cumulative effect of these encounters that pushed Diebenkorn down a new path, leading him to experiment with and test the boundaries of abstraction and composition with a new sense of purpose, direction, and confidence.

Diebenkorn's early *Ocean Park* paintings maintain a sense of figuration, as in works such as *Ocean Park #6* (1968, plate 87), where, on close examination, forms resembling bodies seem to huddle together across the composition—an association made clearer by the scale of the canvas, which is more than life-size. One can recognize the influence of Matisse's abstracted figurative paintings of the mid-1930s, such as *Large Reclining Nude* and *Seated Pink Nude* (1935–36, plate 88), both of which feature obvious traces of reworking and transformation. Matisse arranged to have these paintings photographed while they were in progress, documenting their subtle evolution from traditional depictions of female nudes to more abstract, modern muses; traces of the works' development are also evident to the naked eye.[39] Diebenkorn would have known about the use of photographs in the creation of Matisse's *Large Reclining Nude* from Barr's publication, where six of them are reproduced.[40] The artist's process of multiple revisions is also clearly visible throughout the *Ocean Park* series. In *Ocean Park #12* (1968, plate 90)—a partially abstracted interior made up of bold areas of cool and warm colors, with a small vase of flowers at lower right and a large window that opens to a tree set against a bright blue sky—reworking is evident in the variations in color and form that lie just beneath the surface of the paint. A recurring theme in Diebenkorn's representational works, the view through a window also links the subjects of many of his compositions with those explored by Matisse in the 1910s and during his Nice and Vence periods (plates 1, 4, and 92).

Another window composition, Diebenkorn's *Untitled (View from Studio, Ocean Park)* (1969, plate 89) is a small but powerful work that in its attention to architectural features exhibits the focus on geometry and structure he would explore throughout his *Ocean Park* series. Diebenkorn once commented that he had been largely unaware of the influence of his new studio's windows until it was brought to his attention: "In the other studio, there were these transom windows. . . . I still have them, but they're more like that window, and [they] have this very strong diagonal, and friends have come and looked at my pictures and [said], 'Well, I see here you really got the windows in this one, haven't you?'"[41]

Hints of representational elements had mostly disappeared from the *Ocean Park* paintings by 1970, although the sense of an interior space remains in *Ocean Park #27* of that same year (plate 91), where one can read the two planes of blue and green on the bottom half of the canvas as the floor; the upper quadrants of yellow, lavender, orange, and blue as the back wall; and the field of rose-colored pigment outlined in a lighter shade as the right wall (the architecture of the composition is very similar to that in *Ocean Park #12*). One has the sense of entering a space filled with color and line, struggle and conclusion, and this feeling produces a composition that is mesmerizing and elegant. *Ocean Park #29* (1970, plate 93) eschews the sense of creating a space to enter and instead focuses on the purity of shape and line. Cool tones of varying shades of blue are offset by a striking yellow band at left, all the colors carefully chosen to both hush and excite the senses. One can look to Matisse's *The Piano Lesson* as inspiration for some elements seen in Diebenkorn's *Ocean Park* works. Particularly notable in *The Piano Lesson* are the flattening of compositional space, the combination of bright and subtle hues, and the use of geometric planes of vibrant, thinly painted color to break open the work's gray interior. Matisse's *On the Terrace* (1912, plate 94), which Diebenkorn saw during his trip to the Soviet Union, was certainly also a resonant work in its abstracted geometric background and use of colorful, thinly layered paint.

Diebenkorn introduced an even more complex use of bands of color in two *Ocean Park* works that are almost like mirror images of each other: *Ocean Park #54* (1972, plate 95), with its cool tones of light blue and stone and injections of yellow, green, and darker blue; and the grand *Ocean Park #79* (1975, plate 97), which is a symphony of blues and greens punctuated with pops of yellow and red. By using multiple layers of thin paint in the *Ocean Park* series, Diebenkorn found the freedom to experiment with his palette, producing an innovative array of chromatic combinations with which to explore light and structure. He would begin each canvas with a decision as to whether it was to have an overall cool or warm tone, and from there on it was a journey of trial and error.[42] According to Martin Facey, a former student of the artist's who spent a great deal of time with him in his studio during the Ocean Park years, Diebenkorn worked on each composition until he felt it was just right. He was always in the process of painting several large canvases at once, and he spent many hours and days contemplating his works in progress, looking for the next move, as if in a game of chess. His studio had two chairs set up for this contemplation—one for the artist and the other for the occasional visitor—and he considered it an essential step in the creation of his work.[43]

In 1975 Diebenkorn moved into his third Ocean Park studio, a space that had been designed to his specifications. This new environment was equally inspiring, and he continued the series uninterrupted, as he had found his muse in Santa Monica. Some canvases began to take on a bit of the depth and patina of old stone architecture, as in the small but potent *Ocean Park #93* (1976, plate 103) and the transcendent *Ocean Park #94* (1976, plate 99), which can be seen as an image of building blocks with a view through a window. Within the series, a sense of time is present, and evidence of the artist's process still lingers. A new focus on the horizontal line within a vertical framework began to emerge at the end of the decade, with a blue and green palette highlighted with oranges and yellows in the monumental *Ocean Park #105* (1978, plate 101), followed two years later by the sunny and warm *Ocean Park #122* (1980, plate 104), which harkens back to Matisse's sun-soaked Nice interiors of the 1920s, such as *Interior at Nice* (1919 or 1920, plate 4). Even Diebenkorn's abstracted and seemingly blossoming image of a heraldic club (part of his decades-long fascination with clubs and spades) painted over the veils of scaffolding of a drawing beneath (1980, plate 105) recalls Matisse's own pared-down view of foliage seen through a window in *The Blue Window* (1913, plate 25), a work the younger artist had known for decades.

From the moment Diebenkorn first exhibited a selection from the *Ocean Park* series, in 1968, the paintings were linked with Matisse's oeuvre, with one critic seeing Diebenkorn as the inheritor of the French master's vision,[44] a legacy that was both a pleasure and, perhaps, a bit of a burden. In 1988 Diebenkorn and his wife returned to Northern California, moving to Healdsburg. Unfortunately, ill health plagued him in his new home, making it too difficult to work with large canvases. He continued to paint on a smaller scale, primarily producing abstractions, until his death in 1993. In an interview conducted during the last decade of his life, after a long career filled with great critical success, Diebenkorn freely discussed Matisse's importance, acknowledging his great interest in the older artist's work with easy enthusiasm: "Matisse always surprises me, he's so rich. One may expect, for example, a certain enhancing at a particular point, but then one looks and finds it's all pretty drab there. He has this marvelous cool, he manages to resist all that jazz, yet he's as sumptuous a painter as there is. It's the restraint coupled with the sensuousness that's so utterly exceptional. It's a musical thing: this transition here, this color here, a wild surprise here that becomes, a little farther up—well, just a gentle part of the harmony."[45] One could certainly link those attributes equally well with the art of Richard Diebenkorn.

Notes

1. Richard Diebenkorn quoted in Dan Hofstadter, "Profiles: Almost Free of the Mirror," *New Yorker*, September 7, 1987, 64. Although Diebenkorn refers here to his high regard for Willem de Kooning, the sentiment is equally pertinent to his respect for Henri Matisse.
2. For further discussion of the drawings of Diebenkorn and Matisse, see the essay by Jodi Roberts on pages 86–94 in this publication.
3. For a thorough examination of Diebenkorn's *Berkeley* paintings, see Timothy Anglin Burgard, Steven A. Nash, and Emma Acker, *Richard Diebenkorn: The Berkeley Years, 1953–1966*, exh. cat. (San Francisco: Fine Arts Museums of San Francisco, 2013).
4. William Luers, letter to Gretchen Diebenkorn Grant, December 31, 2015. Luers, who was a junior diplomat at the U.S. Embassy in Moscow in 1964, served as the escort for the artist and his wife during their visit to the USSR. This letter is full of interesting information about the Diebenkorns' trip and the close relationship between Luers and Richard and Phyllis Diebenkorn. With grateful thanks to Gretchen Diebenkorn Grant and Richard Grant for generously sharing this letter with Janet Bishop and the author via email, January 3, 2016. According to Luers, his time with the Diebenkorns in the USSR lasted about two weeks. William Luers, interview by the author, January 22, 2016. Daisy Murray Holman, director of archives, Richard Diebenkorn Foundation, has indicated that the entire trip to the USSR probably lasted six weeks to two months. Daisy Murray Holman, email to the author, August 12, 2015.
5. Luers to Grant, 2015.
6. Ibid., and Phyllis Diebenkorn, interview by Ben Grant, #4, ca. 2003–4, Richard Diebenkorn Foundation archives.
7. Luers, interview by the author, 2016. Luers notes that the artist was looking for something new to inspire him when he agreed to take the trip and feels that the experience of being in the USSR at that time was both difficult and transformative for Diebenkorn.
8. Alfred H. Barr Jr., *Matisse: His Art and His Public* (New York: The Museum of Modern Art, 1951). Diebenkorn informed Bruce Grenville, a graduate student

researching the influence of Matisse on abstract expressionist artists, that he purchased his copy of Barr's book in 1954. Richard Diebenkorn, letter to Bruce Grenville, November 8, 1981. For further discussion of the Grenville letter, see note 6 in Janet Bishop's essay in this publication. Grateful thanks to Gail Stavitsky for sharing this letter with the author via email, January 29, 2015.
9. According to Gretchen Diebenkorn Grant, this drawing is an accurate representation of the Diebenkorn family dining table at the time. The tablecloth was an Indian bedspread. Gretchen Diebenkorn Grant, "The Insights of the Life and Art of Her Father, Richard Diebenkorn" (lecture, Cubberley Auditorium, Stanford University, Stanford, California, November 4, 2015).
10. Phyllis Diebenkorn, interview by Ben Grant, #5, August 21, 2003, Richard Diebenkorn Foundation archives.
11. Diebenkorn to Grenville, 1981.
12. Luers to Grant, 2015.
13. Ibid., and Phyllis Diebenkorn, interview by Grant, #5.
14. Luers, interview by the author, 2016.
15. Luers to Grant, 2015.
16. Ibid., and Luers, interview by the author, 2016.
17. Richard Diebenkorn, interview by Susan Larsen, June 2, 1977, Archives of American Art, Smithsonian Institution, Washington, D.C. Oral history interviews of Diebenkorn were also conducted by Larsen as part of the Archives of American Art's Oral History Project between May 1, 1985, and December 15, 1987.
18. Diebenkorn quoted in Hofstadter, "Profiles," 68–69. Diebenkorn discussed the same painting and its conservation issues in the interview by Larsen, 1977. His recollections of the painting's fragile state were correct. The conservation effort, which lasted for four years, was finally completed in 1965. See Kasper Monrad, ed., *Henri Matisse: Four Great Collectors*, exh. cat. (Copenhagen: Statens Museum for Kunst, 1999), 242.
19. Phyllis Tuchman, interview by the author, January 19, 2016.
20. Richard Diebenkorn in "Oral history interview with Richard Diebenkorn, May 1, 1985–December 15, 1987," conducted by Susan Larsen. Archives of American Art, Smithsonian Institution, Washington, D.C. See session 3, May 7, 1985.
21. Christopher Diebenkorn, conversation with Janet Bishop and Lily Pearsall, October 13, 2015.
22. Clement Greenberg, "Matisse in 1966," in *The Collected Essays and Criticism, Volume 4: Modernism with a Vengeance, 1957–1969*, ed. John O'Brian (Chicago: The University of Chicago Press, 1995), 221.
23. Diebenkorn to Grenville, 1981.
24. Nancy Marmer, "Matisse and the Strategy of Decoration," *Artforum* 4, no. 7 (March 1966): 32.
25. Stephanie D'Alessandro and John Elderfield, *Matisse: Radical Invention, 1913–1917*, exh. cat. (Chicago: The Art Institute of Chicago, 2010), 233–35.
26. Diebenkorn to Grenville, 1981. For more information, see the essay by Janet Bishop on pages 18–30 in this publication.
27. Diebenkorn, "Oral history interview," conducted by Larsen, May 7, 1985.
28. Diebenkorn noted the Los Angeles Matisse retrospective as one of his key interactions with the French artist's work. Diebenkorn to Grenville, 1981.
29. For an in-depth discussion of the making of Matisse's *The Yellow Dress*, see Yve-Alain Bois, ed., *Matisse in the Barnes Foundation* (London: Thames & Hudson in association with the Barnes Foundation, 2015), 108–12.
30. Diebenkorn, "Oral history interview," conducted by Larsen, December 15, 1987.
31. Discussing several Matisse works while looking through publications on the artist, Diebenkorn pointed out the unusual depiction of the hands in *Portrait of the Artist's Wife*: "I have to think that these odd, unfinished-looking things in Matisse were done toward the beginning, and the painting finished around them. It seems that in time the painting—oh, *accepted* them. . . . Stuff like this is so outrageous, but there's a deeper rightness to it. Sometimes it happens to me in a painting that I just have one dumb little area to fix up, and I do it, and, boom, the painting's gone—for the time being, anyway. Matisse refrained from this sort of thing, and his very refraining became a kind of seeing." Diebenkorn quoted in Hofstadter, "Profiles," 69.
32. Luers to Grant, 2015.
33. Diebenkorn stated that he first saw *The Piano Lesson* in 1947 at The Museum of Modern Art, New York. Diebenkorn to Grenville, 1981.
34. *The Piano Lesson*, along with other Matisse paintings that embrace the line between abstraction and figuration, such as *Bathers by a River* (1909–17), was an important part of Diebenkorn's teaching during this period. He encouraged his students to paint in a flat, pared-down manner rather than an illusionistic one, and from time to time he brought in Matisse publications from his library to assist them. Martin Facey, a former student of Diebenkorn's at UCLA, recalls the artist mentioning *The Piano Lesson* and *Bathers by a River* during their interactions. Martin Facey, interview by the author, November 23, 2015. Another former student, Jan Wurm, also recalled that Diebenkorn brought up *The Piano Lesson* in her discussions with him at UCLA. Jan Wurm, interview by the author and Janet Bishop, April 24, 2014.
35. Diebenkorn, "Oral history interview," conducted by Larsen, May 2, 1985.
36. Richard Diebenkorn quoted in John Gruen, "Richard Diebenkorn: The Idea Is to Get Everything Right," *Art News* 85, no. 9 (November 1986): 86.
37. For a thorough examination of Diebenkorn's *Ocean Park* series, see Sarah C. Bancroft, ed., *Richard Diebenkorn: The Ocean Park Series*, exh. cat. (Newport Beach, CA: Orange County Museum of Art, 2011).
38. For example, see Jane Livingston, "The Art of Richard Diebenkorn," in *The Art of Richard Diebenkorn*, exh. cat., ed. Jane Livingston (New York: Whitney Museum of American Art, 1997), 62–64; and Gerald Nordland, *Richard Diebenkorn*, 2nd ed. (New York: Rizzoli, 2001), 144.
39. For images of the twenty-two states of *Large Reclining Nude* in process, see Jack Flam, *Matisse in The Cone Collection: The Poetics of Vision* (Baltimore: The Baltimore Museum of Art, 2001), 104–5. For images of the thirteen states of *Seated Pink Nude* in process, see Pierre Schneider, *Matisse* (New York: Rizzoli, 1984), 364.
40. Barr, *Matisse: His Art and His Public*, 472.
41. Diebenkorn, interview by Larsen, 1977.
42. Facey, interview by the author, 2015.
43. Ibid.
44. In 1968 Diebenkorn exhibited paintings from his *Ocean Park* series for the first time at the Poindexter Gallery in New York. John Canaday reviewed the show in the *New York Times* and linked the new series with Matisse's example, citing *View of Notre Dame* and *French Window at Collioure*, in particular, as impetuses for his new work. He stated: "Structurally, it is as if Matisse at this juncture had developed as an abstract painter in the person of his protégé-by-example." John Canaday, "Richard Diebenkorn: Still Out of Step," *New York Times*, May 26, 1968, D37.
45. Diebenkorn quoted in Hofstadter, "Profiles," 69.

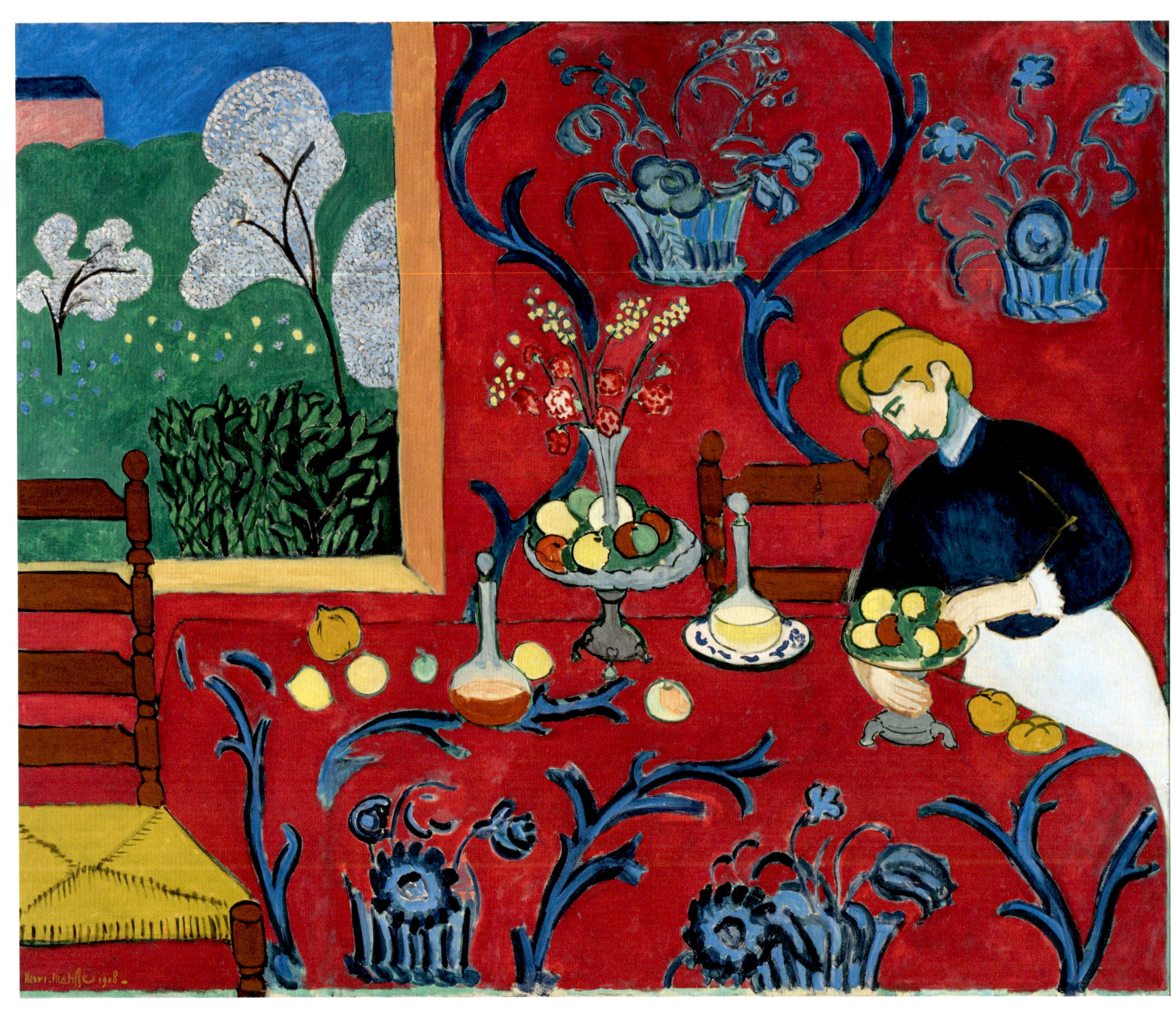

Plate 71. Henri Matisse, *Red Room (Harmony in Red)*, 1908. Oil on canvas, 71⅛ x 87 in. (180.5 x 221 cm). The State Hermitage Museum, Saint Petersburg

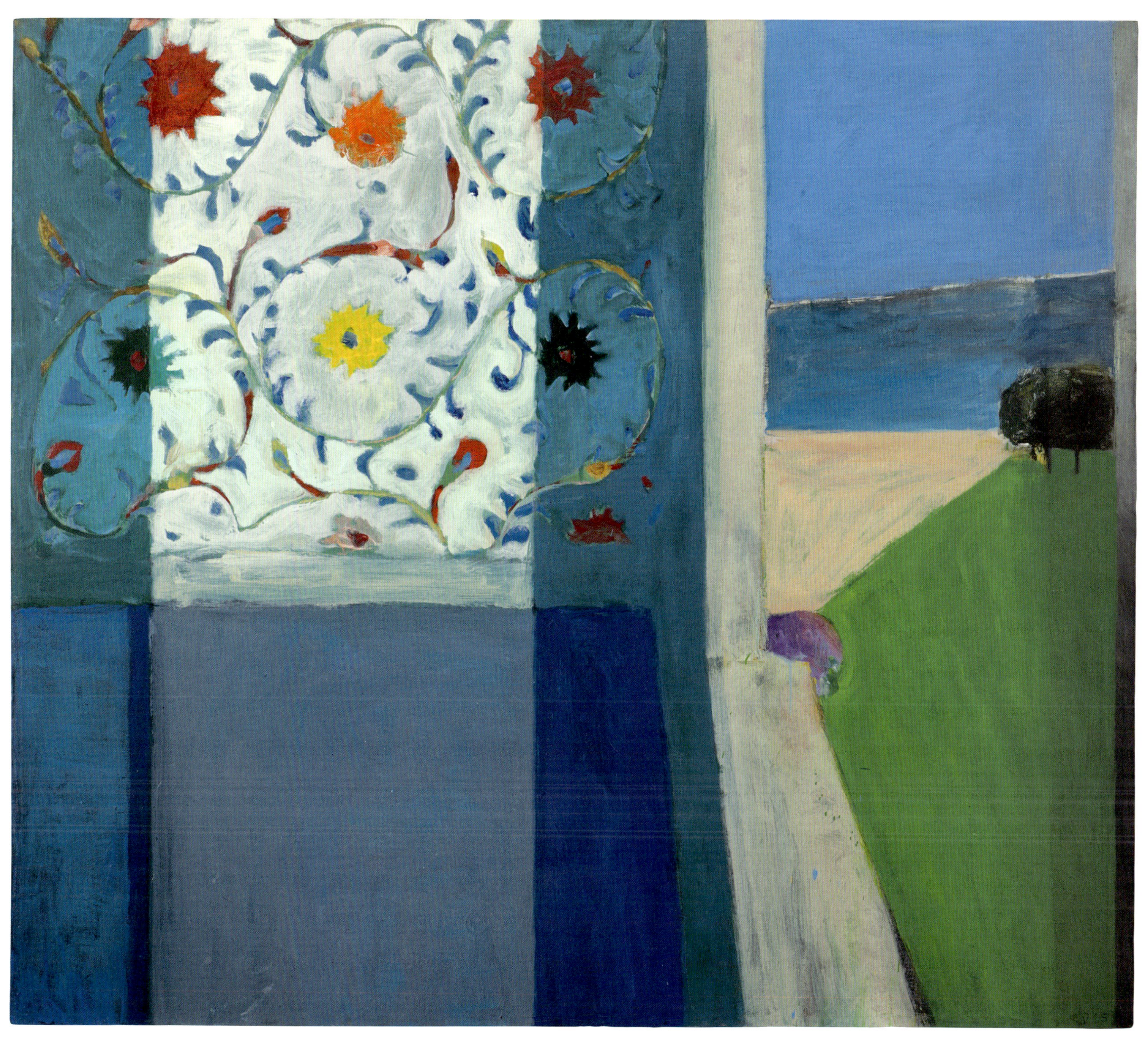

Plate 72. Richard Diebenkorn, *Recollections of a Visit to Leningrad,* 1965. Oil on canvas, 73 x 84 in. (185.4 x 213.4 cm). Private collection

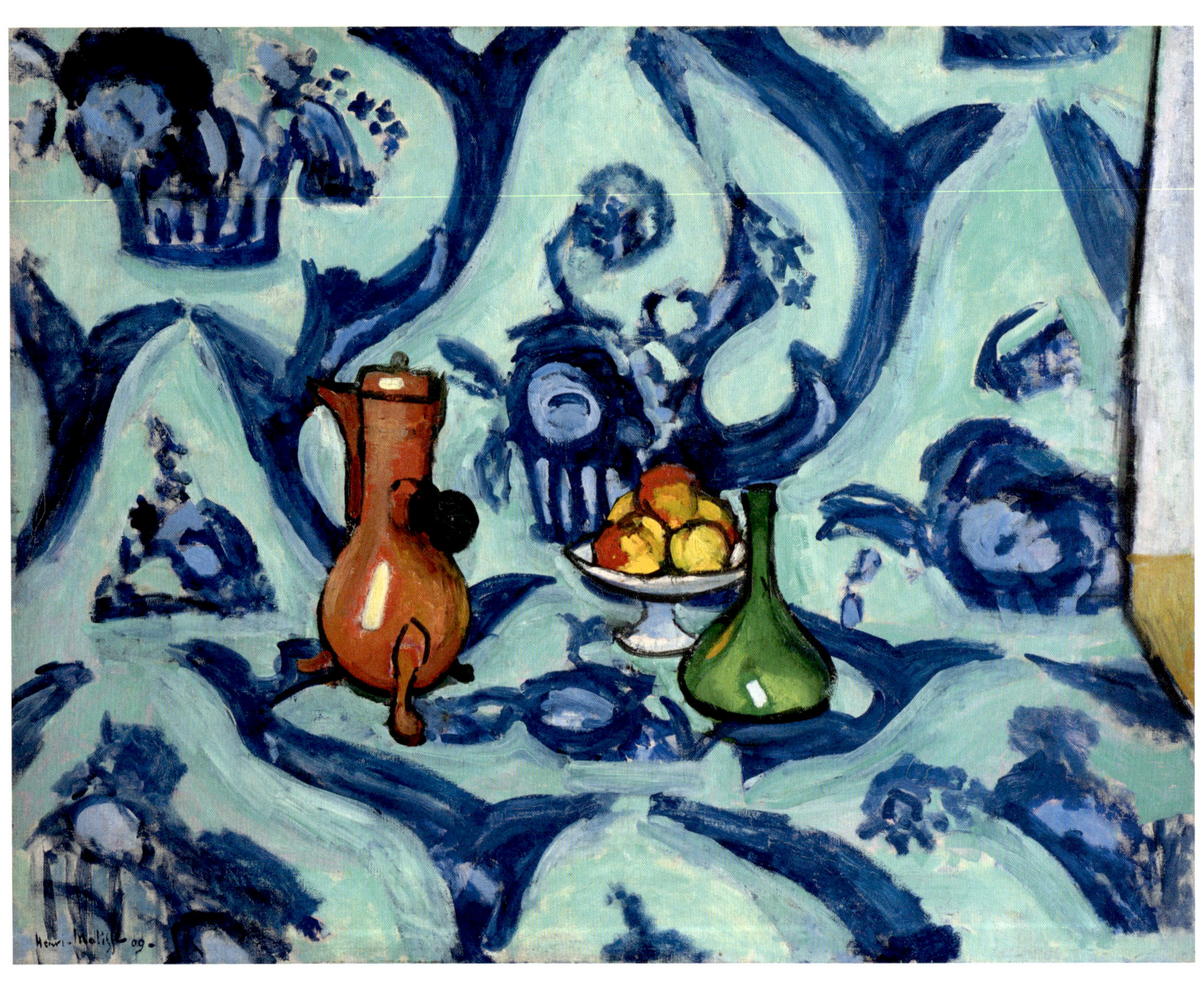

Plate 73. Henri Matisse, *Still Life with Blue Tablecloth,* 1909. Oil on canvas, 34⅝ x 46½ in. (88 x 118 cm).
The State Hermitage Museum, Saint Petersburg

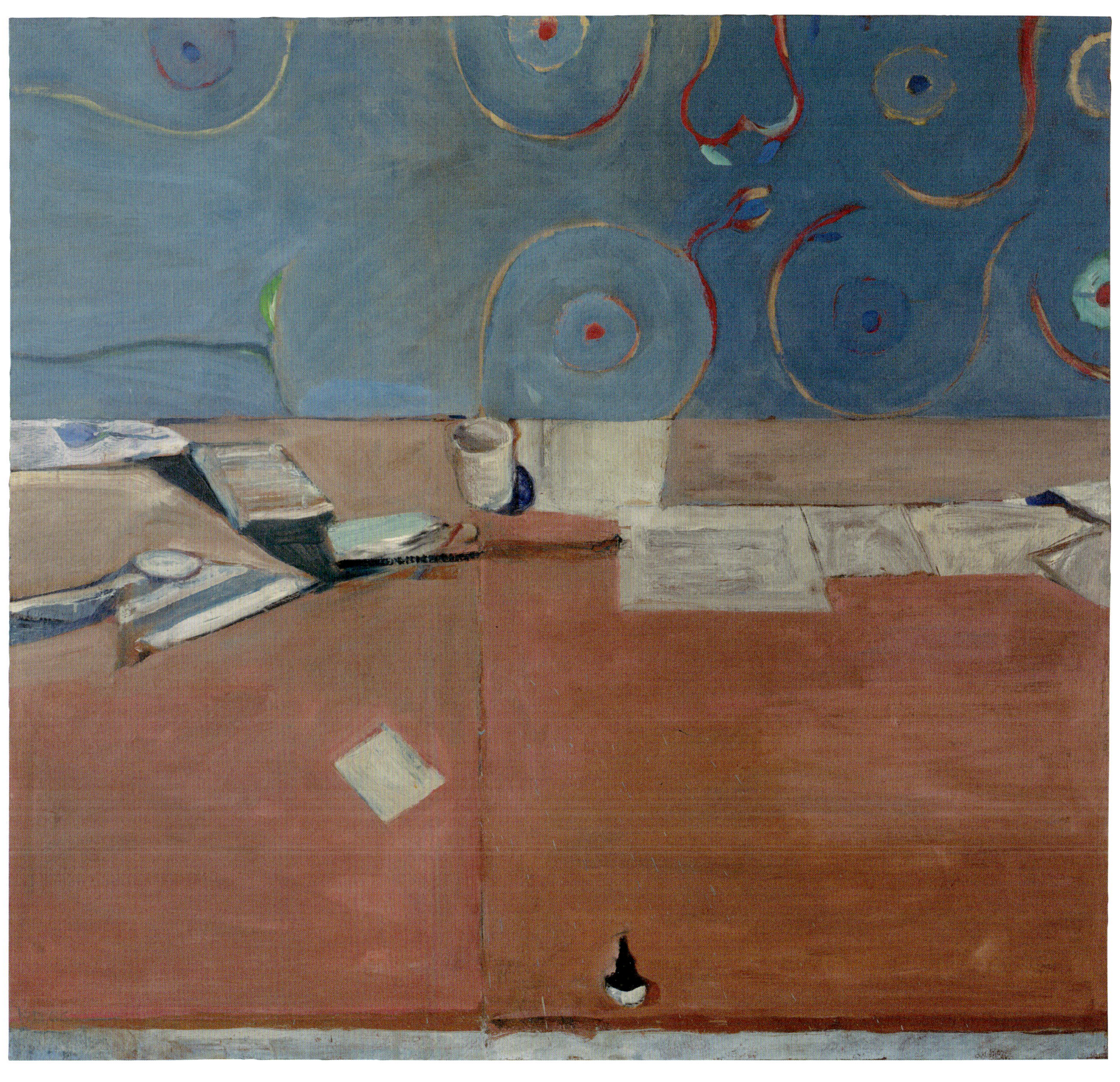

Plate 74. Richard Diebenkorn, *Large Still Life,* 1966. Oil on canvas, 64½ x 70¼ in. (163.8 x 178.4 cm). The Museum of Modern Art, New York, gift of the family of Richard Diebenkorn

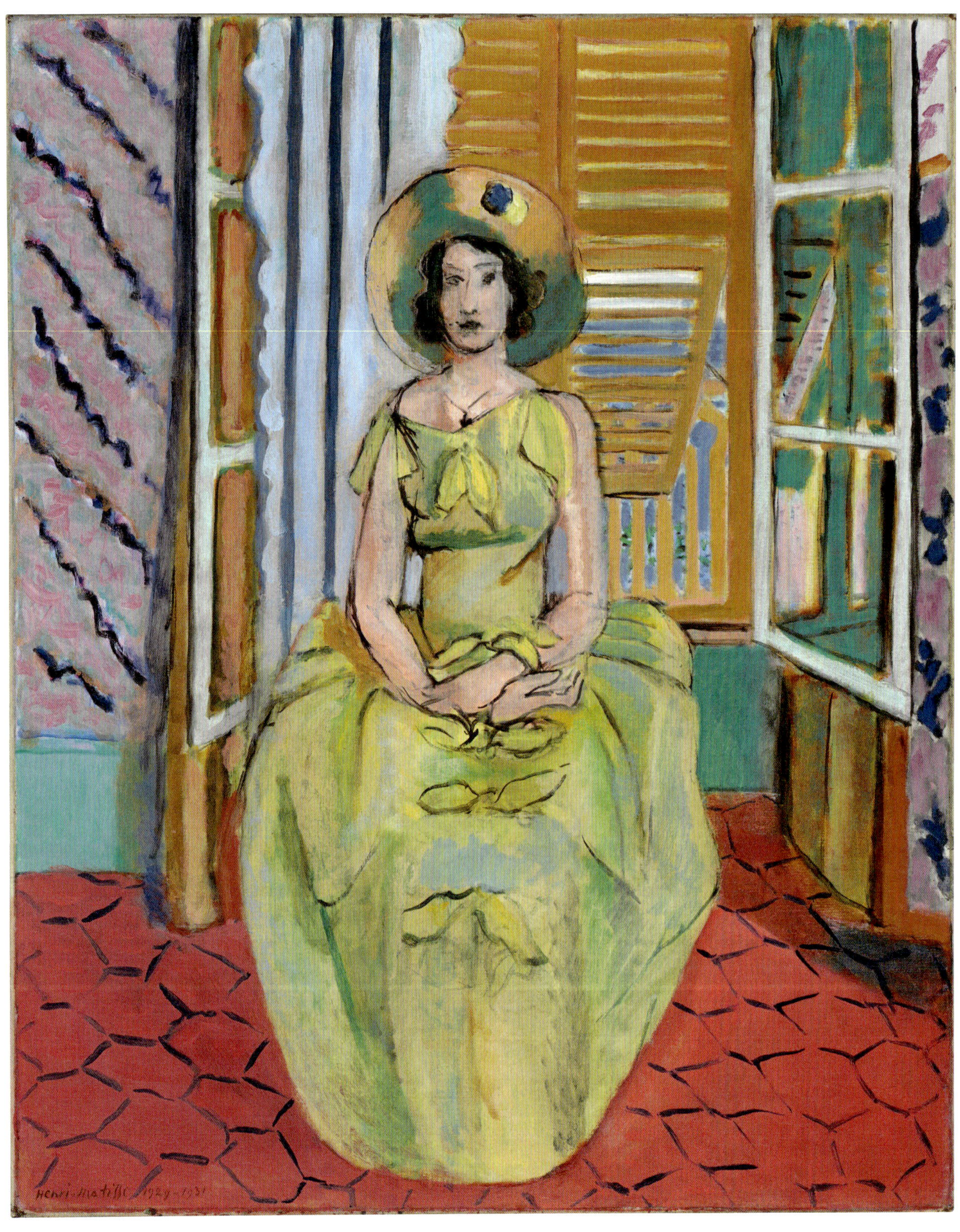

Plate 75. Henri Matisse, *The Yellow Dress,* 1929–31. Oil on canvas, 39⅝ x 32⅛ in. (100.6 x 81.6 cm).
The Baltimore Museum of Art: The Cone Collection, formed by Dr. Claribel Cone and Miss Etta Cone of Baltimore, Maryland

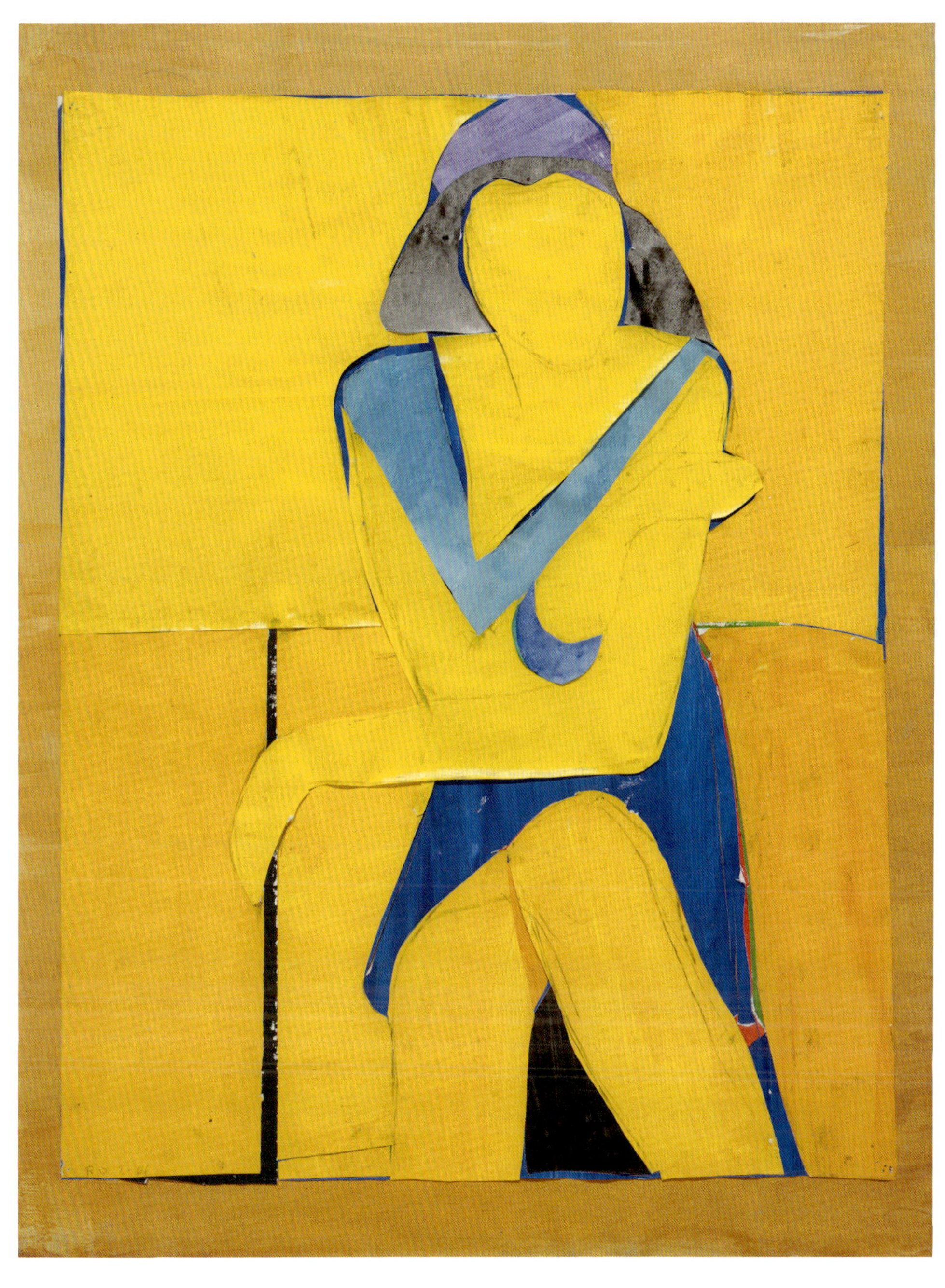

Plate 76. Richard Diebenkorn, *Untitled (Yellow Collage)*, 1966. Pasted paper, gouache, and ink on paper, 28¾ x 22 in. (73 x 55.9 cm). The Grant Family Collection

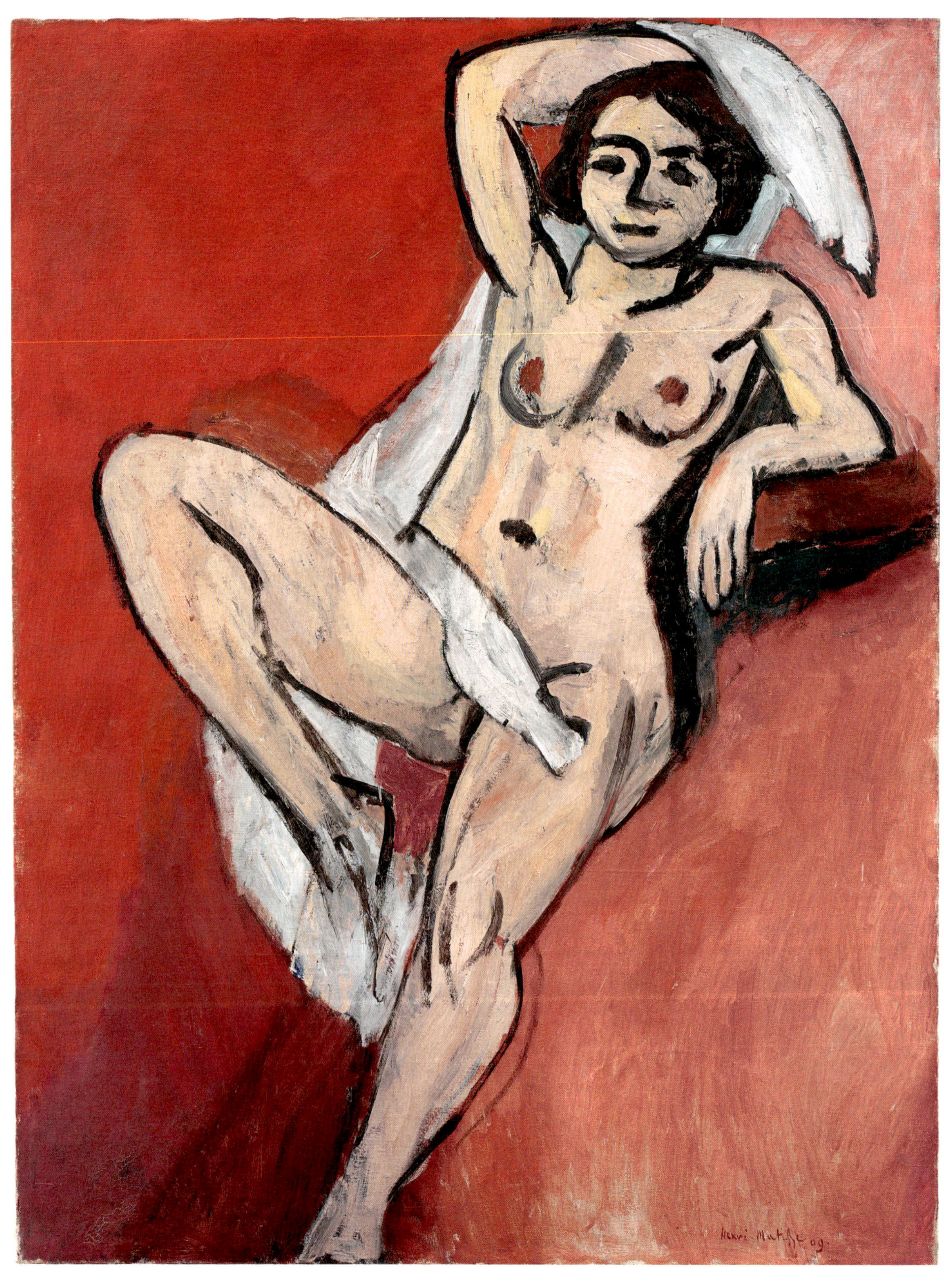

Plate 77. Henri Matisse, *Nude with a White Scarf,* 1909. Oil on canvas, 45⅞ x 35⅛ in. (116.5 x 89.2 cm). Statens Museum for Kunst, Copenhagen

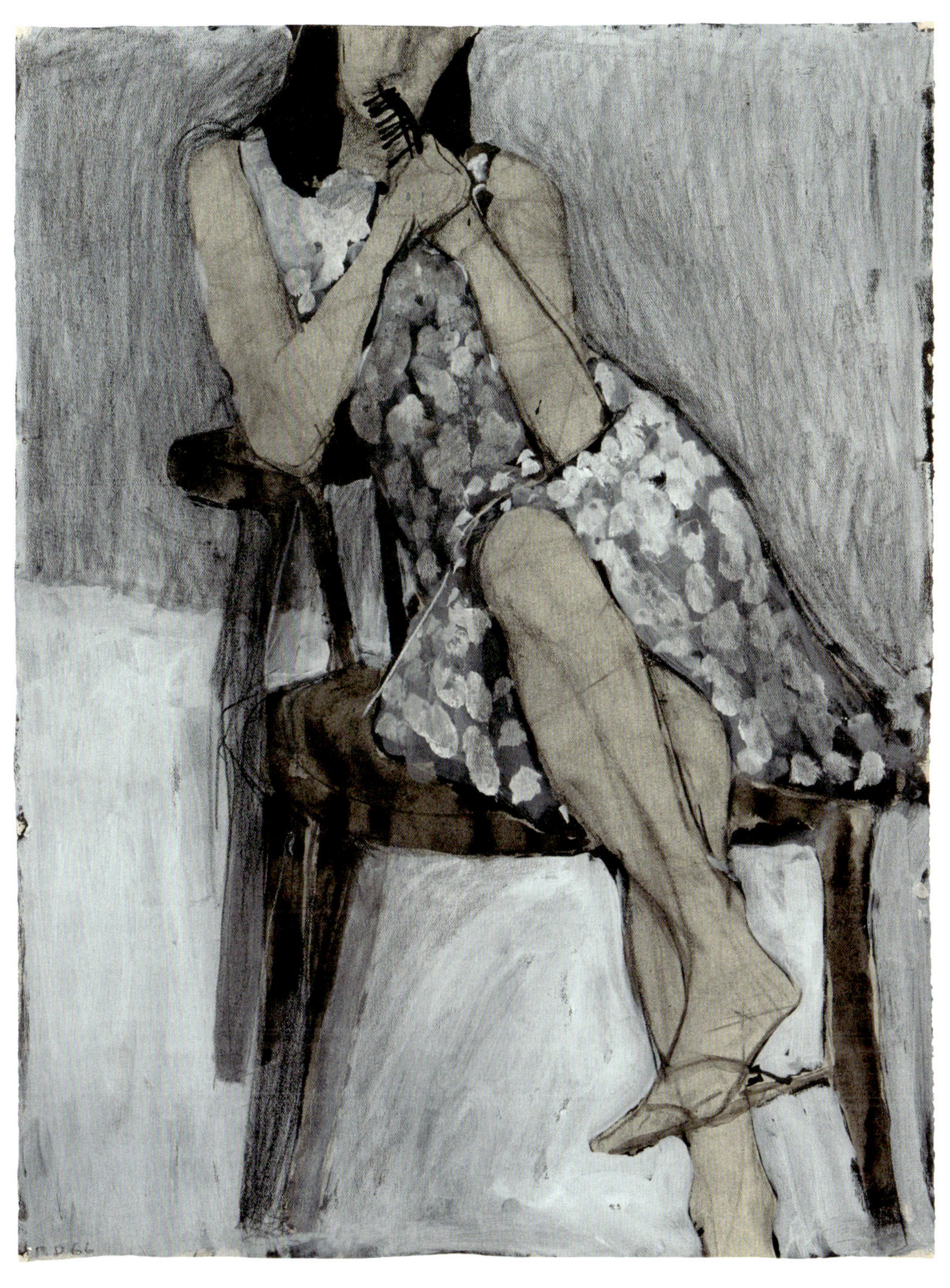

Plate 78. Richard Diebenkorn, *Untitled (Seated Woman, Patterned Dress)*, 1966.
Gouache, crayon, and ink on paper, 30¼ x 23¼ in. (76.8 x 59.1 cm). University Art Museum, University at Albany, State University of New York, purchase of Student Art Council

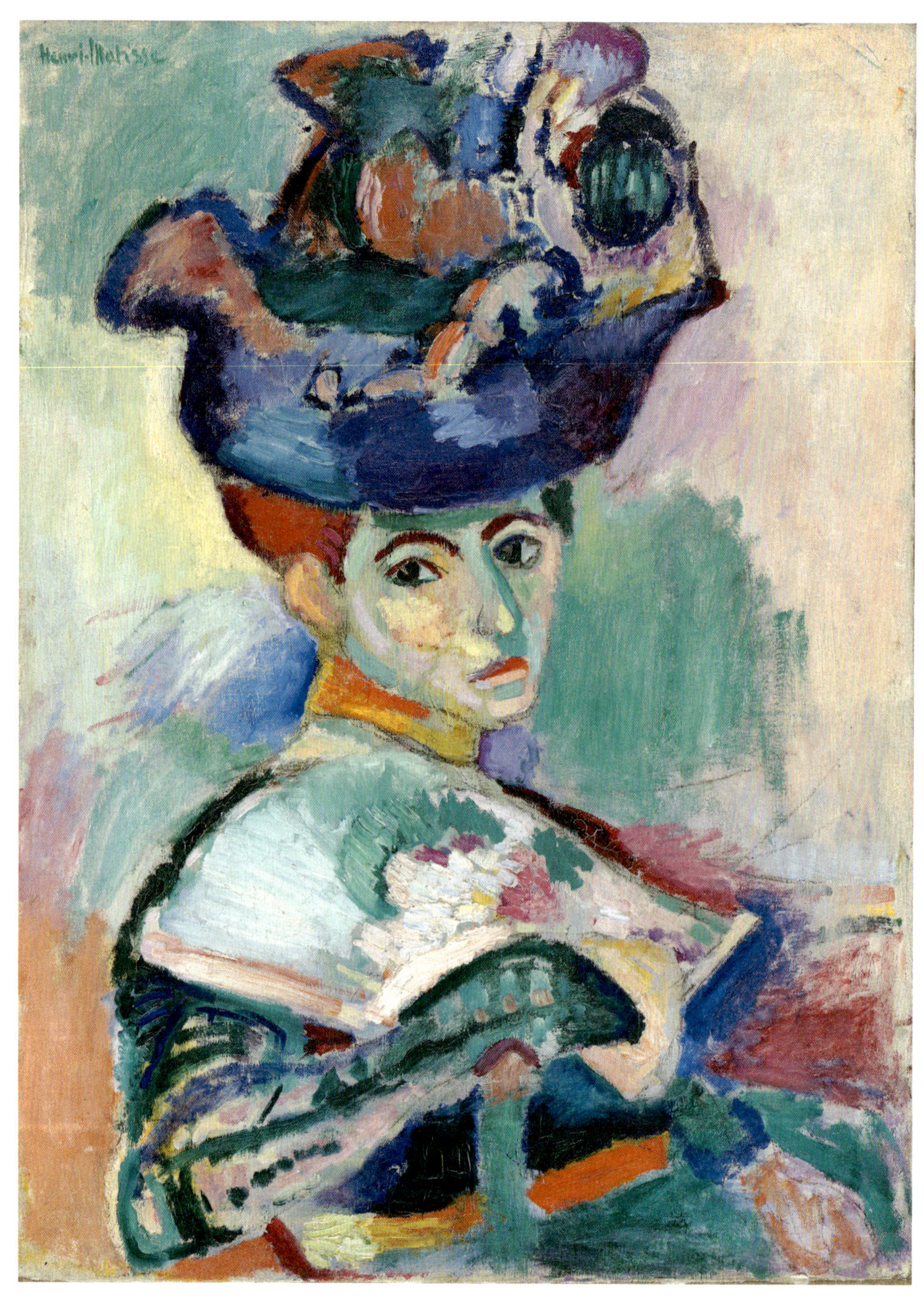

Plate 79. Henri Matisse, *Woman with a Hat,* 1905. Oil on canvas, 31¾ x 23½ in. (80.7 x 59.7 cm). San Francisco Museum of Modern Art, bequest of Elise S. Haas

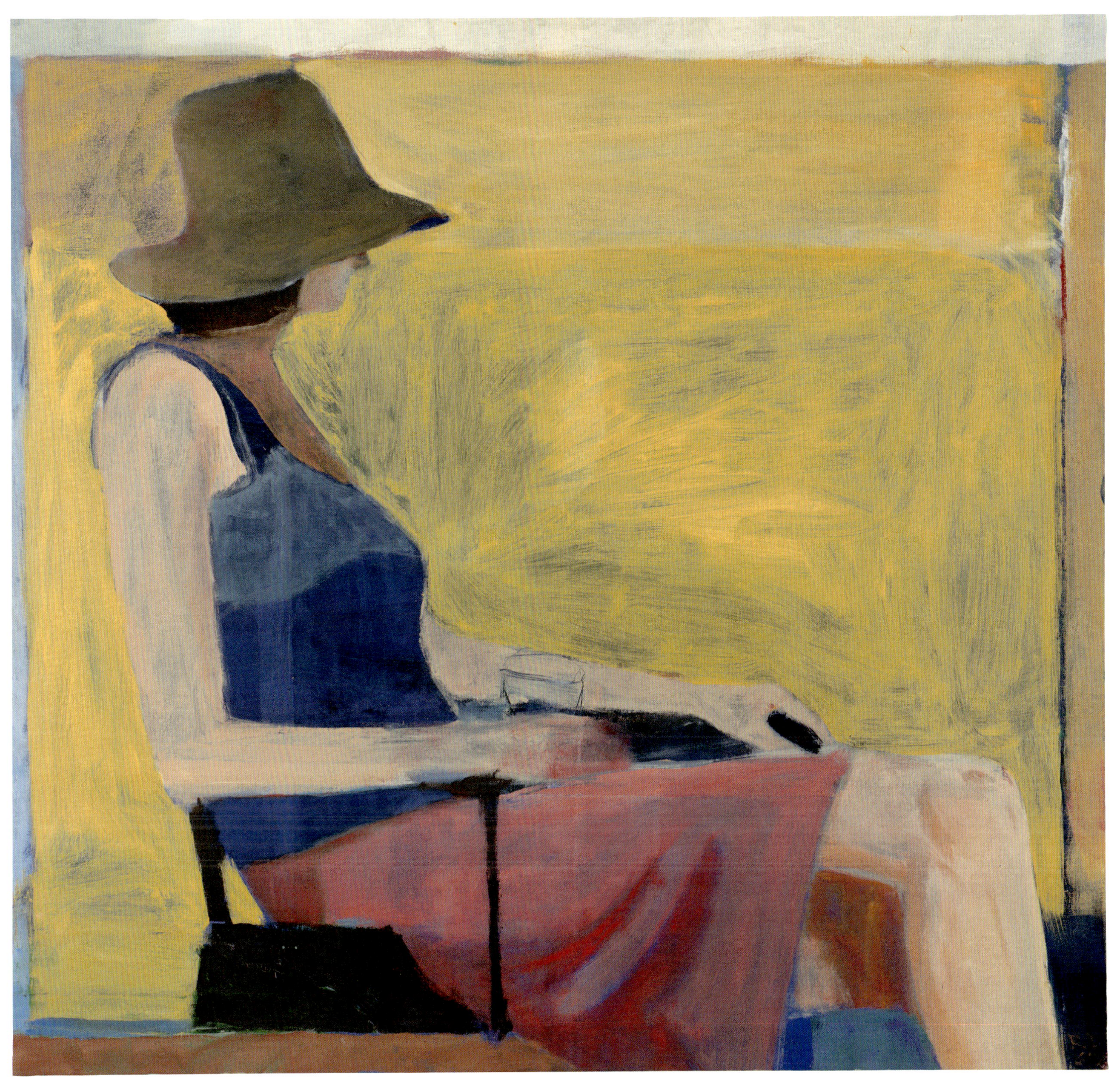

Plate 80. Richard Diebenkorn, *Seated Figure with Hat,* 1967. Oil on canvas, 57¾ x 61¾ in. (146.7 x 156.8 cm). National Gallery of Art, Washington, D.C., gift of the Collectors Committee and Mr. and Mrs. Lawrence Rubin

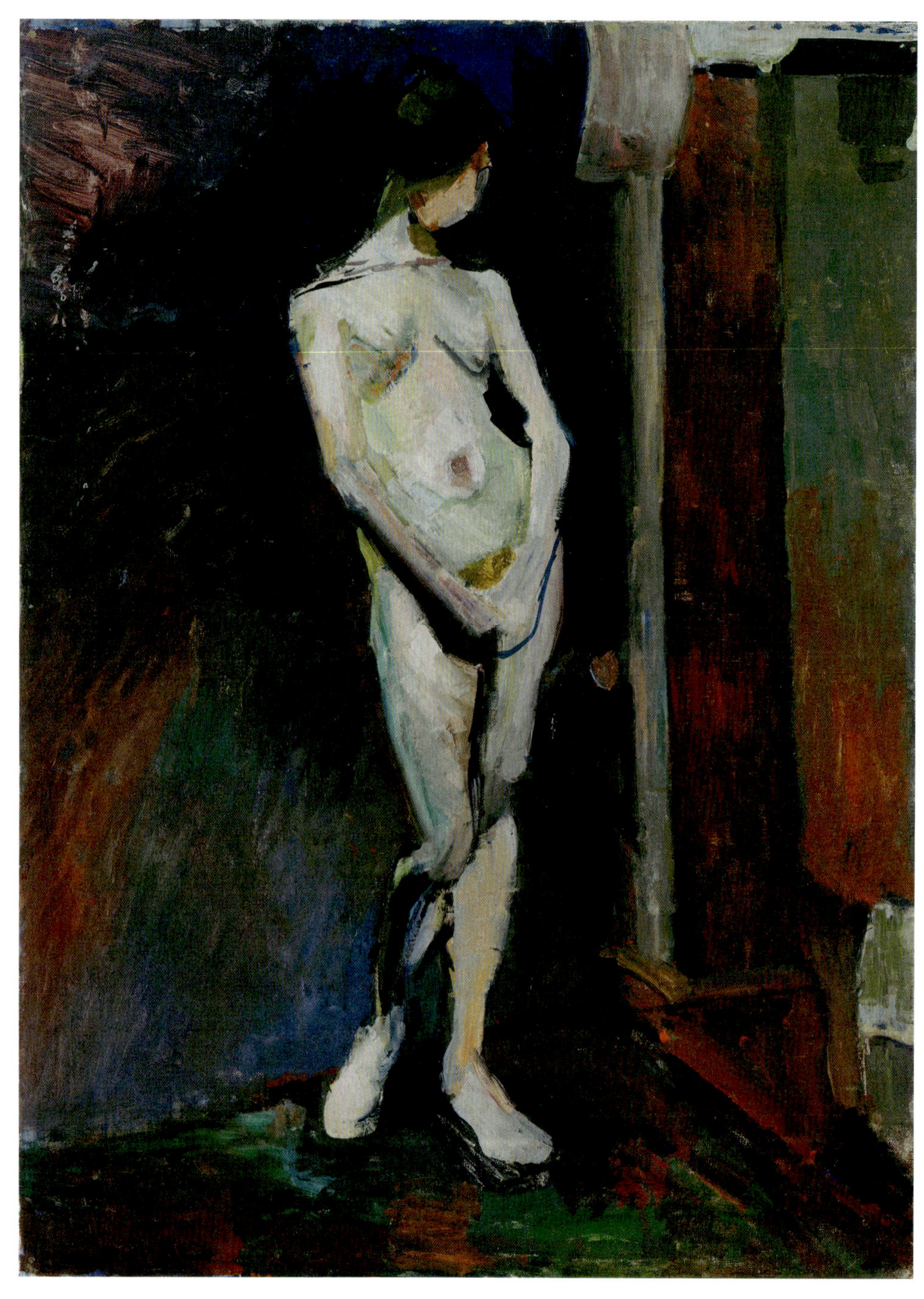

Plate 81. Henri Matisse, *Nude Study in Blue,* ca. 1899–1900. Oil on canvas, 28¾ x 21⅜ in. (73 x 54.3 cm). Tate, London, bequeathed by C. Frank Stoop

OPPOSITE
Plate 82. Richard Diebenkorn, *Nude on Blue Ground,* 1966. Oil on canvas, 81¼ x 59¼ in. (206.4 x 150.5 cm). Private collection

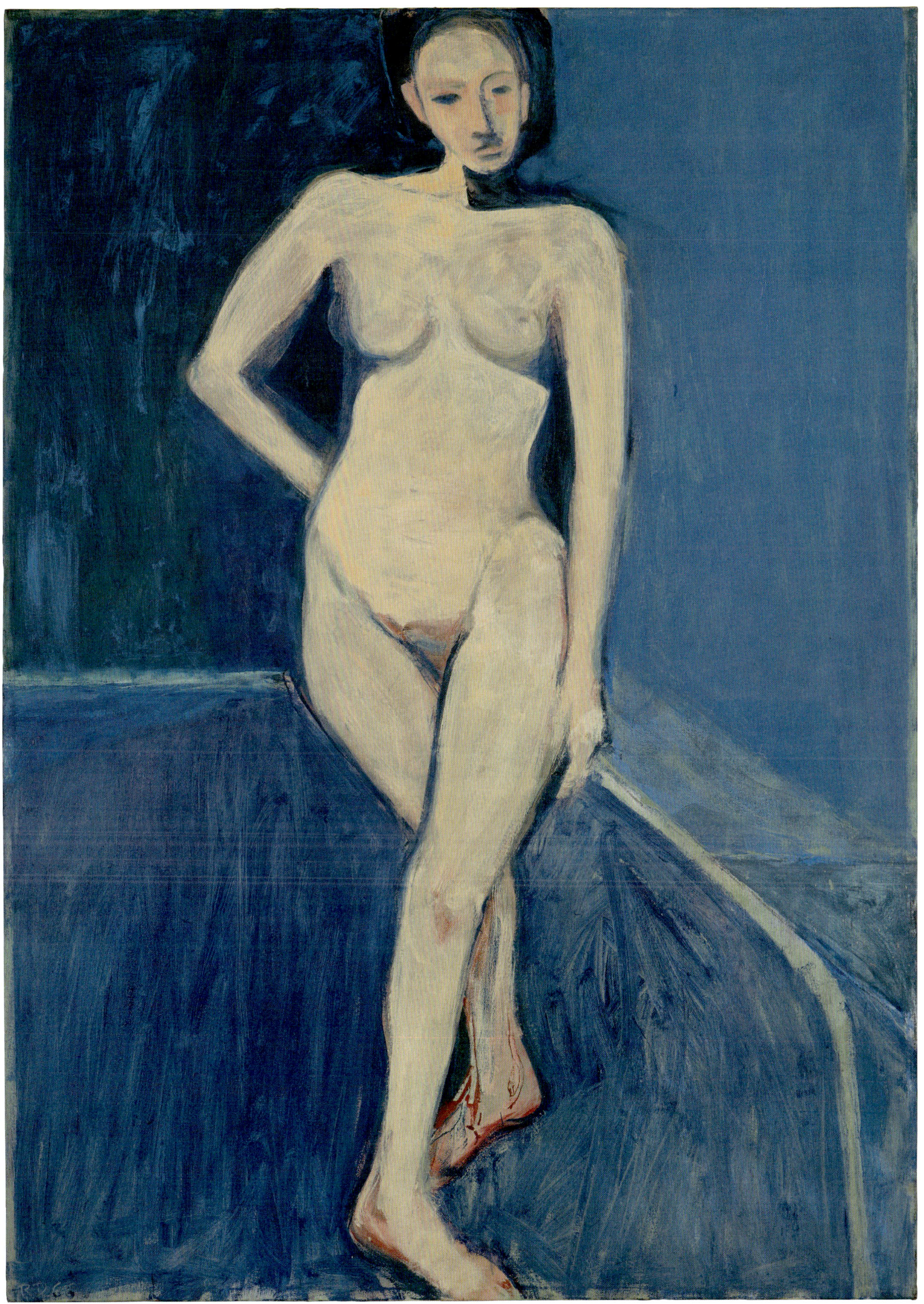

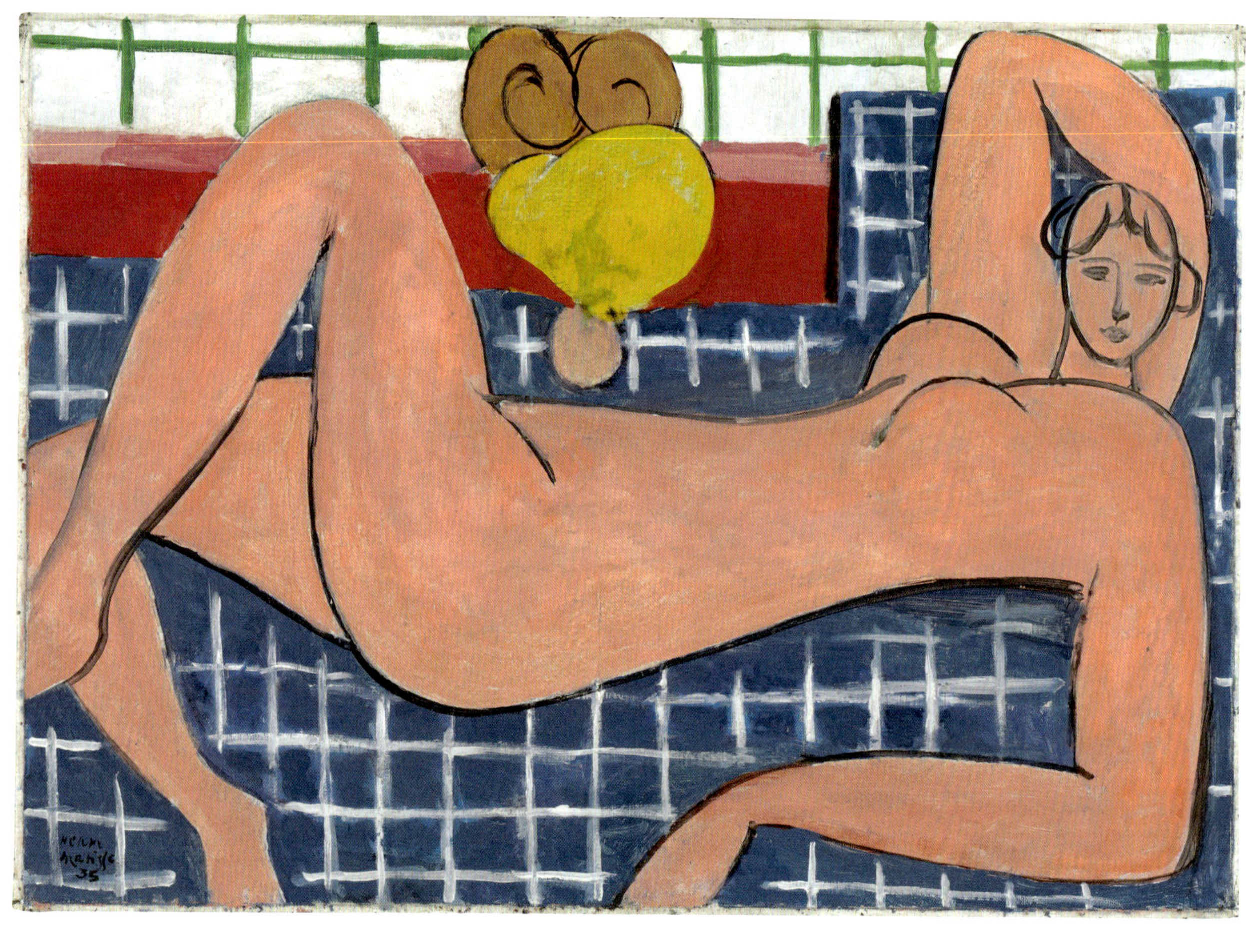

Plate 83. Henri Matisse, *Large Reclining Nude,* 1935. Oil on canvas, 26⅛ x 36¾ in. (66.4 x 93.3 cm). The Baltimore Museum of Art: The Cone Collection, formed by Dr. Claribel Cone and Miss Etta Cone of Baltimore, Maryland

OPPOSITE
Plate 84. Richard Diebenkorn, *Window,* 1967. Oil and graphite on canvas, 92 x 80 in. (233.7 x 203.2 cm). Iris & B. Gerald Cantor Center for Visual Arts at Stanford University, Stanford, California, gift of Mr. and Mrs. Richard Diebenkorn and anonymous donors

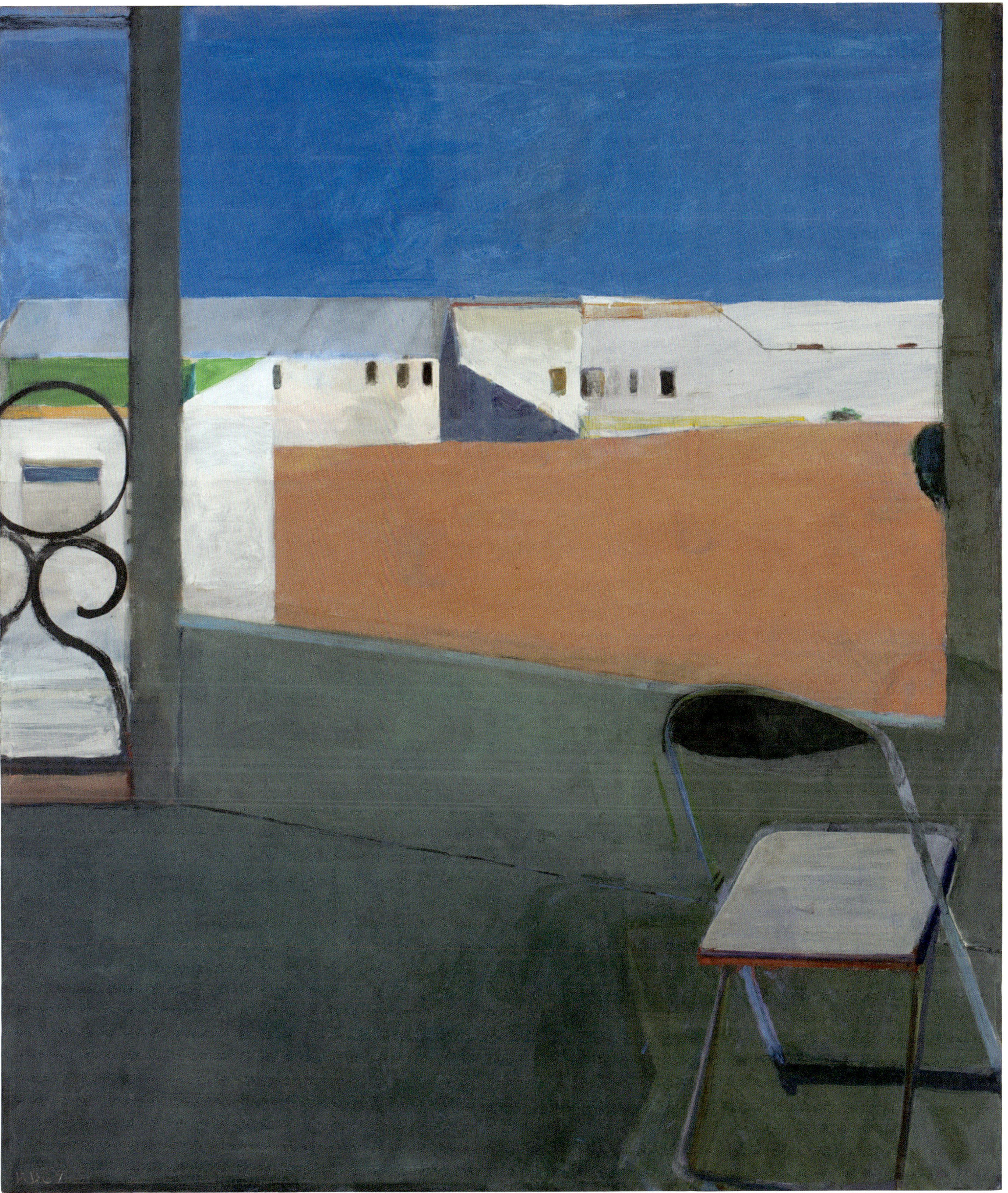

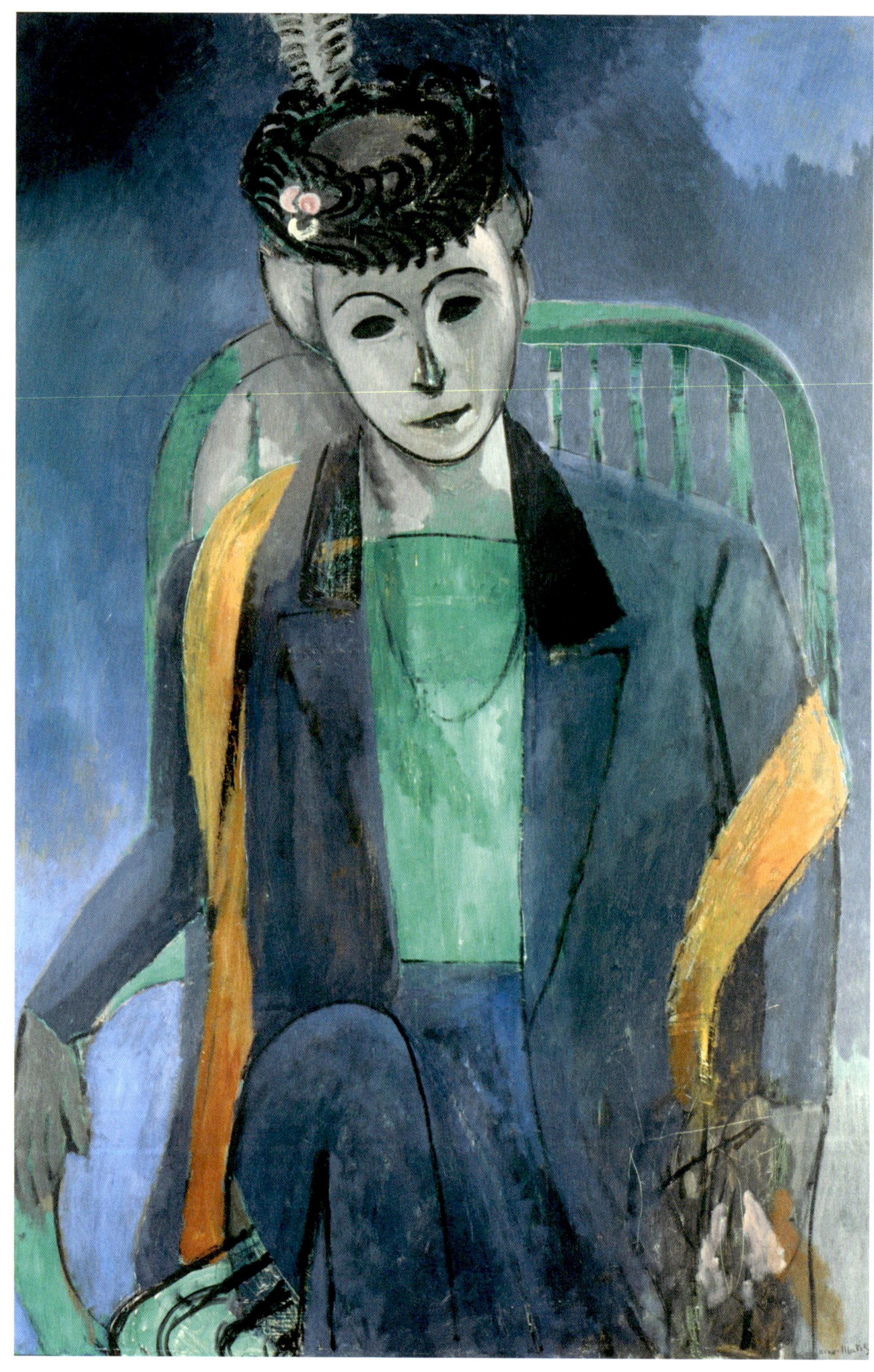

Plate 85. Henri Matisse, *Portrait of the Artist's Wife,* 1913. Oil on canvas, 57 x 38⅛ in. (145 x 97 cm). The State Hermitage Museum, Saint Petersburg

OPPOSITE
Plate 86. Richard Diebenkorn, *Seated Woman,* 1967. Oil on canvas, 90 x 80⅛ in. (228.6 x 203.5 cm). Collection of Gretchen and John Berggruen, San Francisco

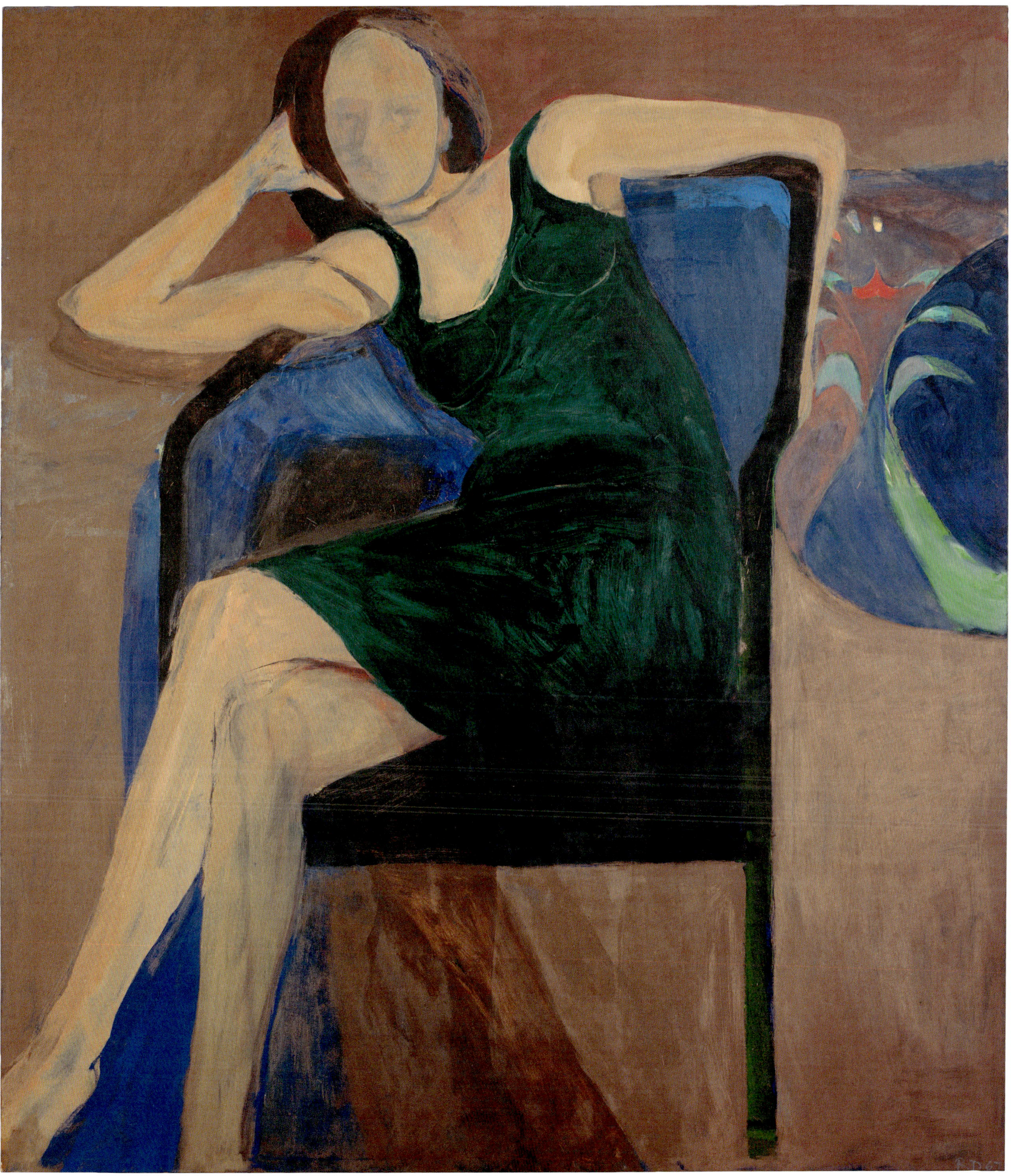

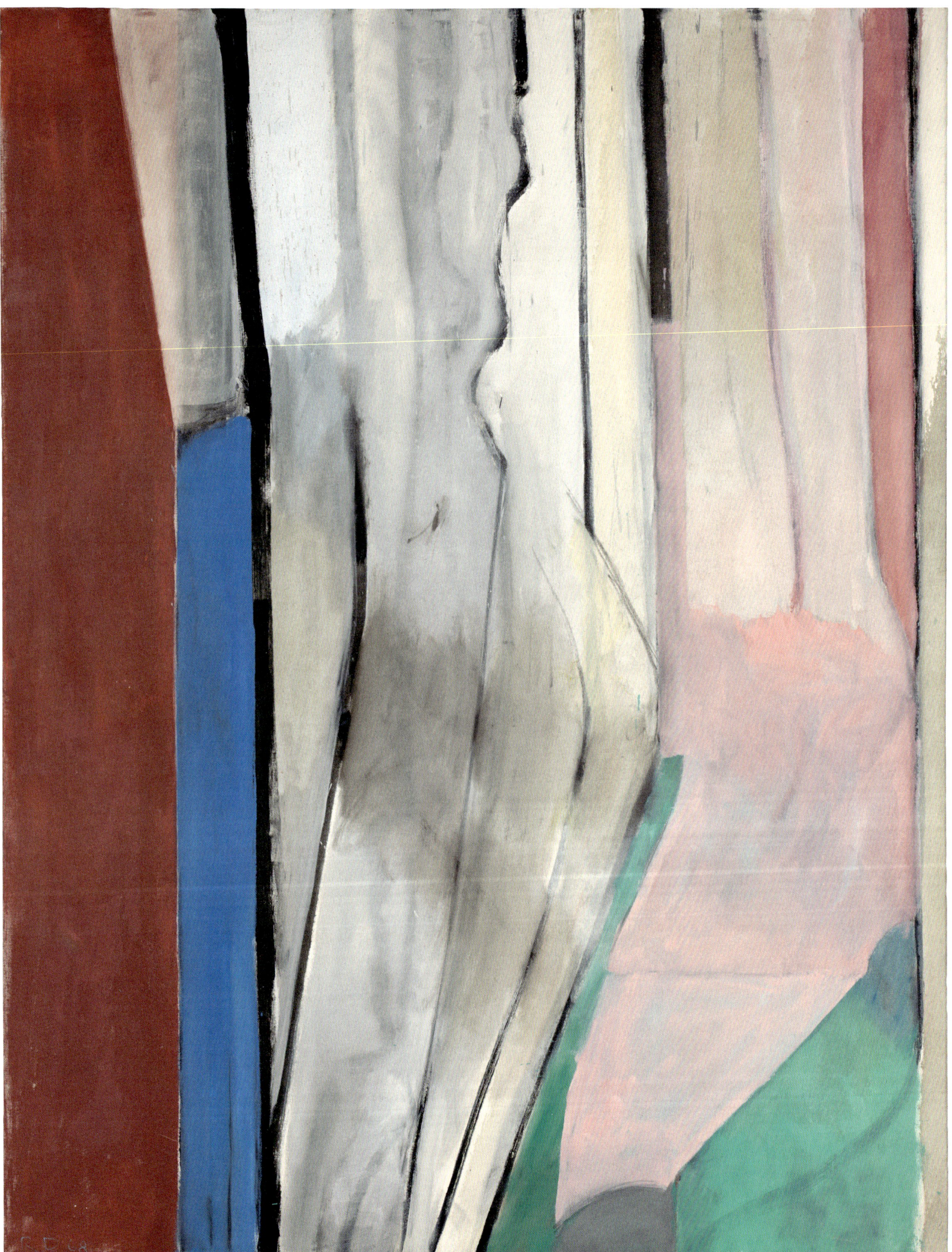

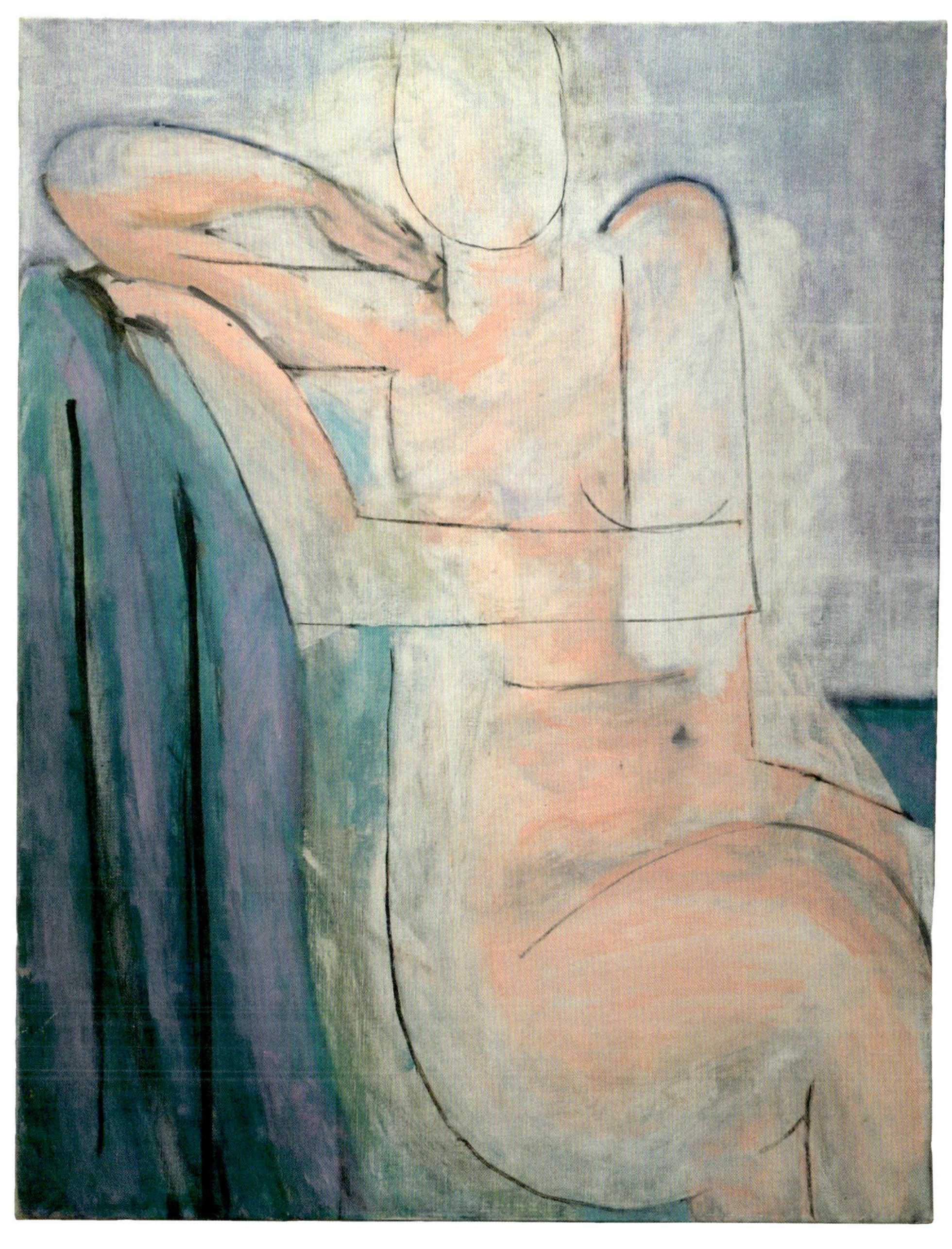

OPPOSITE
Plate 87. Richard Diebenkorn, *Ocean Park #6,* 1968. Oil on canvas, 92 x 72 in. (233.7 x 182.9 cm). Smithsonian American Art Museum, Washington, D.C., gift of Arthur J. Levin in memory of his beloved wife Edith

Plate 88. Henri Matisse, *Seated Pink Nude,* 1935–36. Oil on canvas, 36¼ x 28¾ in. (92 x 73 cm). Musée national d'art moderne/Centre de création industrielle, Centre Georges Pompidou, Paris

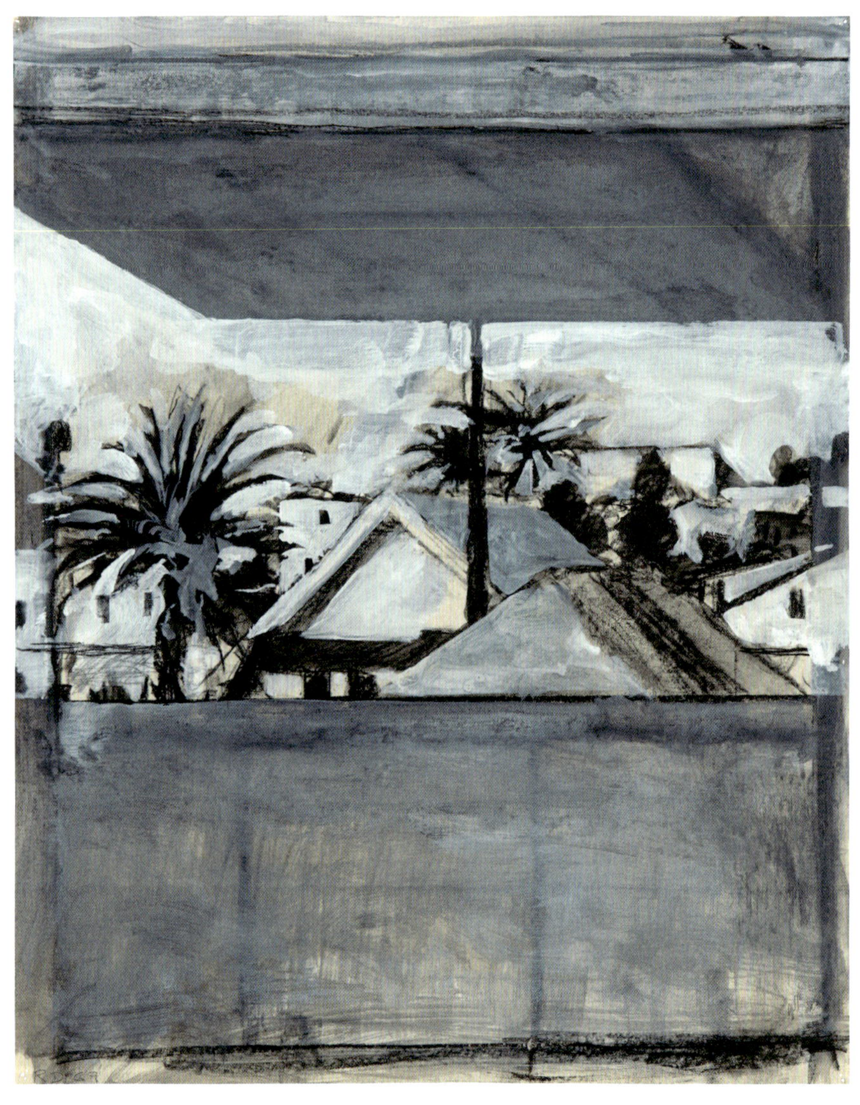

Plate 89. Richard Diebenkorn, *Untitled (View from Studio, Ocean Park)*, 1969. Gouache, charcoal, and ink on paper, 17 x 13¾ in. (43.2 x 34.9 cm). The Grant Family Collection

OPPOSITE
Plate 90. Richard Diebenkorn, *Ocean Park #12*, 1968. Oil and charcoal on canvas, 92½ x 80 in. (235 x 203.2 cm). Private collection

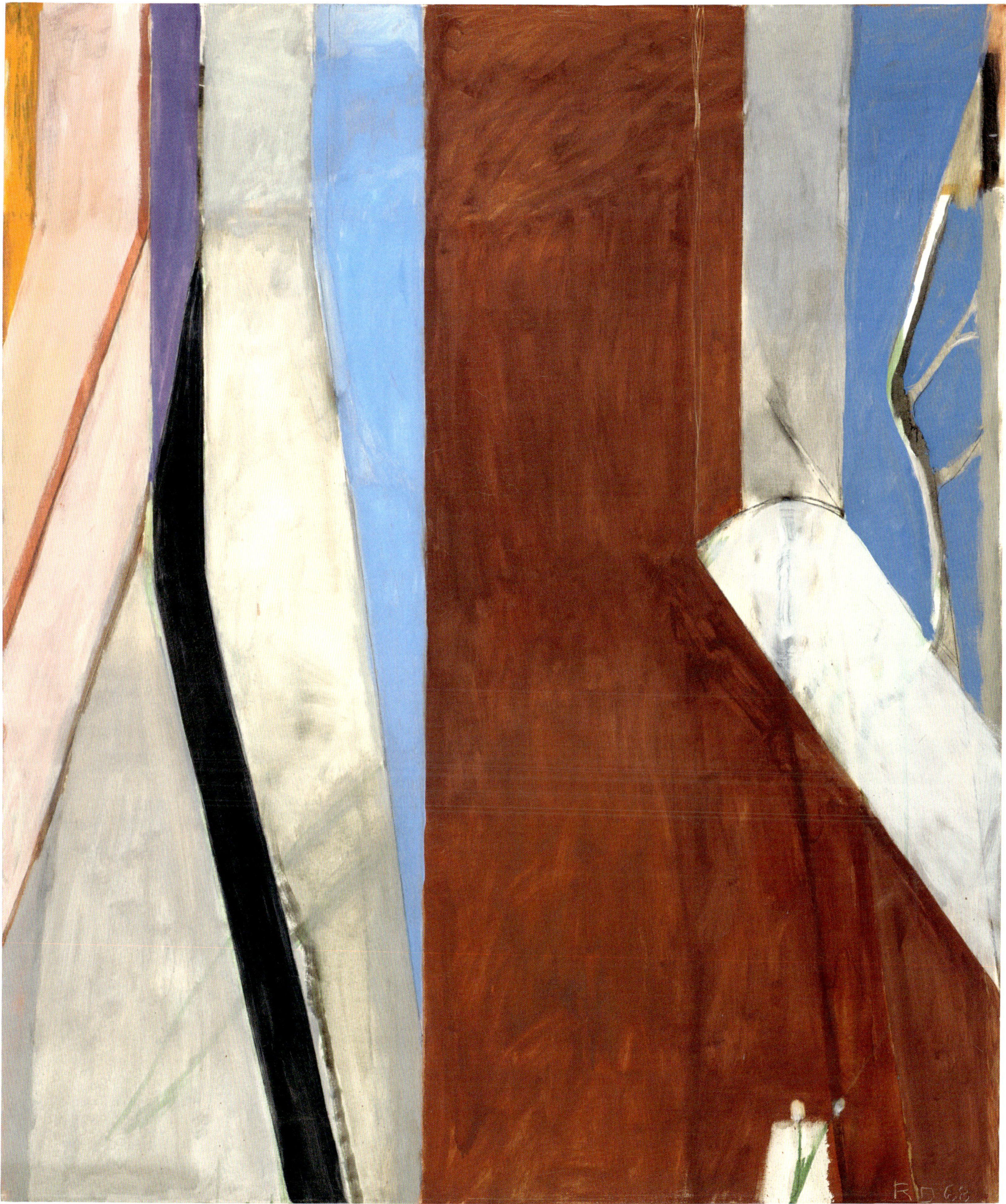
RD 68

Plate 91. Richard Diebenkorn, *Ocean Park #27*, 1970. Oil and charcoal on canvas, 100 x 80 in. (254 x 203.2 cm). Brooklyn Museum, gift of the Roebling Society and Mr. and Mrs. Charles H. Blatt and Mr. and Mrs. William K. Jacobs Jr.

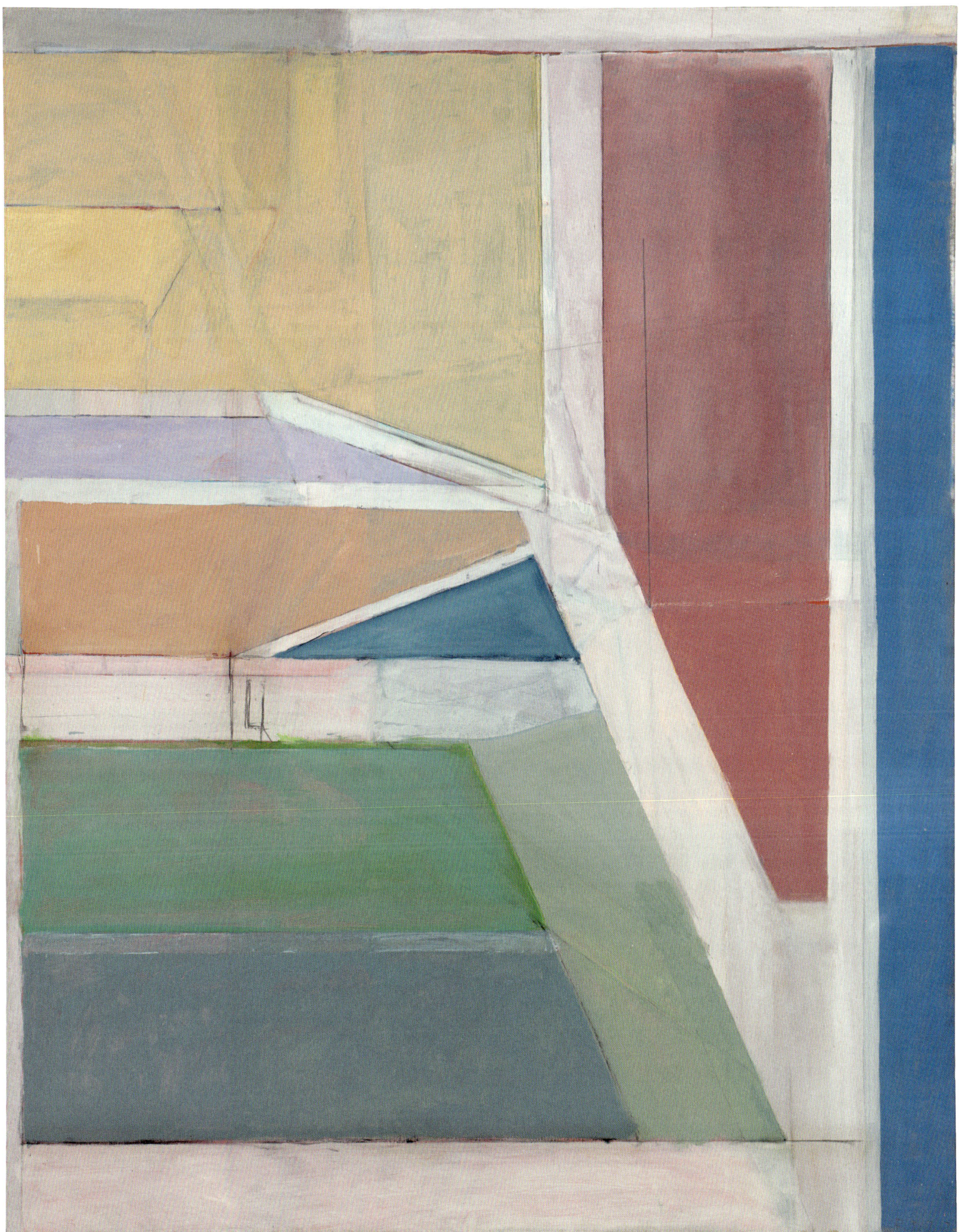

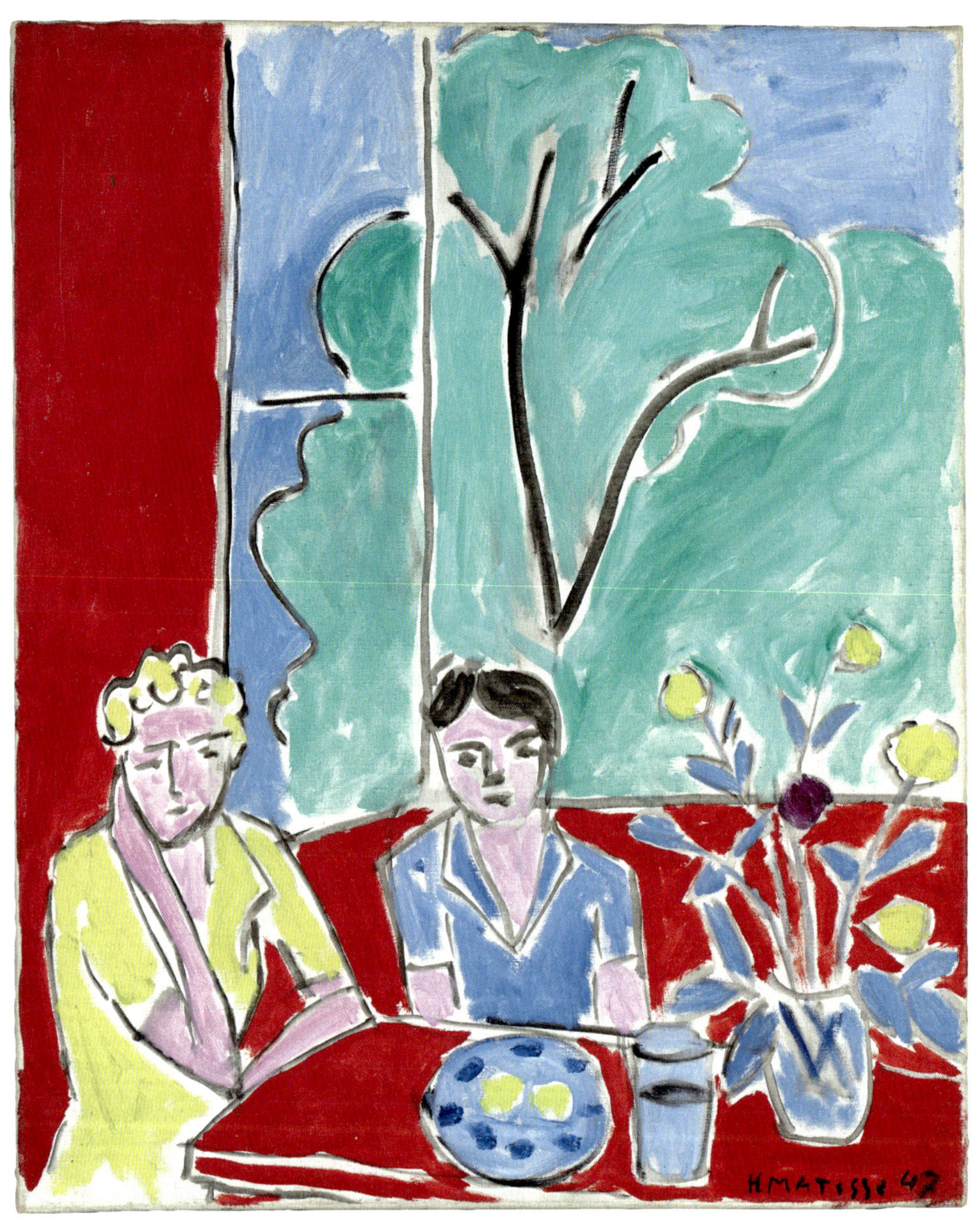

Plate 92. Henri Matisse, *Two Girls, Red and Green Background,* 1947.
Oil on canvas, 22⅛ x 18¼ in. (56.2 x 46.4 cm). The Baltimore Museum of Art: The Cone Collection, formed by Dr. Claribel Cone and Miss Etta Cone of Baltimore, Maryland

OPPOSITE
Plate 93. Richard Diebenkorn, *Ocean Park #29,* 1970. Oil and charcoal on canvas, 100⅛ x 81⅛ in. (254.3 x 206.1 cm). Dallas Museum of Art, gift of the Meadows Foundation, Incorporated

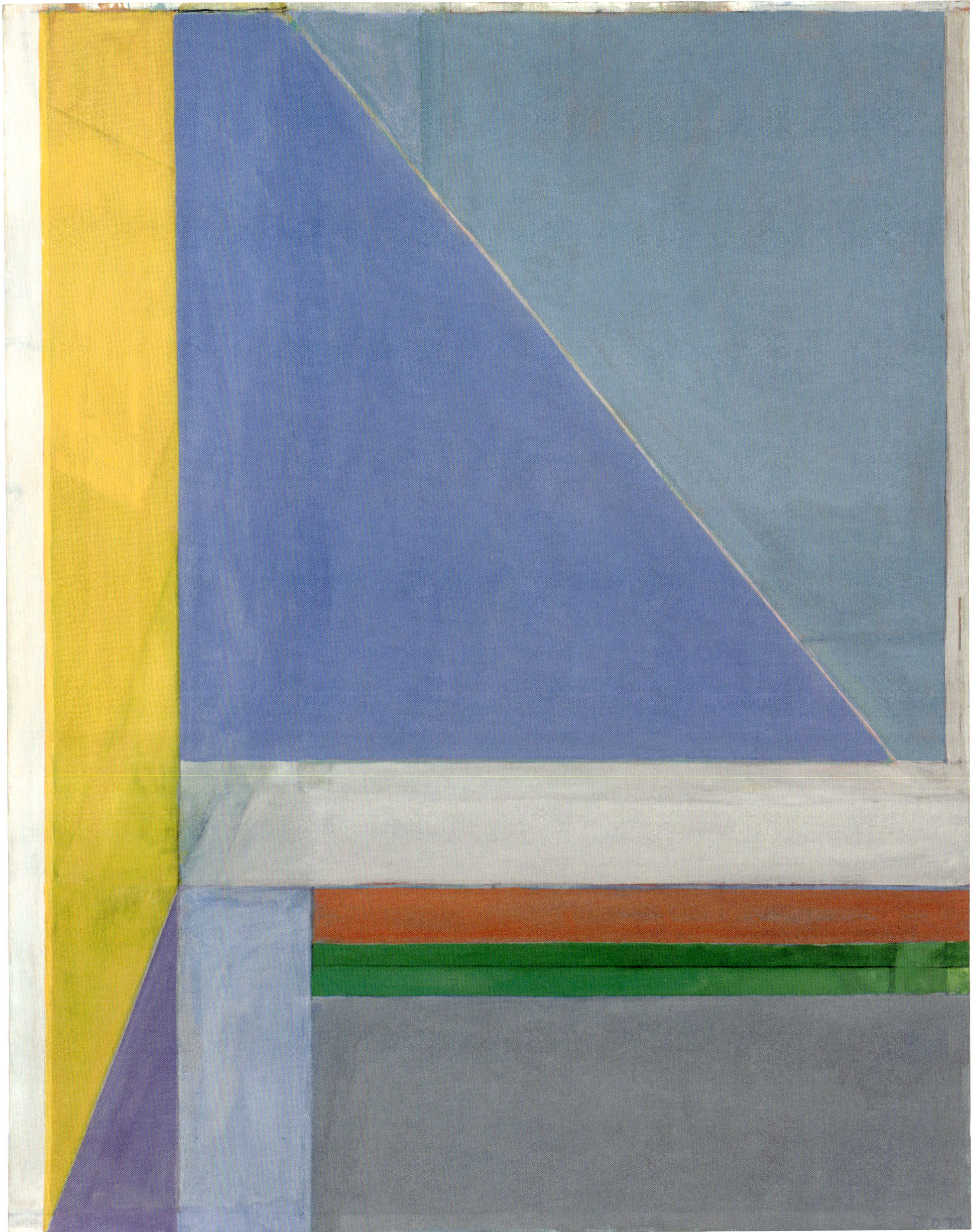

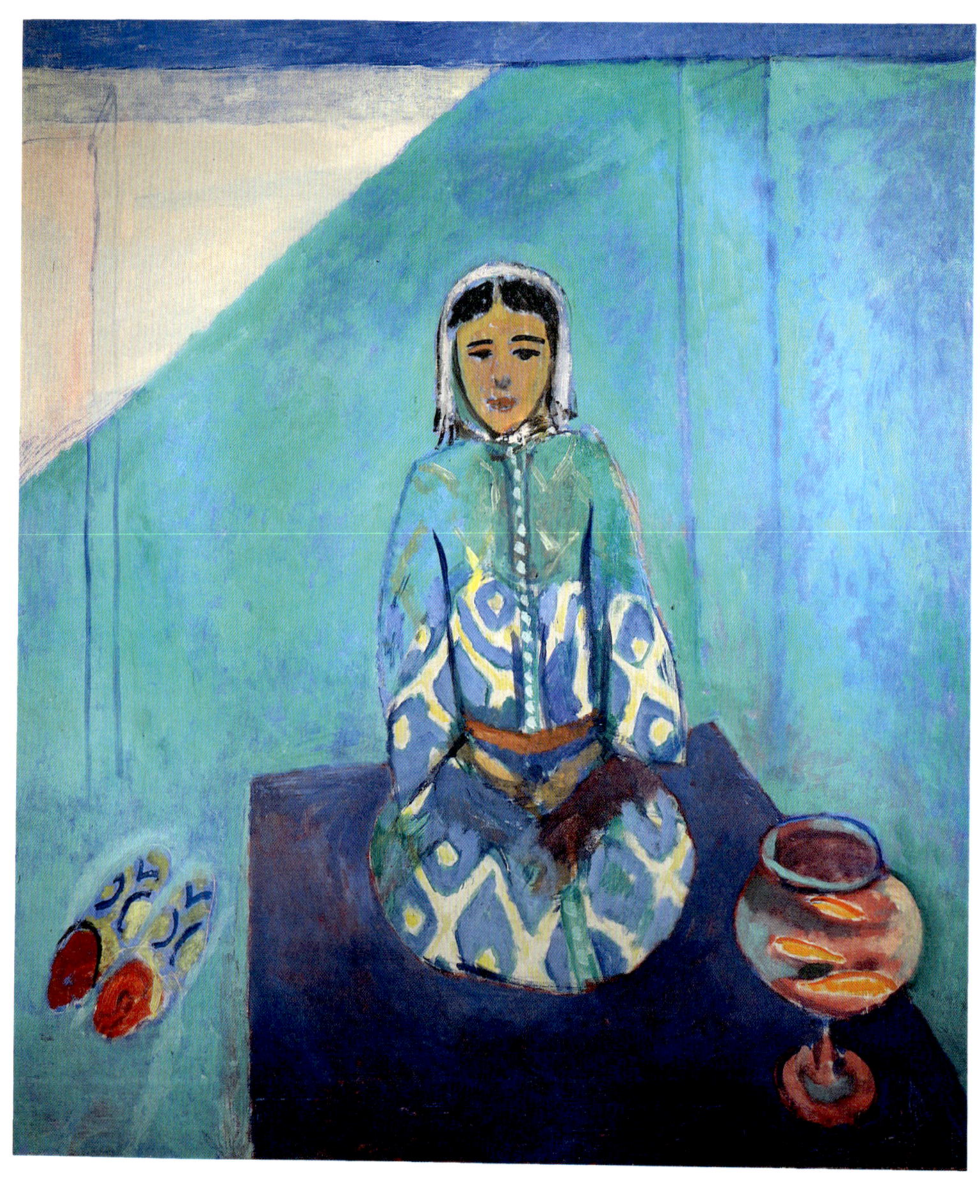

Plate 94. Henri Matisse, *On the Terrace,* 1912. Oil on canvas, 45¼ x 39⅛ in. (115 x 100 cm). The Pushkin State Museum of Fine Arts, Moscow

OPPOSITE
Plate 95. Richard Diebenkorn, *Ocean Park #54,* 1972. Oil and charcoal on canvas, 100 x 81 in. (254 x 205.7 cm). San Francisco Museum of Modern Art, gift of Friends of Gerald Nordland

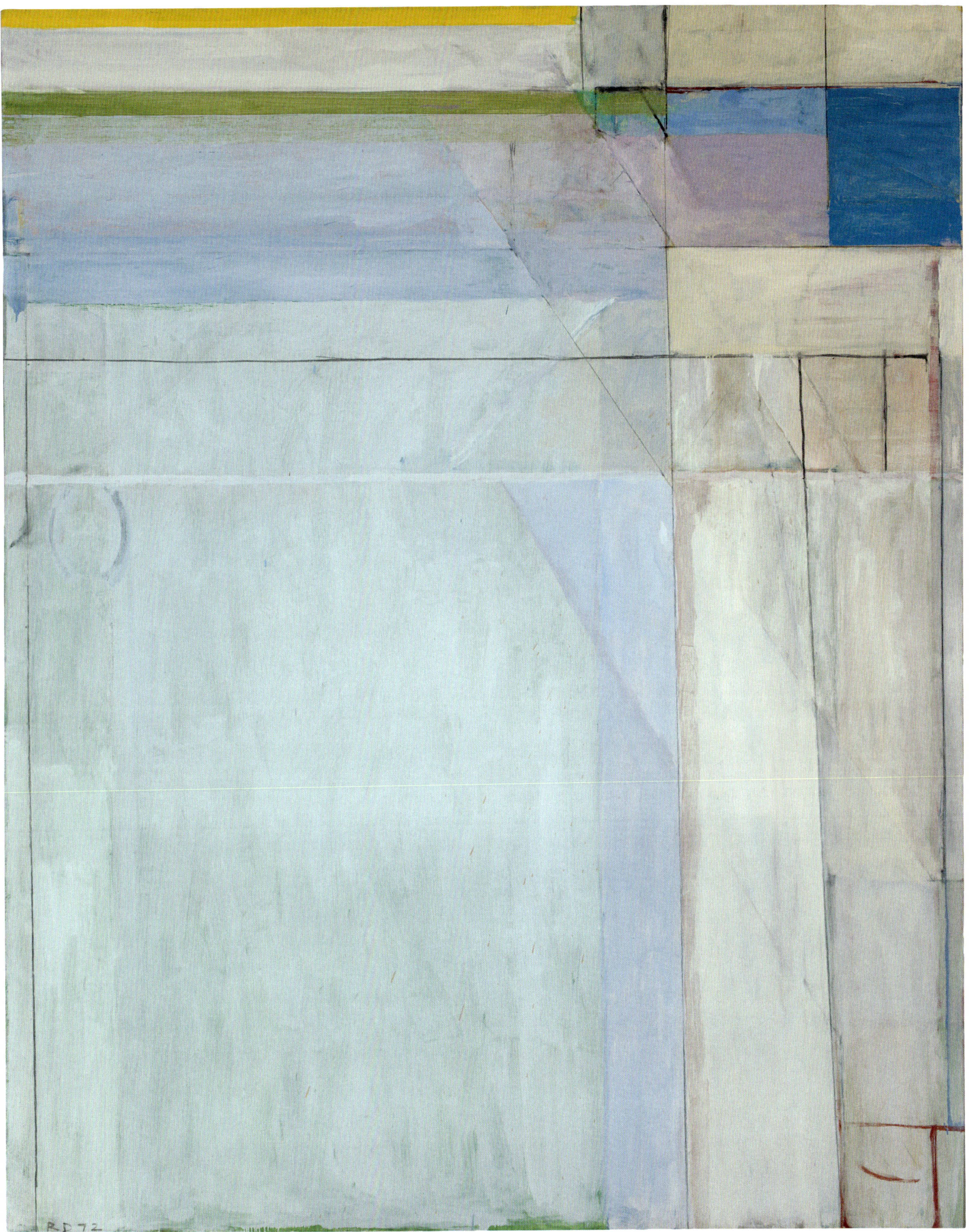

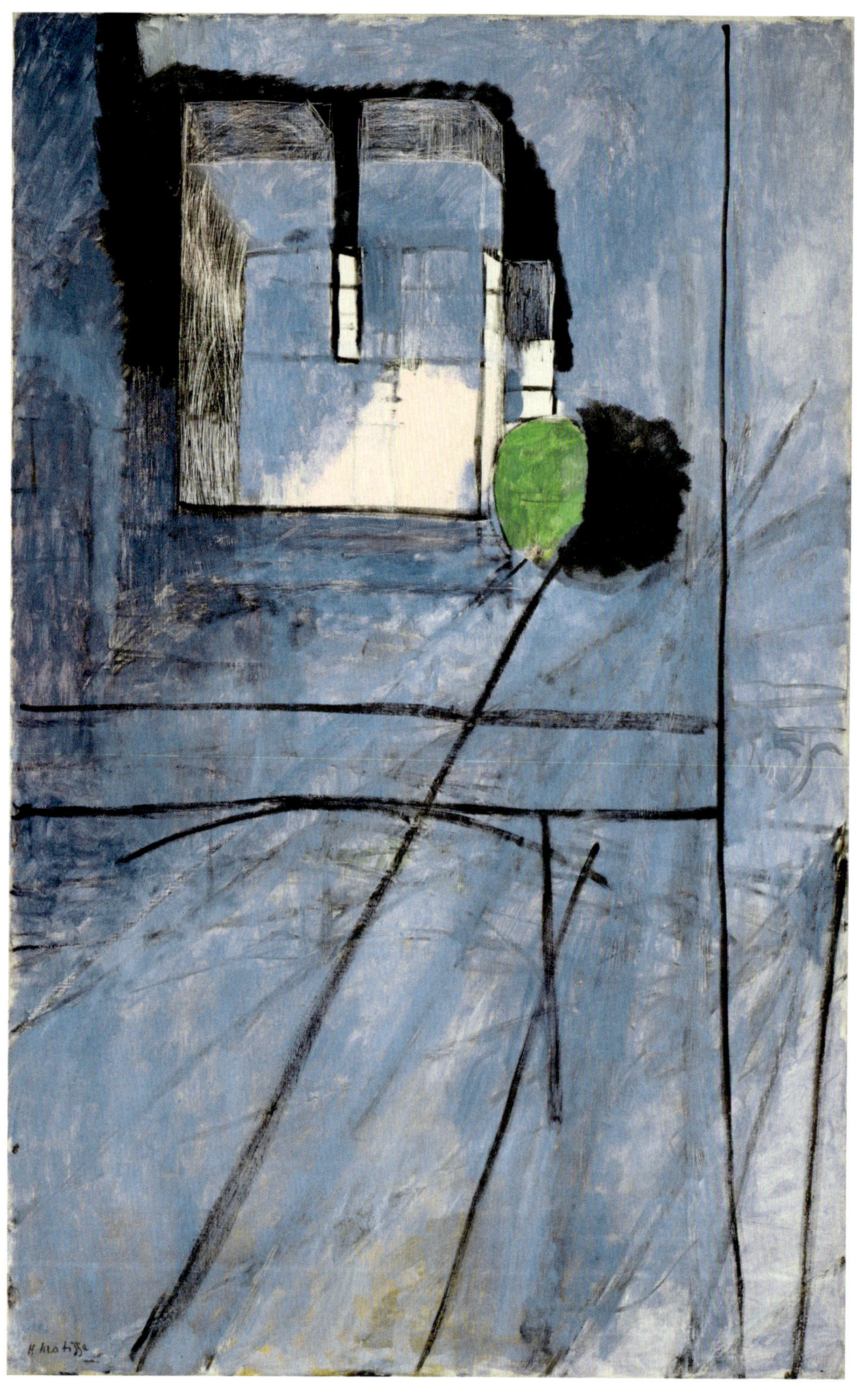

Plate 96. Henri Matisse, *View of Notre Dame,* 1914. Oil on canvas, 58 x 37⅛ in. (147.3 x 94.3 cm). The Museum of Modern Art, New York, acquired through the Lillie P. Bliss Bequest, and the Henry Ittleson, A. Conger Goodyear, Mr. and Mrs. Robert Sinclair Funds, and the Anna Erickson Levene Bequest given in memory of her husband, Dr. Phoebus Aaron Theodor Levene

OPPOSITE

Plate 97. Richard Diebenkorn, *Ocean Park #79,* 1975. Oil and charcoal on canvas, 93 x 81 in. (236.2 x 205.7 cm). Philadelphia Museum of Art, purchased with a grant from the National Endowment for the Arts and with funds contributed by private donors

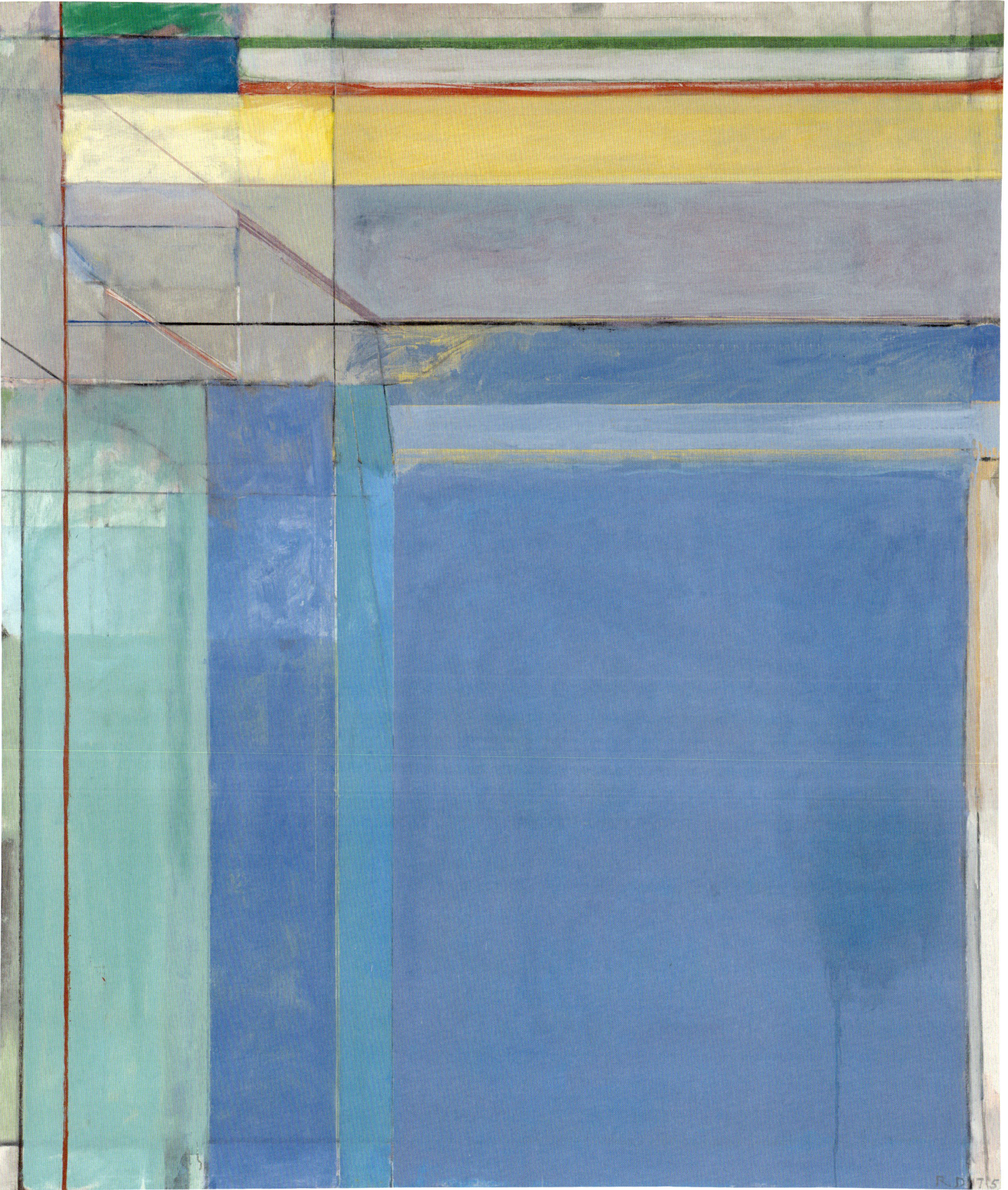

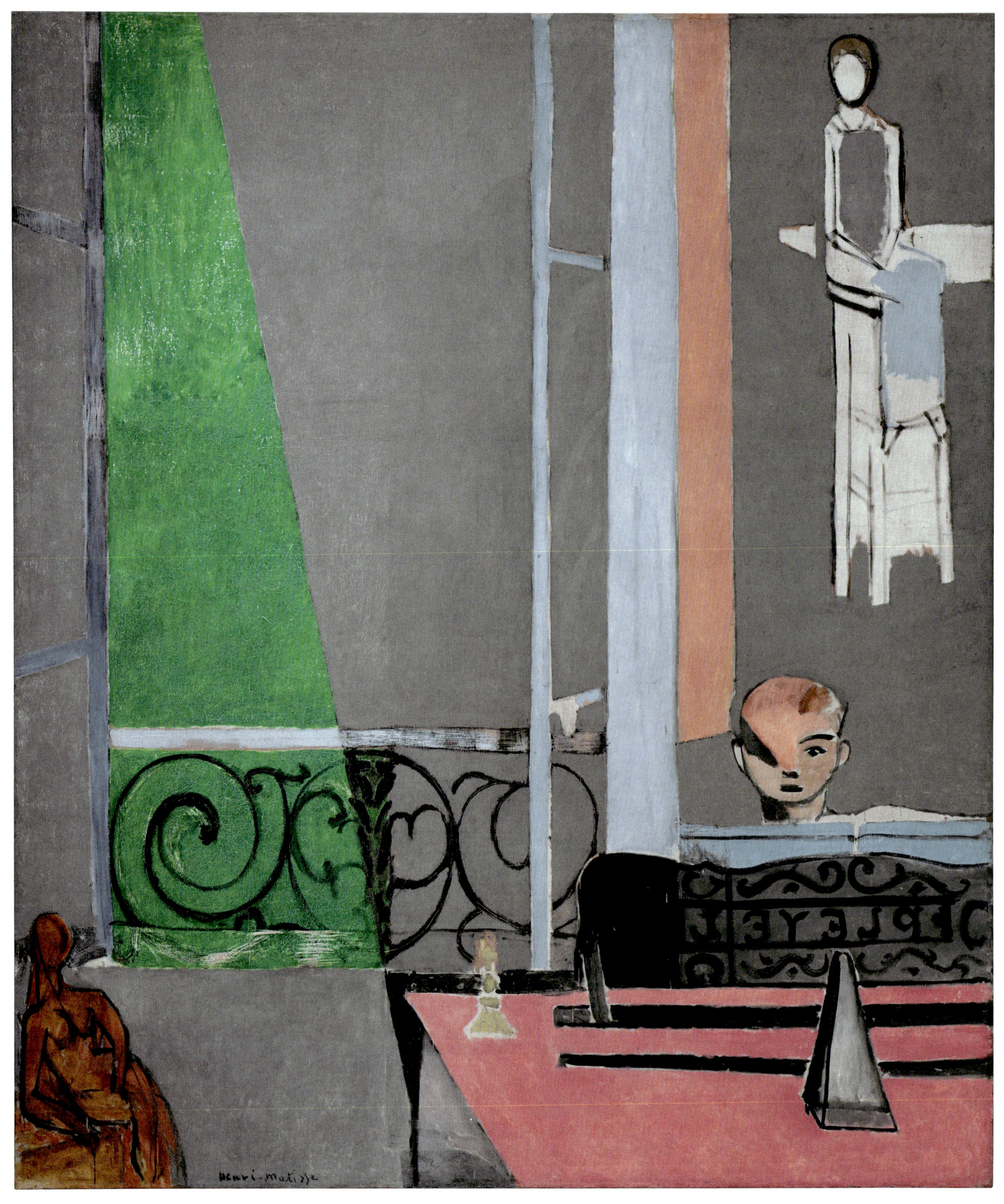

Plate 98. Henri Matisse, *The Piano Lesson,* 1916. Oil on canvas, 95¾ x 83 in. (245.1 x 212.7 cm).
The Museum of Modern Art, New York, Mrs. Simon Guggenheim Fund

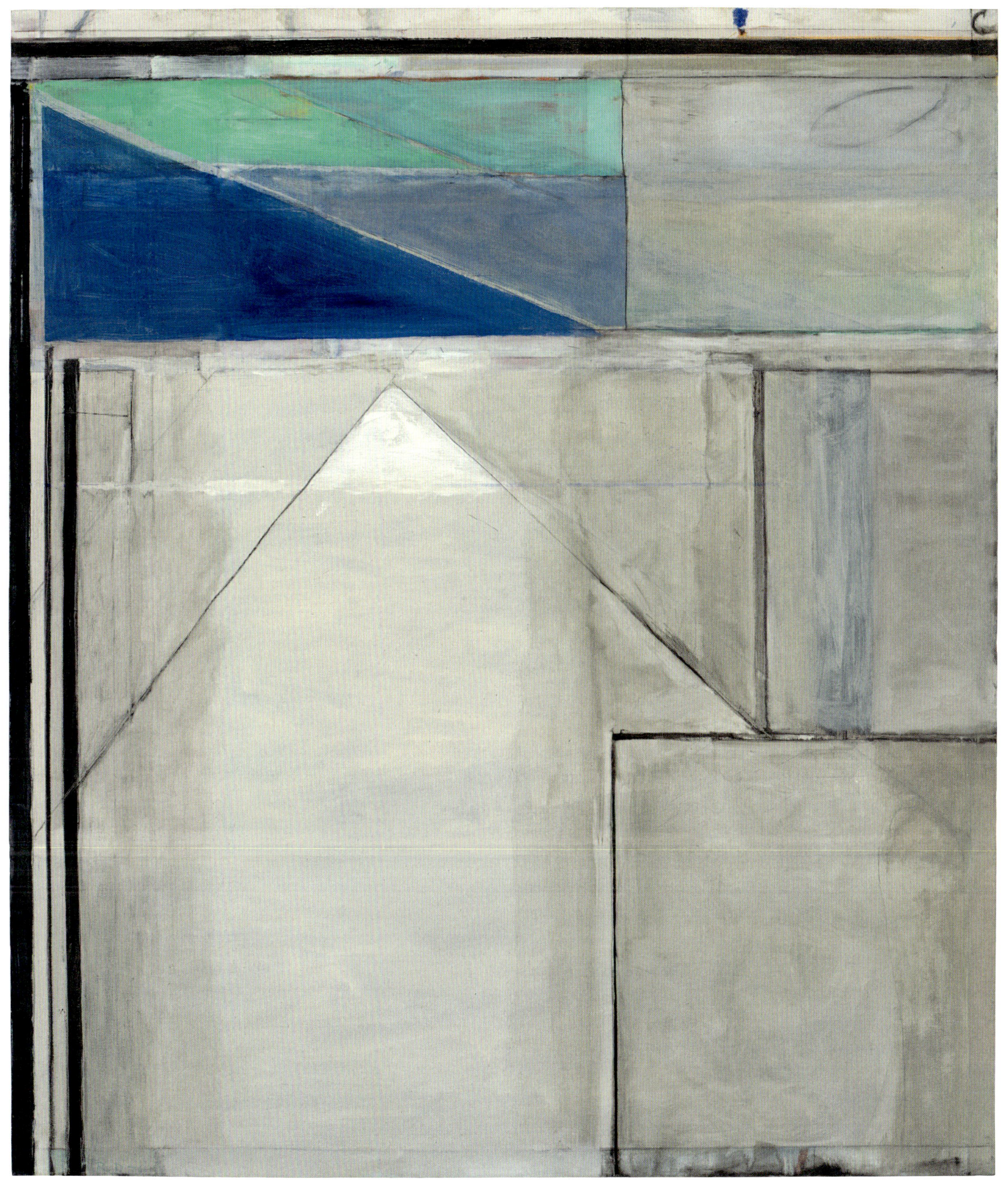

Plate 99. Richard Diebenkorn, *Ocean Park #94,* 1976. Oil and charcoal on canvas, 93⅛ x 81⅛ in. (236.5 x 206.1 cm). Iris & B. Gerald Cantor Center for Visual Arts at Stanford University, Stanford, California, gift of Phyllis G. Diebenkorn

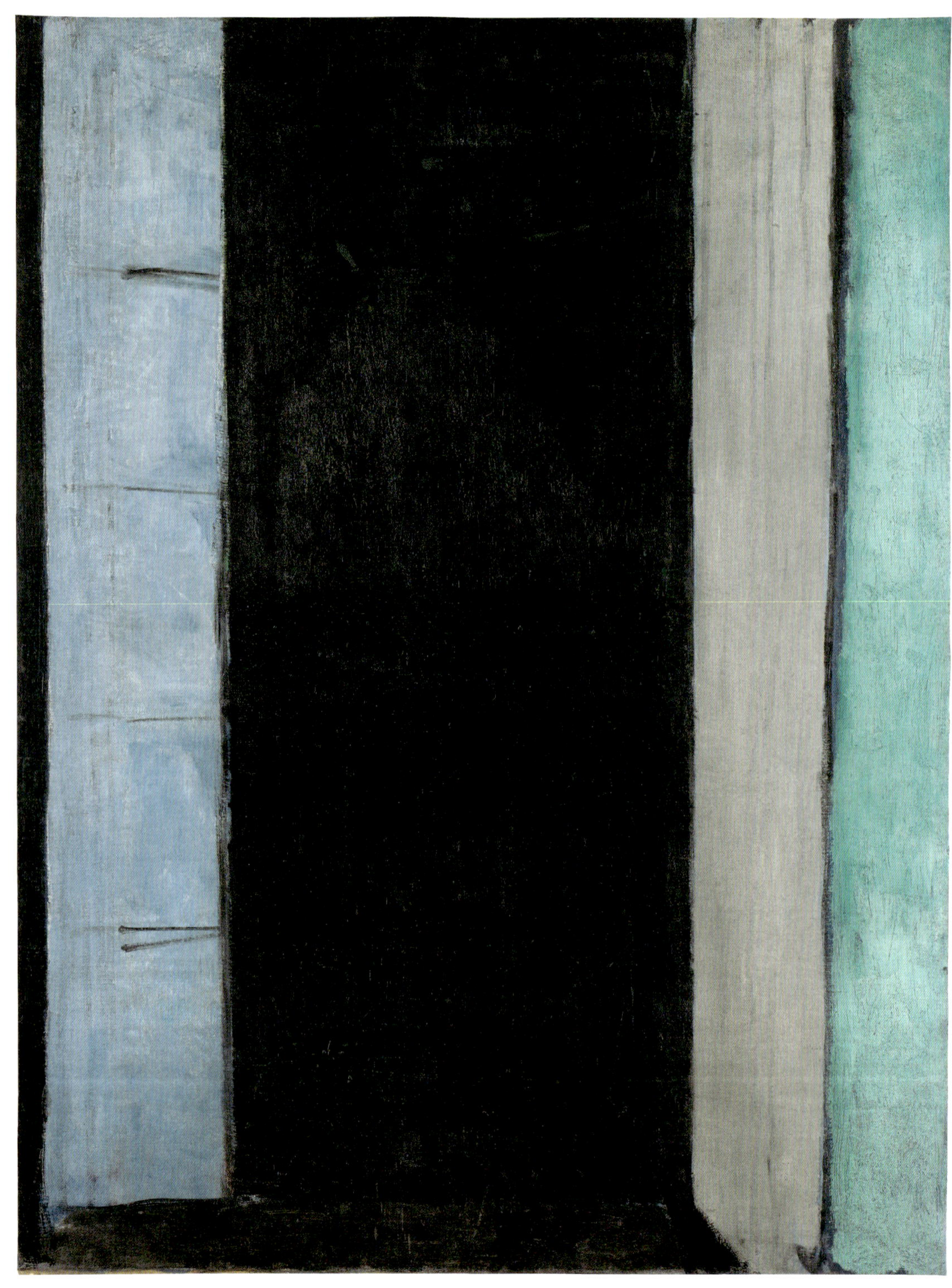

Plate 100. Henri Matisse, *French Window at Collioure,* 1914. Oil on canvas, 45⅞ x 35⅛ in. (116.5 x 89.2 cm). Musée national d'art moderne/Centre de création industrielle, Centre Georges Pompidou, Paris

OPPOSITE
Plate 101. Richard Diebenkorn, *Ocean Park #105,* 1978. Oil and charcoal on canvas, 100⅛ x 93⅛ in. (254.3 x 236.5 cm). Modern Art Museum of Fort Worth, museum purchase, Sid W. Richardson Foundation Endowment Fund and The Burnett Foundation

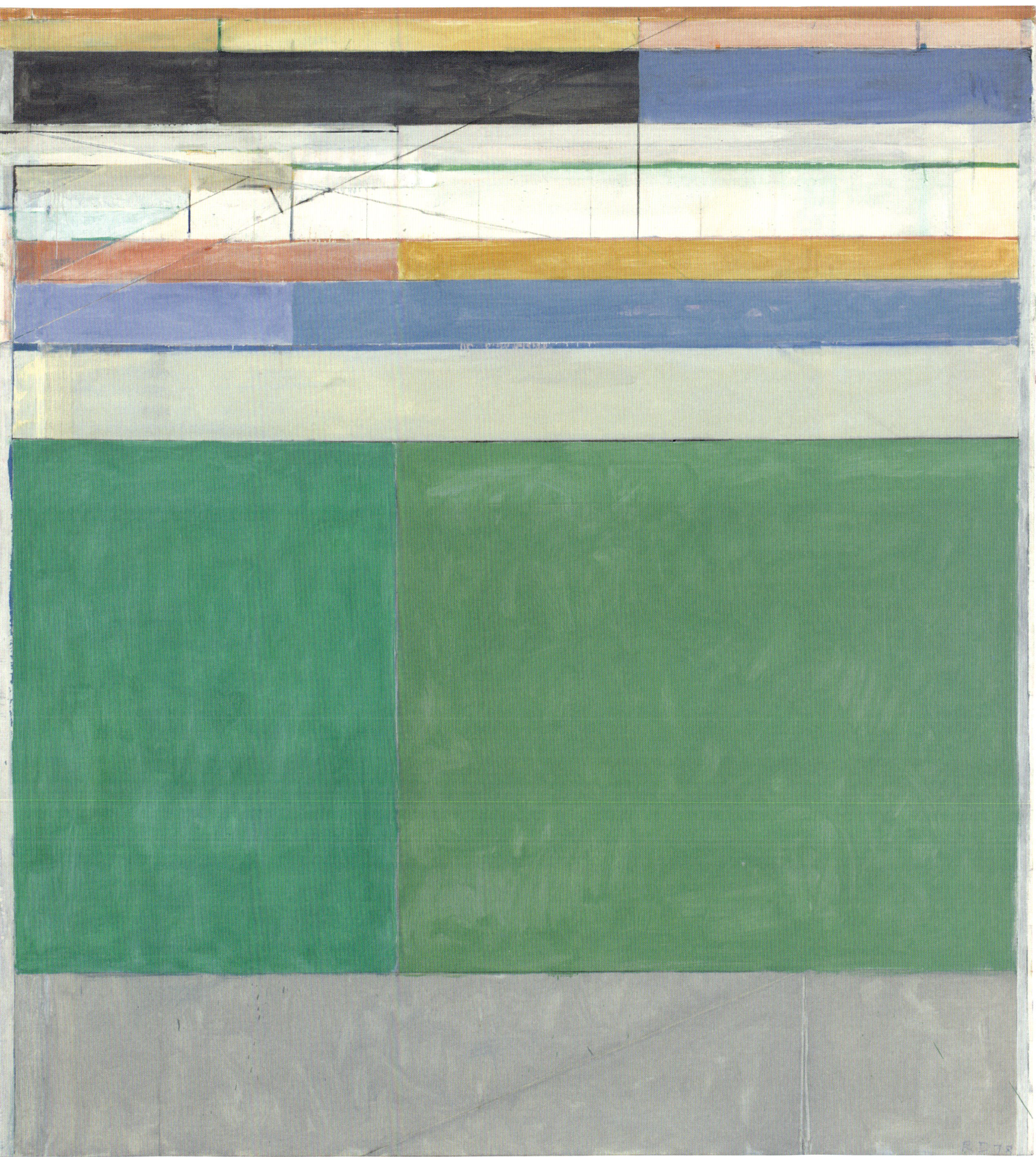

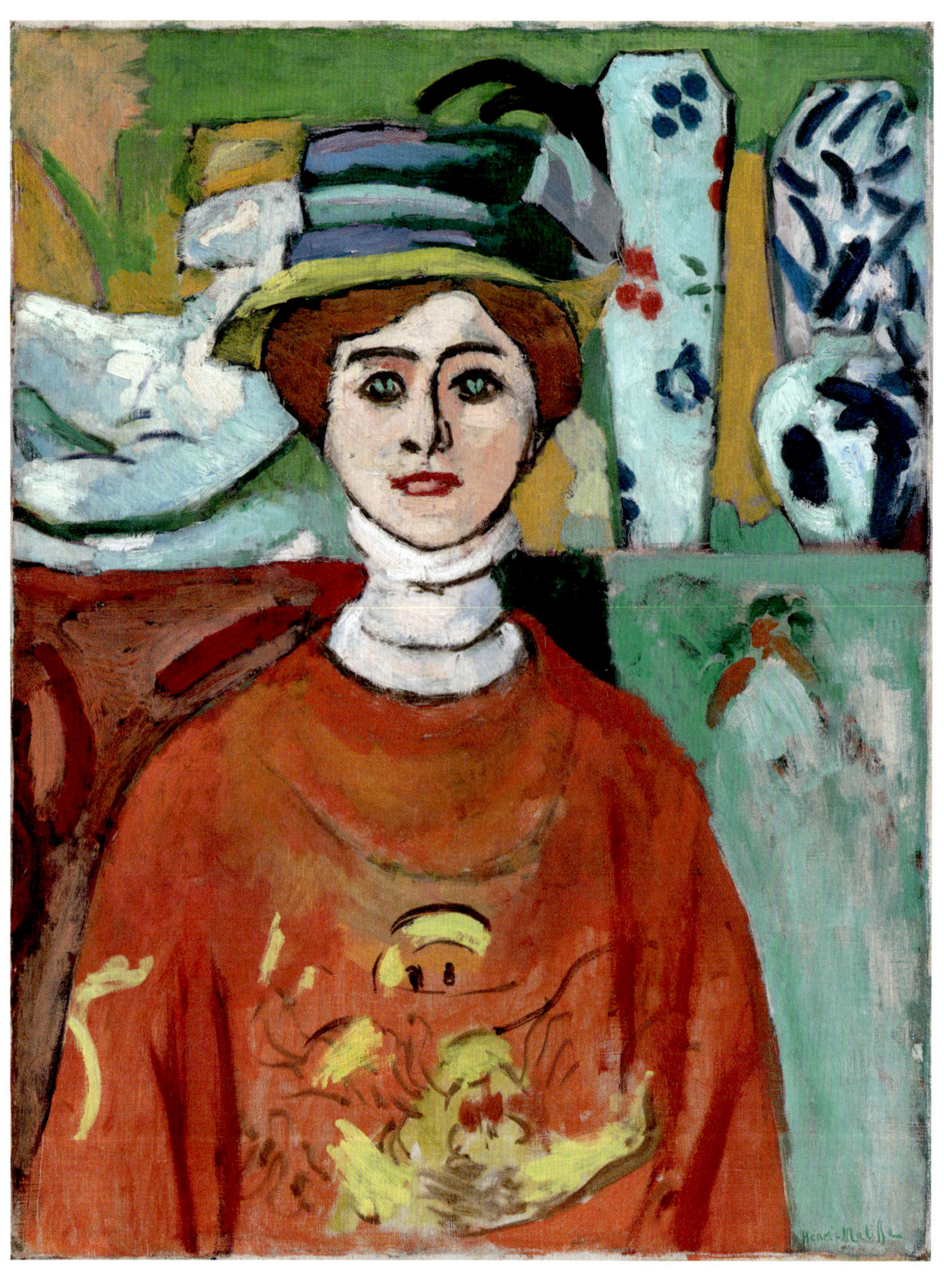

Plate 102. Henri Matisse, *The Girl with Green Eyes,* 1908. Oil on canvas, 26 x 20 in. (66 x 50.8 cm). San Francisco Museum of Modern Art, bequest of Harriet Lane Levy

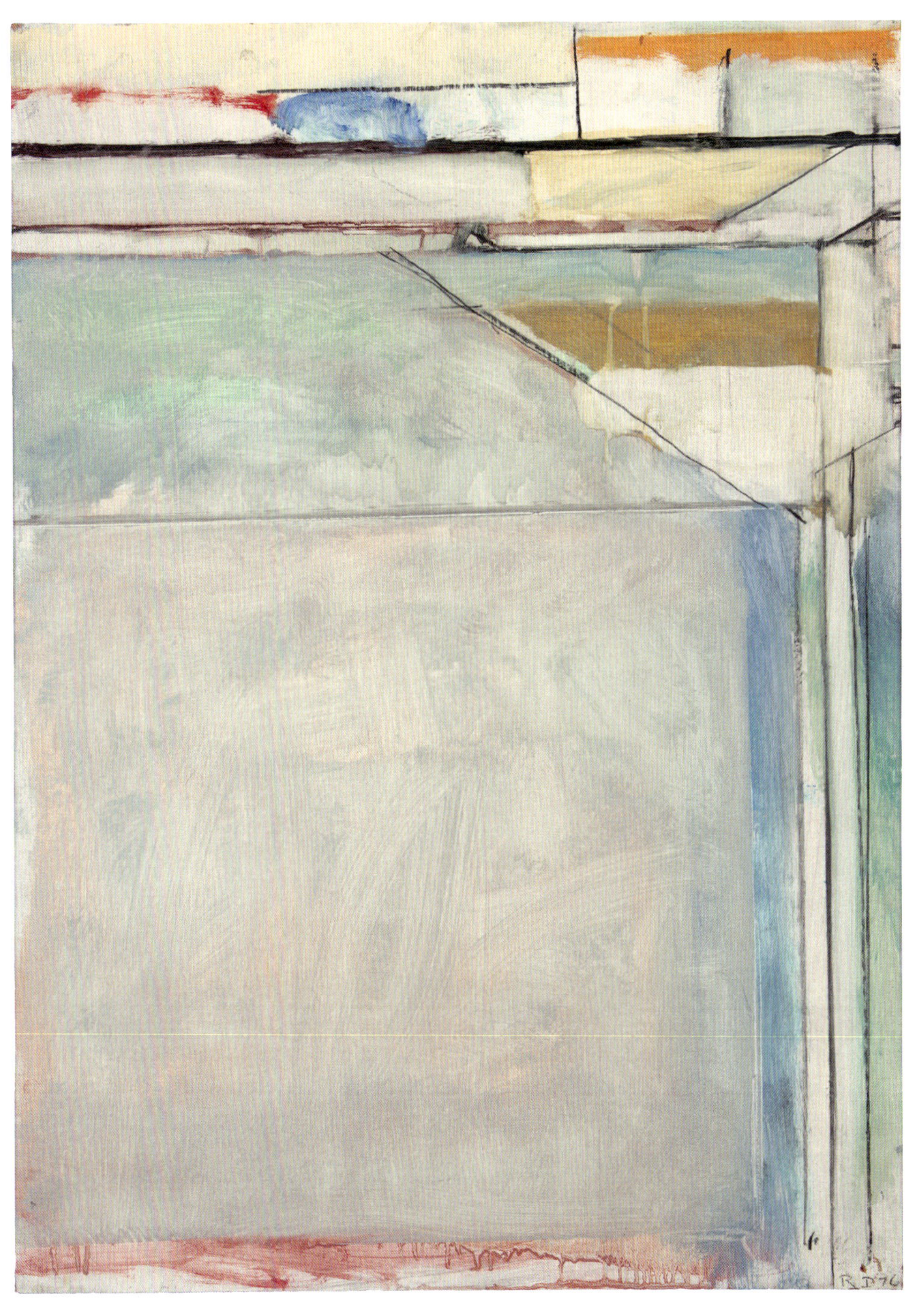

Plate 103. Richard Diebenkorn, *Ocean Park #93,* 1976. Oil on hardboard, 29 x 21 in. (73.7 x 53.3 cm). The Grant Family Collection

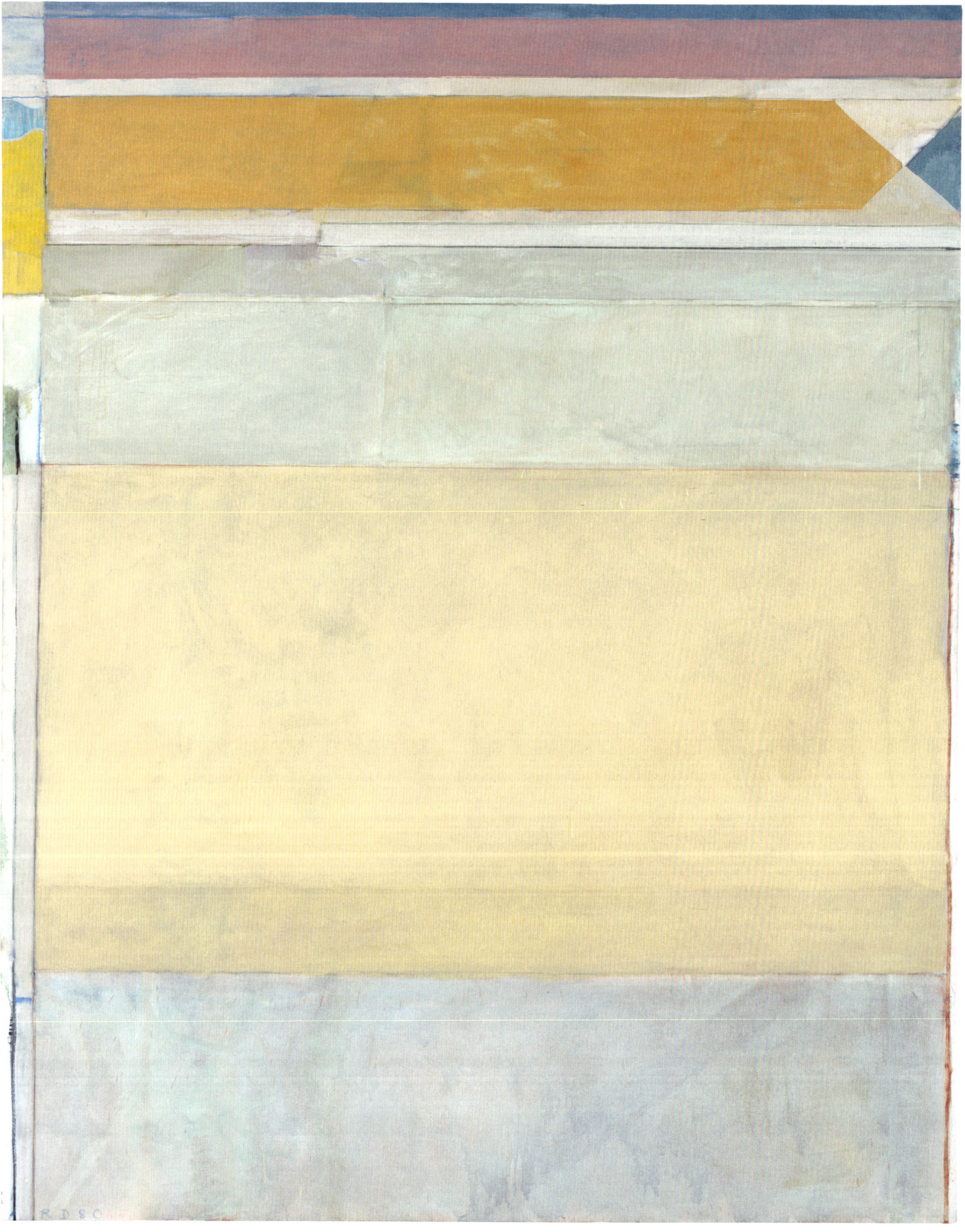
RD 80

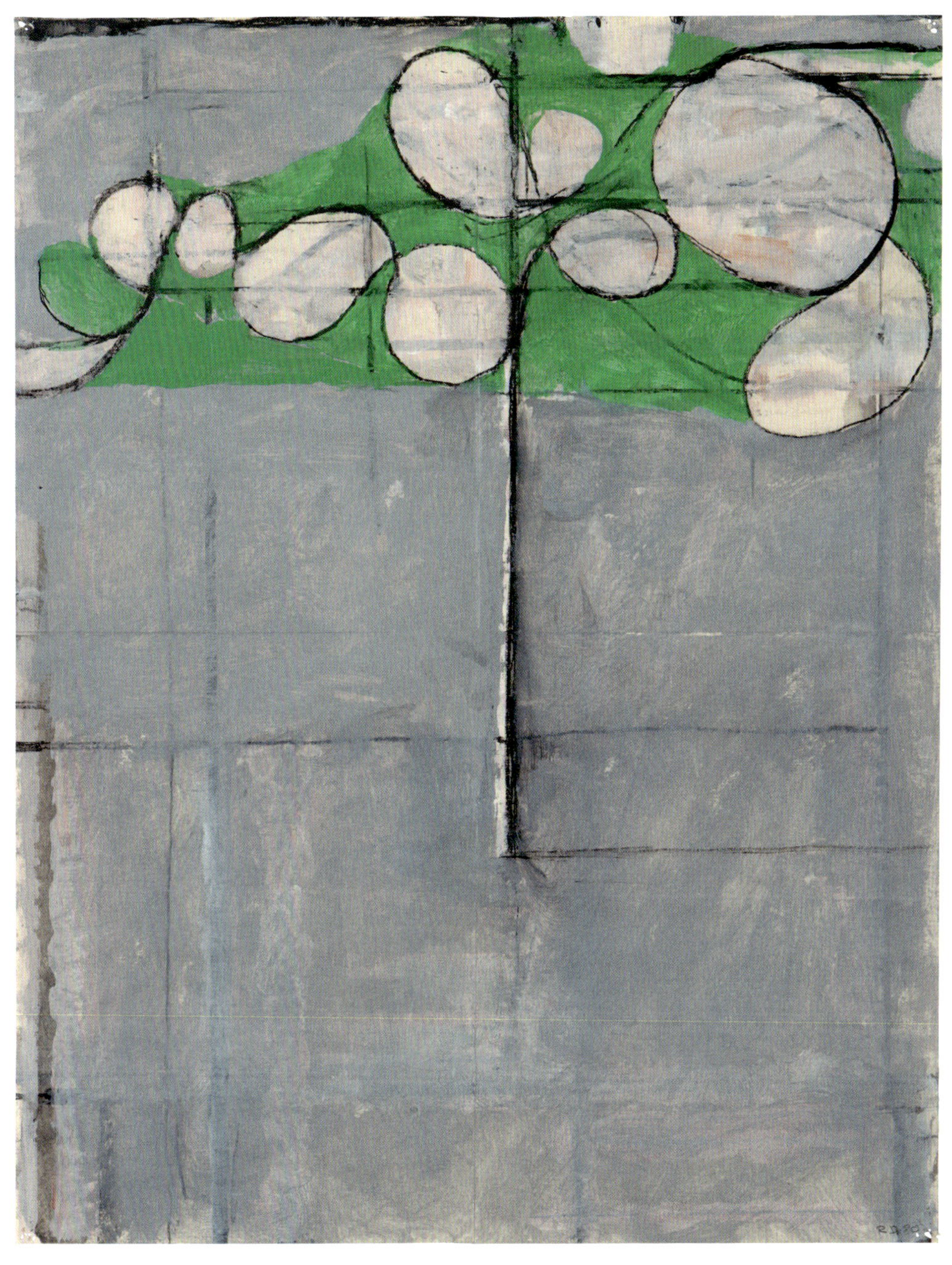

OPPOSITE

Plate 104. Richard Diebenkorn, *Ocean Park #122,* 1980. Oil and charcoal on canvas, 100¼ x 81¼ in. (254.6 x 206.4 cm). San Francisco Museum of Modern Art, Charles H. Land Family Foundation Fund purchase

Plate 105. Richard Diebenkorn, *Untitled,* 1980. Acrylic and charcoal on paper, 22⅜ x 17⅜ in. (56.8 x 44.1 cm). Estate of the artist

Richard Diebenkorn's Library: A Bibliography of Matisse Publications

Over the course of his lifetime, Richard Diebenkorn amassed dozens of publications on Henri Matisse—more than on any other artist. While Matisse, with his wife Amélie's approval, sold one of her rings to buy a *Bathers* painting by Paul Cézanne,[1] Diebenkorn did not set out to purchase Matisse's work for inspiration. Rather, he actively collected books about the artist to peruse and use as references. When Diebenkorn was interviewed for a major profile published in the *New Yorker* in 1987, he moved with great familiarity through two of the Matisse monographs in his personal art library, discussing images he found especially compelling.[2]

The first Matisse book Diebenkorn recalled purchasing was Alfred H. Barr Jr.'s *Matisse: His Art and His Public* (1951), in 1954, which he noted as being "probably the most important to [him]—in [the] '50s anyhow."[3] From that point forward, the artist explained, "I've been continually on the alert for new publications and don't think I've missed many."[4] As inscriptions and cards inserted into many of Diebenkorn's Matisse books reveal, friends and family members often gave the volumes to him as gifts. His wife, Phyllis, was always pleased when a new catalogue was published in time for Christmas.[5]

These publications were essential to Diebenkorn's ongoing connection with Matisse, allowing him to examine images of many paintings and drawings he had not been able to see in person and to refresh his memories of those he had. Though sometimes Diebenkorn consulted the books in his studio, it was more typical for him to pore over them in the evening after a day's work, while relaxing in an armchair with a drink in hand.

Diebenkorn's Matisse publications show varying degrees of wear. He used Barr's volume, especially, as a scrapbook. As he encountered reproductions of Matisse works that were not already among its plates or color images of works pictured in black and white, the artist glued them onto blank pages for ready access, sometimes adding titles and dimensions. The books are also filled with loose inserts, including postcards, notes, articles, reviews, restaurant cards, and shopping lists, some of which were undoubtedly tucked between their pages by Phyllis after her husband's passing.

The *Matisse/Diebenkorn* curators, with the assistance of curatorial team members Jared Ledesma and Kate Mendillo, reviewed these publications while conducting research for the exhibition at both the Diebenkorn residence in Healdsburg, California, and the Richard Diebenkorn Foundation archives in San Francisco. We extend our thanks to the late Phyllis Diebenkorn, Gretchen Diebenkorn Grant, Richard Grant, Carl Schmitz, and Pennington Ahlstrand for facilitating our visits.

The following list documents the books in Diebenkorn's Matisse library. They are organized by publication date, suggesting an approximate order in which the artist might have obtained and begun using them. For consistency, the volumes from the 1920s and 1930s appear first, though they were certainly acquired decades after they were published.

Janet Bishop, Jared Ledesma, and Katherine Rothkopf

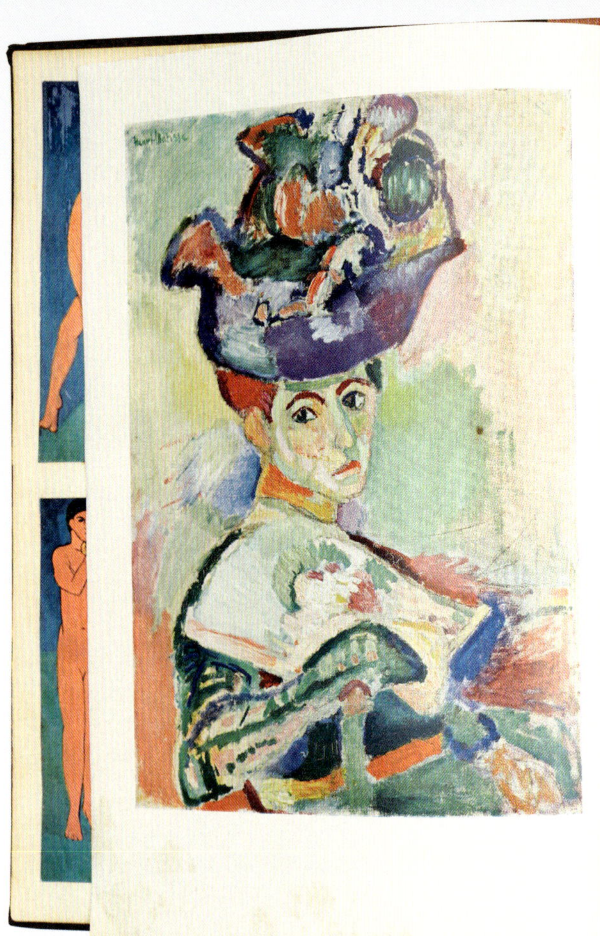

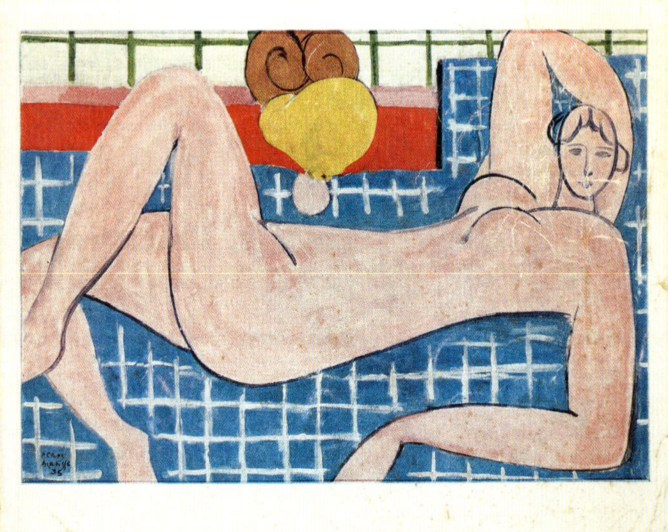

Alfred H. Barr Jr., *Matisse: His Art and His Public,* 1951. Richard Diebenkorn Foundation archives

Jean Leymarie, Herbert Read, and William S. Lieberman, *Henri Matisse: Retrospective, 1966,* 1966. Richard Diebenkorn Foundation archives

George, Waldemar. *Henri-Matisse: Dessins*. Paris: Éditions des quatre chemins, 1925.

Owner's signature, front flyleaf, top right: "R Diebenkorn"
Given by Diebenkorn to the curator John Elderfield, 1983[6]

Fry, Roger. *Henri-Matisse*. Paris: Éditions des chroniques du jour; New York: E. Weyhe, 1930.

Formerly in the collection of the Anne Bremer Memorial Library, California School of Fine Arts (now the San Francisco Art Institute)

Cassou, Jean. *Paintings and Drawings of Matisse*. Paris: Les éditions Braun; New York: Tudor Publishing, 1939.

Owner's signature, front flyleaf, top right: "R Diebenkorn"

Barr, Alfred H., Jr. *Matisse: His Art and His Public*. New York: The Museum of Modern Art, 1951.

Owner's signature, front flyleaf, top right: "R Diebenkorn"
Pasted inserts: color reproductions of Matisse works, including an unidentified painting of Pont Saint-Michel, Paris; *View of Notre Dame* (1902); *Guitarist* (1902–3); *Still Life* (1905); *Bathers with a Turtle* (1908); *Dance* (1909–10); *Music* (1910); *Large Landscape, Mont Alban* (1918); *The Painting Session* (1919); *The Painter and His Model: Studio Interior* (1921); and *Still Life, Pink Tablecloth, Vase of Anemones, Lemons, and Pineapple* (1925)

Lejard, André. *Matisse*. Paris: Fernand Hazan, 1952.

Owner's signature, inside cover, top right: "R Diebenkorn"

Lieberman, William S. *Etchings by Matisse*, exh. cat. New York: The Museum of Modern Art, 1955.

Portraits: Henri Matisse*. Monte Carlo, Monaco: André Sauret, 1955.

Owner's signature, inside cover, middle right: "R Diebenkorn"
Loose inserts: note from Diebenkorn's wife, Phyllis, undated, alongside Matisse's *The Girl with Green Eyes* (1908), "Surprise Happy Birthday and Love P G D"; postcard from Diebenkorn's daughter, Gretchen, dated 1987, Paris, featuring a photograph of Matisse in his studio; excerpt from an unidentified magazine article on Matisse; color reproductions of Matisse's *Nasturtiums with the Painting "Dance" I* (1912), *View of Notre Dame* (1914), and *Anemones and Mirror* (1920, with a color reproduction of an unidentified Pierre Bonnard still life on the back)

***Henri Matisse: Jazz*. Munich: R. Piper & Co. Verlag, 1957.**

Two copies in Diebenkorn's library

Diehl, Gaston. *Henri Matisse*. Paris: Éditions Pierre Tisné; New York: Universe Books, 1958.

Owner's signature, inside cover, top right: "R Diebenkorn"
Pasted insert: color reproduction of Matisse's *The Terrace, Saint-Tropez* (1904)
Loose insert: Christmas card from *Vogue* magazine, undated, featuring details of Matisse's *The Virgin and Child* (1948–49) and *Tree* (1951)

Barnes, Albert C., and Violette de Mazia. *The Art of Henri Matisse*. Merion, PA: Barnes Foundation Press, 1959.

Lassaigne, Jacques. *Matisse: Biographical and Critical Study*. Geneva: Éditions d'art Albert Skira, 1959.

Owner's signature, front flyleaf, top right: "R Diebenkorn"

Escholier, Raymond. *Matisse, from the Life*. London: Faber and Faber, 1960.

Wheeler, Monroe. *The Last Works of Henri Matisse: Large Cut Gouaches*, exh. cat. New York: The Museum of Modern Art, 1961.

Matisse, Henri. *Chapelle du Rosaire des Dominicaines de Vence*. Vence, France: Chapelle du Rosaire, 1963.

Owner's signature, title page, top right: "Diebenkorn"

Leymarie, Jean, Herbert Read, and William S. Lieberman. *Henri Matisse: Retrospective, 1966*, exh. cat. Berkeley and Los Angeles: University of California Press, 1966.

Owner's signature, inside cover, top right: "R Diebenkorn"

***Henri Matisse, 1869–1954: Drawings*, exh. cat. London: Victor Waddington Galleries, 1967.**

Gowing, Lawrence. *Matisse, 1869–1954: A Retrospective Exhibition at the Hayward Gallery*, exh. cat. London: Arts Council of Great Britain, 1968.

Owner's signature, inside cover, top center: "R Diebenkorn"

Di San Lazzaro, G., ed. *Homage to Henri Matisse*. Special issue of *XXe siècle*. New York: Tudor Publishing, 1970.

Owner's signature, front flyleaf, top right: "R Diebenkorn"
Book jacket flipped inside out
Taped insert: note from Gretchen and her family, undated, written on a Brentano's bookstore stationery card and attached inside cover, "Love and Merry Christmas from Gretchen, Dick, P[hyllis] and [Ben]"

Finsen, Hanne, Denys Sutton, and Pierre Soulages. *Matisse: En retrospektiv udstilling*, exh. cat. Copenhagen: Statens Museum for Kunst, 1970.

***Henri Matisse: Reproductions*. 2 vols. Paris: Grand Palais, 1970.**

Carlson, Victor I. *Matisse as a Draughtsman*, exh. cat. Baltimore: The Baltimore Museum of Art, 1971.

Meyer, Franz. *Henri Matisse: Zwanzig auserlesene Werke: Eröffnungsausstellung (Henri Matisse: Twenty Important Paintings: Inaugural Exhibition)*, exh. cat. Zurich and New York: Marlborough Galerie, 1971.

Aragon, Louis. *Henri Matisse: A Novel*. 2 vols. New York: Harcourt Brace Jovanovich, 1972.

Owner's signature and date, front flyleaf, top right, both volumes: "R Diebenkorn / 9.19.77"

Greenberg, Clement. *Henri Matisse*, exh. cat. New York: Acquavella Galleries, 1973.

Jacobus, John. *Henri Matisse*. New York: Harry N. Abrams, 1973.

Owner's signature, front flyleaf, top right: "R Diebenkorn"
Book jacket flipped inside out
Loose inserts: postcard from former San Francisco Museum of Art (now the San Francisco Museum of Modern Art) director Gerald Nordland, dated September 5, 1975, featuring a color reproduction of Matisse's *Nude Study in Blue* (ca. 1899–1900) and a discussion of the Matisse works Nordland saw during his visit to the Tate, London; postcards featuring color reproductions of Matisse's *Purple Robe and Anemones* (1937) and *Young Girl with Anemones on a Purple Background* (1944)

***Art in America* 63, no. 4 (July–August 1975).**

Special issue on Matisse

Cowart, Jack, Jack D. Flam, Dominique Fourcade, et al. *Henri Matisse: Paper Cut-Outs*, exh. cat. Saint Louis: Saint Louis Art Museum; Detroit: Detroit Institute of Arts, 1977.

Inscription, front flyleaf: "To Phyllis + Dick / Merry Christmas 1977, John Berggruen"

Elderfield, John. *Matisse in The Collection of the Museum of Modern Art*. New York: The Museum of Modern Art, 1978.

Owner's signature, front flyleaf, top right: "Diebenkorn"

Wadley, Nicholas. *An Important Exhibition of Works by Henri Matisse*, exh. cat. London: Marlborough Fine Art, 1978.

Lassaigne, Jacques. *Matisse*. Paris: Éditions de vergeures, 1981.

Baumann, Felix, Margrit Hahnloser-Ingold, and Klaus Schrenk. *Henri Matisse*, exh. cat. Zurich: Kunsthaus Zürich/Städtische Kunsthalle Düsseldorf, 1982.

Loose inserts: card from a restaurant in Düsseldorf, used as a bookmark; notecard from Diebenkorn's friends Bill and Roselle Davenport, undated, "Merry Xmas dear Dick & Phyllis and a reunion in the new year / Love, B & R"; exhibition review (John Russell, "Even Now, Fresh Insights into Matisse," *New York Times*, January 2, 1983, H1); color reproduction of Matisse's *Portrait of Auguste Pellerin (II)* (1917)

***XIX and XX Century Master Paintings*, exh. cat. New York: Acquavella Galleries, 1982.**

Elderfield, John. *The Drawings of Henri Matisse*, exh. cat. New York: The Museum of Modern Art in association with the Arts Council of Great Britain, 1984.

Loose insert: card from the author, undated, "With compliments of John Elderfield"

***XIX and XX Century Master Drawings and Watercolors*, exh. cat. New York: Acquavella Galleries, 1984.**

Schneider, Pierre. *Matisse*. New York: Rizzoli, 1984.

Loose inserts: excerpt from an article on Matisse (John Russell, "Final Flowering of Henri Matisse, Invincible Artist," *Smithsonian Studies in American Art* 8, no. 6 [1977]); invitation from The Phillips Collection, Washington, D.C., to the member preview for its 1988–89 exhibition *The Pastoral Landscape*, featuring a color reproduction of Matisse's *By the Sea* (1904) on the front; black-and-white reproduction of Matisse's *Large Odalisque in Striped Pantaloons* (1925)

Bell, Tiffany. *After Matisse*, exh. cat. New York: Independent Curators Incorporated, 1986.

Cowart, Jack, and Dominique Fourcade. *Henri Matisse: The Early Years in Nice, 1916–1930*, exh. cat. Washington, D.C.: National Gallery of Art, 1986.

Flam, Jack. *Matisse: The Man and His Art, 1869–1918*. Ithaca, NY, and London: Cornell University Press, 1986.

Delectorskaya, Lydia. *With Apparent Ease . . . Henri Matisse: Paintings from 1935–1939*. Paris: Adrien Maeght éditeur, 1988.

Loose inserts: bookmark on pages with Matisse's studies for *Nymph in the Forest (Greenery)* (1935–42/43); bookmark on pages with Matisse's ink studies of female nudes (1936)

Monod-Fontaine, Isabelle, Anne Baldassari, and Claude Laugier. *Matisse: Oeuvres de Henri Matisse*, exh. cat. Paris: Centre Georges Pompidou, 1989.

Loose inserts: card from John Elderfield and his then-wife, the painter Jill Moser, "for Dick / with fondest regards, Christmas 1989, and with best wishes for a great New Year and new decade of painting"; bookmark on a page with the drawing *Study for the Portrait of Madame Colette* (1950); bookmark at the introduction to the sculpture section; Christmas card signed "Trixie" (MoMA assistant curator Beatrice Kearnan), undated

---

Cowart, Jack, Pierre Schneider, John Elderfield, et al. *Matisse in Morocco: The Paintings and Drawings, 1912–1913*, exh. cat. Washington, D.C.: National Gallery of Art, 1990.

Loose inserts: letter from the gallerist John Berggruen, undated, discussing the *Matisse in Morocco* exhibition, "We thought of you many times while we were at the preview as well as when we visited the exhibition"; color reproduction of Matisse's *On the Terrace* (1912) with a sticky note from friend and interior designer Maybelle Bayly Wolfe, undated, "Dear Dick—when I opened H&G. [*House & Garden* magazine] to this Matisse I did a double take—the colors of the ground were so similar to my drawing—no doubt by June you can pop back and see the show / Love & K[isses] Mibs"

Bernier, Rosamond. *Matisse, Picasso, Miró: As I Knew Them*. New York: Alfred A. Knopf, 1991.

Elderfield, John. *Henri Matisse: A Retrospective*, exh. cat. New York: The Museum of Modern Art, 1992.

Notes

1. For a thorough description of Matisse's purchase of Cézanne's *Three Bathers* (ca. 1879–82), see Hilary Spurling, *The Unknown Matisse: A Life of Henri Matisse—The Early Years, 1869–1908* (New York: Alfred A. Knopf, 1998), 180–82.
2. Dan Hofstadter, "Profiles: Almost Free of the Mirror," *New Yorker*, September 7, 1987, 69–70.
3. Richard Diebenkorn, letter to Bruce Grenville, November 8, 1981.
4. Ibid.
5. Phyllis Diebenkorn, conversation with Janet Bishop and Katherine Rothkopf, January 11, 2013.
6. See the essay by John Elderfield on pages 12–16 in this publication.

Works in the Exhibition

This listing represents the San Francisco and Baltimore presentations of *Matisse/Diebenkorn* and reflects the information available at the time of publication. All works are exhibited at both venues unless otherwise noted. Catalogue raisonné (CR) numbers are provided for Diebenkorn works. In addition to the artworks below, the exhibition includes a selection of publications from Richard Diebenkorn's personal library, courtesy the estate of the artist.

Henri Matisse
French, 1869–1954

Corsican Landscape (plate 19)
1898
Oil on canvas
15⅛ x 18¼ in. (38.4 x 46.4 cm)
San Francisco Museum of Modern Art, bequest of Harriet Lane Levy, 1950

Nude Study in Blue (plate 81)
ca. 1899–1900
Oil on canvas
28¾ x 21⅜ in. (73 x 54.3 cm)
Tate, London, bequeathed by C. Frank Stoop, 1933
[San Francisco only]

Still Life with Blue Jug (plate 35)
ca. 1900–1903
Oil on canvas
23 x 25 in. (58.4 x 63.5 cm)
San Francisco Museum of Modern Art, bequest of Matilda B. Wilbur in honor of her daughter, Mary W. Thacher, 2008

Notre Dame, a Late Afternoon (plate 45)
1902
Oil on paper mounted on canvas
28½ x 21½ in. (72.4 x 54.6 cm)
Albright-Knox Art Gallery, Buffalo, gift of Seymour H. Knox Jr., 1927

Fruit Dish (plate 23)
1902–3
Oil on canvas
10⅝ x 13⅞ in. (27 x 35.3 cm)
San Francisco Museum of Modern Art, bequest of Harriet Lane Levy, 1950

Pansies (plate 47)
ca. 1903
Oil on paper mounted on paperboard
19¼ x 17¾ in. (48.9 x 45.1 cm)
The Metropolitan Museum of Art, New York, bequest of Joan Whitney Payson, 1975, 1976.201.22

Carmelina (plate 50)
1903
Oil on canvas
32 x 23¼ in. (81.3 x 59 cm)
Museum of Fine Arts, Boston, Tompkins Collection—Arthur Gordon Tompkins Fund, RES.32.14

Woman with a Hat (plate 79)
1905
Oil on canvas
31¾ x 23½ in. (80.7 x 59.7 cm)
San Francisco Museum of Modern Art, bequest of Elise S. Haas, 1991
[San Francisco only]

Yellow Pottery from Provence (plate 15)
1905
Oil on canvas
21⅞ x 18⅜ in. (55.6 x 46.7 cm)
The Baltimore Museum of Art: The Cone Collection, formed by Dr. Claribel Cone and Miss Etta Cone of Baltimore, Maryland, BMA 1950.227

Landscape: Broom (plate 8)
1906
Oil on panel
12 x 15⅝ in. (30.5 x 39.7 cm)
San Francisco Museum of Modern Art, bequest of Elise S. Haas, 1991

Marguerite in Three Poses (plate 53)
1906
Ink on paper
10 x 15⅝ in. (25.4 x 39.7 cm)
San Francisco Museum of Modern Art, bequest of Elise S. Haas, 1991

The Girl with Green Eyes (plate 102)
1908
Oil on canvas
26 x 20 in. (66 x 50.8 cm)
San Francisco Museum of Modern Art, bequest of Harriet Lane Levy, 1950

Nude with a White Scarf (plate 77)
1909
Oil on canvas
45⅞ x 35⅛ in. (116.5 x 89.2 cm)
Statens Museum for Kunst, Copenhagen, KMSr81

The Blue Window (plate 25)
1913
Oil on canvas
51½ x 35⅝ in. (130.8 x 90.5 cm)
The Museum of Modern Art, New York, Abby Aldrich Rockefeller Fund, 1939

French Window at Collioure (plate 100)
1914
Oil on canvas
45⅞ x 35⅛ in. (116.5 x 89.2 cm)
Musée national d'art moderne/Centre de création industrielle, Centre Georges Pompidou, Paris, gift 1983, AM 1983-508

Goldfish and Palette (plate 6)
1914
Oil on canvas
57¾ x 44¼ in. (146.7 x 112.4 cm)
The Museum of Modern Art, New York, gift and bequest of Florene M. Schoenborn and Samuel A. Marx, 1964

View of Notre Dame (plate 96)
1914
Oil on canvas
58 x 37⅛ in. (147.3 x 94.3 cm)
The Museum of Modern Art, New York, acquired through the Lillie P. Bliss Bequest, and the Henry Ittleson, A. Conger Goodyear, Mr. and Mrs. Robert Sinclair Funds, and the Anna Erickson Levene Bequest given in memory of her husband, Dr. Phoebus Aaron Theodor Levene, 1975

Laurette in a Green Robe, Black Background (plate 30)
1916
Oil on canvas
28¾ x 21⅜ in. (73 x 54.3 cm)
The Metropolitan Museum of Art, New York, Jacques and Natasha Gelman Collection, 1998, 1999.363.43

Sarah Stein (plate 37)
1916
Oil on canvas
28½ x 22¼ in. (72.4 x 56.5 cm)
San Francisco Museum of Modern Art, Sarah and Michael Stein Memorial Collection, gift of Elise S. Haas, 1954

Studio, Quai Saint-Michel (plate 1)
1916
Oil on canvas
58¼ x 46 in. (148 x 116.8 cm)
The Phillips Collection, Washington, D.C., 1940, 1307

Study of Sarah Stein (plate 67)
1916
Graphite on paper
19⅛ x 12⅝ in. (48.6 x 32.1 cm)
San Francisco Museum of Modern Art, gift of Mr. and Mrs. Walter A. Haas, 1962

The Pewter Jug (plate 43)
1917
Oil on canvas
36⅜ x 25½ in. (92.4 x 64.8 cm)
The Baltimore Museum of Art: The Cone Collection, formed by Dr. Claribel Cone and Miss Etta Cone of Baltimore, Maryland, BMA 1950.230

Interior with a Violin (plate 39)
1918
Oil on canvas
45⅝ x 35 in. (115.9 x 88.9 cm)
Statens Museum for Kunst, Copenhagen, KMSr83

Interior at Nice (plate 4)
1919 or 1920
Oil on canvas
52 x 35 in. (132.1 x 88.9 cm)
The Art Institute of Chicago, gift of Mrs. Gilbert W. Chapman, 1956.339

Reclining Model with a Flowered Robe (plate 59)
ca. 1923–24
Black chalk on paper
18⅞ x 24¾ in. (47.9 x 62.9 cm)
The Baltimore Museum of Art: The Cone Collection, formed by Dr. Claribel Cone and Miss Etta Cone of Baltimore, Maryland, BMA 1950.12.52

Nude in Armchair (plate 63)
ca. 1924
Charcoal on paper
24⅞ x 19⅛ in. (63 x 48.6 cm)
The Baltimore Museum of Art: Bequest of Blanche Adler, BMA 1941.196

Interior, Flowers and Parakeets (plate 33)
1924
Oil on canvas
46¼ x 29 in. (117.5 x 73.7 cm)
The Baltimore Museum of Art: The Cone Collection, formed by Dr. Claribel Cone and Miss Etta Cone of Baltimore, Maryland, BMA 1950.252

Lemons on a Pewter Plate (plate 21)
1926, reworked 1929
Oil on canvas
21⅝ x 26⅛ in. (55 x 66.4 cm)
The Art Institute of Chicago, a Millennium Gift of the Sara Lee Corporation, 1999.371

Seated Odalisque, Left Knee Bent, Ornamental Background and Checkerboard (plate 12)
1928
Oil on canvas
21⅝ x 14⅞ in. (54.9 x 37.8 cm)
The Baltimore Museum of Art: The Cone Collection, formed by Dr. Claribel Cone and Miss Etta Cone of Baltimore, Maryland, BMA 1950.255

The Yellow Dress (plate 75)
1929–31
Oil on canvas
39⅝ x 32⅛ in. (100.6 x 81.6 cm)
The Baltimore Museum of Art: The Cone Collection, formed by Dr. Claribel Cone and Miss Etta Cone of Baltimore, Maryland, BMA 1950.256

The Blue Eyes (plate 32)
1935
Oil on canvas
15 x 18 in. (38.1 x 45.7 cm)
The Baltimore Museum of Art: The Cone Collection, formed by Dr. Claribel Cone and Miss Etta Cone of Baltimore, Maryland, BMA 1950.259

Large Reclining Nude (plate 83)
1935
Oil on canvas
26⅛ x 36¾ in. (66.4 x 93.3 cm)
The Baltimore Museum of Art: The Cone Collection, formed by Dr. Claribel Cone and Miss Etta Cone of Baltimore, Maryland, BMA 1950.258

Seated Pink Nude (plate 88)
1935–36
Oil on canvas
36¼ x 28¾ in. (92 x 73 cm)
Musée national d'art moderne/Centre de création industrielle, Centre Georges Pompidou, Paris, gift 2001, AM 2001-215

Model Resting on Her Arms (plate 55)
1936
Graphite on paper
Two joined sheets, overall: 17¼ x 20 in. (43.8 x 50.8 cm)
The Baltimore Museum of Art: The Cone Collection, formed by Dr. Claribel Cone and Miss Etta Cone of Baltimore, Maryland, BMA 1950.12.49

Seated Nude, Head on Arms (plate 57)
1936
Charcoal on paper
28¾ x 21 in. (73 x 53.3 cm)
Private collection
[Baltimore only]

Reclining Nude with Arm behind Head (plate 65)
1937
Charcoal on paper
15 x 19 in. (37.9 x 48.3 cm)
The Baltimore Museum of Art: The Cone Collection, formed by Dr. Claribel Cone and Miss Etta Cone of Baltimore, Maryland, BMA 1950.12.50

The Conversation (plate 17)
1938
Oil on canvas
18⅜ x 21¾ in. (46.7 x 55.3 cm)
San Francisco Museum of Modern Art, bequest of Mr. James D. Zellerbach, 1993

Two Girls, Red and Green Background (plate 92)
1947
Oil on canvas
22⅛ x 18¼ in. (56.2 x 46.4 cm)
The Baltimore Museum of Art: The Cone Collection, formed by Dr. Claribel Cone and Miss Etta Cone of Baltimore, Maryland, BMA 1950.264

Richard Diebenkorn
American, 1922–1993

Urbana #2 (The Archer) (plate 3)
1953
Oil on canvas
64½ x 47½ in. (163.8 x 120.7 cm)
Estate of the artist
CR 1245

Urbana #4 (plate 2)
1953
Oil on canvas
66 x 49 in. (167.6 x 124.5 cm)
Colorado Springs Fine Arts Center, gift of Julianne Kemper Gilliam, 1977.20
CR 1247

Urbana #5 (Beach Town) (plate 5)
1953
Oil on canvas
68 x 53½ in. (172.7 x 135.9 cm)
Collection of Joann K. Phillips
CR 1248

Urbana #6 (plate 7)
1953
Oil on canvas
69¼ x 58 in. (175.9 x 147.3 cm)
Modern Art Museum of Fort Worth, museum purchase, Sid W. Richardson Foundation Endowment Fund, 1996.01.P.P.
CR 1249

Berkeley #5 (plate 9)
1953
Oil on canvas
53 x 53 in. (134.6 x 134.6 cm)
Private collection
CR 1254

Berkeley #7 (plate 10)
1953
Oil on canvas
47¾ x 43 in. (121.3 x 109.2 cm)
Mildred Lane Kemper Art Museum, Washington University in St. Louis, gift of Joseph Pulitzer Jr., 1962
CR 1256

Berkeley #22 (plate 11)
1954
Oil on canvas
59 x 57 in. (149.9 x 144.8 cm)
Hirshhorn Museum and Sculpture Garden, Smithsonian Institution, Washington, D.C., Regents Collections Acquisition Program, 1986
CR 1346

Berkeley #23 (plate 13)
1955
Oil on canvas
62 x 54¾ in. (157.5 x 139 cm)
San Francisco Museum of Modern Art, gift of the Women's Board, 1958
CR 1470

Berkeley #47 (plate 16)
1955
Oil on canvas
58⅞ x 65⅞ in. (149.5 x 167.3 cm)
The Doris and Donald Fisher Collection at the San Francisco Museum of Modern Art
CR 1486

Berkeley #57 (plate 14)
1955
Oil on canvas
58¾ x 58¾ in. (149.2 x 149.2 cm)
San Francisco Museum of Modern Art, bequest of Joseph M. Bransten in memory of Ellen Hart Bransten, 1980
CR 1492

Berkeley #58 (plate 18)
1955
Oil on canvas
64 x 58¾ in. (162.6 x 149.2 cm)
Private collection
CR 1493

Chabot Valley (plate 20)
1955
Oil on canvas
19½ x 18¾ in. (49.5 x 47.6 cm)
Collection of Christopher Diebenkorn
CR 1582

Still Life with Orange Peel (plate 22)
1955
Oil on canvas
29¼ x 24½ in. (74.3 x 62.2 cm)
San Francisco Museum of Modern Art, bequest of Barbara E. Foster, 2016
CR 1588

Still Life with Orange Peel II (plate 24)
1955/1956
Oil on canvas
15⅛ x 18⅜ in. (38.4 x 46.7 cm)
Private collection
CR 1587

Woman by the Ocean (plate 27)
1956
Oil on canvas
79 x 59 in. (200.7 x 149.9 cm)
Collection of the Lisa and Douglas E. Goldman family
CR 2080
[San Francisco only]

Man and Woman in a Large Room (plate 31)
1957
Oil on canvas
71⅛ x 62½ in. (180.7 x 158.8 cm)
Hirshhorn Museum and Sculpture Garden, Smithsonian Institution, Washington, D.C., gift of the Joseph H. Hirshhorn Foundation, 1966
CR 2184

Untitled (plate 52)
1958
Charcoal on paper
12 x 8⅞ in. (30.5 x 22.5 cm)
Santa Cruz Island Foundation
CR 2496

Woman on a Porch (plate 26)
1958
Oil on canvas
72 x 72 in. (182.9 x 182.9 cm)
New Orleans Museum of Art, museum purchase through the National Endowment for the Arts Matching Grant, 77.64
CR 2540

Cane Chair—Outside (plate 41)
1959
Oil on canvas
32 x 27 in. (81.3 x 68.6 cm)
Promised gift of a private collection to the San Francisco Museum of Modern Art
CR 2718

Coffee (plate 29)
1959
Oil on canvas
57½ x 52¼ in. (146.1 x 132.7 cm)
San Francisco Museum of Modern Art, fractional and promised gift of Barbara and Gerson Bakar, 1994
CR 2720
[San Francisco only]

View from the Porch (plate 28)
1959
Oil on canvas
70 x 66 in. (177.8 x 167.6 cm)
Collection of Harry W. and Mary Margaret Anderson
CR 2725

Untitled (plate 54)
ca. 1960–66
Ink and charcoal on paper
17 x 14 in. (43.2 x 35.6 cm)
Private collection, courtesy Van Doren Waxter
CR 2996

Girl with Plant (plate 34)
1960
Oil on canvas
80 x 69½ in. (203.2 x 176.5 cm)
The Phillips Collection, Washington, D.C., 1961, 0519
CR 2772

Untitled (plate 56)
ca. 1961–62
Ink, charcoal, and graphite on paper
13⅞ x 16⅞ in. (35.2 x 42.9 cm)
Collection of John and Sally Van Doren, courtesy Van Doren Waxter
CR 3115

Seated Nude, Hands behind Head (plate 36)
1961
Oil on canvas
84 x 69 in. (213.4 x 175.3 cm)
Collection of Jane Wenner
CR 3178
[San Francisco only]

Sleeping Woman (plate 38)
1961
Oil on canvas
70 x 58 in. (177.8 x 147.3 cm)
Kalamazoo Institute of Arts, Michigan, Director's Fund Purchase, 1968/9.86
CR 3171

Ashtray and Doors (plate 44)
1962
Oil on canvas
29 x 20⅜ in. (73.7 x 51.8 cm)
Estate of the artist
CR 3251

Girl with Flowered Background (plate 42)
1962
Oil on canvas
40 x 34 in. (101.6 x 86.4 cm)
Modern Art Museum of Fort Worth, museum purchase, Sid W. Richardson Foundation Endowment Fund, 1991.11
CR 3275

Interior with Doorway (plate 40)
1962
Oil on canvas
70⅜ x 59½ in. (178.8 x 151.1 cm)
Pennsylvania Academy of the Fine Arts, Philadelphia, Henry D. Gilpin Fund, 1964.3
CR 3255

Untitled (plate 58)
1962
Ink and graphite on paper
17 x 12½ in. (43.2 x 31.8 cm)
San Francisco Museum of Modern Art, purchase through anonymous funds and the Albert M. Bender Bequest Fund, 1964
CR 3236

Untitled (Standing Nude) (plate 61)
1962
Conté crayon on paper
17 x 11 in. (43.2 x 27.9 cm)
The Baltimore Museum of Art:
Thomas E. Benesch Memorial Collection, BMA 1970.21.4
CR 3234

Cityscape #1 (plate 49)
1963
Oil on canvas
60¼ x 50½ in. (153 x 128.3 cm)
San Francisco Museum of Modern Art, purchase with funds from Trustees and friends in memory of Hector Escobosa, Brayton Wilbur, and J. D. Zellerbach, 1964
CR 3373

Ingleside (plate 46)
1963
Oil on canvas
81¾ x 69½ in. (207.6 x 176.5 cm)
Grand Rapids Art Museum, museum purchase, 1967.1.1
CR 3377

Studio Wall (plate 51)
1963
Oil on canvas
45⅜ x 42½ in. (115.3 x 108 cm)
U.C. Berkeley Art Museum and Pacific Film Archive, gift of Richard and Phyllis Diebenkorn
CR 3366

Untitled (Woman Seated in a Chair) (plate 60)
1963
Ink, conté crayon, and charcoal on paper
17 x 13⅞ in. (43.2 x 35.2 cm)
The Baltimore Museum of Art:
Thomas E. Benesch Memorial Collection, BMA 1970.21.3
CR 3328

Untitled (plate 62)
1964
Graphite and ink on paper
13⅞ x 16⅞ in. (35.2 x 42.9 cm)
Collection of Leslie A. Feely, New York
CR 3415

Untitled (plate 48)
1964
Gouache and graphite on paper
13⅜ x 13⅞ in. (34 x 35.2 cm)
Collection of John and Sally Van Doren, courtesy Van Doren Waxter
CR 3464

Recollections of a Visit to Leningrad (plate 72)
1965
Oil on canvas
73 x 84 in. (185.4 x 213.4 cm)
Private collection
CR 3642

Untitled (Seated Woman) (plate 64)
1965
Conté crayon on paper
16⅞ x 14 in. (42.9 x 35.6 cm)
Collection of Eve Benesch-Goldschmidt
CR 3567

Untitled (Seated Woman) (plate 66)
1965
Charcoal on paper
23¾ x 19 in. (60.3 x 48.3 cm)
Collection of Susan and David Gersh, Los Angeles
CR 3595

Large Still Life (plate 74)
1966
Oil on canvas
64½ x 70¼ in. (163.8 x 178.4 cm)
The Museum of Modern Art, New York, gift of the family of Richard Diebenkorn, 315.2004
CR 3643

Nude on Blue Ground (plate 82)
1966
Oil on canvas
81¼ x 59¼ in. (206.4 x 150.5 cm)
Private collection
CR 3647
[San Francisco only]

Untitled (Interior with Mirror) (plate 69)
1966
Watercolor, charcoal, and conté crayon on paper
16⅞ x 14 in. (42.9 x 35.6 cm)
Private collection
CR 3653

Untitled (Seated Nude) (plate 68)
1966
Charcoal on paper
33 x 23½ in. (83.8 x 59.7 cm)
San Francisco Museum of Modern Art, gift of the Diebenkorn family and purchase through a gift of Leanne B. Roberts, Thomas W. Weisel, and the Mnuchin Foundation, 1996
CR 3712

Untitled (Seated Woman, Patterned Dress) (plate 78)
1966
Gouache, crayon, and ink on paper
30¼ x 23¼ in. (76.8 x 59.1 cm)
University Art Museum, University at Albany, State University of New York, purchase of Student Art Council, 1970
CR 3694

Untitled (Yellow Collage) (plate 76)
1966
Pasted paper, gouache, and ink on paper
28¾ x 22 in. (73 x 55.9 cm)
The Grant Family Collection
CR 3693
[Baltimore only]

Seated Figure with Hat (plate 80)
1967
Oil on canvas
57¾ x 61¾ in. (146.7 x 156.8 cm)
National Gallery of Art, Washington, D.C., gift of the Collectors Committee and Mr. and Mrs. Lawrence Rubin, 1991.176.1
CR 3908

Seated Woman (plate 86)
1967
Oil on canvas
90 x 80⅛ in. (228.6 x 203.5 cm)
Collection of Gretchen and John Berggruen, San Francisco
CR 3907
[San Francisco only]

Sink (plate 70)
1967
Ink, charcoal, and watercolor on paper
24¾ x 18¾ in. (62.9 x 47.6 cm)
The Baltimore Museum of Art: Thomas E. Benesch Memorial Collection, BMA 1969.2
CR 3899

Window (plate 84)
1967
Oil and graphite on canvas
92 x 80 in. (233.7 x 203.2 cm)
Iris & B. Gerald Cantor Center for Visual Arts at Stanford University, Stanford, California, gift of Mr. and Mrs. Richard Diebenkorn and anonymous donors, 1969.125
CR 3906

Ocean Park #6 (plate 87)
1968
Oil on canvas
92 x 72 in. (233.7 x 182.9 cm)
Smithsonian American Art Museum, Washington, D.C., gift of Arthur J. Levin in memory of his beloved wife Edith, 1999.17
CR 3979

Ocean Park #12 (plate 90)
1968
Oil and charcoal on canvas
92½ x 80 in. (235 x 203.2 cm)
Private collection
CR 3984
[San Francisco only]

Untitled (View from Studio, Ocean Park) (plate 89)
1969
Gouache, charcoal, and ink on paper
17 x 13¾ in. (43.2 x 34.9 cm)
The Grant Family Collection
CR 3995

Ocean Park #27 (plate 91)
1970
Oil and charcoal on canvas
100 x 80 in. (254 x 203.2 cm)
Brooklyn Museum, gift of the Roebling Society and Mr. and Mrs. Charles H. Blatt and Mr. and Mrs. William K. Jacobs Jr., 72.4
CR 4016

Ocean Park #29 (plate 93)
1970
Oil and charcoal on canvas
100⅛ x 81⅛ in. (254.3 x 206.1 cm)
Dallas Museum of Art, gift of the Meadows Foundation, Incorporated, 1981.106
CR 4018

Ocean Park #54 (plate 95)
1972
Oil and charcoal on canvas
100 x 81 in. (254 x 205.7 cm)
San Francisco Museum of Modern Art, gift of Friends of Gerald Nordland, 1972
CR 4117

Ocean Park #79 (plate 97)
1975
Oil and charcoal on canvas
93 x 81 in. (236.2 x 205.7 cm)
Philadelphia Museum of Art, purchased with a grant from the National Endowment for the Arts and with funds contributed by private donors, 1977, 1977-28-1
CR 4195

Ocean Park #93 (plate 103)
1976
Oil on hardboard
29 x 21 in. (73.7 x 53.3 cm)
The Grant Family Collection
CR 4263

Ocean Park #94 (plate 99)
1976
Oil and charcoal on canvas
93⅛ x 81⅛ in. (236.5 x 206.1 cm)
Iris & B. Gerald Cantor Center for Visual Arts at Stanford University, Stanford, California, gift of Phyllis G. Diebenkorn, 1998.142
CR 4264

Ocean Park #105 (plate 101)
1978
Oil and charcoal on canvas
100⅛ x 93⅛ in. (254.3 x 236.5 cm)
Modern Art Museum of Fort Worth, museum purchase, Sid W. Richardson Foundation Endowment Fund and The Burnett Foundation, 1991.12.P.P.
CR 4338

Ocean Park #122 (plate 104)
1980
Oil and charcoal on canvas
100¼ x 81¼ in. (254.6 x 206.4 cm)
San Francisco Museum of Modern Art, Charles H. Land Family Foundation Fund purchase, 1980
CR 4431

Untitled (plate 105)
1980
Acrylic and charcoal on paper
22⅜ x 17⅜ in. (56.8 x 44.1 cm)
Estate of the artist
CR 4415

Index

Numbers in *italics* refer to images and their captions.

Image Credits

All artworks by Richard Diebenkorn are copyright © The Richard Diebenkorn Foundation. All artworks by Henri Matisse are copyright © 2016 Succession H. Matisse / Artists Rights Society (ARS), New York. Page 4: © 2016 by the Morley Baer Photography Trust, Santa Fe. Used by permission—all reproduction rights reserved. Pages 18, 116: © The Estate of Leo Holub. Page 92: © 1991 Hans Namuth Estate.

All artworks by Richard Diebenkorn are reproduced courtesy the Richard Diebenkorn Foundation unless otherwise indicated. Additional photography credits are provided below.

PLATES
Listed by plate number
2: Colorado Springs Fine Arts Center. 4, 21: © The Art Institute of Chicago. 6, 25, 96, 98: © The Museum of Modern Art / Licensed by SCALA / Art Resource, NY. 8: Katherine Du Tiel. 12, 15, 32–33, 43, 55, 59–61, 63, 65, 70, 75, 83, 92: Mitro Hood, courtesy The Baltimore Museum of Art. 17, 19, 23, 35, 37, 58, 79, 102: Ben Blackwell. 30: Malcolm Varon / Image copyright © The Metropolitan Museum of Art / Image source: Art Resource, NY. 39, 77: © SMK Photo. 45: Tom Loonan. 46: Grand Rapids Art Museum. 47: © The Metropolitan Museum of Art / Image source: Art Resource, NY. 50: © 2016 Museum of Fine Arts, Boston. 52: Santa Cruz Island Foundation. 53, 67: Don Ross. 57: Juan Trujillo. 71, 73, 85: © The State Hermitage Museum / Photo by Vladimir Terebenin. 81: © Tate, London 2015. 88: Georges Meguerditchian © CNAC / MNAM / Dist. RMN-Grand Palais / Art Resource, NY. 94: Scala / Art Resource, NY. 100: Philippe Migeat © CNAC / MNAM / Dist. RMN-Grand Palais / Art Resource, NY.

OTHER
Listed by page number
4: Morley Baer Photography Trust, Santa Fe, New Mexico. 12: © The Museum of Modern Art / Licensed by SCALA / Art Resource, NY / Photographer: Mali Olatunji. 18, 116: Courtesy Estate of Leo Holub. 20–21: David and Barbara Block family archives. 22: Courtesy The Phillips Collection, Washington, D.C. 25, 86, 118: Courtesy the Richard Diebenkorn Foundation. 26–27: © 2016 The Barnes Foundation. 87: Courtesy Cantor Arts Center. 89 (top): François Fernandez. 92: Courtesy Center for Creative Photography, University of Arizona. 119: © Centre Pompidou, MNAM-CCI / Service de la documentation photographique du MNAM. 120–21: Scala / Art Resource, NY. 125: Art Resource, NY. 168: Johnna Arnold.

This catalogue is published on the occasion of the exhibition *Matisse/Diebenkorn*, held at The Baltimore Museum of Art, October 23, 2016–January 29, 2017, and at the San Francisco Museum of Modern Art, March 11–May 29, 2017.

Matisse/Diebenkorn is organized by The Baltimore Museum of Art and the San Francisco Museum of Modern Art.

Major sponsorship for the exhibition is provided by

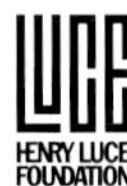

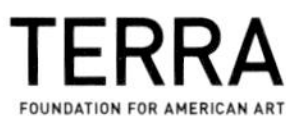

The exhibition is supported by an indemnity from the Federal Council on the Arts and the Humanities.

At The Baltimore Museum of Art, the exhibition is made possible by the following: Ellen W. P. Wasserman, Jeanette C. and Stanley H. Kimmel, and the National Endowment for the Arts.

Corporate sponsorship is provided by

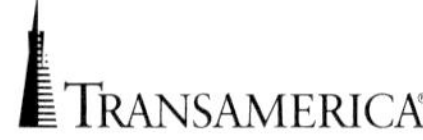

Education Partner

TRANSAMERICA

At the San Francisco Museum of Modern Art, the exhibition is made possible by

Presenting Sponsor

Evelyn D. Haas
EXHIBITION FUND

Additional support is provided by The Bernard and Barbro Osher Exhibition Fund.

Head of Publications: Kari Dahlgren
Senior Editor and Project Editor:
Amanda Glesmann
Publications Associate and Assistant Editor:
Lucy Medrich
Curatorial Research Assistants:
Laura Albans and Jared Ledesma
Indexer: Kathleen Preciado
Proofreader: Dianne Woo
Designers: Miko McGinty and
Claire Bidwell, Miko McGinty Inc.
Typesetter: Tina Henderson

Printed and bound in Italy by Trifolio SRL, Verona, featuring their extended gamut system AreaW4

Published in 2016 by The Baltimore Museum of Art, the San Francisco Museum of Modern Art, and DelMonico Books • Prestel

DelMonico Books, an imprint of Prestel Publishing, a member of Verlagsgruppe Random House GmbH

Prestel Verlag
Neumarkter Strasse 28
81673 Munich

Prestel Publishing Ltd.
14-17 Wells Street
London W1T 3PD

Prestel Publishing
900 Broadway, Suite 603
New York, NY 10003

www.prestel.com

Page 4: Richard Diebenkorn's Hillcrest studio, Berkeley, 1966. Photograph by Morley Baer

Image credits appear on page 183.

Library of Congress Cataloging-in-Publication Data

Names: Bishop, Janet C., editor. | Rothkopf, Katherine, editor. | Baltimore Museum of Art, organizer, host institution. | San Francisco Museum of Modern Art, organizer, host institution.
Title: Matisse/Diebenkorn / edited by Janet Bishop and Katherine Rothkopf.
Other titles: Matisse Diebenkorn
Description: San Francisco : San Francisco Museum of Modern Art, 2016. | "This catalogue is published by The Baltimore Museum of Art and the San Francisco Museum of Modern Art in association with DelMonico Books • Prestel Munich, London, and New York, on the occasion of the exhibition Matisse/Diebenkorn, held at The Baltimore Museum of Art, October 23, 2016–January 29, 2017, and at the San Francisco Museum of Modern Art, March 11–May 29, 2017." | Includes bibliographical references and index.
Identifiers: LCCN 2016017928 | ISBN 9783791355344 (hardback)
Subjects: LCSH: Diebenkorn, Richard, 1922–1993—Exhibitions. | Matisse, Henri, 1869–1954—Exhibitions. | Matisse, Henri, 1869–1954—Influence—Exhibitions. | BISAC: ART / Individual Artists / Monographs. | ART / Collections, Catalogs, Exhibitions / Group Shows.
Classification: LCC N6537.D447 A4 2016 | DDC 709.2/2—dc23 LC record available at https://lccn.loc.gov/2016017928

A CIP catalogue record for this book is available from the British Library.

ISBN: 978-3-7913-5534-4